The Old-House Journal Buyer's Guide

The Old-House Journal Buyer's Guide

COMPILED BY THE EDITORS OF THE OLD-HOUSE JOURNAL

DOUBLEDAY & COMPANY • GARDEN CITY, NEW YORK • 1984

The Old-House Journal Buyer's Guide

Doubleday Edition   1984

Library of Congress Cataloging in Publication Data
Main entry under title:

The Old-house journal buyer's guide.

   1. Building materials—Catalogs. 2. Building fittings
—Catalogs. 3. Dwellings—Remodeling—Catalogs.
I. Old-house journal.
TH455.042   1984   690'.837'029473
ISBN 0-385-18746-7

Library of Congress Catalog Card Number 83-45964

CONTENTS

Compiled and Edited by the staff of The
Old-House
Journal

How To Love An Old House
(In 10 Easy Lessons)

This Buyer's Guide is about love. When you love an old house, you're sensitive to what's good for it and what isn't. That's why the products in this Buyer's Guide have been carefully screened to make sure they are appropriate for restoration or rehabilitation of houses built before 1939.

You won't find aluminum siding, vinyl shutters, or any of the phoney "olde time" gadgets that clutter the advertising pages of the home magazines. What you *will* find here are authentic designs, good materials, and quality craftsmanship. Products that couldn't meet these criteria (and there were many that didn't) weren't listed.

Any house built before 1939 deserves a bronze plaque just for surviving in our throw-away culture. Your old house is special, even if it wasn't designed by a famous architect, even if no famous event ever took place there. Beyond that, pre-1939 houses have better materials, better workmanship, and richer detailing than you can find in newer houses. So even if you own "just a plain old house," it's worth treating it as a cultural treasure . . . because it is one.

Restoring an old house is fun: challenging and creative fun. In the process, you learn about social and art history, construction skills, architecture, preservation technology, and restoration philosophy. And when you're through, you'll have found that nothing equals the satisfaction of taking a building that's been neglected or abused, and restoring its former integrity.

But beware of jumping in too fast! If you don't understand your particular old house, you might wind up "remuddling" it. (A remuddling — from "remodelling" — is a misguided "improvement" that destroys some of the old character.) The ten basic principles that follow will guide you toward a meaningful relationship with your special old house. And that's the first step in your love affair.

1. Develop Sensitivity

Working on an old house requires respect — for the people who built it and for the structure itself. In a sense, an old house doesn't belong to you, no matter what the deed says. It fulfilled a dream 50, 100, or 200 years ago for the people who created it. Successive generations left their own mark, too. By virtue of having survived so many decades, the house has acquired a history and personality all its own. You are a caretaker . . . holding the property in trust for future generations. Because it is a tangible record of human life, an old house, once destroyed, can never be replaced at any cost.

Of course, this doesn't mean that a house can't be changed. A house is a dynamic organism that always reflects the life of its occupants. But sensitivity suggests that your changes respect the basic style and character of the house.

Your goal is not to make the house "look like new." After all, it is an *old* house. Here's a rule of thumb told to us by one sensitive old-house lover:

> *If it's a mark of abuse, repair it.*
> *If it's a mark of wear, leave it alone.*

It's the accumulation of all those wear marks that gives an old house its character. That's probably what attracted you to old-house living in the first place. So don't be afraid to leave some of those worn spots.

2. Don't Rush In

More damage can be done to an old house during two weeks of hasty "restoration" than would be caused by two decades of neglect. A new owner always feels an irresistible urge to produce immediate results. It's very satisfying to make the plaster dust fly and see a

Here is an "ordinary" old house that has been sensitively maintained. It hasn't been covered with aluminum or vinyl siding, so all of the ornamental wooden trim around windows and eaves has survived. Because the porch has been kept in good repair, all of its distinctive sawn wood ornament is intact. A carefully maintained house never needs major restoration.

trash hauler fill up with debris. Making the house over makes it yours.

Resist that urge! Most mistakes are made in this period of initial enthusiasm, when people act before they have compiled sufficient information about their house. By the time realization dawns, it's often too late. What you wish you'd saved has already gone to the dump.

So go ahead and inspect, clean, scour, scrub, and plan. If at all possible, live in the house a while before you start big projects or make irreversible decisions. It's guaranteed that after a few months you'll start feeling differently about the house and what you want to do to it.

You'll need patience even beyond the first few months, of course. Fixing up an old house is not everyone's idea of fun. Here's a quick test: What would your reaction be on a Saturday — just before a big party — if the front hall ceiling fell on your newly varnished

floor? If you'd laugh . . . because it hurts too much to cry . . . then you're a real old-house person!

3. Learn About YOUR House

There's no old house exactly like yours. Even if the house next door was a twin originally, successive generations of occupants have given each house its own unique character.

Your house represents a specific point in architectural history. Its shape, roofline, windows, porches, bays, chimneys, siding materials, and ornamental details are all part of an architectural style, that in turn is a reflection of the times that produced it. Part of the fun of owning an old house is reading everything you can about the times in which it was built — and the effect that social trends had on the appearance of domestic dwellings.

Periodicals such as The Old-House Journal can help you learn about the basic architectural styles and the trends that influenced them. Books in your local library can be a great source of information about the social history surrounding your house. Your local historical society may have a photo archive that will show houses like yours — or perhaps even your house itself — in earlier times. And if your house has been remuddled, you may be able to find a similar house in your neighborhood to provide clues as to what might be missing.

In addition, the structure itself can speak volumes — when you know what to look for. Original paint colors, alterations to room layouts, mouldings and architectural trim that may have been removed, original wallcoverings and decoration . . all these can often be discovered by careful inspection of your building. These discoveries won't necessarily mean that you'll want to re-create everything that was original. But having this information in hand allows you to make more intelligent choices about what you *will* do.

Photo: Jim Kalett

BEFORE: A typical old-house dilemma. An 1880's house had been converted to a multiple dwelling, with doors chopped through walls, deteriorated flooring, and damaged plaster everywhere.

4. Memorize The Two Golden Rules

The many fine points of old-house restoration could fill a book. But at The Old-House Journal, we think these two Golden Rules express all the dos and don'ts:

THOU SHALT NOT DESTROY GOOD OLD WORK.

In most cases, new work that is put into an old house will be inferior to the original, both in quality of materials and workmanship. Thus, when original material is ripped out during a renovation, the building suffers a downgrading in quality. Contractors, especially, are often too eager to pronounce old materials "beyond repair" and urge total replacement.

After a series of seemingly minor replacements, significant changes in the building's character can result. Ironically, these alterations rob the building of the antique charm that attracted the buyer to it in the first place.

Of course, value judgments are involved when deciding what constitutes "good old work." In general, work can be called "good" if: (1) It is fabricated from good quality materials; (2) The workmanship is good; (3) The design is typical of a particular style, or works in harmony with the rest of the house.

TO THINE OWN STYLE BE TRUE.

Your house possesses a unique architectural style. Be proud of it. Learn everything you can about that style — and then plan your rehabilitation or restoration so it brings out the character and flavor of that style.

Don't try to make your house over into something it never was. Most especially, don't try to "antique" it in an attempt to make it look older than it actually is. A few years ago, a common mistake was to try to make a Victorian house look colonial by adding fake shutters, pedimented doorways, and the like. Today, we're equally likely to see someone take a turn-of-century house and try to Victorianize it with stencilling and inappropriate 19th century hardware.

5. Know Your Goal

Your approach to rehabilitation is not going to be the same as a museum curator. A house is to be lived in; you can't impose a purist philosophy on it, or freeze time. Yet the definitions that follow are important, even if you have an "average" old house. Your approach will fall into one of these categories, whether you're conscious of it or not.

Unfortunately, these words are used interchangeably by many house owners, contractors, and magazines. Imprecise use of words causes confusion. If our ideas are fuzzy, our work will always reflect that confusion.

PRESERVATION — Keeping an existing building in its current state by a careful program of maintenance and repair.

REHABILITATION — To make a structure sound and usable again, without attempting to restore any particular period appearance. Rehabilitation respects the original architectural elements of a building and retains them whenever possible. Sometimes also called "Reconditioning."

AFTER: The plaster surfaces were carefully restored to their original condition. To complete the interpretive restoration, the room was stencilled with patterns typical of the late Victorian period.

RENOVATION — Similar to "Rehabilitation," except that in renovation work there is a greater proportion of new materials and elements introduced into the building.

REMODELLING — Changing the appearance and style of a structure, inside or out, by removing or covering over original details and substituting new materials and forms. Also called "Modernizing."

RESTORATION — Repairing or re-creating the original architectural elements in a building so that it closely resembles the appearance it had at some previous point in time.

"Interpretive Restoration" is less scholarly than "Historic Restoration." It involves keeping all of the original architectural features intact, and reconstructing missing elements as faithfully as budget allows. Decoration and furnishings of interior spaces are appropriate to the style of the house — without attempting to duplicate what was in the house originally. Restored houses that function as homes are usually of the interpretive variety.

6. Put Your Plans On Paper

Planning seems so boring when you could be doing really exciting things like knocking down walls. But planning can save a lot of wasted energy — and regret. You don't want to discover *after* you've painted and papered the front parlor that you've got to rip up a wall to install new plumbing lines for the top-floor bathroom.

Your Master Plan has to take two major requirements into account: (1) the living needs of you and your family; and (2) the need to treat the structure sensitively. When these two needs conflict, you have to work out the best compromise, keeping in mind that the house will be around a lot longer than you.

Some sort of organized system is essential for assembling your plan. Some people like file folders. Others find three-ring binders most convenient. The method isn't important; just use *some* system. Keep records according to specific areas of the house: north facade, front parlor, back bathroom, and so on.

Start planning with a careful inventory of the structure. Note any special problems such as structural cracks, missing elements, and water damage that will require repair. Next, historical information — original paint colors, scraps of wallpaper, dates written on plaster — can be added to the file. Be sure to include "before" photos, too. Not only are they valuable records, but they'll provide an endless source of wonder once your work is complete.

7. Don't Do Anything That Can't Be Undone

Preservation professionals say that the work you do on an old house should be *reversible*. That means that any new work installed should be easy to change if a later owner wishes to restore the house to its original appearance. For example, paints and wallcoverings are completely reversible. If someone doesn't like your paint job, he or she can paint over it. Tearing out original woodwork, however, is *irreversible*. Once that woodwork has been hauled off to the dump, it's gone for good.

Putting aluminum or vinyl siding on an old house often results in irreversible damage. Many houses, especially those built in the 19th century, have wooden decoration around eaves, windows, and doors. Fitting vinyl or aluminum siding around architectural detail is difficult, so installation contractors simply chop the mouldings off. The character of the house is drastically altered — irreversibly.

8. Repair Rather Than Replace; Restore Rather Than Remodel

This rather stiff admonition is simply a guideline for retaining charm and character as you fix up your old house. In general, it is better to fix the old rather than remove it and put in new. And when pieces are missing or truly unsalvageable, it's better to replace them in kind ("restore") rather than change the character ("remodel").

Minor miracles are worked with simple repair materials: patching plaster, putty, caulk, linseed oil, and paint. Many repairs can be accomplished by a dedicated, patient do-it-yourselfer. Repairs cause less disruption and often cost less than replacements.

When replacement is necessary, of course, the new element should match the original as closely as possible. Try to match the visual qualities such as shape, color, texture, and proportion. Often it's acceptable (or even preferable) to use a modern material rather than the traditional one. But the finished product should *look* the same and last as long or longer than the original.

9. Be Proud Of Your Work

Don't compromise on quality. If you make a mistake, tear it out and do it again. Don't inflict your errors on the house . . . and all subsequent owners. If it's an expensive mistake, the next project may have to

Tudor Revival is just one example of the post-Victorian house styles that are beginning to receive serious attention. Once regarded as unworthy of restoration, such houses have recently been recognized not only for their architectural merit, but also for their comfort and quality of construction.

wait. So be it. As we pointed out earlier, one of the cardinal virtues that an old-house owner can possess is *patience*.

The materials and workmanship in an old house are superior to that found in new buildings. Therefore, the work you put into an old house should be at least as good as what's already there. Otherwise, you'll be downgrading the house's intrinsic worth.

10. Watch Your Contractors

It's not easy to find contractors who will do high quality work worthy of your house. Left to their own devices, most will work to the slipshod standards of modern construction. The responsibility is on the old-house owner to know precisely what has to be done, and to have a pretty clear idea of how to do it. The homeowner who relies on the expertise of the average contractor is asking for trouble. If you don't indicate in advance that you know what good work is, you're not likely to get it.

Many contractors are unfamiliar with old houses. They haven't developed a sensitivity toward the special requirements of old houses or a respect for old workmanship. Their recommendation always will be to "rip out this old stuff, and put in nice new material." If you haven't mastered principles 1 through 9, it's easy to be bulldozed by the advice of a seeming "expert."

Armed with the 10 basic principles — plus the products and services you'll find in this Buyer's Guide — you and your old house should have a long happy life together!

Catalog Editor . . . Joni Monnich
Designer . . . Charles Eanet
Editorial Assistant . . . Christina Plattner

©1983 The Old-House Journal Corporation
Editorial Director . . . Patricia Poore
Publisher . . . Clem Labine

How To Use This Book

This Buyer's Guide Catalog lists 1,251 companies. Most of them are cited several times, for each of the various products they sell. We haven't repeated the detailed ordering information with each listing — that would make a very fat book. Instead, we separated this Buyer's Guide into two major sections: a Product & Service Directory and a Company Directory. The Product & Service Directory tells you what companies offer which products. The Company Directory lists all the companies in alphabetical order; here's where you will find the complete address, phone number, and further information for each company.

The series of steps below shows you how to use this Buyer's Guide most efficiently. First, look up the product or service you require. Second, among the companies that offer that product, select the one that is closest to you and best serves your needs. Third, look up specific information on that company — its address, phone number, even the cost of its catalog or brochure (if it offers one).

The directions below also explain special features of this Buyer's Guide: the product displays and a helpful new listing of companies by city and state.

Step 1: Finding The Product

To locate the product or service you need, consult the Alphabetical Index on page 193. The index contains numerous cross-references that take into account common synonyms for the same item.

The Alphabetical Index will refer you to the appropriate page in the Product & Service Directory.

```
Coal Grates.............................69
Coal Scuttles...........................69
Coat Hooks, ............................63
Coat Racks and Umbrella Stands...........56
Collars, Stove Pipe — see Stove Pipe & Fittings
Columns, Exterior.......................22
Columns, Interior.......................45
Columns, Porch.........................26
Commode Seats.........................60
Composition Ornaments .................51
Concrete Roofing Tiles .................17
    (under Other Roofing Materials)
Conductor Heads — see Leaders & Leader Boxes
Conservator's Tools.....................89
Consolidants, Wood — see Rot Patching Materials
Consulting Services ....................103
Contour Gauges.........................89
```

from the Alphabetical Index to Products & Services

Step 2: Selecting The Right Company

In the Product & Service Directory, you'll find the heading for the item you're after. Below that heading will be the names of all the companies whom the editors have validated as providing that product or service.

In addition to the listings, you'll also find useful product displays from companies who supply that type of item.

```
┌─ Sub-categories ─────────────────────┐
│  SHAKES & SHINGLES, WOOD             │
│    (1)  Handsplit                    │
│    (2)  Machine Cut                  │
│  Brewster's Lumberyard (CT) ........... 2 │
│  Crawford's Old House Store (WI) ...... 2 │
│  Essex Tree Service (WA) ........... 1,2 │
│  Hendricks Tile Mfg. Co., Inc. (VA)  │
│  Koppers Co. (PA) ...................... 2 │
│  Mad River Wood Works (CA) ........... 2 │
│  Puget Sound Shake Brokers (WA)      │
│  Renovator's Supply (MA)             │
│  Shakertown Corporation (WA) ........ 2 │
└──────────────────────────────────────┘
```

More information is available in a product display

After each company name is a two-letter state abbreviation. This helps you find nearby suppliers when there are many companies in a category. If you have any difficulty deciphering these standard Post Office abbreviations, you will find the key on page 12.

The small numbers after the company name in some categories tell which of the sub-categories the firm sells.

A company's name in **boldface** means they have placed a product display that you can consult for additional details. If the display isn't adjacent to the company's listing, refer to the Index to Product Displays on page 199.

Step 3: Contacting The Company

The basic information about each company is found in the Company Directory that starts on page 113.

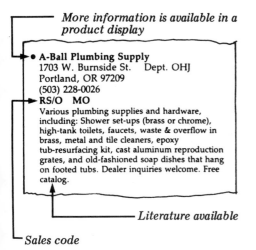

More information is available in a product display

● **A-Ball Plumbing Supply**
1703 W. Burnside St.   Dept. OHJ
Portland, OR 97209
(503) 228-0026
RS/O   MO
Various plumbing supplies and hardware, including: Shower set-ups (brass or chrome), high-tank toilets, faucets, waste & overflow in brass, metal and tile cleaners, epoxy tub-resurfacing kit, cast aluminum reproduction grates, and old-fashioned soap dishes that hang on footed tubs. Dealer inquiries welcome. Free catalog.

Literature available

Sales code

A boldface bullet (●) next to the company name means the company has placed a product display to provide you with more data.

KEY TO ABBREVIATIONS

MO	**sells by Mail Order**
RS/O	**sells through Retail Store or Office**
DIST	**sells through Distributors**
ID	**sells only through Interior Designers or Architects**

The Sales Code tells HOW the company sells its products. Some sell nationwide by mail order (MO). Others sell through their local distributors (DIST). Some companies will sell direct to consumers from a retail store or office (RS/O), while a few sell only to interior designers and architects (ID).

For Further Information . . .

When you've located a company that has the product-display code (●), refer to the Index to Product Displays on page 199. These displays supplement the editorial listings, providing such things as product illustrations and additional ordering information.

from the Product Displays Index

You'll find a brand-new feature in this edition of our Buyer's Guide — introduced by popular demand. In The Company Directory By State, which begins on page 185, we've listed companies according to their location. For each state, companies are listed alphabetically *by city*. The new listing will tell you at a glance who the restoration suppliers are in your area.

If you know other good sources for old-house products and services, please let us know about them. We'll send them a questionnaire and give them the opportunity to be listed in the next edition.

Editor's Tips On Contacting Suppliers

Here are a few tried-and-true hints to help you deal with mail-order companies.

1. Before writing and saying, "send catalog," check the write-up in the Company Directory to see if they have literature — and if there's a charge. It wastes your time and theirs if the company has to write back to tell you there is a charge for literature.

2. Don't send form-letter inquiries to dozens of companies. Many companies will ignore these.

3. Write 'Catalog Request,' 'Order,' or similar clarifying phrase on the outside of your envelope to help with handling.

4. If you're asking for more information than their catalog can provide, telephoning is usually the fastest and most satisfactory way to get the answer.

5. If you do write to a company asking a non-routine question, enclosing a self-addressed, stamped envelope (SASE) is a thoughtful gesture. (It may mean the difference between getting an answer and not.)

6. Be patient. With mail being what it is, it can take 4 weeks or longer for catalogs or merchandise to arrive.

7. Always mention The Old-House Journal Buyer's Guide when you write. It helps identify you as part of the 'family.'

A Note About State Abbreviations

Alabama	AL	Nebraska	NE
Alaska	AK	Nevada	NV
Arizona	AZ	New Hampshire	NH
Arkansas	AR	New Jersey	NJ
California	CA	New Mexico	NM
Canada	CAN	New York	NY
Colorado	CO	North Carolina	NC
Connecticut	CT	North Dakota	ND
Delaware	DE	Ohio	OH
District of Columbia	DC	Oklahoma	OK
Florida	FL	Oregon	OR
Georgia	GA	Pennsylvania	PA
Hawaii	HI	Puerto Rico	PR
Idaho	ID	Rhode Island	RI
Illinois	IL	South Carolina	SC
Indiana	IN	South Dakota	SD
Iowa	IA	Tennessee	TN
Kansas	KS	Texas	TX
Kentucky	KY	United Kingdom	
Louisiana	LA	(England)	UK
Maine	ME	Utah	UT
Maryland	MD	Vermont	VT
Massachusetts	MA	Virginia	VA
Michigan	MI	Washington	WA
Minnesota	MN	West Virginia	WV
Mississippi	MS	Wisconsin	WI
Missouri	MO	Wyoming	WY
Montana	MT		

After each company name in the Product & Service Directory, you'll find a two-letter state code. This indicates the state in which the company is located. The state code helps you find nearby suppliers when there is a long list of companies within a category.

The full name, address, and telephone number of every company can be found in the Company Directory starting on page 113.

THE PRODUCT & SERVICE DIRECTORY

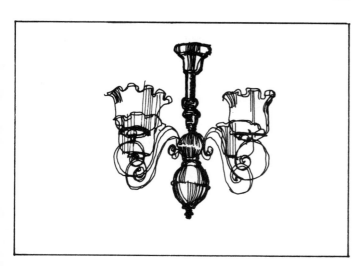

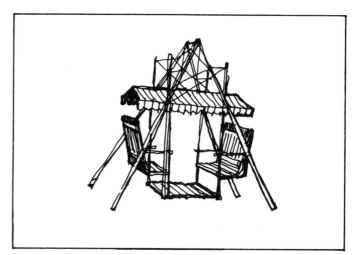

PRODUCT & SERVICE DIRECTORY

Exterior Building Materials & Supplies

Building Maintenance Materials & Supplies

BASEMENT WATERPROOFING PAINTS & COMPOUNDS

Benjamin Moore Co. (NJ)
Chapman Chemical Co. (TN)
Rutland Products (VT)
Thoro System Products (FL)
United Gilsonite Laboratories (PA)
U.S. Gypsum Company (IL)

BIRD & PEST CONTROL PRODUCTS

Bird — X, Inc. (IL)
Nixalite of America (IL)
Paramount Exterminating Co. (NY)

MASONRY CLEANERS & PAINT STRIPPERS

American Building Restoration (WI)
Diedrich Chemicals-Restoration Technologies, Inc. (WI)
Hydrochemical Techniques, Inc. (CT)
North Coast Chemical Co. (WA)
ProSoCo, Inc. (KS)
Vermont Marble Co. (VT)

MASONRY SEALERS

American Building Restoration (WI)
Building Materials Inc. (MA)
Diedrich Chemicals-Restoration Technologies, Inc. (WI)
Hydrozo Coatings Co. (NE)
ProSoCo, Inc. (KS)
Rutland Products (VT)
Thoro System Products (FL)
United Gilsonite Laboratories (PA)
U.S. Gypsum Company (IL)
Watco - Dennis Corporation (CA)
Wood and Stone, Inc. (VA)

PAINTS, EXTERIOR—MASONRY

Cabot Stains (MA)
Rutland Products (VT)
Thoro System Products (FL)
U.S. Gypsum Company (IL)

PRESERVATIVES, WOOD

American Building Restoration (WI)
Cabot Stains (MA)
Chapman Chemical Co. (TN)
E & B Marine Supply (NJ)
Hydrozo Coatings Co. (NE)
Minwax Company, Inc. (NJ)
Watco - Dennis Corporation (CA)

STAINS, EXTERIOR

Barnard Chemical Co. (CA)
Cabot Stains (MA)

VARNISHES, EXTERIOR

Barnard Chemical Co. (CA)
E & B Marine Supply (NJ)
North Coast Chemical Co. (WA)
Rutland Products (VT)
United Gilsonite Laboratories (PA)

Masonry & Supplies

BRICKS, HANDMADE

(1) New
(2) Salvage
Binghamton Brick Co., Inc. (NY) 1
Boren Clay Products Company (NC) 1
Continental Clay Company (PA) 1
Cushwa, Victor & Sons Brick Co. (MD) 1
Glen - Gery Corporation (PA) 1
Kane-Gonic Brick Corp. (NH) 1
Old Carolina Brick Co. (NC) 1
Pennsylvania Barnboard Company (PA) 2
Royal River Bricks Co., Inc. (ME) 1
Sky Lodge Farm (MA) 2

See Company Directory for Addresses & Phone Numbers

SPECIALTY MORTARS & CEMENTS

Lehigh Portland Cement Co. (PA)
Riverton Corporation (VA)
Wood and Stone, Inc. (VA)

STONE

(1) Bluestone
(2) Granite
(3) Limestone
(4) Marble
(5) Sandstone (Brownstone)
(6) Slate
(7) Other Stone

Briar Hill Stone Co. (OH) 5
Building Materials Inc. (MA) 1
Cathedral Stone Company (DC) 3,5
Chester Granite Co. (MA) 2
Delaware Quarries, Inc. (PA) 2,3,4,5,6
Evergreen Slate Co. (NY) 6
Hilltop Slate Co. (NY) 6
Materials Unlimited (MI)
Mr. Slate - Smid Incorporated (VT) 6
Pasvalco (NJ) 5
Rising & Nelson Slate Co. (VT) 6
Sculpture Associates, Ltd. (NY) 4,7
Shaw Marble & Tile Co., Inc. (MO) 4
Structural Slate Company (PA) 6
Tatko Bros. Slate Co. (NY) 6
Vermont Marble Co. (VT) 4
Vermont Soapstone Co. (VT) 7
Vermont Structural Slate Co. (VT) 5,6

STUCCO PATCHING MATERIALS

Building Materials Inc. (MA)
Thoro System Products (FL)
U.S. Gypsum Company (IL)

Roofing Materials & Supplies

METAL ROOFING

(1) Galvanized
(2) Terne
(3) Other

Berridge Manufacturing Co. (TX) 1,2,3
Conklin Tin Plate & Metal Co. (GA) 1,2,3
Follansbee Steel (WV) 2
Norman, W.F., Corporation (MO)

SHAKES & SHINGLES, WOOD

(1) Handsplit
(2) Machine Cut

Blue Ridge Shingle Co. (VA) 2
Brewster's Lumberyard (CT) 2
Cedar Valley Shingle Systems (CA)
Crawford's Old House Store (WI) 2
Essex Tree Service (WA) 1,2
Hendricks Tile Mfg. Co., Inc. (VA)
Koppers Co. (PA) 2
Mad River Wood Works (CA) 2
Puget Sound Shake Brokers (WA)
Shakertown Corporation (WA) 2
Shingle Mill, Inc. (MA) 2
South Coast Shingle Co. (CA) 2
Southington Specialty Wood Co. (CT) 2

SHINGLES, METAL

Berridge Manufacturing Co. (TX)
Conklin Tin Plate & Metal Co. (GA)
Norman, W.F., Corporation (MO)

TILES, ASBESTOS

Supradur Mfg. Corp. (NY)

You'll get better service when contacting companies if you mention The Old-House Journal Catalog

TILES, SLATE

Buckingham-Virginia Slate Corporation (VA)
Evergreen Slate Co. (NY)
Hilltop Slate Co. (NY)
Millen Roofing Co. (WI)
Mr. Slate - Smid Incorporated (VT)
Rising & Nelson Slate Co. (VT)
Structural Slate Company (PA)
Supradur Mfg. Corp. (NY)
Vermont Structural Slate Co. (VT)
Walker, Dennis C. (OH)

See Company Directory for Addresses & Phone Numbers

TILES, TERRA COTTA & CERAMIC

Architectural Terra Cotta and Tile, Ltd. (IL)
Gladding, McBean & Co. (CA)
Hendricks Tile Mfg. Co., Inc. (VA)
Ludowici-Celadon Co. (OH)
Virtue, W.D., Co., Inc. (NJ)

OTHER ROOFING

Duro Fiber Co. (MA)
Hendricks Tile Mfg. Co., Inc. (VA)
Monier (CA)
Raleigh, Inc. (IL)

Siding Materials & Supplies

CLAPBOARDS, BEADED EDGE AND OTHER OLD STYLES

SHINGLES, SPECIAL ARCHITECTURAL SHAPES

Cedar Valley Shingle Systems (CA)
Kingsway (CO)
Mad River Wood Works (CA)
Puget Sound Shake Brokers (WA)
Shakertown Corporation (WA)
Shingle Mill, Inc. (MA)
South Coast Shingle Co. (CA)

See Company Directory for
Addresses & Phone Numbers

You'll get better service
when contacting companies
if you mention
The Old-House Journal
Catalog

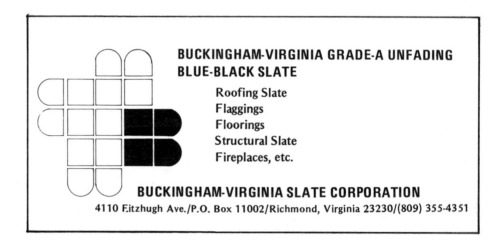
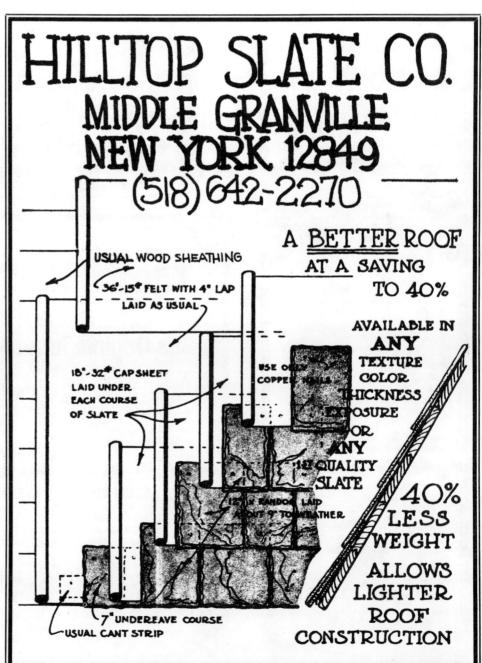

SHAKES & SHINGLES, CUSTOM-CUT

Essex Tree Service (WA)
Homestead Supply (ME)
Mad River Wood Works (CA)
Puget Sound Shake Brokers (WA)
Shakertown Corporation (WA)
Shingle Mill, Inc. (MA)

SIDING, BARN

(1) Salvage
(2) New

Barn People, The (VT) *1*
Belcher, Robert W. (GA) *1*
Castle Burlingame (NJ) *1*
Littlefield Lumber Co., Inc. (NH) *2*
Old-Home Building & Restoration (CT) *1*
Pennsylvania Barnboard Company (PA) *1*
Structural Antiques (OK) ....:............... *1*
Vermont Weatherboard, Inc. (VT) *2*
Vintage Lumber Co. (MD) *2*
Walker, Dennis C. (OH) *2*

SALVAGE BUILDING MATERIALS (BOARDS, BEAMS, POSTS, ETC.)

Architectural Accents (GA)
Barn People, The (VT)
Belcher, Robert W. (GA)
Castle Burlingame (NJ)
Croton, Evelyn — Architectural Antiques (NY)
Materials Unlimited (MI)
Old-Home Building & Restoration (CT)
Pelnik Wrecking Co., Inc. (NY)
Pennsylvania Barnboard Company (PA)
Sky Lodge Farm (MA)
Vintage Lumber Co. (MD)
Walker, Dennis C. (OH)

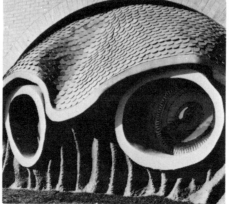

FANCY IDEAS.
With Shakertown Fancy Cuts Cedar Shingles.

Create your own unique patterns and textural effects for walls, ceilings and roofs. Interior and exterior.

Ideal for accents and combining with other materials for special surface treatments.

We'd like to send you a sample and design kit full of Fancy Cuts fancy ideas for your home. For the package send $4 to Shakertown Corp., Dept. OH, Winlock, WA 98596.

Available in 9 styles.

FISH-SCALE   HALF-COVE   DIAMOND   DIAGONAL   ROUND   OCTAGONAL   ARROW   HEXAGONAL   SQUARE

ARCHITECTURAL MILLWORK

See Company Directory for
Addresses & Phone Numbers

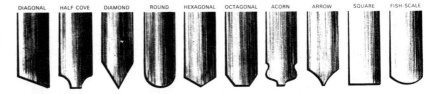

BRACKETS, BUTTRESSES & CORBELS—EXTERIOR

(1) Stone
(2) Stamped Metal
(3) Wood
Art Directions (MO)
ART, Inc. (NJ) *1*
ByGone Era Architectural Antiques (GA)
Chester Granite Co. (MA) *1*
Croton, Evelyn — Architectural Antiques
  (NY)
Crowe Company (CA) *3*
Cumberland Woodcraft Co., Inc. (PA) *3*
Gingerbread House (NC) *3*
Hallelujah Redwood Products (CA) *3*
Kenneth Lynch & Sons, Inc. (CT) *2*
Leslie Brothers Lumber Company (WV) *3*
Leyva's Ornamental Staff & Stone (CA) *1*
Maine Architectural Millwork (ME) *3*
Materials Unlimited (MI)
Navedo Woodcraft, Inc. (NY) *3*
**Pagliacco Turning & Milling Architectural
  Wood Turning (CA)** *3*
Renovation Products (TX) *3*
W.N. Russell and Co. (NJ) *1*
Silverton Victorian Millworks (CO) *3*
Turncraft (OR) *3*
Vintage Wood Works (TX) *3*
Wrecking Bar, Inc. (TX)

COLUMNS & CAPITALS—EXTERIOR

(1) Wood
(2) Stone
(3) Plaster
(4) Iron
(5) Fiberglass
(6) Metal
American Wood Column (NY) *1*
Architectural Sculpture (NY) *5*
Biagiotti, L. (NY) *3*
ByGone Era Architectural Antiques (GA)
Campbellsville Industries (KY) *6*
Chester Granite Co. (MA) *2*
Chilstone Garden Ornament (UK) *2*
Croton, Evelyn — Architectural Antiques
  (NY)
Decorators Supply Corp. (IL) *3*
Designer Resource (CA) *1,3*
Duro Fiber Co. (MA) *5*
Elk Valley Woodworking Company (OK) ... *1*
Felber, Inc. (PA) *3*
Hartmann-Sanders Column Co. (GA) *1,5*
Henderson Black & Greene, Inc. (AL) *1*
Lachin, Albert & Assoc., Inc. (LA) *2*
Leeke, John — Woodworker (ME) *1*
Leyva's Ornamental Staff & Stone (CA) ...*2,3*
Moore, E.T., Jr. Co. (VA) *1*
Moultrie Manufacturing Company (GA) *6*
Nord, E.A. Company (WA) *1*
**Pagliacco Turning & Milling Architectural
  Wood Turning (CA)** *1*
Pennsylvania Barnboard Company (PA) *1*
Renovation Concepts, Inc. (MN)
Russell Restoration of Suffolk (NY) *3,5*
W.N. Russell and Co. (NJ) *2*
San Francisco Victoriana (CA) *3*
Schwerd Manufacturing Co. (PA) *1*
Somerset Door & Column Co. (PA) *1*
**Southern Heritage Metal Amenities, Ltd.
  (AL)** *4*
Tennessee Fabricating Co. (TN) *4*
Turncraft (OR) *1*
Verine Products & Co. (UK) *5*
Wrecking Bar, Inc. (TX)

CORNICES—EXTERIOR

(1) Wood
(2) Stamped Metal
(3) Fiberglass
Campbellsville Industries (KY) *2*
Cumberland Woodcraft Co., Inc. (PA) *1*
Designer Resource (CA)
Downstate Restorations (IL) *2,3*
Fypon, Inc. (PA)
Hallelujah Redwood Products (CA) *1*
House of Moulding (CA) *1*
Kenneth Lynch & Sons, Inc. (CT) *2*
J.C. Lauber Co. (IN) *2*
Maine Architectural Millwork (ME) *1*
Russell Restoration of Suffolk (NY) *3*
Wagner, Albert J., & Son (IL) *2*

FINIALS

(1) Composition
(2) Metal
(3) Wood
Dovetail, Inc. (MA) *1*
Moultrie Manufacturing Company (GA) *2*
Norman, W.F., Corporation (MO) *2*
Renovation Products (TX) *1,3*
Vintage Wood Works (TX) *3*

GINGERBREAD TRIM—WOOD

(1) Stock Items
(2) Custom Fabrication
Cumberland Woodcraft Co., Inc. (PA) *1*
Emporium, The (TX) *1*
Gazebo and Porchworks (WA) *1*
Gingerbread House (NC) *1,2*
Hallelujah Redwood Products (CA) *1,2*
Mad River Wood Works (CA) *2*
Marsh Stream Enterprise (ME) *2*
North Pacific Joinery (CA) *2*
**Pagliacco Turning & Milling Architectural
  Wood Turning (CA)** *2*
Rejuvenation House Parts Co. (OR)
Renovation Concepts, Inc. (MN)
Renovation Products (TX) *1*
Silverton Victorian Millworks (CO) *1,2*
Victorian Building & Repair (IL) *2*
Vintage Wood Works (TX) *1,2*

**See Company Directory for
Addresses & Phone Numbers**

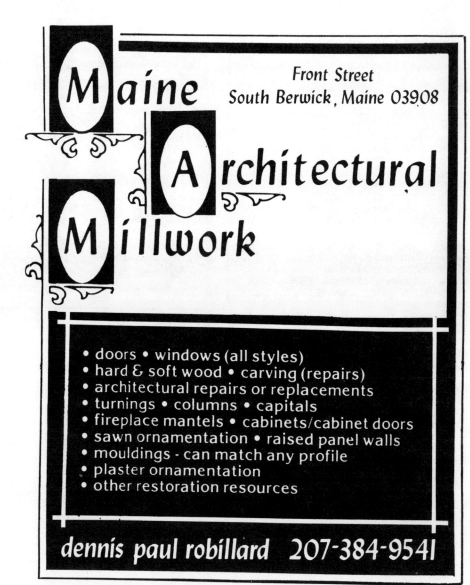

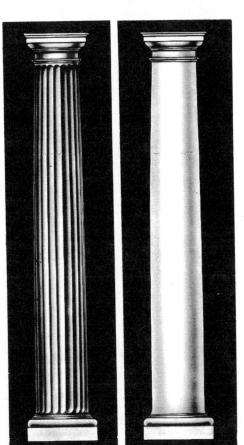

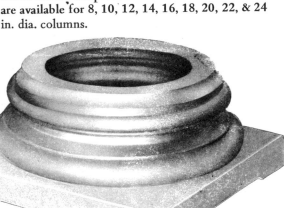

GUTTERS, LEADERS & LEADER BOXES

(1) Wood
(2) Copper
(3) Lead
(4) Other

Alte, Jeff Roofing, Inc. (NJ) 2
Conklin Tin Plate & Metal Co. (GA) 2,4
Copper Sales, Inc. (MN) 2,4
Kenneth Lynch & Sons, Inc. (CT) 2,3
J.C. Lauber Co. (IN) 4
Nostalgia, Inc. (GA)
Wagner, Albert J., & Son (IL) 2
Windham Millworks (ME) 1

MOULDINGS, EXTERIOR WOOD

(1) Stock Items
(2) Custom-Made

American Wood Column (NY) 2
Bailey Architectural Millwork (NJ) 2
Bendix Mouldings, Inc. (NJ) 1
Center Lumber Company (NJ) 2
Depot Woodworking, Inc. (VT) 1,2
Designer Resource (CA) 1,2
Driwood Moulding Company (SC) 1
Drums Sash & Door Co., Inc. (PA) 2
Elliott Millwork Co. (IL) 1
Fireplace Mantel Shop, Inc. (MD) 1,2
Hallelujah Redwood Products (CA) 1
House of Moulding (CA) 1
Leeke, John — Woodworker (ME) 2
Mad River Wood Works (CA) 2
Maine Architectural Millwork (ME) 2
Merit Moulding, Ltd. (NY) 2
Michael's Fine Colonial Products (NY) 2
Millwork Supply Company (WA) 1,2
Navedo Woodcraft, Inc. (NY) 2
North Pacific Joinery (CA) 2
Piscataqua Architectural Woodwork, Co.
   (NH) 2
Renovation Concepts, Inc. (MN)
Silverton Victorian Millworks (CO) 1,2
W. P. Stephens Lumber Co. (GA) 1,2
Turnbull's Lumber Company (MI) 2
Walbrook Mill & Lumber Co., Inc. (MD) 2
Wood Designs (OH) 2
Wood Masters, Inc. (NJ) 2

MOULDINGS, EXTERIOR

(1) Ceramic
(2) Fiberglass
(3) Plaster
(4) Terra Cotta
(5) Stone
(6) Other

Architectural Sculpture (NY) 3
Architectural Terra Cotta and Tile, Ltd. (IL) 4
ART, Inc. (NJ) 4,5
Biagiotti, L. (NY) 3,6
Decorators Supply Corp. (IL) 3
Designer Resource (CA) 3
Duro Fiber Co. (MA) 2
Felber, Inc. (PA) 2,3
Fypon, Inc. (PA) 6
Gladding, McBean & Co. (CA) 4
J.O. Holloway & Company (OR) 2,6
Lachin, Albert & Assoc., Inc. (LA) 5
Leyva's Ornamental Staff & Stone (CA) ... 3,5
Orlandini Studios Ltd. Decorative Plaster
   Supply Co. (WI) 3
Russell Restoration of Suffolk (NY) 2,3
W.N. Russell and Co. (NJ) 5
Virtue, W.D., Co., Inc. (NJ) 4

Vintage Wood Works . . .

HAS A SISTER!

You probably know us as one of the country's major producers of handcrafted Victorian Gingerbread. But now we are more.

Our sister company, Vintage Gazebos, is in full production. The pre-assembled, bolt together "Dolly Bryan" is already being acclaimed "The finest production Gazebo available."

The Dolly Bryan —
Victorian Gazebo

Fully illustrated information on both of our Gazebo models, **together with our complete Gingerbread and Fretwork line**, is available in a 36-page descriptive

Catalog.

That's like two catalogs for the price of one!

Send $2. To

Dept. 183, Box 1157 • Fredericksburg, TX 78624 • 512/997-9513

- WE SHIP PROMPTLY NATIONWIDE -

PORCH PARTS

(1) Stock Items
(2) Custom Work

Abaroot Mfg., Co. (CA) 2
Cumberland Woodcraft Co., Inc. (PA) *1,2*
Dixon Bros. Woodworking (MA) 2
Gazebo and Porchworks (WA) *1,2*
Gingerbread House (NC) *1,2*
Great American Salvage (NY,VT)
Hallelujah Redwood Products (CA) *1,2*
Henderson Black & Greene, Inc. (AL) *1*
Maine Architectural Millwork (ME) 2
Mansion Industries, Inc. (CA) *1*
Michael's Fine Colonial Products (NY) 2
Nord, E.A. Company (WA) *1*
North Pacific Joinery (CA) 2
Pagliacco Turning & Milling Architectural
  Wood Turning (CA) *1,2*
Renovation Concepts, Inc. (MN) *1*
Renovation Products (TX) *1,2*
Taft Wood Products Co. (OH) 2
Turncraft (OR) *1,2*
Vintage Wood Works (TX) *1*

SHUTTERS & BLINDS, EXTERIOR WOOD

(1) New (Stock Items)
(2) Custom-Made

Architectural Components (MA) 2
Bank Architectural Antiques (LA) *1*
Beauti-home (CA) 2
Iberia Millwork (LA) 2
Island City Wood Working Co. (TX) 2
LaPointe, Chip, Cabinetmaker (NY) 2
Maurer & Shepherd, Joyners (CT) 2
Michael's Fine Colonial Products (NY) 2
Nord, E.A. Company (WA) *1*
Piscatagua Architectural Woodwork, Co.
  (NH) 2
Restoration Fraternity (PA) 2

EXTERIOR DOORS, REPRODUCTION

(1) Early American
(2) Victorian
(3) Turn-of-Century
(4) Custom-Made
(5) Other

Architectural Components (MA)
Bel-Air Door Co. (CA) *1,2,3,5*
Cascade Mill & Glass Works (CO) *4*
Driwood Moulding Company (SC) *4*
Drums Sash & Door Co., Inc. (PA) ... *1,2,3,4*
Elliott Millwork Co. (IL)
Feather River Wood and Glass Co. (CA) 2
Gibbons, John — Cabinetmaker (WI) *3,4*
International Wood Products (CA) *2,3,4*
Kingsway (CO) 2
Maine Architectural Millwork (ME) *4*
Maurer & Shepherd, Joyners (CT) *4*
Millwork Supply Company (WA) *4*
Nord, E.A. Company (WA) *1,2,3*
North Pacific Joinery (CA) *4*
Old'N Ornate Wooden Reproductions (OR)
  .... *2,4*
Old Wagon Factory (VA)
Piscatagua Architectural Woodwork, Co.
  (NH) *1,4*
Pocahontas Hardware & Glass (IL) *2*
Renovation Concepts, Inc. (MN) *2,3*
Renovation Products (TX) *2,3*
Restoration Fraternity (PA) *4*
Richmond Doors (NH) *1,4*

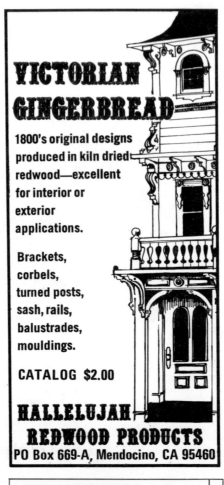

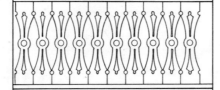

EXTERIOR DOORS, ANTIQUE (SALVAGE)

Architectural Antiques Exchange (PA)
Architectural Antique Warehouse, The (CAN)
Architectural Archives (TX)
Artifacts, Inc. (VA)
Bank Architectural Antiques (LA)
ByGone Era Architectural Antiques (GA)
Canal Co. (DC)
Castle Burlingame (NJ)
Croton, Evelyn — Architectural Antiques (NY)
Joe Ley Antiques, Inc. (KY)
Materials Unlimited (MI)
Monroe Coldren and Sons (PA)
Olde Bostonian Architectural Antiques (MA)
Red Baron's Peachtree Antique Emporium (GA)
United House Wrecking Corp. (CT)
Westlake Architectural Antiques (TX)
Wrecking Bar, Inc. (TX)

custom sash & door work
hardwood French and
frame & panel doors
divided lite windows
arch top doors, sashes
& jambs

Gibbons Cabinetry
2070 Helena Street
Madison, WI 53704

brochure $1

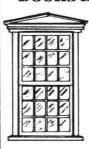
You'll get better service
when contacting companies
if you mention
The Old-House Journal
Catalog

See Company Directory for
Addresses & Phone Numbers

SCREEN DOORS

Cascade Mill & Glass Works (CO)
Combination Door Co. (WI)
Creative Openings (WA)
Gingerbread House (NC)
JMR Products (CA)
Mad River Wood Works (CA)
Maine Architectural Millwork (ME)
Moser Brothers, Inc. (PA)
Old'N Ornate Wooden Reproductions (OR)
Old Wagon Factory (VA)
Remodelers & Renovators (ID)
Renovation Products (TX)
Restoration Fraternity (PA)

ENTRYWAYS & DOOR FRAMING WOODWORK—REPRODUCTION

(1) Early American
(2) Victorian
(3) Stock Items
(4) Salvage
(5) Custom-Made

Burt Millwork Corp (NY) 5
C—E Morgan (WI) 3
Drums Sash & Door Co., Inc. (PA) 1,2,5
Fireplace Mantel Shop, Inc. (MD) 1,2
Fypon, Inc. (PA) 1
Gibbons, John — Cabinetmaker (WI) 5
Great American Salvage (NY,VT) 4
Henderson Black & Greene, Inc. (AL) ... 1,3
Island City Wood Working Co. (TX) 2
Kingsway (CO) 2
Littlefield Lumber Co., Inc. (NH) 5
Materials Unlimited (MI) 4
Maurer & Shepherd, Joyners (CT) 5
Michael's Fine Colonial Products (NY) 5
Restoration Fraternity (PA) 5
Somerset Door & Column Co. (PA) 5
Strobel Millwork (CT) 5
United House Wrecking Corp. (CT) 4
Jack Wallis' Doors (KY) 5
Woodstone Co. (VT) 5

WINDOW BALANCES (REPLACEMENT CHANNELS)

Crawford's Old House Store (WI)
Quaker City Manufacturing Co. (PA)

WINDOW FRAMES & SASH—PERIOD

(1) Early American
(2) Victorian
(3) New (Stock Items)
(4) Salvage
(5) Custom-Made

Air-Flo Window Contracting Corp. (NY) 3
Architectural Components (MA) 5
Bow House, Inc. (MA) 1
Burt Millwork Corp (NY) 5
Crawford's Old House Store (WI) 1,2,5
Drums Sash & Door Co., Inc. (PA) 5
Englander Millwork Corp. (NY) 3,5
Gibbons, John — Cabinetmaker (WI) 5
Glass & Aluminum Construction Services,
Inc. (NH) 5
Hallelujah Redwood Products (CA) 3
Hank, Dennis V. (FL) 3,5
Island City Wood Working Co. (TX) 5
Keddee Woodworkers (RI) 5
Kenmore Industries (MA)
Kingsway (CO) 2
Lavoie, John F. (VT)
Littlefield Lumber Co., Inc. (NH) 5
Maine Architectural Millwork (ME) 5
Marvin Windows (MN) 3,5
Maurer & Shepherd, Joyners (CT) 5
Michael's Fine Colonial Products (NY) 1,5
Millwork Supply Company (WA) 5
Restoration Fraternity (PA) 5
RUSCO (PA) 3
Silverton Victorian Millworks (CO) 5
Somerset Door & Column Co. (PA) 5
Strobel Millwork (CT) 5
Wes-Pine Millwork, Inc. (MA) 5
Window Grille Specialists (MN) 3
Woodstone Co. (VT)

WINDOWS, SPECIAL ARCHITECTURAL SHAPES (ROUNDS, OVALS, FANLIGHTS, TRANSOMS, ETC.)

Architectural Components (MA)
Bullseyes Unltd. (MA)
Crawford's Old House Store (WI)
Hank, Dennis V. (FL)
Kenmore Industries (MA)
Kraatz/Russell Glass (NH)
Lavoie, John F. (VT)
Pompei Stained Glass (MA)
Woodstone Co. (VT)

WINDOW GLASS, CLEAR—HANDMADE

(1) New
(2) Antique (Salvage)
Bendheim, S.A. Co., Inc. (NY) 1
Bienenfeld Ind. Inc. (NY) 1
Blenko Glass Co., Inc. (WV) 1
Coran — Sholes Industries (MA)
Englander Millwork Corp. (NY) 1
Kraatz/Russell Glass (NH)
Vintage Lumber Co. (MD) 2
Whittemore-Durgin Glass Co. (MA) 1

WINDOW GLASS, CURVED

Shadovitz Bros. Distributors, Inc. (NY)

Hardware, Exterior

DOOR HARDWARE, EXTERIOR

(1) Brass & Bronze
(2) Wrought Iron
(3) Door Knockers
(4) Rim Locks
(5) Mortised Locks
(6) Latches, Hand Forged
(7) Mail Slots
(8) Hinges
(9) Strap Hinges

18th Century Hardware Co. (PA) *3,6,9*
Acorn Manufacturing Co., Inc. (MA) *2,8,9*
Arden Forge (PA) *1,2,6,8,9*
Baldwin Hardware Mfg. Corp. (PA) *1,3,4,5,6,7*
Ball and Ball (PA) *1,2,3,4,5,6,8,9*
Barnett, D. James — Blacksmith (PA) *6,8*
Bona Decorative Hardware (OH) *1,3,5*
Broadway Collection (MO) *1,3,4*
Canal Co. (DC) *1*
Castle Burlingame (NJ) *9*
Colonial Lock Company (CT) *2,4*
Crawford's Old House Store (WI) *1,3,4,8*
Decorative Hardware Studio (NY) *1,3,4,7*
Dover Furniture Stripping (DE)
Guerin, P.E. Inc. (NY) *1,3*
Guthrie Hill Forge, Ltd. (PA) *2,6,8,9*
Horton Brasses (CT) *3*
Howard Palmer, Inc. (CA) *1,3,4*
Howland, John — Metalsmith (CT) *1,2,8*
Hunrath , Wm. Co., Inc. (NY)
Kayne, Steve & Son Custom Forged
   Hardware (NC) *1,2,3,6,9*
Kingsway (CO) *1,3,7,8*
Merritt's Antiques, Inc. (PA) *7*
Mill River Hammerworks (MA) *6,8,9*
Millham, Newton — Blacksmith (MA)
   .... *2,3,6,8,9*
Omnia Industries, Inc. (NJ) *3*
Pfanstiel Hardware Co. (NY) *1,3*
Reproduction Distributors, Inc. (IL) *8*
Restoration Hardware (CA) *3*
Restoration Works, Inc. (NY) *7*
Ritter & Son Hardware (CA) *3*
San Francisco Victoriana (CA) *1*
Sign of the Crab (CA) *1*
Smithy, The (VT) *2,3,6,8,9*
Strafford Forge (VT) *2,3,6,8,9*
Wallin Forge (KY) *2,3,6,8,9*
Weaver, W. T. & Sons, Inc. (DC) *1,3,4*
Williamsburg Blacksmiths, Inc. (MA)
   .... *2,3,6,8,9*
Wolchonok, M. and Son, Inc. (NY) *1,4,5*

EXTERIOR HARDWARE, CUSTOM-MADE

(1) Cast Brass & Bronze
(2) Hand-Forged Iron
(3) Cast Iron

18th Century Hardware Co. (PA) *1,2*
Arden Forge (PA) *1,2*
Ball and Ball (PA) *1,2,3*
Bronze et al (NY) *1*
Cassidy Bros. Forge (MA) *2*
Guthrie Hill Forge, Ltd. (PA) *2*
Kayne, Steve & Son Custom Forged
   Hardware (NC) *1,2*
G. Krug & Son, Inc. (MD) *3*
Leo, Brian (MN) *1*
Mill River Hammerworks (MA) *2*
Millham, Newton — Blacksmith (MA) *2*
RAM's Forge (PA) *2*
Schwartz's Forge & Metalworks (NY) *2*
Smithy, The (VT) *2*
Strafford Forge (VT) *2*
Tennessee Fabricating Co. (TN) *3*
Travis Tuck, Inc. — Metal Sculptor (MA) .. *2*
Wallin Forge (KY) *2*
Woodbury Blacksmith & Forge Co. (CT) *2*

DOORBELLS—PERIOD DESIGNS

(1) Electric
(2) Mechanical

Antique Bldrs. Hardware (AR)
Ball and Ball (PA)
Bona Decorative Hardware (OH) *2*
Cumberland General Store (TN) *2*
Dover Furniture Stripping (DE) *2*
Period Furniture Hardware Co., Inc. (MA) . *1*
Restoration Works, Inc. (NY) *2*
Sign of the Crab (CA)
Victorian Reproductions Enterprises, Inc.
   (MN) *2*

SHUTTER HARDWARE (HINGES, HOLDBACKS, ETC.)

Acorn Manufacturing Co., Inc. (MA)
Ball and Ball (PA)
Crawford's Old House Store (WI)
Decorative Hardware Studio (NY)
Dover Furniture Stripping (DE)
Guthrie Hill Forge, Ltd. (PA)
Millham, Newton — Blacksmith (MA)
Smithy, The (VT)
Weaver, W. T. & Sons, Inc. (DC)
Williamsburg Blacksmiths, Inc. (MA)
Wrightsville Hardware (PA)

Ironwork, Exterior

BALUSTERS & HANDRAILS, IRON—PERIOD DESIGNS

(1) Cast Iron
(2) Wrought Iron

Benjamin Eastwood Co. (NJ) *1*
Braun, J.G. Co. (IL) *1*
Cassidy Bros. Forge (MA) *2*
Gorsuch Foundry (IN) *1*
G. Krug & Son, Inc. (MD) *1,2*
Lawler Machine & Foundry (AL) *1*
Schwartz's Forge & Metalworks (NY) *2*
Southern Heritage Metal Amenities, Ltd.
   (AL) *1*
Tennessee Fabricating Co. (TN)
Travis Tuck, Inc. — Metal Sculptor (MA) .. *2*

Hand Forged Iron House Hardware
and furnishings: H-L hinges, straps, butterflies, shutter hardware, interior and exterior latches — candlestands, rushlights, betty lamps, andirons, cranes, spits, broilers, toasters.

Catalogue $1.00

Newton Millham
672 Drift Road
Westport, Mass. 02790

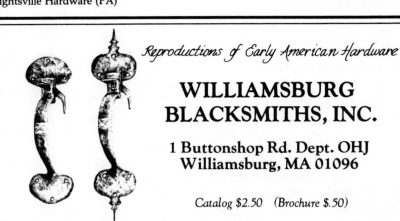

CAST ALUMINUM, EXTERIOR ORNAMENTAL

Braun, J.G. Co. (IL)
Campbellsville Industries (KY)
Colonial Foundry & Mfg. Co. (CT)
Lawler Machine & Foundry (AL)
Moultrie Manufacturing Company (GA)
Norcross Galleries (GA)
**Southern Heritage Metal Amenities, Ltd.
(AL)**
Swiss Foundry, Inc. (MD)

CAST IRON, EXTERIOR ORNAMENTAL

Architectural Iron Company (PA)
Benjamin Eastwood Co. (NJ)
Lawler Machine & Foundry (AL)
Oliver, Bradley C. (PA)
Robinson Iron Corporation (AL)
**Southern Heritage Metal Amenities, Ltd.
(AL)**
Stewart Manufacturing Company (KY)
Swiss Foundry, Inc. (MD)
Tennessee Fabricating Co. (TN)

CAST IRON, CUSTOM CASTING

Architectural Iron Company (PA)
Benjamin Eastwood Co. (NJ)
Clarksville Foundry & Machine Works (TN)
Gorsuch Foundry (IN)
G. Krug & Son, Inc. (MD)
Robinson Iron Corporation (AL)
Swiss Foundry, Inc. (MD)
Tennessee Fabricating Co. (TN)

CRESTING

(1) Cast Iron
(2) Fiberglass
Architectural Iron Company (PA) *1*
Rejuvenation House Parts Co. (OR) *1*
Robinson Iron Corporation (AL) *1*
Tennessee Fabricating Co. (TN) *1*

RAILINGS, BALCONIES & WINDOW GRILLES

(1) Cast Iron
(2) Wrought Iron
Architectural Antiques Exchange (PA)
Architectural Antique Warehouse, The
(CAN) *1*
Braun, J.G. Co. (IL) *1*
Gorsuch Foundry (IN) ....,..... *1*
Lawler Machine & Foundry (AL) *1*
Memico House (CA) *2*
Mill River Hammerworks (MA)
RAM's Forge (PA) *2*
Robinson Iron Corporation (AL) *1*
Schwartz's Forge & Metalworks (NY) *2*
**Southern Heritage Metal Amenities, Ltd.
(AL)** *1*
Tennessee Fabricating Co. (TN) *1*
Travis Tuck, Inc. — Metal Sculptor (MA) .. *2*

WROUGHT IRON ORNAMENTS, STOCK ITEMS

Tennessee Fabricating Co. (TN)

WROUGHT IRON, CUSTOM FABRICATION

Antares Forge and Metalworks (NY)
Architectural Iron Company (PA)
Arden Forge (PA)
Cassidy Bros. Forge (MA)
Iron Anvil Forge (CO)
Kayne, Steve & Son Custom Forged
  Hardware (NC)
Kentucky Ornamental Iron (KY)
G. Krug & Son, Inc. (MD)
Millham, Newton — Blacksmith (MA)
RAM's Forge (PA)
Schwartz's Forge & Metalworks (NY)
Smithy, The (VT)
Strafford Forge (VT)
Tennessee Fabricating Co. (TN)
Travis Tuck, Inc. — Metal Sculptor (MA)
Wallin Forge (KY)
Williamsburg Blacksmiths, Inc. (MA)
Woodbury Blacksmith & Forge Co. (CT)

Other Exterior Ornament & Details

AWNINGS

Astrup Company (OH)
Industrial Fabrics Association International
  (MN)

AWNING HARDWARE

Astrup Company (OH)

BALUSTRADES, ROOF

Campbellsville Industries (KY)
Lachin, Albert & Assoc., Inc. (LA)

CHIMNEY POTS

Superior Clay Corporation (OH)
Victorian Reproductions Enterprises, Inc.
  (MN)

CUPOLAS

Campbellsville Industries (KY)
Cape Cod Cupola Co., Inc. (MA)
Duro Fiber Co. (MA)
International Building Components (NY)
Kenneth Lynch & Sons, Inc. (CT)
Kool-O-Matic Corp. (MI)
Old And Elegant Distributing (WA)
Sun Designs (WI)
Tennessee Fabricating Co. (TN)

FENCES & GATES—PERIOD DESIGNS

(1) Cast Iron
(2) Wrought Iron
(3) Wood
(4) Antique
(5) Cast Aluminum

1890 Iron Fence Co. (IN) 2
Architectural Accents (GA) 4
Architectural Antiques Exchange (PA)
Architectural Antique Warehouse, The
  (CAN) 1
Architectural Iron Company (PA) 1,2
Artifacts, Inc. (VA) 4
Belcher, Robert W. (GA) 3
Braun, J.G. Co. (IL) 1,5
ByGone Era Architectural Antiques (GA) .. 4
Canal Co. (DC) 4
Canal Works Architectural Antiques (OH) .. 4
Colonial Charm (OH) 3
Croton, Evelyn — Architectural Antiques
  (NY) 4
Kenneth Lynch & Sons, Inc. (CT) 1
Kentucky Ornamental Iron (KY) 2
G. Krug & Son, Inc. (MD) 2
Lawler Machine & Foundry (AL) 1,5
Joe Ley Antiques, Inc. (KY) 4
Mad River Wood Works (CA) 3
Moultrie Manufacturing Company (GA) 5
Oliver, Bradley C. (PA) 4
Robinson Iron Corporation (AL) 1
Salvage One (IL) 4
Schwartz's Forge & Metalworks (NY) 2
Stewart Manufacturing Company (KY) 2
Tennessee Fabricating Co. (TN) 1,2
Travis Tuck, Inc. — Metal Sculptor (MA) .. 2
Westlake Architectural Antiques (TX) 2,4
Wrecking Bar of Atlanta (GA) 2,4
Wrecking Bar, Inc. (TX) 4

GARDEN ORNAMENT

(1) Fountains
(2) Statuary
(3) Planters
(4) Urns & Vases
(5) Other

Bench Manufacturing Co. (MA) 3
Betsy's Place (PA) 5
Biagiotti, L. (NY) 4
Chilstone Garden Ornament (UK) 2,3,4,5
Dan Wilson & Company, Inc. (NC) 3
International Terra Cotta, Inc. (CA) 1,2,3,4
Kenneth Lynch & Sons, Inc. (CT) 1,2,4
Lachin, Albert & Assoc., Inc. (LA) 1
Lawler Machine & Foundry (AL) 3,4
Joe Ley Antiques, Inc. (KY)
Moultrie Manufacturing Company (GA) . 1,3,4
Norcross Galleries (GA) 1,4
Orlandini Studios Ltd. Decorative Plaster
    Supply Co. (WI) 2
Richardson, Matthew Coppersmith (MA) ... 1
Ritter & Son Hardware (CA) 5
Robinson Iron Corporation (AL) 1,2,3,4
Roman Marble Co. (IL) 2
Silver Dollar Trading Co. (CO) 1
**Southern Heritage Metal Amenities, Ltd.
    (AL)** 1,2
Spring City Electrical Mfg. Co (PA) 1
Tennessee Fabricating Co. (TN) 1,2,3,4
Verine Products & Co. (UK) 3
Victorian Reproductions Enterprises, Inc.
    (MN)

GAZEBOS

Bench Manufacturing Co. (MA)
Cedar Gazebos, Inc. (IL)
Gazebo and Porchworks (WA)
Vintage Wood Works (TX)
Welsbach (CT)

LAWN AND PORCH FURNITURE

(1) Cast Iron
(2) Wood
(3) Wicker
(4) Wrought Iron
(5) Cast Aluminum

British-American Marketing Services, Ltd.
  (PA) 2
Colonial Foundry & Mfg. Co. (CT) 5
Dan Wilson & Company, Inc. (NC) 2
Gazebo and Porchworks (WA) 2
Kings River Casting (CA) 5
Lawler Machine & Foundry (AL) 1
Mexico House (CA) 4
Moultrie Manufacturing Company (GA) 5
Norcross Galleries (GA) 5
Robinson Iron Corporation (AL) 1
Rocker Shop of Marietta, GA (GA) 2
Southern Heritage Metal Amenities, Ltd.
  (AL) 1,4,5
Tennessee Fabricating Co. (TN) 1
Welsbach (CT) 5

LIGHTNING RODS, OLD-FASHIONED

Victorian Reproductions Enterprises, Inc.
  (MN)

MAIL BOXES — PERIOD DESIGNS

Mel-Nor Marketing (TX)
Norcross Galleries (GA)
Sign of the Crab (CA)
Silver Dollar Trading Co. (CO)

PLAQUES & HISTORIC MARKERS

Jaxon Co., Inc. (AL)
Lake Shore Markers (PA)
Meierjohan — Wengler, Inc. (OH)
Smith-Cornell Homestead, Inc. (IN)
Weaver, W. T. & Sons, Inc. (DC)

PORCH SWINGS

Cumberland General Store (TN)
Renovation Products (TX)

SHEET METAL ORNAMENT, EXTERIOR

Authentic Designs Inc. (VT)
Campbellsville Industries (KY)
Kenneth Lynch & Sons, Inc. (CT)
J.C. Lauber Co. (IN)
Wagner, Albert J., & Son (IL)

SIGNS, OLD-FASHIONED

Custom Sign Co. (MD)
Shelley Signs (NY)
Vintage Wood Works (TX)

TURNBUCKLE STARS

Ainsworth Development Corp. (MD)

WEATHERVANES—NEW & REPRODUCTION

Campbellsville Industries (KY)
Cape Cod Cupola Co., Inc. (MA)
Copper House (NH)
Cumberland General Store (TN)
Friend, The (ME)
Good Directions (CT)
Kayne, Steve & Son Custom Forged
    Hardware (NC)
Kenneth Lynch & Sons, Inc. (CT)
Kingsway (CO)
Old And Elegant Distributing (WA)
Period Furniture Hardware Co., Inc. (MA)
RAM's Forge (PA)
Richardson, Matthew Coppersmith (MA)
Sign of the Crab (CA)
Smithy, The (VT)
Travis Tuck, Inc. — Metal Sculptor (MA)
United House Wrecking Corp. (CT)

STREETSCAPE EQUIPMENT

(1) Bollards and Stanchions
(2) Promenade Benches
(3) Street Clocks
(4) Tree Grates
(5) Street Lamps

Antique Street Lamps (TX) 5
Bench Manufacturing Co. (MA) 2,5
Canterbury Designs, Inc. (CA) 2,3,4
Charleston Battery Bench, Inc. (SC) 2
Chilstone Garden Ornament (UK) 2
Colonial Foundry & Mfg. Co. (CT) 5
Kenneth Lynch & Sons, Inc. (CT) 1,2,4
Mel-Nor Marketing (TX) 1,2,5
Norcross Galleries (GA) 5
**Southern Heritage Metal Amenities, Ltd.
    (AL)** 1
Spring City Electrical Mfg. Co (PA) 1,5
Vermont Iron (VT) 2
Welsbach (CT) 1,2,5

OTHER EXTERIOR ORNAMENT

Gargoyles — New York (NY)

See Company Directory for Addresses & Phone Numbers

Building Materials For Interiors

BASEBOARDS

Bangkok Industries, Inc. (PA)
Bendix Mouldings, Inc. (NJ)
Dixon Bros. Woodworking (MA)
Drums Sash & Door Co., Inc. (PA)
House of Moulding (CA)
Old World Moulding & Finishing Co., Inc. (NY)
Renovation Products (TX)
Silverton Victorian Millworks (CO)

BEAMS, HAND-HEWN

(1) Antique (Recycled)
(2) New
Barn People, The (VT) 1
Belcher, Robert W. (GA) 1
Broad-Axe Beam Co. (VT) 2
ByGone Era Architectural Antiques (GA) .. 1
Castle Burlingame (NJ) 1
Depot Woodworking, Inc. (VT) 2
Industrial Woodworking, Inc. (IL) 2
Moore, E.T., Jr. Co. (VA) 2
Mountain Lumber Company (VA)
Old-Home Building & Restoration (CT) 1
Old World Moulding & Finishing Co., Inc. (NY) 2
Pagliacco Turning & Milling Architectural Wood Turning (CA) 1,2
Pennsylvania Barnboard Company (PA) 1
Period Pine (GA) 1
Southington Specialty Wood Co. (CT) 2
Structural Antiques (OK) 1
Walker, Dennis C. (OH) 2

BOARDS, SALVAGE

Barn People, The (VT)
Mountain Lumber Company (VA)
Old-Home Building & Restoration (CT)
Pennsylvania Barnboard Company (PA)
Period Pine (GA)
Vintage Lumber Co. (MD)

CASINGS & FRAMES FOR DOORS & WINDOWS

(1) Stock Items
(2) Custom Made
Architectural Components (MA) 2
Drums Sash & Door Co., Inc. (PA) 2
Elliott Millwork Co. (IL) 1
House of Moulding (CA) 1
Michael's Fine Colonial Products (NY) 2
Restoration Fraternity (PA) 2
San Francisco Victoriana (CA) 1,2
Silverton Victorian Millworks (CO) 2

CEILINGS, WOOD—CUSTOM MANUFACTURED

Architectural Paneling, Inc. (NY)
Cumberland Woodcraft Co., Inc. (PA)
Quality Woodworks, Inc. (FL)

CHAIR RAILS

(1) Stock Items
(2) Custom Made
Bartley's Mill — Victorian Woodwork (CA) 1,2
Bendix Mouldings, Inc. (NJ) 1
California Heritage Wood Products, Ltd. (CA) 2
Cumberland Woodcraft Co., Inc. (PA)
Dimension Lumber Co. (NY) 2
Dixon Bros. Woodworking (MA) 2
Drums Sash & Door Co., Inc. (PA) 2
Elliott Millwork Co. (IL)
Fireplace Mantel Shop, Inc. (MD)
House of Moulding (CA) 1
Industrial Woodworking, Inc. (IL) 1,2
Maurer & Shepherd, Joyners (CT) 2
Michael's Fine Colonial Products (NY) 2
Old World Moulding & Finishing Co., Inc. (NY) 1
Piscataqua Architectural Woodwork, Co. (NH) 1,2
Quality Woodworks, Inc. (FL) 2
Renovation Concepts, Inc. (MN) 1
San Francisco Victoriana (CA) 1,2
Silverton Victorian Millworks (CO)
Turnbull's Lumber Company (MI) 2

You'll get better service when contacting companies if you mention The Old-House Journal Catalog

DOORS, INTERIOR

(1) Antique (Salvage)
(2) Reproduction
(3) Early American
(4) Victorian
(5) Turn-of-Century
(6) Custom-Made
(7) Other
Architectural Antiques Exchange (PA)
Architectural Antique Warehouse, The (CAN) 1
Architectural Components (MA) 2
Art Directions (MO) 1
Bow House, Inc. (MA) 3
ByGone Era Architectural Antiques (GA) .. 1
C—E Morgan (WI) 3
Canal Co. (DC)
Cascade Mill & Glass Works (CO) 2,6
Castle Burlingame (NJ) 1
Cohen's Architectural Heritage (CAN) 1
Croton, Evelyn — Architectural Antiques (NY) 1
Depot Woodworking, Inc. (VT) 6
Driwood Moulding Company (SC) 6
Drums Sash & Door Co., Inc. (PA) 6
Fireplace Mantel Shop, Inc. (MD) 2
Great American Salvage (NY,VT) 1
Ideal Millwork Co. (TX)
International Wood Products (CA) 4,5,6
Leeke, John — Woodworker (ME) 6
Joe Ley Antiques, Inc. (KY) 1
Maurer & Shepherd, Joyners (CT) 6
Millwork Supply Company (WA) 6
Nord, E.A. Company (WA)
Olde Bostonian Architectural Antiques (MA) 1
Pelnik Wrecking Co., Inc. (NY) 1
Piscataqua Architectural Woodwork, Co. (NH) 3,6
Renovation Concepts, Inc. (MN) 2,4,5
Restoration Fraternity (PA) 6
Richmond Doors (NH) 2,3,6
Salvage One (IL) 1
Second Chance (GA) 1
Somerset Door & Column Co. (PA) 6
Structural Antiques (OK) 1
United House Wrecking Corp. (CT) 1
Westlake Architectural Antiques (TX) 1,4,5
Wood Designs (OH) 6
Woodstone Co. (VT) 3
Wrecking Bar, Inc. (TX) 1

DUMBWAITERS & BUILT-INS

Blue Frog Enterprises (CA)
Dorz Mfg. Co. (WA)
Econol Stairway Lift Corp. (IA)
Henderson Black & Greene, Inc. (AL)
Ideal Millwork Co. (TX)
Iron-A-Way, Inc. (IL)
Sedgwick Machine Works, Inc. (NY)
Vincent — Whitney Co. (CA)

FLOORING, WOOD

(1) Hardwood Strip
(2) Heart Pine
(3) Parquet
(4) Wide Board
(5) Other

Architectural Accents (GA) 2
Bangkok Industries, Inc. (PA) 1,3,4
Bruce Hardwood Floors (TX) 1,3
ByGone Era Architectural Antiques (GA) ..2
Carlisle Restoration Lumber (NH) 4
Castle Burlingame (NJ) 4
Craftsman Lumber Co. (MA) 4
Depot Woodworking, Inc. (VT) 1,2,3,4
Harris Manufacturing Company (TN) 3,4
Hartco (TN) 3
Hoboken Wood Floors Corp. (NJ) 1,4
Kentucky Wood Floors, Inc. (KY) 1,3,4
Lee Woodwork Systems (PA) 1
Legacy Pine Ltd. (GA) 2
Leslie Brothers Lumber Company (WV)
Littlefield Lumber Co., Inc. (NH)
Maurer & Shepherd, Joyners (CT) 5
Memphis Hardwood Flooring Co. (TN) 1
Moore, E.T., Jr. Co. (VA) 2
Mountain Lumber Company (VA) 2,4
Nassau Flooring Corp. (NY) 1,3,4
Pennsylvania Barnboard Company (PA) 2
Period Pine (GA) 2
Quality Woodworks, Inc. (FL) 2
Robinson Lumber Company (LA) 2
Southington Specialty Wood Co. (CT) 4
Tiresias, Inc. (SC) 2,4
Turnbull's Lumber Company (MI) 1
Vintage Lumber Co. (MD) 2
Vintage Pine Co., Inc. (VA) 2,4

FLOORING, LINOLEUM

Bangor Cork Co., Inc. (PA)
Lauria, Tony (PA)
Mannington Mills, Inc. (NJ)

FLOORING, STONE & CERAMIC

(1) Slate, Marble & Other Stone
(2) Ceramic Tile
A.R.D. (NY)
American Olean Tile Company (PA) 2
Brooklyn Tile Supply (NY) 2
Country Floors, Inc. (NY) 2
Evergreen Slate Co. (NY) 1
Mid-State Tile Company (NC) 1
Mr. Slate - Smid Incorporated (VT) 1
New York Marble Works, Inc. (NY) 1
Structural Slate Company (PA) 1
Tatko Bros. Slate Co. (NY) 1
Tile Distributors, Inc. (NY) 2
Vermont Marble Co. (VT) 1
Vermont Structural Slate Co. (VT) 1

See Company Directory for Addresses & Phone Numbers

SEDGWICK RESIDENCE ELEVATORS

A Sedgwick Residence Elevator adds something very special to a fine home. It adds a touch of elegance...and a real measure of comfort and ease.

Sedgwick Residence Elevators are easily and quickly installed in most homes. They are simple to operate and safe to use. They provide the smoothest, quietest, most stable ride available. And they are more affordable than you think.

Ask for our free brochure.

Specializing in Residence Elevators Since 1920
P.O. Box 630,
Poughkeepsie, N.Y. 12602
914-454-5400 • Toll Free: 800-431-8262

GRILLES FOR HOT-AIR REGISTERS

(1) New
(2) Antique (Original)
A-Ball Plumbing Supply (OR) 1
Bryant Stove Works (ME) 2
Croton, Evelyn — Architectural Antiques
(NY) 2
Materials Unlimited (MI) 2
The Reggio Register Co. (MA) 1

HARDWOODS SUPPLIERS

Amherst Woodworking & Supply (MA)
Center Lumber Company (NJ)
Constantine, Albert and Son, Inc. (NY)
Craftsman Lumber Co. (MA)
Depot Woodworking, Inc. (VT)
Kaymar Wood Products, Inc. (WA)
Littlefield Lumber Co., Inc. (NH)
J.H. Monteath Co. (NY)
Morgan Woodworking Supplies (KY)
Mountain Lumber Company (VA)
Native American Hardwood Ltd. (NY)
Potlatch Corp. — Townsend Unit (AR)
Quality Woodworks, Inc. (FL)
Southington Specialty Wood Co. (CT)
Willis Lumber Co. (OH)

OVERDOOR TREATMENTS

Bel-Air Door Co. (CA)
California Heritage Wood Products, Ltd.
(CA)
Driwood Moulding Company (SC)
Fypon, Inc. (PA)
Kenmore Industries (MA)
Verine Products & Co. (UK)

STAIRCASES

American Stair Builder (NY)
C—E Morgan (WI)
Cooper Stair Co. (IL)
Curvoflite (NH)
Dean, James R. (NY)
Dixon Bros. Woodworking (MA)
Driwood Moulding Company (SC)
Drums Sash & Door Co., Inc. (PA)
H & M Stair Builders, Inc. (MD)
Housejoiner, Ltd. (VT)
Steptoe and Wife Antiques Ltd. (CAN)
Taney Supply & Lumber Corp. (MD)
Woodstone Co. (VT)

SPIRAL STAIRCASES

(1) Wood
(2) Metal
American General Products (MI)
American Ornamental Corporation (TX) 2
Cooper Stair Co. (IL) 1
Curvoflite (NH) 1
Duvinage Corporation (MD) 1,2
H & M Stair Builders, Inc. (MD) 1
International Building Components (NY) 1
Midwest Spiral Stair Company, Inc. (IL) ..1,2
Remodelers & Renovators (ID) 2
Rich Woodturning and Stair Co. (FL) 1
San Francisco Victoriana (CA)
Schwartz's Forge & Metalworks (NY)
Spiral Manufacturing, Inc. (LA) 1
Stair-Pak Products Co. (NJ) 1
Steptoe and Wife Antiques Ltd. (CAN) 2
Taney Supply & Lumber Corp. (MD) 1

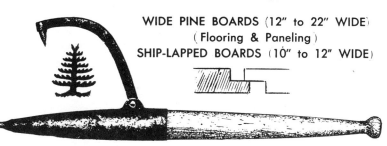

STAIRCASE PARTS

(1) Balusters, Antique (Original)
(2) Balusters, New
(3) Balusters, Custom-Made
(4) Handrails
(5) Newel Posts
(6) Other

Abaroot Mfg., Co. (CA) 3,5
American Stair Builder (NY)
Architectural Accents (GA) 1
Artifacts, Inc. (VA) 1
Bailey Architectural Millwork (NJ)
Bank Architectural Antiques (LA) 4,5
ByGone Era Architectural Antiques (GA)
.... 1,4,5
C—E Morgan (WI) 2,4,5
Canal Co. (DC) 1,5
Croton, Evelyn — Architectural Antiques
(NY) 1,5
Crowe Company (CA)
Cumberland Woodcraft Co., Inc. (PA) ...2,4,5
Curvoflite (NH) 3
Dean, James R. (NY)
Depot Woodworking, Inc. (VT) 2,3,4,5
Dixon Bros. Woodworking (MA) 3,4
Drums Sash & Door Co., Inc. (PA) 6
Elk Valley Woodworking Company (OK) ...2
Gazebo and Porchworks (WA) 2
Great American Salvage (NY,VT) 1
H & M Stair Builders, Inc. (MD) 2,4,5
Haas Wood & Ivory Works (CA) 3,4,5
Harris Manufacturing Company (TN) 6
Henderson Black & Greene, Inc. (AL) 2
House of Moulding (CA) 2,4,5
Industrial Woodworking, Inc. (IL) 4,5
Island City Wood Working Co. (TX) 3

Kingsway (CO) 2,5,6
Leeke, John — Woodworker (ME)
Legacy Pine Ltd. (GA) 3,5
Joe Ley Antiques, Inc. (KY) 5
Mansion Industries, Inc. (CA) 2,4,5
Materials Unlimited (MI) 1
Michael's Fine Colonial Products (NY) ..3,4,5
Miles Lumber Co, Inc. (VT) 3
Millwork Supply Company (WA) 3
Nelson-Johnson Wood Products, Inc. (MN) 2
Nord, E.A. Company (WA) 2
North Pacific Joinery (CA) 3,4,5
Olde Bostonian Architectural Antiques (MA)
.... 5
Pagliacco Turning & Milling Architectural
Wood Turning (CA) 2,3,5
Renovation Products (TX) 2,4,5
Rich Woodturning and Stair Co. (FL) 3
Second Chance (GA) 1,5
Somerset Door & Column Co. (PA) 3,5
Taft Wood Products Co. (OH) 3
Taney Supply & Lumber Corp. (MD) .. 2,3,4,5
Vintage Pine Co., Inc. (VA) 6
Wrecking Bar, Inc. (TX) 5

TIN CEILINGS

AA-Abbingdon, Inc. (NY)
Ceilings, Walls & More, Inc. (TX)
Chelsea Decorative Metal Co. (TX)
Designer Resource (CA)
Hi-Art East (GA)
Klinke & Lew Contractors (CO)
Norman, W.F., Corporation (MO)
Ohman, C.A. (NY)
Remodelers & Renovators (ID)
Renovation Concepts, Inc. (MN)
Shanker—Glendale Steel Corp. (NY)
Steptoe and Wife Antiques Ltd. (CAN)
Structural Antiques (OK)

VENEERS & INLAYS

Artistry in Veneers, Inc. (NY)
Boseman Veneer & Supply Co. (TX)
Constantine, Albert and Son, Inc. (NY)
Depot Woodworking, Inc. (VT)
Dover Furniture Stripping (DE)
Gaston Wood Finishes, Inc. (IN)
Homecraft Veneer (PA)
Morgan Woodworking Supplies (KY)
Woodworkers' Store, The (MN)

THE BARCLAY

THE KENSINGTON

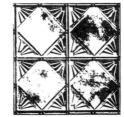

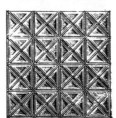
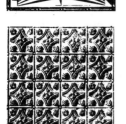

WAINSCOTTING

(1) Antique (Salvage)
(2) New

Amerian Woodworking (CA) 2
Art Directions (MO) 1
Canal Works Architectural Antiques (OH) .. 1
Carlisle Restoration Lumber (NH) 2
Craftsman Lumber Co. (MA) 2
Cumberland Woodcraft Co., Inc. (PA) 2
Depot Woodworking, Inc. (VT) 2
Dixon Bros. Woodworking (MA) 2
Elliott Millwork Co. (IL) 2
Kingsway (CO) 2
Lee Woodwork Systems (PA) 2
Materials Unlimited (MI) 1
Maurer & Shepherd, Joyners (CT)
Old World Moulding & Finishing Co., Inc.
  (NY) 2
Olde Bostonian Architectural Antiques (MA)
  1
Quality Woodworks, Inc. (FL) 2
Renovation Concepts, Inc. (MN)
Restoration Fraternity (PA) 2
Robinson Lumber Company (LA) 2
San Francisco Victoriana (CA) 2
Silverton Victorian Millworks (CO) 2
Sunshine Architectural Woodworks (AR) ... 2

WALL PANELLING, WOOD—PERIOD

(1) Antique (Salvage)
(2) New—Stock Items
(3) Custom-Made

Amerian Woodworking (CA) 2
Architectural Antiques Exchange (PA)
Architectural Components (MA) 3
Architectural Paneling, Inc. (NY) 3
Art Directions (MO) 1
Bangkok Industries, Inc. (PA) 2
Canal Works Architectural Antiques (OH) .. 1
Carlisle Restoration Lumber (NH) 3
Cooper Stair Co. (IL) 2
Craftsman Lumber Co. (MA) 3
Cumberland Woodcraft Co., Inc. (PA) 2
Curvoflite (NH) 3
Depot Woodworking, Inc. (VT) 2,3
Dixon Bros. Woodworking (MA) 3
Driwood Moulding Company (SC) 2
Great American Salvage (NY,VT) 1
Industrial Woodworking, Inc. (IL) 2,3
Johnson, Walter H. (NY) 3
LaPointe, Chip, Cabinetmaker (NY) 3
Leeke, John — Woodworker (ME) 3
Legacy Pine Ltd. (GA) 3
Leslie Brothers Lumber Company (WV) 2,3
Maurer & Shepherd, Joyners (CT) 3
Moore, E.T., Jr. Co. (VA) 3
Mountain Lumber Company (VA) 1
Old World Moulding & Finishing Co., Inc.
  (NY) 2,3
Period Pine (GA) 2
Piscatagua Architectural Woodwork, Co.
  (NH) 3
Quality Woodworks, Inc. (FL) 3
Restoration Fraternity (PA) 3
Restorations Unlimited, Inc. (PA) 3
Salvage One (IL) 1
Somerset Door & Column Co. (PA) 3
Southington Specialty Wood Co. (CT) 2
Sunshine Architectural Woodworks (AR) . 2,3
Tiresias, Inc. (SC) 2
Vermont Weatherboard, Inc. (VT) 2
Walker, Dennis C. (OH) 3
Wrecking Bar, Inc. (TX) 1

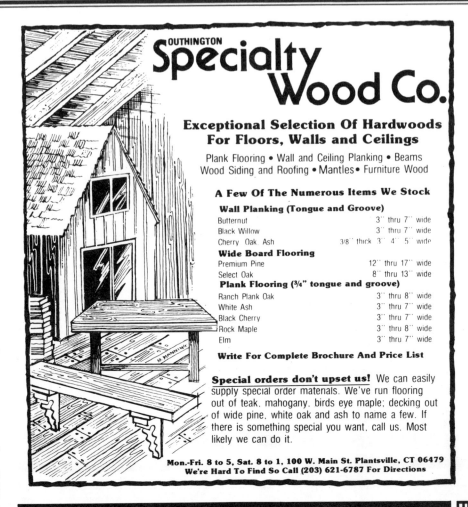
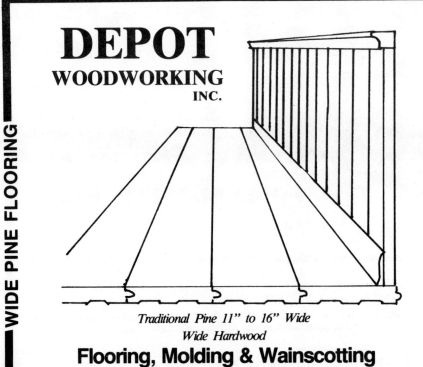

Ceilings, Walls & More, Inc. (TX)
Giles & Kendall, Inc. (AL)

It takes a rare lumber company to bring you quality heart pine.

You can buy longleaf heart pine from several companies, but when you want the best, come to Mountain Lumber. We concentrate exclusively on the selection and milling of superior heart pine and other rare wood products to insure the widest choice for the discriminating buyer.

Because we hand select our heart pine of only the best sources, and because we kiln dry every piece to stabilize the wood against shrinkage or warping, you can be sure of Mountain Lumber quality. Our milling craftsmen are second to none, so we can design and build beautiful custom cabinetry, doors and mouldings for any installation.

What's more, all our wood is precisely graded for grain, sap content, defects, and shake, and comes in standard widths. There's nothing more beautiful than authentic longleaf heart pine for flooring, paneling, trim, mouldings, custom millwork and the best place to get it is Mountain Lumber. To learn more about this unique wood, call or write for our brochure and price list.

MOUNTAIN LUMBER

1327 Carlton Avenue, Dept. OHJ   Charlottesville, Virginia 22901   (804) 295-1922 or 295-1757

**See Company Directory for
Addresses & Phone Numbers**

**You'll get better service
when contacting companies
if you mention
The Old-House Journal
Catalog**

Decorative Interior Materials & Supplies

BRACKETS & CORBELS—INTERIOR

ByGone Era Architectural Antiques (GA)
Croton, Evelyn — Architectural Antiques (NY)
Cumberland Woodcraft Co., Inc. (PA)
Decorators Supply Corp. (IL)
Dovetail, Inc. (MA)
Elk Valley Woodworking Company (OK)
Haas Wood & Ivory Works (CA)
Hallelujah Redwood Products (CA)
House of Moulding (CA)
Leyva's Ornamental Staff & Stone (CA)
Pagliacco Turning & Milling Architectural Wood Turning (CA)
Renovation Products (TX)
Vintage Wood Works (TX)

CEILING MEDALLIONS

(1) Non-Plaster
(2) Plaster
Architectural Sculpture (NY) 2
Biagiotti, L. (NY) 2
Crawford's Old House Store (WI) 2
Decorators Supply Corp. (IL) 2
Designer Resource (CA) 2
Dovetail, Inc. (MA) 2
Entol Industries, Inc. (FL) 1
Felber, Inc. (PA) 2
Fischer & Jirouch Co. (OH) 2
Focal Point, Inc. (GA) 1
Giannetti Studios (MD) 1,2
J.O. Holloway & Company (OR) 1
House of Moulding (CA) 1
Lachin, Albert & Assoc., Inc. (LA) 2
Leyva's Ornamental Staff & Stone (CA) 2
Nostalgia, Inc. (GA) 2
Orlandini Studios Ltd. Decorative Plaster Supply Co. (WI) 2
Ornamental Design Studios (NY) 2
Renovation Concepts, Inc. (MN) 1,2
Restoration Hardware (CA) 1
Russell Restoration of Suffolk (NY) 2
San Francisco Victoriana (CA) 2
J.P. Weaver Co. (CA) 1
Weaver, W. T. & Sons, Inc. (DC) 1
Windmill Interiors (CA) 2

COLUMNS & CAPITALS—INTERIOR

(1) Composition
(2) Plaster
(3) Wood
American Wood Column (NY) 3
Architectural Sculpture (NY) 2
Biagiotti, L. (NY) 1,2
ByGone Era Architectural Antiques (GA) .. 3
Cumberland Woodcraft Co., Inc. (PA) 3
Decorators Supply Corp. (IL) 2,3
Designer Resource (CA) 1,2
Dovetail, Inc. (MA) 2
Elk Valley Woodworking Company (OK) ... 3
Felber, Inc. (PA) 2
Fischer & Jirouch Co. (OH) 2
Giannetti Studios (MD) 1,2
Haas Wood & Ivory Works (CA) 3
Hartmann-Sanders Column Co. (GA) 3
J.O. Holloway & Company (OR) 1
Kingsway (CO) 1
Lachin, Albert & Assoc., Inc. (LA) 2
Leyva's Ornamental Staff & Stone (CA) 2
Pagliacco Turning & Milling Architectural Wood Turning (CA) 3
Renovation Concepts, Inc. (MN) 2,3
Russell Restoration of Suffolk (NY) 2
Schwerd Manufacturing Co. (PA) 1
Second Chance (GA) 3
Turncraft (OR) 3
J.P. Weaver Co. (CA) 1
Wrecking Bar, Inc. (TX)

Timeless Designs Go Right To The Top. Focal Point.

Focal Point® cornice mouldings of tough, lightweight, fire-retardant Endure-all.™ They make master craftsmanship feasible for today's homes. They're molded in single members, install with hammer and nails, come ready to paint or stain! We have the largest selection available of historically documented patterns to suit any style. Take your interior designs right to the top. With Focal Point. Send $3 for our brochures.

Dept. OHC4/2005 Marietta Road, N.W.
Atlanta, Georgia 30318/404-351-0820

Focal Point Inc.
There is only one.

CERAMIC TILE

(1) Antique
(2) Dutch
(3) Encaustic
(4) Hand-Painted
(5) Period Styles—New
(6) Small White Hexagonal (Bathroom)
(7) Custom-Made

ARJ Assoc. — Reza Jahedi (MA) 4,7
American Olean Tile Company (PA) 5
Amsterdam Corporation (NY) 2,4
Architectural Terra Cotta and Tile, Ltd. (IL) 3
Backlund Moravian Tile Works (FL) 4,5,7
Berkshire Porcelain Studios Ltd. (MA) 4,7
Brooklyn Tile Supply (NY) 6
Country Floors, Inc. (NY) 5
Dutch Products & Supply Co. (PA) 2,4
Elon, Inc. (NY) 4
FerGene Studio (IN) 5
H & R Johnson Tile Ltd./ Highgate Tile
  Works 5,7
Hearthstone Tile Studio (NY) 7
Jackson, Wm. H. Co. (NY) 4
Sculptured Tiles (NY) 4,7
Second Chance (GA) 1
Summitville Tiles, Inc. (OH) 3,6
Terra Designs, Inc. (NJ) 4,5,7
Tile Distributors, Inc. (NY) 6
Tootie's Tile & Trim (TX) 5
Up Your Alley (PA) 1
Virtue, W.D., Co., Inc. (NJ) 7
Helen Williams—Delft Tiles (CA) 1,2

CORNER BEAD MOULDING

Crawford's Old House Store (WI)
Renovation Products (TX)

FRETWORK & GRILLES, WOOD

ByGone Era Architectural Antiques (GA)
Croton, Evelyn — Architectural Antiques
  (NY)
Cumberland Woodcraft Co., Inc. (PA)
Emporium, The (TX)
Gazebo and Porchworks (WA)
Gingerbread House (NC)
North Pacific Joinery (CA)
Renovation Concepts, Inc. (MN)
Victorian Reproductions Enterprises, Inc.
  (MN)
Vintage Wood Works (TX)

GLASS, CURVED—FOR CHINA CABINETS

Blaschke Cabinet Glass (CT)
Furniture Revival (OR)
Morgan & Company (NY)
Shadovitz Bros. Distributors, Inc. (NY)

**See Company Directory for
Addresses & Phone Numbers**

GLASS, ART—ANTIQUE (STAINED, BEVELLED, ETCHED, ETC.)

Architectural Accents (GA)
Architectural Antiques Exchange (PA)
Architectural Archives (TX)
Art Directions (MO)
Artifacts, Inc. (VA)
Bank Architectural Antiques (LA)
ByGone Era Architectural Antiques (GA)
Canal Co. (DC)
Canal Works Architectural Antiques (OH)
Cohen's Architectural Heritage (CAN)
Electric Glass Co. (VA)
Florida Victoriani Architectural Antiques (FL)
Great American Salvage (NY,VT)
Master's Stained and Etched Glass Studio
  (CA)
Materials Unlimited (MI)
Pelnik Wrecking Co., Inc. (NY)
Red Baron's Peachtree Antique Emporium
  (GA)
Salvage One (IL)
Spiess, Greg (IL)
Structural Antiques (OK)
Such Happiness, Inc. (MA)
Sunset Antiques, Inc. (MI)
United House Wrecking Corp. (CT)
Westlake Architectural Antiques (TX)
Wilson, H. Weber, Antiquarian (MD)
Wrecking Bar of Atlanta (GA)
Wrecking Bar, Inc. (TX)

GLASS, LEADED & STAINED—NEW

(1) New Work
(2) Restoration & Repair

Bel-Air Door Co. (CA) 1
Botti Studio of Architectural Arts (IL) 1,2
Boulder Stained Glass Studios (CO) 1,2
CasaBlanca Glass, Ltd. (GA) 1
Contois Stained Glass Studio (WV)
Crowe Company (CA) 1
Crown Glass Co. (CO) 2
Curran, Patrick J. (MA) 1
Franklin Art Glass Studios (OH) 1
Glassmasters Guild (NY) 1
Golden Age Glassworks (NY) 1,2
Greenland Studio, Inc., The (NY) 1,2
Greg Monk Stained Glass (HI) 1,2
Lyn Hovey Studio, Inc. (MA) 2
Lamb, J & R Studios (NY) 1,2
LaRoche Stained Glass (MA) 1,2
Manor Art Glass Studio (NY) 1,2
Master's Stained and Etched Glass Studio
  (CA) 1
Melotte-Morse Studios (IL) 1,2
Morgan Bockius Studios, Inc. (PA) 1,2
Nast, Vivian (NY) 1
Newe Daisterre Glas (OH) 1,2
Phoenix Studio, Inc. (ME) 1,2
Pike Stained Glass Studios, Inc. (NY) 1,2
Pompei Stained Glass (MA) 1,2
Porcelli, Ernest (NY) 1,2
Ragland Stained Glass (IN) 1,2
Rambusch (NY) 2
Ring, J. Stained Glass, Inc. (MN) 1,2
Rohlf's Stained & Leaded Glass (NY) 1,2
Southeastern Art Glass Studio (GA) 1
Spiess, Greg (IL) 1
Stained Panes (CT) 1
Studio Workshop, Ltd. (CT) 2
Such Happiness, Inc. (MA) 1,2
Sunburst Stained Glass Co. (IN) 1,2
Sunset Antiques, Inc. (MI) 1,2
Unique Art Glass Co. (MO) 1,2
Victorian Glassworks (MD) 1,2
Jack Wallis' Doors (KY) 1
Willet Stained Glass Studio, Inc. (PA) 1,2
Wilson, H. Weber, Antiquarian (MD) 1,2
Windle Stained Glass Studio (NC) 1,2

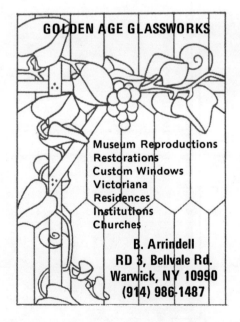

GLASS, ETCHED—NEW

GLASS, SPECIALTY—NEW

(1) Bevelled
(2) Carved & Cut
(3) Engraved
(4) Glue-Chip
(5) Slumping & Bending

Turn a hole-in-the-wall fireplace...

into this – with a Readybuilt® Mantel.

MANTELS

(1) Antique (Original)
(2) New (Reproduction)
(3) Cast Iron
(4) Marble
(5) Slate
(6) Wood
(7) Other

Amerian Woodworking (CA) *2,6*
Architectural Accents (GA) *1*
Architectural Antiques Exchange (PA) *1,6*
Architectural Archives (TX)
Architectural Paneling, Inc. (NY) *2,6*
Art Directions (MO) *1*
Artifacts, Inc. (VA) *1*
Bank Architectural Antiques (LA) *1*
ByGone Era Architectural Antiques (GA)
.... *1,3,4,5,6*
C—E Morgan (WI) *6*
Canal Co. (DC) *1*
Canal Works Architectural Antiques (OH) .. *1*
Cohen's Architectural Heritage (CAN) *1*
Crawford's Old House Store (WI) *2,4,6*
Decorators Supply Corp. (IL) *2*
Designer Resource (CA) *6*
Driwood Moulding Company (SC) *2*
Drums Sash & Door Co., Inc. (PA) *2*
Feather River Wood and Glass Co. (CA) ..*2,6*
Fireplace Mantel Shop, Inc. (MD) *2,6*

Florida Victoriani Architectural Antiques (FL)
.... *1*
Henderson Black & Greene, Inc. (AL) *2*
International Building Components (NY) *6*
Jackson, Wm. H. Co. (NY) *6*
Joe Ley Antiques, Inc. (KY) *1*
Materials Unlimited (MI) *1*
Millwork Supply Company (WA) *6*
Monroe Coldren and Sons (PA) *1*
Moore, E.T., Jr. Co. (VA) *6*
New York Marble Works, Inc. (NY) *4*
Old Colony Crafts (ME) *7*
Old World Moulding & Finishing Co., Inc.
(NY) *2*
Olde Bostonian Architectural Antiques (MA)
.... *1*
Pelnik Wrecking Co., Inc. (NY) *1*
Purcell, Francis J., II (PA) *1*
Quality Woodworks, Inc. (FL) *2,6*
Readybuilt Products, Co. (MD) *2,6*
Remodelers & Renovators (ID) *2*
Renovation Concepts, Inc. (MN) *2*
Restoration Fraternity (PA) *2*
Restoration Hardware (CA) *2*
Roman Marble Co. (IL) *1,4*
Salvage One (IL) *1*
Second Chance (GA) *1*
Southington Specialty Wood Co. (CT) *2,6*
Spiess, Greg (IL) *1*
Structural Antiques (OK) *1,3,6*

Sunset Antiques, Inc. (MI) *1*
Sunshine Architectural Woodworks (AR) . *2,6*
Trump R.T., & Co., Inc. (PA) *1*
United House Wrecking Corp. (CT) *1,6*
Verine Products & Co. (UK) *2*
Westlake Architectural Antiques (TX) *1,3,4,5,6*
Windmill Interiors (CA) *2,7*
Wrecking Bar of Atlanta (GA) *1*
Wrecking Bar, Inc. (TX) *1*
Ye Olde Mantel Shoppe (FL) *3,6,7*

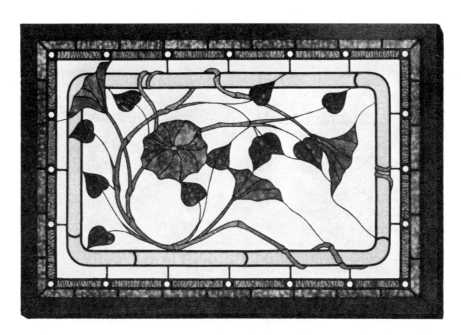

Ernest Porcelli/Stained Glass

333 Flatbush Avenue, Brooklyn, New York 11217 — (212) 857-6888

**Custom designed, leaded and stained glass windows, door panels, side lights, skylights
For Commercial and Residential Use**

Repairs and Restoration — Estimates with SASE, send dimensions

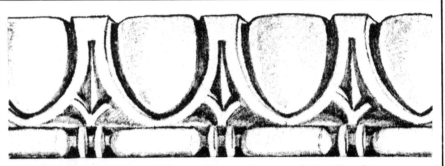

MARBLE, REPLACEMENT (FINISHED PIECES)

New York Marble Works, Inc. (NY)
Shaw Marble & Tile Co., Inc. (MO)
Vermont Marble Co. (VT)

MOULDINGS & CORNICES—INTERIOR DECORATIVE

(1) Composition
(2) Plaster
(3) Wood
(4) Custom Cast

American Wood Column (NY) 3
Architectural Paneling, Inc. (NY) 3
Architectural Sculpture (NY) 4
Bartley's Mill — Victorian Woodwork (CA) . 3
Bendix Mouldings, Inc. (NJ) 3
Biagiotti, L. (NY) *1,2,4*
California Heritage Wood Products, Ltd.
   (CA) 3
Casey Architectural Specialties (WI) *2,4*
Cumberland Woodcraft Co., Inc. (PA) 3
Decorators Supply Corp. (IL) *1,2,3*
Designer Resource (CA) *1,2,3*
Dixon Bros. Woodworking (MA) 3
Dovetail, Inc. (MA) 2
Driwood Moulding Company (SC) 3
Elliott Millwork Co. (IL) 3
Englewood Hardware Co. (NJ)
Entol Industries, Inc. (FL) *1*
Felber, Inc. (PA) *2,4*
Fireplace Mantel Shop, Inc. (MD) 3
Fischer & Jirouch Co. (OH) 2
Focal Point, Inc. (GA) *1*
Frenzel Specialty Moulding Co. (MO) *3,4*
Giannetti Studios (MD) *1,2,4*
Greensboro Art Foundry & Machine Co.
   (NC) 4
Haas Wood & Ivory Works (CA) 3
Hallelujah Redwood Products (CA) 3
J.O. Holloway & Company (OR) *1,4*
House of Moulding (CA) 3
Industrial Woodworking, Inc. (IL) 3
Kingsway (CO) *1,3*
Klise Manufacturing Company (MI) 3
Lachin, Albert & Assoc., Inc. (LA) *2,4*
Merit Moulding, Ltd. (NY) 3
Michael's Fine Colonial Products (NY) *3,4*
Moore, E.T., Jr. Co. (VA) 3
Navedo Woodcraft, Inc. (NY) 3
Nelson-Johnson Wood Products, Inc. (MN) 3
Nostalgia, Inc. (GA) 2
Old Colony Crafts (ME)
Old World Moulding & Finishing Co., Inc.
   (NY) 3
Orlandini Studios Ltd. Decorative Plaster
   Supply Co. (WI) 4
Ornamental Design Studios (NY) *2,4*
Period Pine (GA) 3
Piscatagua Architectural Woodwork, Co.
   (NH) 3

(continued)

See Company Directory for Addresses & Phone Numbers

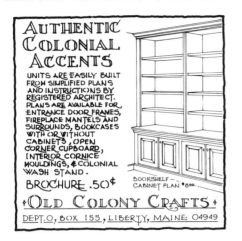
ORNAMENTS

BED HANGINGS

CANDLESTANDS & HOLDERS

CLOCKS

CHAIRS, VICTORIAN REPRODUCTION

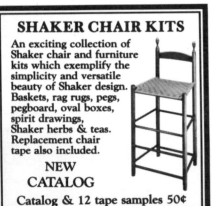

CHAIRS, EARLY AMERICAN REPRODUCTION

(1) Colonial Wooden Side Chairs
(2) Rockers
(3) Other
Cohasset Colonials by Hagerty (MA)
Colonial Williamsburg Foundation Craft House (VA) 1
Cornucopia, Inc. (MA) 1,2
Country Bed Shop (MA) 1
Furniture Traditions, Inc. (NC) 1
Greenfield Village and Henry Ford Museum (MI) 1
Habersham Plantation Corp. (GA) 1,2
Heritage Design (IA) 2
Lea, James — Cabinetmaker (ME) 1
Mazza Frame and Furniture Co., Inc. (NY)
.... 1,3
Rocker Shop of Marietta, GA (GA) 2
Shaker Workshops (MA) 1,2
Whitley Studios (PA) 2
Yield House, Inc. (NH)

CHRISTMAS DECORATIONS

Amazon Vinegar & Pickling Works Drygoods (IA)
Gerlachs of Lecha (PA)
Hurley Patentee Lighting (NY)
Museum of the City of New York (NY)
Victorian Accents (NY)

CLOTHING, PERIOD

(1) Patterns
(2) Custom-Made
(3) Ready-To-Wear
Amazon Vinegar & Pickling Works Drygoods (IA) 1,3
Arriaga, Nelson (NY) 2,3
Old World Sewing Pattern Co. (MN) 1
Past Patterns (MI) 1
Patchmakers (NY) 1
Sunflower Studio (CO) 2

DRAPERY & CURTAINS

(1) Curtains, Ready-Made
(2) Curtains, Custom-Made
(3) Drapes, Custom-Made

Beck, Nelson of Wash. Inc. (DC) 2,3
Nancy Borden, Period Textiles (NH) 2
Cohasset Colonials by Hagerty (MA) 1
Country Curtains (MA) 1
Dentelle de France (CA) 1
Dorothy's Ruffled Originals (NC) 1,2
Grilk Interiors (IA) 2,3
Home Fabric Mills, Inc. (MA) 3
Norman's of Salisbury (NC) 2
Old Colony Curtains (NJ) 1
Quaker Lace Co. (NY) 1
Rue de France (RI) 1

DRAPERY & CURTAIN PATTERNS—PERIOD DESIGNS

Colonial Weavers (ME)

DRAPERY HARDWARE

(1) Wood Poles & Brackets
(2) Metal Poles & Brackets
(3) Decorative Tie-Backs

Ball and Ball (PA) 2,3
Cohasset Colonials by Hagerty (MA) 1
Country Curtains (MA) 1
Decorative Hardware Studio (NY) 3
Gould-Mesereau Co., Inc. (NY) 1,2,3
Guerin, P.E. Inc. (NY) 2,3
Hunrath , Wm. Co., Inc. (NY) 2
Standard Trimming Co. (NY) 3

DRAPERY TRIMMINGS

Colonial Williamsburg Foundation Craft
    House (VA)
Meyer, Kenneth Co. (CA)
Scalamandre, Inc. (NY)
Standard Trimming Co. (NY)

**See Company Directory for
Addresses & Phone Numbers**

FABRIC, REPRODUCTION

(1) Early American
(2) Victorian
(3) Turn-of-Century

Nancy Borden, Period Textiles (NH) 1
Brunschwig & Fils, Inc. (NY) 1,2,3
Cohasset Colonials by Hagerty (MA) 1
Colonial Williamsburg Foundation Craft
    House (VA) 1
Cowtan & Tout, Inc. (NY) 1,2,3
Hexter, S. M. Company (OH) 1
Historic Charleston Reproductions (SC)
Johnson, R.L. Interiors (MT)
LEE JOFA (NY) 1,2
Scalamandre, Inc. (NY) 1,2,3
Sunflower Studio (CO) 1
Thibaut, Richard E., Inc. (NJ) 1,2
Waverly Fabrics (NY) 1,2

FABRIC, TRADITIONAL

(1) Tapestry
(2) Crewel
(3) Handwoven
(4) Linen, Cotton
(5) Horsehair
(6) Silk, Velvet, Damask
(7) Other

Brown, Carol (VT) 4,7
Brunschwig & Fils, Inc. (NY) 1,4,5,6
Colonial Williamsburg Foundation Craft
    House (VA) 4,6
Cowtan & Tout, Inc. (NY) 6
Cyrus Clark Co., Inc. (NY) 4
Dentelle de France (CA) 7
Gill Imports (CT) 2
Gurian's (NY) 2
Heirloom Rugs (RI)
Home Fabric Mills, Inc. (MA) 6
Homespun Weavers (PA) 4
S. & C. Huber, Accoutrements (CT) 2,3,4
Johnson, R.L. Interiors (MT)
LEE JOFA (NY) 2,4
Lovelia Enterprises, Inc. (NY) 1
Scalamandre, Inc. (NY) 2,4,5,6
Sunflower Studio (CO) 3,4
Tioga Mill Outlet (PA) 6
Waverly Fabrics (NY) 4

FURNITURE, REPRODUCTION — CUSTOM-MADE

Artistic Woodworking, Inc. (MI)
Biggs Company (VA)
Campbell, Marion (PA)
Carolina Leather House, Inc. (NC)
Congdon, Johns/Cabinetmaker (VT)
Crowfoot's Inc. (AZ)
Curry, Gerald — Cabinetmaker (ME)
Dixon Bros. Woodworking (MA)
Gaudio Custom Furniture (NY)
LaPointe, Chip, Cabinetmaker (NY)
Lea, James — Cabinetmaker (ME)
Master Wood Carver (NJ)
Mead Associates Woodworking, Inc. (NY)
Millbranth, D.R. (NH)
Newby, Simon (MA)
Nutt, Craig, Fine Wood Works (AL)
Whitley Studios (PA)

Our Ruffled Originals
and Old Houses...
made for each other.

Just imagine our custom-made curtains
or
coverlets, shams, dust ruffles
or
placemats, tablecloths, napkins,
chairpads
or
lampshades or wreaths
in
Ask about our DYNASTY
fabric curtains · standard
size (96"L.x180"W.) $58.pr. Your Old House
36 · Page Catalog & Swatches $4.00

Dorothy's Ruffled Originals, Inc.

6721 Market St. Wilmington, NC 28405 (Dpt.OHJ)
(919) 791·1296   Mst. Ch. Visa Am. Ex.
Toll·free 1·800·334·2593   In NC: 1·800·672·2947

FURNITURE & ACCESSORIES — PERIOD STYLES

*The chair
is Shaker,
the fabric is
Brunschwig.*

*DOMMEL: mohair velvet.
Chair: Shaker Museum Collection, Old Chatham, NY.*

Brunschwig & Fils, Inc.

410 East 62 Street • New York, N.Y. 10021 • Through designers and fine stores.

You'll get better service
when contacting companies
if you mention
The Old-House Journal
Catalog

**See Company Directory for
Addresses & Phone Numbers**

LAMP SHADES — FRINGE

Rumplestiltskin Designs (CA)

LAMP SHADES — PERIOD STYLES

Burdoch Silk Lampshade Co. (CA)
Country Window, The (PA)
Custom House (CT)
Dilworthtown Country Store (PA)
Light Fantastic (WA)
Lundberg Studios (CA)
Menerey, E. W. (MI)
Pacific Lamp & Stove Co. (WA)
Shades of the Past (CA)
Victorian Reproductions Enterprises, Inc.
(MN)
Yestershades (OR)

NEEDLEWORK KITS

(1) Crewel Chair Kits
(2) Rug Braiding & Hooking
(3) Needlepoint
(4) Quilt Patterns
Colonial Williamsburg Foundation Craft
House (VA) *1,3*

PEDESTALS & PLANT STANDS

(1) Cast Iron
(2) Marble
(3) Wood
(4) Wrought Iron
Magnolia Hall (GA) 3
New York Marble Works, Inc. (NY) 2
Wolchonok, M. and Son, Inc. (NY) 1,3,4

PICTURE FRAMES

Decorators Market, USA (TX)
Sedgwick House (IN)

PICTURE HANGERS — PERIOD STYLES

Masters Picture Frame Co. (MI)
Novelty Trimming Works, Inc. (NJ)
S & W Framing Supplies, Inc. (NY)

PRINTS & ORIGINAL ART

Creatus (PA)
Facemakers, Inc. (IL)
Gifford, D.K. (GA)
Grilk Interiors (IA)
McGivern, Barbara — Artist (WI)

RUGS & CARPETS

(1) Ingrain
(2) Oriental
(3) Traditional
(4) Documentary Reproductions
(5) Custom-Made
(6) Other
Colefax and Fowler *3,5*
Couristan, Inc. (NY) *2*
Jacobsen, Charles W., Inc. (NY) *2*
Johnson, R.L. Interiors (MT) *3*
Langhorne Carpet Co. (PA) *3,4,5*
Patterson, Flynn, & Martin, Inc. (NY) *3*
Peerless Imported Rugs (IL) *2,3*
Rastetter Woolen Mill (OH) *3*
Scalamandre, Inc. (NY) *1,3*
Stark Carpet Corp. (NY) *2,6*
Sunflower Studio (CO) *1,5*
Victorian Collectibles Ltd. (WI) *6*

RUGS, FOLK

(1) Braided
(2) Floorcloths
(3) Straw Matting
(4) Hooked
(5) Needlework
(6) Woven
(7) Other
Adams and Swett (MA) *1,4*
Brown, Carol (VT) *6*
Cole, Diane Jackson (ME) *6*
Cornucopia, Inc. (MA) *1*
Country Braid House (NH) *1*
Floorcloths Incorporated (MD) *2*
Good Stenciling (NH) *2*
Heirloom Rugs (RI) *4*
Heritage Rugs (PA)
S. & C. Huber, Accoutrements (CT) *1,4,5,6*
Import Specialists, Inc. (NY) *3*
Peerless Imported Rugs (IL) *1,6*
Pemaquid Floorcloths (ME) *2*
Rastetter Woolen Mill (OH) *4,6*
Shaker Workshops (MA) *6*
Sunflower Studio (CO) *6*

SHADES, BLINDS, & SCREENS

Devenco Louver Products (GA)
Hudson Venetian Blind Service, Inc. (VA)
Iberia Millwork (LA)
LaForte Design (MA)
Walsh Screen Products (NY)

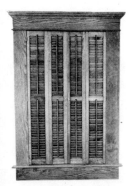

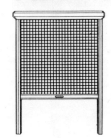

OLD-FASHIONED RESTAURANT FITTINGS

Architectural Antiques Exchange (PA)
Architectural Antique Warehouse, The (CAN)
Art Directions (MO)
Bedlam Brass (NJ)
Bona Decorative Hardware (OH)
Brass Menagerie (LA)
Canal Works Architectural Antiques (OH)
Gargoyles, Ltd. (PA)
Joe Ley Antiques, Inc. (KY)
Spiess, Greg (IL)

UMBRELLA STANDS & COAT RACKS

(1) Umbrella Stands
(2) Coat Racks
Bedlam Brass (NJ) 2
Brass Bed Company of America (CA) 2
Kayne, Steve & Son Custom Forged
    Hardware (NC) 2
Lemee's Fireplace Equipment (MA) 1
Magnolia Hall (GA)
Pacific Lamp & Stove Co. (WA) 2
Swan Brass Beds (CA) 2

WALLCOVERINGS (OTHER THAN WALLPAPER)

(1) Anaglypta
(2) Leather, Genuine
(3) Leather, Imitation
(4) Embossed Vinyl
(5) Other
Bentley Bros. (KY) *1,3,4*
Brown, Carol (VT) *5*
Decor International Wallcovering, Inc. (NY) *1*
Feather River Wood and Glass Co. (CA) *4*
Flexi-Wall Systems (SC) *5*
Kingsway (CO) *1,4*
Rejuvenation House Parts Co. (OR) *1*
Remodelers & Renovators (ID) *1*
Renovation Products (TX) *1*
Restoration Hardware (CA) *1*
San Francisco Victoriana (CA) *1*
Scalamandre, Inc. (NY) *2,3*
Thibaut, Richard E., Inc. (NJ) *3,4*
Victorian Crown, Ltd. (OR) *1,4*

WALLPAPER, EARLY AMERICAN

(1) Documentary Reproduction
(2) Scenic Antique
(3) Scenic Reproduction
(4) Other
Brunschwig & Fils, Inc. (NY) *1*
Colonial Williamsburg Foundation Craft
    House (VA) *1*
Cowtan & Tout, Inc. (NY) *1*
Greenfield Village and Henry Ford Museum
    (MI) *1*
Hexter, S. M. Company (OH) *1*
Scalamandre, Inc. (NY) *1*
Schumacher (NY) *1*
Thibaut, Richard E., Inc. (NJ) *1,3*
The Twigs, Inc. (CA) *1*

WALLPAPER, CUSTOM DUPLICATION

Cowtan & Tout, Inc. (NY)
Hexter, S. M. Company (OH)
Old Stone Mill Corp. (MA)
Scalamandre, Inc. (NY)
The Twigs, Inc. (CA)
Zina Studios, Inc. (NY)

See Company Directory for Addresses & Phone Numbers

Anaglypta and Lincrusta Decorations
Date Back 100 Years

WALLPAPER, SPECIALTY

WALLPAPER, TRADITIONAL

WALLPAPER, VICTORIAN

OTHER DECORATIVE ACCESSORIES

Country Stencil Border Designs

Here is a new extraordinary way to apply colorful stencil borders to your walls without the need for specialty paints, templets and brushes.

These screen-printed stencil designs will readily transfer from clear film to become border designs on your walls in flat washable paints!

See the border designs in the

Countryside

GREENFIELD VILLAGE
HENRY FORD MUSEUM
DEARBORN MICHIGAN

wallcovering collection at better wallcovering dealers and interior designers.

S.M. HEXTER COMPANY

ALARM SYSTEMS—FIRE & SECURITY

Fichet Lock Co. (NY)

BATHROOM ACCESSORIES

(1) Soap Dishes, Etc.
(2) Towel Racks, Etc.
(3) Medicine Cabinets
(4) Other

BATHROOM FAUCETS & FITTINGS

Barclay Products Company
QUALITY BATH ACCESSORIES

**Barclay Products Company
424 North Oakley
Chicago, Illinois 60612
(312) 243-1444**

BATHROOM TOILETS & SEATS — PERIOD STYLES

(1) High-Tank Toilets (New)
(2) High-Tank Toilets (Salvage)
(3) Toilets, Period Styles
(4) Toilets, Period Styles (Salvage)
(5) Toilet Parts
(6) Wooden Toilet Seats

A-Ball Plumbing Supply (OR) 3
Barclay Products Co. (IL) 1
Brass Menagerie (LA) 3
Decorative Hardware Studio (NY) *1,3*
DeWeese Woodworking (MS) 6
Heads Up (CA) *1,3,6*
Jennings Lights of Yesterday (CA) *1,6*
Lena's Antique Bathroom Fixtures (CA) ... *2,4*
Maggiem & Co. (MO) 1
Mayer, Michael, Co. (CA) 6
P & G New and Used Plumbing Supply
   (NY) 2
Restoration Works, Inc. (NY) 1
Rheinschild, S. Chris (CA) *1,3,5*
Russell & Company Victorian Bathrooms
   (CA) *1,6*
Sunrise Specialty & Salvage Co. (CA) 1
Vintage Plumbing (CA) *2,4*
Walker Industries (TN) *1,2,3,4,5,6*

BATHTUBS & SINKS — PERIOD STYLES

(1) Tubs & Sinks, Antique (Salvage)
(2) Sinks, Period Styles — New
(3) Sink Replacement Bowls
(4) Tubs, Period Styles — New
(5) Tub Parts & Fittings
(6) Sink Parts & Fittings
(7) Shower Rings
(8) Shower Curtains, Extra-Size

A-Ball Plumbing Supply (OR) *5,7*
A.R.D. (NY) 3
Artifacts, Inc. (VA)
Barclay Products Co. (IL) *2,5,7,8*
Brass Menagerie (LA) *2,3*
Broadway Collection (MO) *2,3*
Crane Co. (NY) 4
Cumberland General Store (TN) 4
Decorative Hardware Studio (NY) *2,3*
Florida Victoriani Architectural Antiques (FL)
   1
Great American Salvage (NY,VT) 1
Guerin, P.E. Inc. (NY) 2
Lena's Antique Bathroom Fixtures (CA) 1
P & G New and Used Plumbing Supply
   (NY) 1
Period Furniture Hardware Co., Inc. (MA) . 3
Remodelers & Renovators (ID) 2
Renovation Concepts, Inc. (MN) 2
Restoration Hardware (CA) 7
Restore-A-Tub (KY) 1
Rheinschild, S. Chris (CA) *2,5,6*
The Sink Factory (CA) *2,3*
Sterline Manufacturing Corp. (IL) *5,7*
Sunrise Specialty & Salvage Co. (CA) ... *1,5,7*
Surrey Shoppe Interiors (MA) 8
Vintage Plumbing (CA) 1
Walker Industries (TN) *2,3,4,5*
Weaver, W. T. & Sons, Inc. (DC) 3

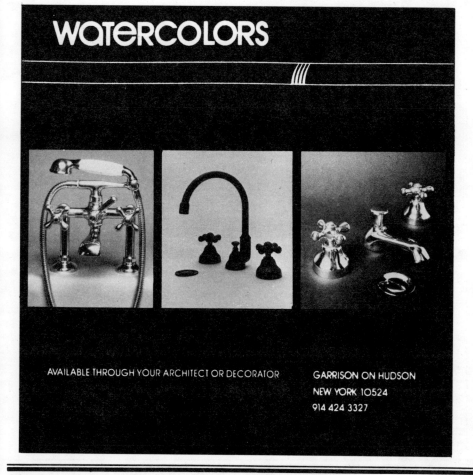

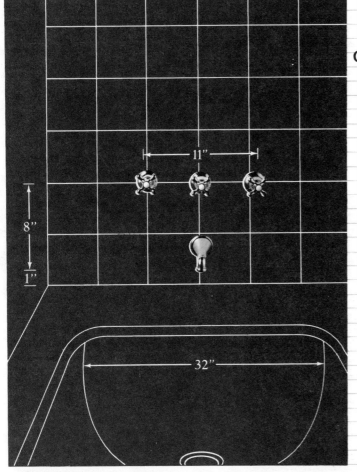

CABINET & FURNITURE HARDWARE — PERIOD

1874 House (OR)
18th Century Hardware Co. (PA)
19th Century Company (CA)
Anglo-American Brass Co. (CA)
Antique Hardware Co. (CA)
Ball and Ball (PA)
Bona Decorative Hardware (OH)
Broadway Collection (MO)
Crawford's Old House Store (WI)
Decorative Hardware Studio (NY)
Dover Furniture Stripping (DE)
Englewood Hardware Co. (NJ)
Faneuil Furniture Hardware (MA)
Furniture Revival (OR)
Gaston Wood Finishes, Inc. (IN)
Guerin, P.E. Inc. (NY)
Guild, The (CA)
Heirloom Enterprises (MN)
Horton Brasses (CT)
Howard Palmer, Inc. (CA)
Hunrath , Wm. Co., Inc. (NY)
Impex Assoc. Ltd., Inc. (NJ)
Klise Manufacturing Company (MI)
Lesco, Inc. (KS)
Merit Metal Products Corp. (PA)
Old And Elegant Distributing (WA)
Omnia Industries, Inc. (NJ)
Paxton Hardware Ltd. (MD)
Period Furniture Hardware Co., Inc. (MA)
Pfanstiel Hardware Co. (NY)
Plexacraft Metals Co. (CA)
Renaissance Decorative Hardware Co. (NJ)
Restoration Hardware (CA)
Ritter & Son Hardware (CA)
Squaw Alley, Inc. (IL)
WSI Distributors (MO)
Weaver, W. T. & Sons, Inc. (DC)
Williamsburg Blacksmiths, Inc. (MA)
Wolchonok, M. and Son, Inc. (NY)

See Company Directory for Addresses & Phone Numbers

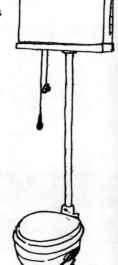

WALKER INDUSTRIES

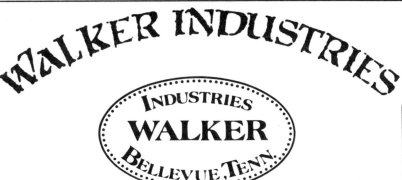

INDUSTRIES
WALKER
BELLEVUE, TENN.

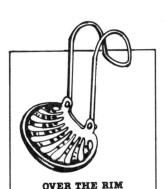

**OVER THE RIM
SOAP DISHES**

**SHOWER MOUNTED
SOAP DISH**

**WOODEN SATURDAY
NIGHT TUB SEATS**

**TUB WASTE
& OVERFLOWS**

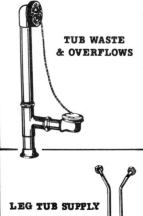

LEG TUB SUPPLY

**MASSIVE DETAILING
ORNATE**

WI-402

WI-403

WI-409

SITZ TUB

These authentic turn of the century "Country Junction" and "Hermitage Collection" period bath tubs are re-created by Walker Industries. The "Hermitage Collection" period bath tub is made out of solid copper, is very strong and durable, and will never rust. The ideal finishing touch for any period or Victorian home. This all solid copper bath tub is made out of No. 15 sheet copper, the joints are supported by solid brass mountings, which terminate into four ornate ornamental feet, the top is capped with a polished hand carved wooden rim (walnut, oak, cherry, or mahogany) 3½ inches wide, 1½ inches thick. The outside and inside of each tub comes fully polished or with a satin finish. All tubs are furnished with a waste and overflow.

The authentic "Country Junction" tub is an all steel bath tub, made out of No. 17 galvanized sheet steel. These tubs are available with the natural (silver gray) finish or coated inside and out with an insoluble blue granite or brown granite country style enameled finish. Easy to keep clean. Complete with pine wooden rim and waste and overflow. Brass cradle-feet and hand carved rim available as an option.

Matching pull chain toilets, brass period plumbing fixtures and hardware, solid brass and copper sinks and bowls. Send for complete catalog, $5.80.

Walker Industries
P.O. Box 129   Bellevue, Tennessee 37221
615-646-5084

CARPET RODS

Baldwin Hardware Mfg. Corp. (PA)
Ball and Ball (PA)
Decorative Hardware Studio (NY)
Guerin, P.E. Inc. (NY)
Hunrath , Wm. Co., Inc. (NY)
Pfanstiel Hardware Co. (NY)
Wolchonok, M. and Son, Inc. (NY)

COAT HOOKS

19th Century Company (CA)
Anglo-American Brass Co. (CA)
Baldwin Hardware Mfg. Corp. (PA)
Kayne, Steve & Son Custom Forged.
   Hardware (NC)
Merritt's Antiques, Inc. (PA)
Omnia Industries, Inc. (NJ)
Restoration Hardware (CA)
Sign of the Crab (CA)
Smithy, The (VT)
Weaver, W. T. & Sons, Inc. (DC)

DOOR HINGES

(1) Brass & Bronze
(2) Iron
(3) Early American
(4) Victorian
(5) Turn-of-Century
(6) Custom-Cast Brass & Bronze
(7) Custom-Wrought Iron
(8) Other

18th Century Hardware Co. (PA) 3
Antares Forge and Metalworks (NY) 7
Arden Forge (PA) 2,3,6,7
Baldwin Hardware Mfg. Corp. (PA) 1
Ball and Ball (PA) 1,2,3,5
Barnett, D. James — Blacksmith (PA) 2
Bona Decorative Hardware (OH) 1,3
Broadway Collection (MO) 1
Cassidy Bros. Forge (MA) 3,7
Cirecast, Inc. (CA) 1,4
The Farm Forge (OH) 7
Guerin, P.E. Inc. (NY) 1,5,6
Guthrie Hill Forge, Ltd. (PA) 2,3
Hammerworks (MA) 7
Horton Brasses (CT) 2
Howard Palmer, Inc. (CA) 1
Howland, John — Metalsmith (CT) 1,2
Kayne, Steve & Son Custom Forged
   Hardware (NC) 2,3
Kingsway (CO) 1
Lee Valley Tools, Ltd. (CAN) 1,2,4,5
Leo, Brian (MN) 4,6
Loose, Thomas — Blacksmith/ Whitesmith
   (PA) 2,3
Merit Metal Products Corp. (PA) 1
Mill River Hammerworks (MA) .꞉....... 1,2,3,6,7
Millham, Newton — Blacksmith (MA) .. 2,3,7
Omnia Industries, Inc. (NJ) 1,3,4
Period Furniture Hardware Co., Inc. (MA)
   1,2
Pfanstiel Hardware Co. (NY) 1,5
Ram's Head Forge (ME) 7
Renovation Concepts, Inc. (MN) 1
Ritter & Son Hardware (CA) 1
Sign of the Crab (CA) 1,3,4
Smithy, The (VT) 7
Strafford Forge (VT) 3,7
WSI Distributors (MO) 1
Wallin Forge (KY) 7
Williamsburg Blacksmiths, Inc. (MA) 2,3
Wolchonok, M. and Son, Inc. (NY) 1
Woodbury Blacksmith & Forge Co. (CT) 7

DOOR LATCHES—WROUGHT IRON

(1) New—Stock Items
(2) Custom-Made

18th Century Hardware Co. (PA) 1
Antares Forge and Metalworks (NY) 2
Arden Forge (PA) 2
Ball and Ball (PA) 1,2
Barnett, D. James — Blacksmith (PA) 1
Bona Decorative Hardware (OH) 1
Broadway Collection (MO) 1
Guthrie Hill Forge, Ltd. (PA) 1,2
Horton Brasses (CT) 1
Kayne, Steve & Son Custom Forged
   Hardware (NC) 1
Mill River Hammerworks (MA) 2
Millham, Newton — Blacksmith (MA) 1,2
Period Furniture Hardware Co., Inc. (MA)   1
RAM's Forge (PA) 2
Smithy, The (VT) 2
Wallin Forge (KY) 2
Williamsburg Blacksmiths, Inc. (MA) 1
Woodbury Blacksmith & Forge Co. (CT) 2

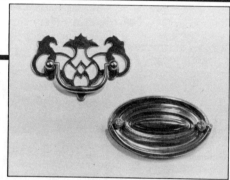
See Company Directory for Addresses & Phone Numbers

You'll get better service when contacting companies if you mention The Old-House Journal Catalog

DOOR KNOBS & ESCUTCHEONS

(1) Brass & Bronze
(2) Porcelain & Glass Knobs
Anglo-American Brass Co. (CA) *1*
Antique Hardware Co. (CA) *1*
Baldwin Hardware Mfg. Corp. (PA) *1*
Broadway Collection (MO)
Cirecast, Inc. (CA) *1*
Crawford's Old House Store (WI) *1,2*
Decorative Hardware Studio (NY) *2*
Englewood Hardware Co. (NJ)
Guerin, P.E. Inc. (NY)
Howard Palmer, Inc. (CA) *1*
Hunrath , Wm. Co., Inc. (NY) *1*
Lee Valley Tools, Ltd. (CAN) *1*
Leo, Brian (MN) *1*
Litchfield House (CT) *2*
Omnia Industries, Inc. (NJ) *1,2*
Renaissance Decorative Hardware Co. (NJ) *1*
Renovation Concepts, Inc. (MN) *1*
Reproduction Distributors, Inc. (IL)
Restoration Hardware (CA) *1,2*
Ritter & Son Hardware (CA) *1*
WSI Distributors (MO)
Weaver, W. T. & Sons, Inc. (DC) *1*

DOOR LOCKS

(1) Brass & Bronze
(2) Iron
(3) Rim Locks
(4) Mortised Locks
(5) Early American
(6) Victorian
(7) Turn-of-Century
(8) Other
Antique Bldrs. Hardware (AR)
Baldwin Hardware Mfg. Corp. (PA) *1,3,4*
Ball and Ball (PA) *1,2,3,4,5,6,7,8*
Bona Decorative Hardware (OH) *1,2,3,4,5*
Brass Menagerie (LA) *1*
Broadway Collection (MO) *1,3*
Colonial Lock Company (CT) *2,3*
Crawford's Old House Store (WI)
.... *1,2,3,4,5,6,7,8*
Decorative Hardware Studio (NY) *4*
Fichet Lock Co. (NY)
Guerin, P.E. Inc. (NY) *1,4,8*
Guthrie Hill Forge, Ltd. (PA) *2*
Howard Palmer, Inc. (CA) *1*
Merit Metal Products Corp. (PA) *1,3,4,6*
Millham, Newton — Blacksmith (MA) *2,5*
Omnia Industries, Inc. (NJ) *1,3,4*
Period Furniture Hardware Co., Inc. (MA)
.... *1,3,4,5*
Pfanstiel Hardware Co. (NY) *1*
Reproduction Distributors, Inc. (IL) *3*
Sign of the Crab (CA) *1,4,5,6*
Weaver, W. T. & Sons, Inc. (DC) *3*
Williamsburg Blacksmiths, Inc. (MA) *2,5*

> **You'll get better service when contacting companies if you mention The Old-House Journal Catalog**

DRY SINKS & LINERS

Oak Post Reproductions (GA)

FANS, CEILING

Brass Fan Ceiling Fan Co. (TX)
CasaBlanca Fan Co. (CA)
Cumberland General Store (TN)
Hunter Ceiling Fans (TN)
Newstamp Lighting Co. (MA)
Progress Lighting (PA)
Royal Windyne Limited (VA)
Worthington Trading Company (MO)

HARDWARE, ANTIQUE (OLD)

Antique Bldrs. Hardware (AR)
Artifacts, Inc. (VA)
Grandpa Snazzy's Hardware (CO)
Lee Valley Tools, Ltd. (CAN)
Monroe Coldren and Sons (PA)
Old And Elegant Distributing (WA)
Pennsylvania Barnboard Company (PA)
Sarah Bustle Antiques, Ltd. (IL)
Tool Works (NY)

HARDWARE, INTERIOR—CUSTOM DUPLICATION

(1) Cast Brass & Bronze
(2) Cast Iron
(3) Wrought Iron
18th Century Hardware Co. (PA)
Anglo-American Brass Co. (CA) *1*
Antares Forge and Metalworks (NY) *3*
Arden Forge (PA) *3*
Ball and Ball (PA) *1*
Blaine Window Hardware, Inc. (MD) *1*
Brass Menagerie (LA) *1*
Bronze et al (NY) *1*
Cassidy Bros. Forge (MA) *3*
Experi-Metals (WI) *1*
The Farm Forge (OH) *3*
Guerin, P.E. Inc. (NY) *1*
Hammerworks (MA) *3*
Howland, John — Metalsmith (CT) *1,3*
Leo, Brian (MN) *1*
New England Brassworks (CT) *1*
Ram's Head Forge (ME) *3*
Smithy, The (VT) *3*
Specialized Repair Service (IL) *1*
Strafford Forge (VT) *3*
Travis Tuck, Inc. — Metal Sculptor (MA) .. *3*
Wallin Forge (KY) *3*

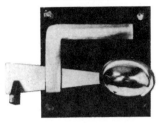

See Company Directory for Addresses & Phone Numbers

HOOSIER HARDWARE

19th Century Company (CA)
Furniture Revival (OR)

ICE BOX HARDWARE

19th Century Company (CA)
Anglo-American Brass Co. (CA)
Antique Hardware Co. (CA)
Ritter & Son Hardware (CA)

KEY BLANKS—FOR ANTIQUE LOCKS

18th Century Hardware Co. (PA)
Ball and Ball (PA)

KITCHEN CABINETS

A.R.D. (NY)
Custom Kitchen and Millwork (MI)
Dixon Bros. Woodworking (MA)
Moser Brothers, Inc. (PA)
Restorations Unlimited, Inc. (PA)
Rich Craft Custom Kitchens, Inc. (PA)

KITCHEN FAUCETS & FITTINGS, OLD STYLES

(1) Antique (Salvage)
(2) Reproduction
Chicago Faucet Co. (IL) 2
Sunrise Specialty & Salvage Co. (CA) 2

KITCHEN SINKS, OLD STYLES

(1) Antique (Salvage)
(2) Reproduction
1874 House (OR) 1
Rheinschild, S. Chris (CA) 2

LIBRARY LADDERS

Putnam Rolling Ladder Co., Inc. (NY)

RADIATORS — PERIOD STYLES

(1) Antique (Salvage)
(2) New
A.A. Used Boiler Supply Co. (NY)
Artifacts, Inc. (VA) 1
Consumer Supply Co. (IL) 1
P & G New and Used Plumbing Supply (NY) 1

See Company Directory for Addresses & Phone Numbers

SHUTTERS & BLINDS, INTERIOR

(1) New—Stock Items
(2) Custom-Made
Architectural Components (MA) 1
Bank Architectural Antiques (LA)
Beauti-home (CA) 2
Devenco Louver Products (GA) 1
Dixon Bros. Woodworking (MA) 2
Historic Windows (VA) 2
Iberia Millwork (LA) 2
LaPointe, Chip, Cabinetmaker (NY) 2
Maurer & Shepherd, Joyners (CT) 2
Michael's Fine Colonial Products (NY) 2
Perkowitz Window Fashions (IL) 1
Piscatagua Architectural Woodwork, Co. (NH) 2
Restoration Fraternity (PA) 2
Sunshine Architectural Woodworks (AR)

SHUTTER HARDWARE

(1) Brass & Bronze
(2) Iron
(3) Custom-Made
Ball and Ball (PA) 1,2,3
Barnett, D. James — Blacksmith (PA) 2
Crawford's Old House Store (WI) 2
Decorative Hardware Studio (NY) 1
Kayne, Steve & Son Custom Forged Hardware (NC) 2
Millham, Newton — Blacksmith (MA) 2
Period Furniture Hardware Co., Inc. (MA) . 1
Smithy, The (VT) 2

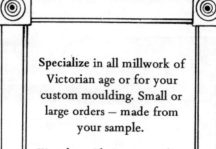

Specialize in all millwork of Victorian age or for your custom moulding. Small or large orders — made from your sample.

We take pride in our quality workmanship as a family business for the last 25 years.

Free Catalog of Trim Patterns

Custom Kitchen & Millwork
2750 W. Bauer Rd., R 2
St. Johns, MI 48879
(517) 593-2244

SLIDING DOOR TRACKS & HARDWARE

Blaine Window Hardware, Inc. (MD)
Decorative Hardware Studio (NY)
Grant Hardware Company Div. of Grant Industries, Inc. (NY)
JGR Enterprises, Inc. (PA)
Sanders, David & Co. (NY)

SWITCH PLATES, PERIOD DESIGNS

A-Ball Plumbing Supply (OR)
Arden Forge (PA)
Decorative Hardware Studio (NY)
Guerin, P.E. Inc. (NY)
Sign of the Crab (CA)
Weaver, W. T. & Sons, Inc. (DC)
Wolchonok, M. and Son, Inc. (NY)

TRUNK HARDWARE

Antique Trunk Supply Co. (OH)
Charolette Ford Trunks (TX)
Dover Furniture Stripping (DE)
Furniture Revival (OR)
WSI Distributors (MO)

WINDOW HARDWARE

You'll get better service when contacting companies if you mention The Old-House Journal Catalog

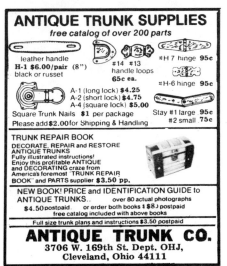

Heating Systems, Fireplaces & Stoves, and Energy-Saving Devices

AUXILIARY FIREPLACE DEVICES TO INCREASE HEAT DISTRIBUTION

Cumberland General Store (TN)
Energy Etcetera (NY)
Iron Craft, Inc. (NH)
Shenandoah Manufacturing Co. (VA)

CENTRAL HEATING SYSTEMS

(1) Wood Fired
(2) Coal Fired
(3) Combination
(4) Other Fuels
Charmaster Products Inc. (MN) *1,3*
Energy Marketing Corporation (VT) *1,2,3*
Heckler Bros. (PA) *2*
Shenandoah Manufacturing Co. (VA) *1,2,3*

CHIMNEY BRUSHES

Ace Wire Brush Co. (NY)
Iron Craft, Inc. (NH)
Mazzeo's Chimney Sweep Suppliers (ME)
Woodmart (WI)

CHIMNEY LININGS

American Boa, Inc. — Ventinox (NY)
Chimney Relining International, Inc. (NH)
Mirror Patented Stove Pipe Co. (CT)
National SUPAFLU Systems, Inc. (NY)
Superior Clay Corporation (OH)
Thermocrete Chimney Lining, Inc. (VT)

COAL GRATES

(1) Coal-Burning
(2) Simulated
Bryant Stove Works (ME) *1*
Cumberland General Store (TN) *1*
Heckler Bros. (PA) *1*
Lemee's Fireplace Equipment (MA) *1*

FIREPLACES, MANUFACTURED

Acme Stove Company (DC)
Jotul U.S.A., Inc. (ME)
Preway, Inc. (WI)
Readybuilt Products, Co. (MD)

FIREPLACE DAMPERS & STRUCTURAL PARTS

Lyemance International (KY)

GAS LOGS

Peterson, Robert H., Co. (CA)
Readybuilt Products, Co. (MD)

HEAT SHIELDS FOR FREE-STANDING STOVES

Hearth Shield (WA)

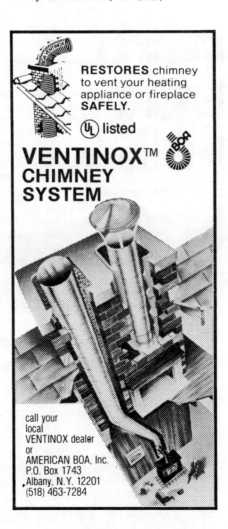

FIREPLACE ACCESSORIES

(1) Andirons
(2) Bellows
(3) Coal Scuttles
(4) Cranes
(5) Fenders
(6) Firebacks
(7) Firegrates
(8) Firescreens
(9) Pokers & Fireplace Tools
(10) Wood Baskets

A.E.S. Firebacks (CT) 6
Acme Stove Company (DC)
Adams Company (IA) 1,10,3,8,9
Auto Hoe, Inc. (WI) 9
Baker, Jim (OH) 8
Ball and Ball (PA) 1,4,5,8,9
Barnett, D. James — Blacksmith (PA) 1
Boren Clay Products Company (NC)
Bryant Stove Works (ME) 7
Buck Creek Bellows (VA) 2
Cassidy Bros. Forge (MA) 1,4,8,9
Colonial Williamsburg Foundation Craft
   House (VA)
The Country Iron Foundry (PA) 6
Eddy, Ian — Blacksmith (VT) 9
Energy Etcetera (NY) 1,10,2,3,6,7,8,9
Essex Forge (CT) 1,9
Hearth Realities (GA) 7
Howland, John — Metalsmith (CT) 1
Hurley Patentee Lighting (NY) 8
Iron Craft, Inc. (NH) 1,2,3,7,9
Jackson, Wm. H. Co. (NY) 1,5,7,9
Kayne, Steve & Son Custom Forged
   Hardware (NC) 1,4,5,7,8,9
Lehman Hardware & Appliances (OH) 3,9
Lemee's Fireplace Equipment (MA)
   1,2,3,4,6,7,8,9
Mexico House (CA) 8
Mill River Hammerworks (MA) 1
Millham, Newton — Blacksmith (MA) .. 1,4,9
Pennsylvania Firebacks, Inc. (PA) 6
Period Furniture Hardware Co., Inc. (MA)
   1,2,3,5,6,8
Peterson, Robert H., Co. (CA) 1,7,8,9
Pine & Palette Studio (CT) 2
RAM's Forge (PA) 1,4,9
Reproduction Distributors, Inc. (IL)
Rustic Home Hardware (PA) 1,7,9
Schwartz's Forge & Metalworks (NY) 1,9
Smithy, The (VT) 9
Smithy Hearth Products (CT) 8
Donald C. Stetson, Sr., Enterprises (MA)
Washington Stove Works (WA) 3
Westlake Architectural Antiques (TX) 1,5,8
Helen Williams—Delft Tiles (CA) 6
Woodbury Blacksmith & Forge Co. (CT) 1,4,9
Ye Olde Mantel Shoppe (FL) 1,5,8

FURNACE PARTS

A.A. Used Boiler Supply Co. (NY)
Heckler Bros. (PA)
Standard Heating Parts, Inc. (IL)

See Company Directory for Addresses & Phone Numbers

STOVES

(1) Heating
(2) Cooking (Kitchen)
(3) Wood-Burning
(4) Coal-Burning
(5) Antique

Acme Stove Company (DC) 3
Aetna Stove Company (PA) 5
Agape Antiques (VT) 5
Bryant Stove Works (ME) 2,5
Coalbrookdale Company (VT) 3,4
Country Comfort Stove Works (MA) 3,4,5
Cumberland General Store (TN) 2,4
Elmira Stove Works (CAN) 3,4
Empire Stove & Furnace Co., Inc. (NY) ... 3,4
Energy Marketing Corporation (VT) 1
Fourth Avenue Stove & Appliance Corp.
   (NY) 1,2,3,4
Hayes Equipment Corp. (CT) 1,3
Heating Research (NH) 3,4,5
House of Webster (AR) 2
Jotul U.S.A., Inc. (ME) 1,3,4
Lehman Hardware & Appliances (OH) 1,2,3,4
Long, E. T., Inc. (VA) 3,5
Malleable Iron Range Co. (WI)
Mohawk Industries, Inc. (MA) 1,3,4
Shenandoah Manufacturing Co. (VA) 1,3,4
Upland Stove Co., Inc. (NY) 1,3
Vermont Iron (VT) 3
Washington Stove Works (WA) 1,2,3,4
Webster Stove (MO) 1,3
West Barnstable Stove Shop (MA) 1,2,3,4,5
Woodstock Soapstone Co., Inc. (VT) 3
Worthington Trading Company (MO) 3,4

STOVE PARTS

(1) Stove Pipe & Fittings
(2) Isinglass For Stove Doors
(3) Parts For Antique Stoves

Aetna Stove Company (PA) 1,2,3
Agape Antiques (VT) 3
American Boa, Inc. — Ventinox (NY) 1
Architectural Iron Company (PA) 3
Bryant Stove Works (ME) 2,3
Castings Unlimited (NY) 3
Country Comfort Stove Works (MA)
Cumberland General Store (TN) 1
Empire Stove & Furnace Co., Inc. (NY) 2,3
Hearth & Home Co. (NJ)
Hearth Realities (GA) 3
Hearth Shield (WA)
Heckler Bros. (PA) 3
Iron Craft, Inc. (NH) 2
Jotul U.S.A., Inc. (ME) 1
Long, E. T., Inc. (VA) 3
Malleable Iron Range Co. (WI) 3
Max-Cast, Inc. (IA) 3
Mohawk Industries, Inc. (MA) 2
Nye's Foundry Ltd. (CAN) 3
Smith, F.E., Castings, Inc. (MI) 3
Tomahawk Foundry (WI) 3
West Barnstable Stove Shop (MA) 3
Worthington Trading Company (MO) 2
Wrightsville Hardware (PA) 1
Xenia Foundry & Machine Co. Specialty
    Castings Dept. (OH) 3

OTHER HEATING EQUIPMENT

A.A. Used Boiler Supply Co. (NY)
Cumberland General Store (TN)
Peterson, Robert H., Co. (CA)

SOLAR HEATING SYSTEMS

Pedersen, Arthur Hall — Design &
    Consulting Engineers (MO)

VENTILATING EQUIPMENT

Kool-O-Matic Corp. (MI)

WATER HEATERS—ALTERNATE FUELS

Cumberland General Store (TN)
Energy Marketing Corpoation (VT)

WINDOW COVERINGS, INSULATING

Appropriate Technology Corp. (VT)
Thermal Wall Insulating Shutters, Inc. (NY)
Window Blanket Company, Inc. (TN)

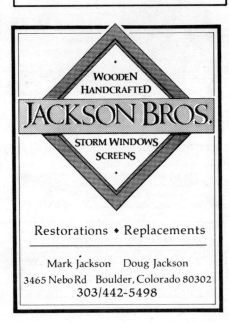
STORM WINDOWS, WOOD

(1) Outside Mounting
(2) Inside Mounting

Air-Flo Window Contracting Corp. (NY) .. 1,2
Combination Door Co. (WI) 1
Crawford's Old House Store (WI) 1
Cusson Sash Company (CT) 1
Drums Sash & Door Co., Inc. (PA) 1
Glass & Aluminum Construction Services,
    Inc. (NH)
Hank, Dennis V. (FL) 1,2
Jackson Bros. (CO) 1
Marvin Windows (MN) 1
Moser Brothers, Inc. (PA) 1,2
Wes-Pine Millwork, Inc. (MA)

STORM WINDOWS, METAL & PLASTIC

(1) Outside Mounting
(2) Inside Mounting

Air-Flo Window Contracting Corp. (NY) .. 1,2
Glass & Aluminum Construction Services,
    Inc. (NH)
Industrial Window Corp. (NY) 2
King Energy Corp. (NJ) 2
Perkasie Industries Corp. (PA) 2
RUSCO (PA) 1
Vecon Energy Systems Corp. (MA) 2

WEATHERSTRIPPING PRODUCTS (INTEGRAL)

Accurate Weatherstripping Co., Inc. (NY)
American Comfort Systems, Inc. (NY)
Pemko Co. (CA)

Lighting Fixtures & Parts

LIGHTING FIXTURES & LAMPS—ANTIQUE

1874 House (OR)
21st Century Antiques (MA)
Architectural Archives (TX)
Art Directions (MO)
Brass & Copper Shop (MO)
Brass Menagerie (LA)
Brasslight Antique Lighting (WI)
ByGone Era Architectural Antiques (GA)
Canal Co. (DC)
Century House Antiques (OH)
City Barn Antiques (NY)
City Knickerbocker, Inc. (NY)
City Lights (MA)
Conservatory, The (MI)
Cosmopolitan International Antiques (NY)
Gem Monogram & Cut Glass Corp. (NY)
Graham's Lighting Fixtures (TN)
Great American Salvage (NY,VT)
Greg's Antique Lighting (CA)
Hexagram (CA)
Illustrious Lighting (CA)
Jefferson Art Lighting, Inc. (MI)
Jennings Lights of Yesterday (CA)
JoEl Enterprises (FL)
John Kruesel's General Merchandise (MN)
Joe Ley Antiques, Inc. (KY)
London Venturers Company (MA)
Mattia, Louis (NY)
McAvoy Antique Lighting (MO)
Moriarty's Lamps (CA)
Neri, C./Antiques (PA)
Ocean View Lighting and Home Accessories (CA)
Old Lamplighter Shop (NY)
Olde Bostonian Architectural Antiques (MA)
Rejuvenation House Parts Co. (OR)
Roberts, Lee & Lynne (NJ)
Roy Electric Co., Inc. (NY)
St. Louis Antique Lighting Co. (MO)
Sandy Springs Galleries (GA)
Sarah Bustle Antiques, Ltd. (IL)
Stanley Galleries (IL)
Wilson, H. Weber, Antiquarian (MD)
Wrecking Bar of Atlanta (GA)
Wrecking Bar, Inc. (TX)
Yankee Craftsman (MA)

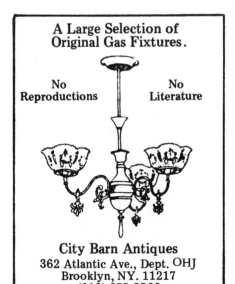
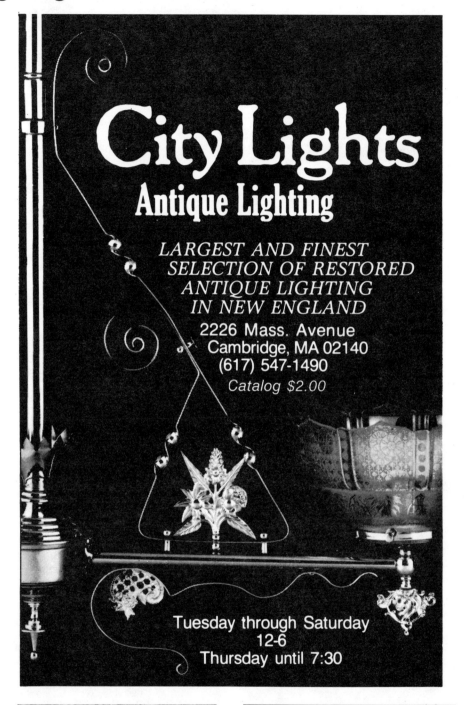
You'll get better service
when contacting companies
if you mention
**The Old-House Journal
Catalog**

**See Company Directory for
Addresses & Phone Numbers**

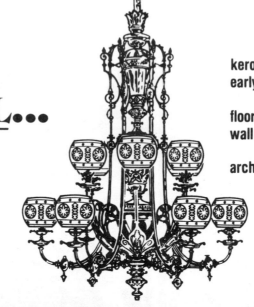
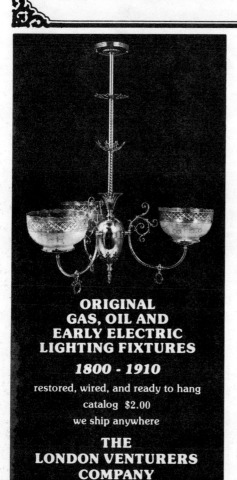

LIGHTING FIXTURES, REPRODUCTION—EARLY AMERICAN

(1) Ceiling & Wall Fixtures
(2) Lamps

A.J.P. Coppersmith (MA)	1
Authentic Designs Inc. (VT)	1,2
Authentic Lighting (NJ)	2
Baldwin Hardware Mfg. Corp. (PA)	1,2
Ball and Ball (PA)	1
Brass Lion (TX)	1
Brass Menagerie (LA)	
Cassidy Bros. Forge (MA)	1,2
Chandelier Wharehouse (NY)	1
Cohasset Colonials by Hagerty (MA)	1,2
Colonial Casting Co., Inc. (CT)	1
Colonial Tin Craft (OH)	1,2
Colonial Williamsburg Foundation Craft House (VA)	1
Copper House (NH)	1
Country Loft (MA)	1,2
Dutch Products & Supply Co. (PA)	1
Essex Forge (CT)	1
Friend, The (ME)	1
Gates Moore (CT)	1
Graham's Lighting Fixtures (TN)	1
Hammerworks (MA)	1,2
Henderson Lighting (CT)	1
Heritage Lanterns (ME)	1
Historic Charleston Reproductions (SC)	2
Hood, R. and Co. (NH)	1,2
Hubbardton Forge Corp. (VT)	1
Hurley Patentee Lighting (NY)	2
Kayne, Steve & Son Custom Forged Hardware (NC)	1
King's Chandelier Co. (NC)	1
Loose, Thomas — Blacksmith/ Whitesmith (PA)	1
New England Brassworks (CT)	1
Newstamp Lighting Co. (MA)	1,2
Nostalgia, Inc. (GA)	1,2
Olde Village Smithery (MA)	1
Period Furniture Hardware Co., Inc. (MA)	1
Period Lighting Fixtures (CT)	1,2
Saltbox (PA)	1,2
Spencer, William, Inc. (NJ)	1
Village Forge (NC)	1,2
Village Lantern (MA)	1
Washington Copper Works (CT)	1,2

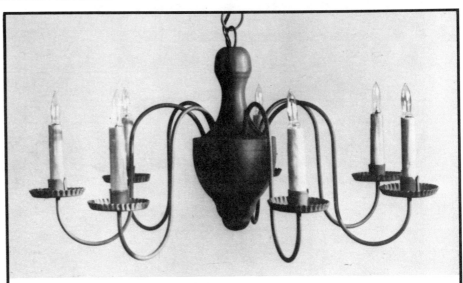

As Shown $165 plus U.P.S. and handling. Dia. 24" H. 11"

HANDCRAFTED
To The Drip On The Tapered Candles

Early American Lighting since 1938; chandeliers, copper lanterns, and wall sconces. Catalog $2 (refundable).

Knowledgeable collectors, Restorations and Museums have been buying our fine fixtures for over 30 years. A list available on request.

GATES MOORE

2 River Rd., Silvermine, Norwalk, Conn. 06850 Tel. (203) 847-3231

You'll get better service when contacting companies if you mention **The Old-House Journal Catalog**

See Company Directory for Addresses & Phone Numbers

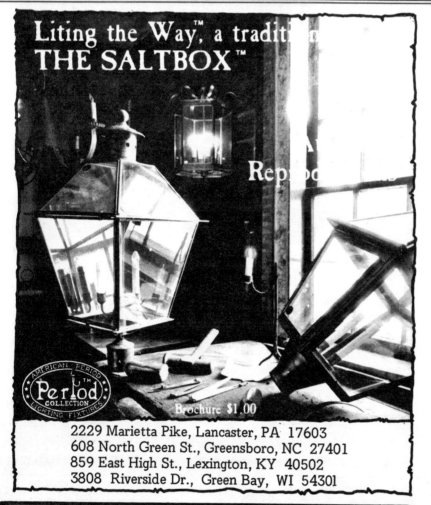

Liting the Way, a tradit...
THE SALTBOX™

Repro...

American Period
Period Collection
Lighting Fixtures

Brochure $1.00

2229 Marietta Pike, Lancaster, PA 17603
608 North Green St., Greensboro, NC 27401
859 East High St., Lexington, KY 40502
3808 Riverside Dr., Green Bay, WI 54301

ROLAND SPIVAK'S CUSTOM LIGHTING
Solid Brass Victorian, Nouveau and Deco Styles

Mail Order Catalog $1
Pendulum Shop
424 South Street Philadelphia, Pa. 19147 (215) 925-4014

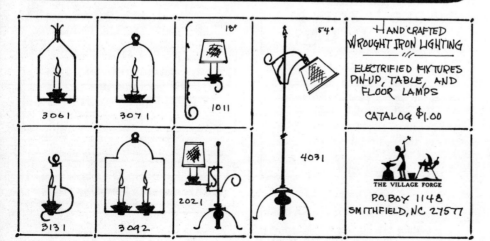

3061
3071
18°
1011
54°

HAND CRAFTED
WROUGHT IRON LIGHTING
///
ELECTRIFIED FIXTURES
PIN-UP, TABLE, AND
FLOOR LAMPS

CATALOG $1.00

3131
3092
2021
4031

THE VILLAGE FORGE
P.O. BOX 1148
SMITHFIELD, NC 27577

LIGHTING FIXTURES, REPRODUCTION—VICTORIAN

Progress Lighting creates the first collection of authentic American Victorian Reproductions

Roger Moss, nationally recognized authority on American chitecture and decorative arts, has authenticated this llection of historically accurate American Victorian eproductions, for Progress Lighting, the world's rgest manufacturer of home lighting fixtures.

ligently researched, attention has been given to e accuracy of the smallest details. Forgotten manu- cturing techniques were rediscovered, old dies and ass molds found, restored or recreated. Ranging in date m 1840 to 1900, the collection includes a selection of styles:

AUTHENTIC
AMERICAN VICTORIAN
REPRODUCTION

Classical Revival, Rococo Revival, Colonial Revival, Art Nouveau and matching wall, hall and street light adaptations.

Minor modifications necessary to meet modern electrical codes have been subtly concealed. The overall scale, the finely detailed castings and the blown glass shades conform so closely to the originals that the many people who formerly sought antiques in vain can use them with confidence. For full color "American Victorian" catalog, send $1.00 to Progress Lighting, G Street and Erie Avenue, Philadephia, Pa., 19134

progress lighting

Subsidiary of Kidde, Inc. **KIDDE** Philadelphia, PA 19134

LIGHTING FIXTURES, REPRODUCTION—EARLY 20TH CENTURY

ELECTRIC CANDLES

KEROSENE LAMPS & LANTERNS

LAMP POSTS & STANDARDS, REPRODUCTION

Antique Street Lamps (TX)
Bradford Consultants (NJ)
Kenneth Lynch & Sons, Inc. (CT)
Saltbox (PA)
Schwerd Manufacturing Co. (PA)
Silver Dollar Trading Co. (CO)
Southern Heritage Metal Amenities, Ltd. (AL)
Spring City Electrical Mfg. Co (PA)
Tennessee Fabricating Co. (TN)
Turncraft (OR)
Welsbach (CT)

LAMPS & LANTERNS, EXTERIOR—REPRODUCTION

A.J.P. Coppersmith (MA)
Authentic Designs Inc. (VT)
Ball and Ball (PA)
Bradford Consultants (NJ)
Colonial Foundry & Mfg. Co. (CT)
Colonial Tin Craft (OH)
Essex Forge (CT)
Gates Moore (CT)
Hammerworks (MA)
Henderson Lighting (CT)
Heritage Lanterns (ME)
Newstamp Lighting Co. (MA)
Nostalgia, Inc. (GA)
Period Lighting Fixtures (CT)
Richardson, Matthew Coppersmith (MA)
Saltbox (PA)
Sign of the Crab (CA)
Silver Dollar Trading Co. (CO)
Travis Tuck, Inc. — Metal Sculptor (MA)
Village Lantern (MA)
Washington Copper Works (CT)
Welsbach (CT)

LIGHTING FIXTURES—GAS BURNING

(1) Antique (Original)
(2) New Reproduction

Bradford Consultants (NJ) 2
Greg's Antique Lighting (CA) 1
Hexagram (CA) 1
Materials Unlimited (MI) 1
Neri, C./Antiques (PA) 1
Nowell's, Inc. (CA) 1,2
Old Lamplighter Shop (NY) 1
Roy Electric Co., Inc. (NY) 1,2
Victorian D'Light (CA) 2

GAS MANTLES

Humphrey Products General Gaslight Co. (MI)
Nowell's, Inc. (CA)
Old Lamplighter Shop (NY)

LIGHTING FIXTURE PARTS—GLASS

(1) Globes
(2) Shades
(3) Prisms
(4) Other (Specify)

Alcon Lightcraft Co. (TX)
Angelo Brothers Co. (PA) 1,2
B & P Lamp Supply Co., Inc. (TN) 1,2,3
Bienenfeld Ind. Inc. (NY) 2
Blenko Glass Co., Inc. (WV) 2
Boulder Stained Glass Studios (CO) 2
Brass & Copper Shop (MO) 1
Brasslight, Inc. (NY) 1,2
Campbell-Lamps (PA) 1,2
City Knickerbocker, Inc. (NY) 1,2
Contois Stained Glass Studio (WV) 2
Crawford's Old House Store (WI) 2,3
Crystal Mountain Prisms (NY) 3
Cumberland General Store (TN) 1,2
Faire Harbour Ltd. (MA) 1,2
Gem Monogram & Cut Glass Corp. (NY) ... 3
Gillinder Brothers, Inc. (NY) 2
Golden Age Glassworks (NY) 2
Greg's Antique Lighting (CA) 1,2
Hexagram (CA) 2
Lyn Hovey Studio, Inc. (MA) 2
Jefferson Art Lighting, Inc. (MI) 2
Larcomb & Wicht (OH) 2
Louis Baldinger & Sons (NY) 3
Luigi Crystal (PA) 1,2,3
Lundberg Studios (CA) 2
Moriarty's Lamps (CA) 2
Nowell's, Inc. (CA) 1,2
Ocean View Lighting and Home Accessories (CA) 1
Old And Elegant Distributing (WA)
Old Lamplighter Shop (NY) 1,2,3
Paxton Hardware Ltd. (MD) 2,3
Pyfer, E.W. (IL) 1,2
Renaissance Marketing, Inc. (MI) 2
Roy Electric Co., Inc. (NY) 1,2
Unique Art Glass Co. (MO) 2
Victorian D'Light (CA) 2
Victorian Lightcrafters, Ltd. (NY) 2
Victorian Reproductions Enterprises, Inc. (MN) 2
Yankee Craftsman (MA) 2

LAMP WICKS & LAMP OIL

Campbell-Lamps (PA)
Cumberland General Store (TN)
Lehman Hardware & Appliances (OH)

LIGHT BULBS, CARBON FILAMENT

Bradford Consultants (NJ)
City Knickerbocker, Inc. (NY)
Kyp-Go, Inc. (IL)
Whittemore-Durgin Glass Co. (MA)

LIGHTING FIXTURE PARTS—METAL

B & P Lamp Supply Co., Inc. (TN)
Barap Specialties (MI)
Campbell-Lamps (PA)
Century House Antiques (OH)
Cumberland General Store (TN)
Faire Harbour Ltd. (MA)
Lundberg Studios (CA)
Moriarty's Lamps (CA)
Old Lamplighter Shop (NY)
Paxton Hardware Ltd. (MD)
Roy Electric Co., Inc. (NY)
Squaw Alley, Inc. (IL)

SWITCHES, ELECTRIC PUSH-BUTTON

Mohawk Electric Supply Co., Inc. (NY)

Paints, Finishes, Removers & Supplies

BLEACH, WOOD

Behlen, H. & Bros. (NY)
Cabot Stains (MA)
Chem-Clean Furniture Restoration Center
    (VT)
Daly's Wood Finishing Products (WA)
Finishing Products (MO)
Janovic/Plaza, Inc. (NY)
Wolf Paints And Wallpapers (NY)

BRASS LACQUER

Behlen, H. & Bros. (NY)
Crawford's Old House Store (WI)
Gaston Wood Finishes, Inc. (IN)
Illinois Bronze Paint Co. (IL)
Janovic/Plaza, Inc. (NY)
Wolf Paints And Wallpapers (NY)

BRONZING & GILDING LIQUIDS

Behlen, H. & Bros. (NY)
Finishing Products (MO)
Gold Leaf & Metallic Powders, Inc. (NY)
Horowitz Sign Supplies (NY)
Janovic/Plaza, Inc. (NY)
Wolf Paints And Wallpapers (NY)

CLEANERS & POLISHES, METAL

(1) Brass & Copper
(2) Silver
(3) Stove Polish
Ball and Ball (PA) *1*
Bradford Derustit Corp. (NY)
Butcher Polish Co. (MA) *3*
Competition Chemicals, Inc. (IA) *1,2*
Cumberland General Store (TN) *3*
**Easy Time Wood Refinishing Products Corp.
    (IL)**
Energy Etcetera (NY) *3*
Goddard & Sons (WI)
Hope Co., Inc. (MO) *3*
Howard Products, Inc. (CA) *1,2*
Iron Craft, Inc. (NH) *3*
Staples, H. F. & Co., Inc. (NH) *3*
Western Wood Doctor (CA) *1*
**Woodcare Corporation Sales & Technical
    Sales Svc. (NJ)** *1,3*

FINISH REVIVERS

Behlen, H. & Bros. (NY)
Cornucopia, Inc. (MA)
Crawford's Old House Store (WI)
Daly's Wood Finishing Products (WA)
**Easy Time Wood Refinishing Products Corp.
    (IL)**
Finish Feeder Company (MD)
Finishing Products (MO)
Finishing Touch (CA)
Furniture Revival (OR)
Hope Co., Inc. (MO)
Howard Products, Inc. (CA)
O'Sullivan Co. (MI)
Sutherland Welles Ltd. (NC)
Western Wood Doctor (CA)
**Woodcare Corporation Sales & Technical
    Sales Svc. (NJ)**

FLATTING OILS

Behlen, H. & Bros. (NY)
Janovic/Plaza, Inc. (NY)

GLASS CLEANERS

Butcher Polish Co. (MA)

GLAZING STAINS & LIQUIDS

Behlen, H. & Bros. (NY)
Benjamin Moore Co. (NJ)
Daly's Wood Finishing Products (WA)
Gaston Wood Finishes, Inc. (IN)
Illinois Bronze Paint Co. (IL)
Janovic/Plaza, Inc. (NY)
Johnson Paint Co. (MA)
Wolf Paints And Wallpapers (NY)

GOLD LEAF

Behlen, H. & Bros. (NY)
Gold Leaf & Metallic Powders, Inc. (NY)
Horowitz Sign Supplies (NY)
Illinois Bronze Paint Co. (IL)
Janovic/Plaza, Inc. (NY)
Swift & Sons, Inc. (CT)
Wolf Paints And Wallpapers (NY)

LACQUERS, CLEAR & COLORED

Barap Specialties (MI)
Behlen, H. & Bros. (NY)
Finishing Products (MO)
Gaston Wood Finishes, Inc. (IN)
Illinois Bronze Paint Co. (IL)
Janovic/Plaza, Inc. (NY)
Wolf Paints And Wallpapers (NY)

MARBLE CLEANERS, SEALERS & POLISHES

Barap Specialties (MI)
Goddard & Sons (WI)
ProSoCo, Inc. (KS)
Sculpture Associates, Ltd. (NY)
TALAS (NY)
Wolf Paints And Wallpapers (NY)

PAINTS—LINSEED OIL BASE

NuBrite Chemical Co., Inc. (MA)
Paints N Papers (ME)

**See Company Directory for
Addresses & Phone Numbers**

WOODCARE CORPORATION
ONE STEP RESTORATION OF WOODS & METALS

WOODCARE CORPORATION manufactures WOOD CARE & METAL CARE PRODUCTS for the restoration of woods and metals. For the wood products, we are distinct from the stripping method in that our products are formulated for one-step restoration. We eliminate the conventional steps of sanding, scraping, washing down, and then staining after a finish has been removed. As our WOODCARE PAINT & VARNISH REMOVER contains no acid or lye it does not raise the grain of wood. It is also completely safe for wood inlay and veneers. It does not dissolve glue around joints. It restores wood without bleaching out the patina that aged wood acquires (and which differentiates it from new wood).

DESCRIPTION OF PRODUCT LINE AND SERVICE:

1. WOODCARE PAINT & VARNISH REMOVER dissolves oil based enamel, varnish, shellac and lacquer. This product can be reused and is highly recommended for the complete restoration of vintage homes. It will not bleach out wood as it contains no acid. Examples: Wood doors, panelling, wainscotting, parquet floors, antiqued wide board flooring, kitchen cabinetry, old furniture, antiques, etc. This product is also recommended for clean-up and a hand-rubbed finish after use of OLD-HOUSE JOURNAL Heat Gun on heavy enamels. (See advertisement.)

2. TUNG OIL FINISH is a penetrating sealer applied over restored patina or a stained surface. Not only does it bring out the natural color of wood but it also is a good wood preservative and a durable finish which can be used even on floors. The method described in the WOODCARE RESTORATION GUIDE allows a high gloss or a hand-rubbed natural finish.

3. WOODCARE COPPER & BRASS CLEANER is recommended for all metals (excluding silver and pewter) and neatly removes the heaviest of tarnish, corrosion, rust and oxidation.

4. METAL CARE CLEAR FILM is a barrier against oxidation and when used on interior metals guarantees a natural metal finish or soft patina for 4-5 years. It does not yellow with age and the finish can be removed easily with detergent and hot water.

5. SIMICHROME POLISH, imported from Germany, is a fine polishing cream for highest lustre on all metals. Shines silver, brass, copper, pewter, tin, bronze, aluminum, stainless steel, chrome, and similar surfaces. Retards tarnish. Meets military specifications. 8.8 oz. can. . .$11.95 (or buy 2 for $21.90).

6. ANTIQUE CARE cleans and brightens wood surfaces without removing the finish. Removes wax build-up and grime that dull finish. Removes alcohol, cosmetic and water staines. No wax build-up when used for polishing furniture. 16 oz. bottle. . .$6.95 (or order 6 for $35.70).

7. BRIWAX is a non-abrasive beeswax imported from England. It cleans and reconditions panelling, cabinetry, woodwork, and metals. One can covers 1000 sq.ft. Available in four shades: clear, light brown, dark brown, and mahogany. Removes water marks, scratches, stains, grease, and oxidation with minimum effort and maximum results. 16 oz. can. . .$11.95 (you can buy 2 for $21.90).

8. PROMPT United Parcel Service Delivery. Woodcare Corp. guarantees fast, same-day shipment on all orders of any size when THE OLD-HOUSE JOURNAL CATALOG is mentioned. Delivery time is 2-4 days.

9. FREE RESTORATION GUIDE available upon request from WOODCARE CORP., PO Box 92, Butler, NJ 07405. Wholesale Price List also available to qualified buyers.

10. Dealers are wanted for the distribution and sales of Woodcare Products at antique shows, flea markets, or retail stores. Contact WOODCARE CORP., PO Box 92, Butler, NJ 07405.

11. All products are UNCONDITIONALLY GUARANTEED to give professional results or your money will be refunded without return of product.

DO IT YOURSELF WITH WOODCARE PAINT & VARNISH REMOVER

EASY — PLEASANT TO USE — NO HARSH FUMES — NO ACIDS — NO WASH — NO SCRUBBING OR SANDING DOES NOT BLEACH OUT PATINA — SAFE FOR GLUES — SOLUTION CAN BE REUSED — SAFE FOR VENEERS & INLAYS — USE TO FINISH & NEUTRALIZE AFTER HARSH STRIPPERS HAVE BEEN USED

☐ 1 qt.   Woodcare Paint & Varnish Remover $6.95
☐ 1 gal.   Woodcare Paint & Varnish Remover 22.95
☐ 1 case   (4 gal.) Paint & Varnish Remover 66.00
☐ 1 8-oz. Tung Oil Natural Finish 2.99
☐ 1 case   (12 8-oz.) Tung Oil Natural Finish 27.00
☐ 1 8-oz. Metal Care Brass & Copper Cleaner. 2.99
☐ 1 case   (12 8-oz.) Brass & Copper Cleaner 27.00
☐ 1 8-oz. Metal Care Clear Film. 2.99
☐ 1 case   (12 8-oz.) Metal Care Clear Film. 27.00
☐ 1 kit   Woodcare Refinishing Kit (contains 2 qts.
           paint & varnish remover, 8 oz. tung oil natural
           finish, dipping jar, and steel wool) 16.49
☐ 1 can   Simichrome Polish (8.8 oz.). 11.95
☐ 2 cans   Simichrome Polish (8.8 oz. each) 21.90
☐ 1 botl. Antique Care (16-oz. bottle) 6.95
☐ 6 botl. Antique Care(16 oz. each). 21.90
☐ 1 can   16 oz. Briwax (in four shades) 11.95
☐ 2 cans   16 oz. Briwax (in four shades) 21.90

         Shipping & Handling (any size order)   2.50
         Total amount enclosed. . . . .$

Send order to: WOODCARE CORPORATION
                  P.O. Box 92
                  Butler, NJ 07405

FOR ORDERS & SERVICE: (201) 838-9536

Please print name & street address:
NAME _____
STREET_____
CITY_____STATE_____ ZIP_____

Send check, order C.O.D., or use credit card. Next day shipment by U.P.S. Delivery is 2-4 days.

VISA☐ MASTERCARD☐ AMERICAN EXPRESS☐
CARD NO. _____
Expiration   Interbank
Date_____to_____Number _____
SIGNATURE
REQUIRED _____

OIL FINISHES, NATURAL

Barap Specialties (MI)
Behlen, H. & Bros. (NY)
Bix Process Systems, Inc. (CT)
Cabot Stains (MA)
Cohasset Colonials by Hagerty (MA)
Daly's Wood Finishing Products (WA)
Deft Wood Finish Products (OH)
Easy Time Wood Refinishing Products Corp. (IL)
Gaston Wood Finishes, Inc. (IN)
Hope Co., Inc. (MO)
McCloskey Varnish Co. (PA)
Minwax Company, Inc. (NJ)
Watco - Dennis Corporation (CA)
Woodcare Corporation Sales & Technical Sales Svc. (NJ)
Woodworkers' Store, The (MN)

PAINTS—PERIOD COLORS

(1) Exterior
(2) Interior

Allentown Paint Mfg. Co., Inc. (PA) *1,2*
Benjamin Moore Co. (NJ) *1,2*
Cohasset Colonials by Hagerty (MA) *2*
Colonial Williamsburg Foundation Craft
   House (VA) *1,2*
Devoe & Raynolds Co. (KY) *1*
Finnaren & Haley, Inc. (PA)
Fuller O'Brien Paints (GA) *1,2*
Greenfield Village and Henry Ford Museum
   (MI)
Janovic/Plaza, Inc. (NY) *1,2*
Munsell Color (MD)
Muralo Company (NJ) *1*
Pratt & Lambert (NY) *2*
Stulb Paint & Chem. Co., Inc. (PA) *1,2*
Sutherland Welles Ltd. (NC) *1,2*
Wolf Paints And Wallpapers (NY) *1,2*

**See Company Directory for
Addresses & Phone Numbers**

**You'll get better service
when contacting companies
if you mention
The Old-House Journal
Catalog**

Authentic American colors look fresh & natural today

Quality finishes in historically-inspired colors from Benjamin Moore Paints.

<u>Inside:</u> Choose authentic historical colors for walls, trim and accents that reflect the dignity and warmth of past generations. Use them naturally, in traditional or colonial settings, or as inspiration for your own style. <u>Outside:</u> You'll find documented 18th & 19th century color combinations that restore the charm of yesterday, with finishes formulated to provide maximum protection today.

See your Benjamin Moore dealer for courteous service & expert advice, to help you create a personal look that is historically correct.

Benjamin Moore PAINTS

NEW

EVERYONE'S TALKING ABOUT THE EXCITING

Palette of
Cape May
Victorian COLORS™

Presented by Fuller-O'Brien Paints with the assistance and endorsement of The Historic District Commission of Cape May, New Jersey.

THIS COLLECTION OF 70 AUTHENTIC VICTORIAN COLORS WAS FORMULATED SPECIALLY FOR HOUSES OF THE VICTORIAN ERA.

For interior and exterior use, these rich colors add interest to Early American and contemporary architecture as well. The Cape May Victorian Color Palatte is available to subscribers of **The Old House Journal** at one half the regular price. For your own copy, send $1.50 with your name and address to:
Fuller-O'Brien Paints
P. O. Box 864, Brunswick, Ga. 31521

FULLER O'BRIEN PAINTS

PAINT STRIPPING CHEMICALS, INTERIOR

Antique Color Supply, Inc. (MA)
Behlen, H. & Bros. (NY)
Bix Process Systems, Inc. (CT)
Chem-Clean Furniture Restoration Center (VT)
Chemical Products Co., Inc. (MD)
Easy Time Wood Refinishing Products Corp. (IL)
North Coast Chemical Co. (WA)
ProSoCo, Inc. (KS)
QRB Industries (MI)
Red Devil, Inc. (NJ)
Staples, H. F. & Co., Inc. (NH)
United Gilsonite Laboratories (PA)
Woodcare Corporation Sales & Technical Sales Svc. (NJ)
Woodworkers' Store, The (MN)

PIGMENTS & TINTING COLORS

Behlen, H. & Bros. (NY)
Benjamin Moore Co. (NJ)
Finishing Products (MO)
Horowitz Sign Supplies (NY)
Janovic/Plaza, Inc. (NY)
Johnson Paint Co. (MA)

PORCELAIN REFINISHING MATERIALS

Janovic/Plaza, Inc. (NY)
Zynolyte Products Co. (CA)

PUTTY, COLORED

Behlen, H. & Bros. (NY)
Daly's Wood Finishing Products (WA)
Rutland Products (VT)

ROT PATCHING & RESTORING MATERIALS

Abatron, Inc. (IL)
Allied Resin Corp. (MA)
Dell Corp. (MD)
E & B Marine Supply (NJ)
Life Industries (NY)
Philadelphia Resins Corp. (PA)
Poxywood, Inc. (VA)

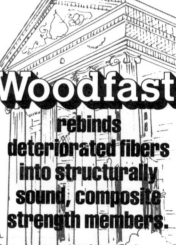

RUST & CORROSION REMOVERS

Bradford Derustit Corp. (NY)
North Coast Chemical Co. (WA)
Woodcare Corporation Sales & Technical Sales Svc. (NJ)

SEALERS, WOOD

Behlen, H. & Bros. (NY)
Benjamin Moore Co. (NJ)
Daly's Wood Finishing Products (WA)
Garrett Wade Company (NY)
Gaston Wood Finishes, Inc. (IN)
Sutherland Welles Ltd. (NC)
Watco - Dennis Corporation (CA)
Woodcare Corporation Sales & Technical Sales Svc. (NJ)

SPECIALTY PAINTS & FINISHES

(1) Calcimine
(2) Casein
(3) Whitewash
(4) Texture Paints
(5) Milk Paint

Antique Color Supply, Inc. (MA) *5*
Barnard Chemical Co. (CA)
Benjamin Moore Co. (NJ) *4*
Chromatic Paint Corp. (NY)
Illinois Bronze Paint Co. (IL)
Janovic/Plaza, Inc. (NY) *2,3,4*
Johnson Paint Co. (MA) *1,5*
Muralo Company (NJ) *1,4*
Old-Fashioned Milk Paint Co. (MA) *5*
Sutherland Welles Ltd. (NC)
U.S. Gypsum Company (IL) *4*
Wolf Paints And Wallpapers (NY) *2*

STAINS, WOOD

Behlen, H. & Bros. (NY)
Benjamin Moore Co. (NJ)
Bix Process Systems, Inc. (CT)
Boseman Veneer & Supply Co. (TX)
Cabot Stains (MA)
Cohasset Colonials by Hagerty (MA)
Daly's Wood Finishing Products (WA)
Deft Wood Finish Products (OH)
Furniture Revival (OR)
Garrett Wade Company (NY)
Gaston Wood Finishes, Inc. (IN)
Illinois Bronze Paint Co. (IL)
Minwax Company, Inc. (NJ)
Sutherland Welles Ltd. (NC)
United Gilsonite Laboratories (PA)
Watco - Dennis Corporation (CA)
Woodcare Corporation Sales & Technical Sales Svc. (NJ)

TEXTILE CLEANERS

TALAS (NY)

TUNG OIL

Behlen, H. & Bros. (NY)
Bix Process Systems, Inc. (CT)
Crawford's Old House Store (WI)
Daly's Wood Finishing Products (WA)
Furniture Revival (OR)
Garrett Wade Company (NY)
Hope Co., Inc. (MO)
Sutherland Welles Ltd. (NC)
Western Wood Doctor (CA)
Wolf Paints And Wallpapers (NY)
**Woodcare Corporation Sales & Technical
    Sales Svc. (NJ)**

VARNISHES

Barnard Chemical Co. (CA)
Behlen, H. & Bros. (NY)
Benjamin Moore Co. (NJ)
Bix Process Systems, Inc. (CT)
Boseman Veneer & Supply Co. (TX)
Daly's Wood Finishing Products (WA)
Deft Wood Finish Products (OH)
Furniture Revival (OR)
Garrett Wade Company (NY)
Illinois Bronze Paint Co. (IL)
McCloskey Varnish Co. (PA)
Minwax Company, Inc. (NJ)
North Coast Chemical Co. (WA)
Stulb Paint & Chem. Co., Inc. (PA)
Sutherland Welles Ltd. (NC)
United Gilsonite Laboratories (PA)

WALLPAPER CLEANERS

TALAS (NY)

WAXES, MICROCRYSTALLINE & OTHER SPECIALTY

Antique Color Supply, Inc. (MA)
Behlen, H. & Bros. (NY)
Black Wax — Pacific Engineering (CT)
Butcher Polish Co. (MA)
Finish Feeder Company (MD)
Janovic/Plaza, Inc. (NY)
Marshall Imports (OH)
O'Sullivan Co. (MI)
Staples, H. F. & Co., Inc. (NH)
Wolf Paints And Wallpapers (NY)
**Woodcare Corporation Sales & Technical
    Sales Svc. (NJ)**

WOOD FILLERS & PATCHING MATERIALS

Abatron, Inc. (IL)
Allied Resin Corp. (MA)
Philadelphia Resins Corp. (PA)
Poxywood, Inc. (VA)

WOOD GRAIN FILLERS

Barap Specialties (MI)
Behlen, H. & Bros. (NY)
Benjamin Moore Co. (NJ)
Daly's Wood Finishing Products (WA)
Garrett Wade Company (NY).
Gaston Wood Finishes,.Inc. (IN)
Janovic/Plaza, Inc. (NY)
Wolf Paints And Wallpapers (NY)

OTHER FINISHES & SUPPLIES

Behlen, H. & Bros. (NY)
Butcher Polish Co. (MA)
Garrett Wade Company (NY)
Hope Co., Inc. (MO)
Life Industries (NY)
Rutland Products (VT)
Sutherland Welles Ltd. (NC)

Tools & Other Supplies

ADZES, FROES & HAND HEWING TOOLS

Avalon Forge (MD)
Cumberland General Store (TN)
Frog Tool Co., Ltd. (IL)
Kayne, Steve & Son Custom Forged
    Hardware (NC)
Woodcraft Supply Corp. (MA)

CANVAS FOR WALLS

Janovic/Plaza, Inc. (NY)
Wolf Paints And Wallpapers (NY)

CHAIR SEAT REPAIR

(1) Caning, Wicker, Etc.
(2) Chair Tapes
(3) Pressed Fiber Replacement Seats
(4) Leather Seats
(5) Other Chair Repair Supplies
Barap Specialties (MI) *1*
Boseman Veneer & Supply Co. (TX) *1*
Cane & Basket Supply Company (CA) *1*
Caning Shop (CA) *1,2,3,5*
Connecticut Cane & Reed Co. (CT) *1,2,5*
Dover Furniture Stripping (DE) *1*
Finishing Products (MO) *1,3*
Finishing Touch (CA) *1,4*
Furniture Revival (OR) *1,3,4*
Jack's Upholstery & Caning Supplies (IL) . *1,5*
Morgan Woodworking Supplies (KY) *1*
Newell Workshop (IL) *1,5*
Poor Richard's Service Co. (NJ) *1*
Pyfer, E.W. (IL) *1*
Shaker Workshops (MA) *2*
Squaw Alley, Inc. (IL) *3*
WSI Distributors (MO) *1,3*

CONSERVATOR'S TOOLS

(1) Contour Gauges
(2) Magnifiers, Portable
(3) Measuring Instruments
(4) Moisture Meters
(5) Telltales
PRG (VA) *1,2,4*

**See Company Directory for
Addresses & Phone Numbers**

GAZEBO & OUTBUILDING PLANS

A.S.L. Associates (CA)
Bow House, Inc. (MA)
Building Conservation (WI)
Native Wood Products, Inc. (CT)
Sun Designs (WI)

GRAINING TOOLS

Janovic/Plaza, Inc. (NY)
Johnson Paint Co. (MA)
Lancaster Paint & Glass Co. (PA)
Wolf Paints And Wallpapers (NY)

HOUSE PLANS, PERIOD DESIGNS

(1) Early American
(2) Victorian
(3) Turn-of-Century
Bow House, Inc. (MA) *1*
Gage, Wm. E., Designer of Homes (MN) *1,2*
Heritage Home Designers (TX) *2*
Historical Replications, Inc. (MS) *2,3*
House Carpenters (MA) *1*
Howard, David, Inc. (NH) *1*
Native Wood Products, Inc. (CT) *1*
New Victorians of Arizona, Inc. (AZ) *2*
Pollitt, E., AIA (CT) *1*
Timberpeg (NH) *1*
Westport Housewrights (MA) *1*

LEADED & STAINED GLASS SUPPLIES & KITS

(1) Tools & Supplies
(2) Lamp Shade Kits
Blenko Glass Co., Inc. (WV) *1*
Coran — Sholes Industries (MA) *1,2*
Glassmasters Guild (NY) *1*
Greg Monk Stained Glass (HI)
Studio Design, Inc., t/a Rainbow Art Glass
   (NJ) *1,2*
Whittemore-Durgin Glass Co. (MA) *1,2*

SUPPLIES FOR MOULDS AND CASTS

(1) Mould-Making Materials
(2) Casting Plastics & Related Materials
(3) Casting Plaster
(4) Casting Repair Kits
Abatron, Inc. (IL) *1,2*
Heritage Studios (NC) *4*
Industrial Plastic Supply Co. (NY) *1,2*
Rutland Products (VT) *3*
Sculpture House (NY) *3*
U.S. Gypsum Company (IL) *3*

NAILS, HAND-MADE

Craftsman Lumber Co. (MA)
Kayne, Steve & Son Custom Forged
   Hardware (NC)
Millham, Newton — Blacksmith (MA)
Tremont Nail Company (MA)

PAINT STRIPPING TOOLS

(1) Hot Air Guns
(2) Mechanical Scrapers
(3) Rotary Tools
Crawford's Old House Store (WI) *1,2,3*
Easy Time Wood Refinishing Products Corp.
(IL) *1*
Goldblatt Tool Co. (KS) *3*
Hyde Manufacturing Company (MA)
Old-House Journal (NY) *1*
Wolf Paints And Wallpapers (NY) *2*
Woodcraft Supply Corp. (MA) *2*

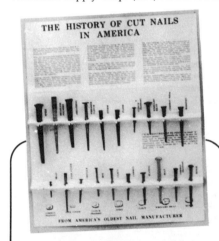

PLANES, WOOD-MOULDING

Cumberland General Store (TN)
Frog Tool Co., Ltd. (IL)
Garrett Wade Company (NY)
Iron Horse Antiques, Inc. (VT)
Williams & Hussey Machine Co. (NH)
Woodcraft Supply Corp. (MA)

PLASTERING & MASONRY TOOLS

Crawford's Old House Store (WI)
Goldblatt Tool Co. (KS)
Hyde Manufacturing Company (MA)
Marshalltown Trowel Co. (IA)
Masonry Specialty Co. (PA)
Mittermeir, Frank Inc. (NY)
Sculpture Associates, Ltd. (NY)
Sculpture House (NY)
Trow & Holden Co. (VT)
Wolf Paints And Wallpapers (NY)

PLASTER PATCHING MATERIALS

Muralo Company (NJ)
Rutland Products (VT)
Sculpture Associates, Ltd. (NY)
U.S. Gypsum Company (IL)
Wolf Paints And Wallpapers (NY)

PLASTER WASHERS & ANCHORS

Charles St. Supply Co. (MA)

SAFETY EQUIPMENT

Direct Safety Company (AZ)
Eastern Safety Equipment Co. (NY)
M.R.S Industries, Inc. (CT)
Masonry Specialty Co. (PA)
Mine Safety Appliance Corp. (NJ)

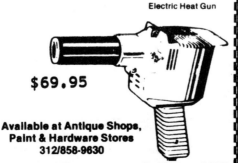
See Company Directory for Addresses & Phone Numbers

FOR INTERIOR STRIPPING
And Small Exterior Jobs

Nearly 10,000 OHJ subscribers have bought the **Master Heavy-Duty Heat Gun**, and discovered the best tool for stripping paint from interior woodwork. This electric-powered heat gun softens paint in a uniform way, so it can be scraped off with a knife. A small amount of chemical cleaner is suggested for tight crevices and clean-up, but the Heat Gun does most of the work. It reduces the hazard of inhaling methylene chloride vapors present in paint removers.

Another major safety feature is the Heat Gun's operating temperature, which is lower than a propane torch or blowtorch. Thus, the danger of vaporizing lead is minimized.

The Master HG-501 Heat Gun is an industrial-grade tool. It operates at 500-750°F, draws 15 amps at 120 volts, and has a rugged, die-cast aluminum body — no plastics! It isn't cheaply made or cheaply priced. But paint remover is going for $15-20 per gallon ... so if you use the Heat Gun just a few times, it pays for itself.

The Heat Gun comes with complete operating and safety instructions, and is backed by The Old-House Journal Guarantee: If your unit should malfunction for any reason within two months of purchase, return it to us and we'll replace it.

You may order your Heat Gun by filling out the Order Form on page 184, or by sending $72.95 (includes fast UPS shipping) to The Old-House Journal, 69A Seventh Ave., Brooklyn, NY 11217.

The Two Best Heat Tools For Stripping Pain

The Heat Gun has been a lifesaver for the 10,000 OHJ subscribers who have to strip paint from ornamental woodwork, shutters, window frames, and similar surfaces. But we're often asked if there's a comparable tool for larger jobs such as exterior clapboards (a task that takes forever with the Heat Gun). After testing all the available tools, the editors of The Old-House Journal are ready to recommend the best tool for the job: the **HYDElectric Heat Plate.**

Drawing 7 amps at 120 volts, the Heat Plate's electric resistance heating coil heats the surface to be stripped to a temperature of 550-800°F. A nickel-plated steel shield reflects the maximum amount of heat from the coil to the surface. And among the Heat Plate's safety features is a wire frame that supports the unit, so you can set it down without having to turn it off.

Gripping the Heat Plate by its cool plastic handle, you hold it close to the paint surface and soften the paint. Then you move the plate along and scrape away the loosened paint with a scraping tool. It's that simple! With a little practice, you can remove paint rapidly in one continuous motion. This procedure may remind you of using the Heat Gun, but that's where the similarity ends. The Heat Plate isn't efficient for the small fussy work that's so simple with the Heat Gun: mouldings, corners, recesses, turned wood such as balusters. What the Heat Plate is designed for — and does better than anything else — are the big jobs: clapboards, shingles, flush doors, large panels, and any flat surface.

The Heat Plate comes complete with operating and safety instructions, and is backed by The Old-House Journal Guarantee: If your unit should malfunction for any reason within two months of purchase, return it to us and we'll replace it.

To get the **HYDElectric Heat Plate**, fill out the Order Form on page 184, or send $39.95 (includes fast UPS shipping) to The Old-House Journal, 69A Seventh Ave., Brooklyn, NY 11217.

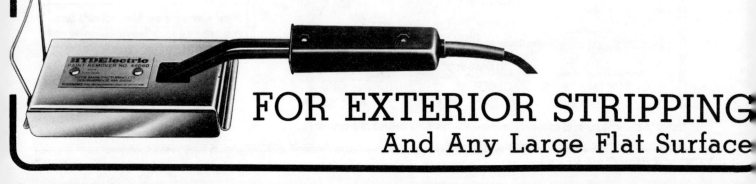

FOR EXTERIOR STRIPPING
And Any Large Flat Surface

SLATE ROOFING TOOLS

Evergreen Slate Co. (NY)

SPECIALTY POWER TOOLS

Dremel/Div. of Emerson Electric (WI)
Garrett Wade Company (NY)
Goldblatt Tool Co. (KS)
Sculpture Associates, Ltd. (NY)
Trow & Holden Co. (VT)
U.S. General Supply Corp. (NY)

STENCILLING SUPPLIES

(1) Brushes
(2) Stencil Paper
(3) Stencils, Drawn or Pre-Cut
(4) Stencil Kits
Behlen, H. & Bros. (NY) *1*
Bishop, Adele, Inc. (VT) *1,3*
Chromatic Paint Corp. (NY)
Cornerstone Antiques (NH) *3*
Hand-Stenciled Interiors (MA) *3*
Horowitz Sign Supplies (NY) *1*
Itinerant Artist (VA) *2,3,4*
Janovic/Plaza, Inc. (NY) *1,2*
Johnson Paint Co. (MA) *1*
Peg Hall Studios (MA)
Stencil House (NH) *3,4*
Stencil School (MA) *3*
Stencil Store (OH) *3*
Timeless Patterns (MA) *3*
Whole Kit & Kaboodle Co., Inc. (NY) *1,3*
Wolf Paints And Wallpapers (NY) *1,3*

UPHOLSTERY TOOLS & SUPPLIES

(1) Upholstery Supplies, Webbing, Batting, Etc.
(2) Upholstery Tools
Barap Specialties (MI)
Dover Furniture Stripping (DE)
Osborne, C. S. & Co. (NJ) *2*

WALLPAPERING & DECORATING TOOLS

Crawford's Old House Store (WI)
Hyde Manufacturing Company (MA)
Red Devil, Inc. (NJ)
Rollerwall, Inc. (MD)
Wolf Paints And Wallpapers (NY)

WOODWORKING TOOLS, HAND

Constantine, Albert and Son, Inc. (NY)
Cumberland General Store (TN)
Fox Maple Tools (ME)
Frog Tool Co., Ltd. (IL)
Garrett Wade Company (NY)
Iron Horse Antiques, Inc. (VT)
Leichtung, Inc. (OH)
The Mechanick's Workbench (MA)
Mittermeir, Frank Inc. (NY)
Nelson-Johnson Wood Products, Inc. (MN)
Sculpture Associates, Ltd. (NY)
Sculpture House (NY)
Tool Works (NY)
U.S. General Supply Corp. (NY)
Universal Clamp Corp. (CA)
Wikkmann House (CA)
Woodcraft Supply Corp. (MA)

OTHER RESTORATION TOOLS & SUPPLIES

Wikkmann House (CA)

See Company Directory for Addresses & Phone Numbers

Antique & Recycled House Parts

ANTIQUE & RECYCLED HOUSE PARTS

1874 House (OR)
Architectural Accents (GA)
Architectural Antique & Salvage Co. of Santa Barbara (CA)
Architectural Antique Warehouse, The ˜ (CAN)
Architectural Antiques Exchange (PA)
Architectural Emporium (IN)
Art Directions (MO)
Artifacts, Inc. (VA)
Baker, A.W. Restorations, Inc. (MA)
Bank Architectural Antiques (LA)
Bedlam Brass (NJ)
The Brass Knob (DC)
ByGone Era Architectural Antiques (GA)
Canal Co. (DC)
Canal Works Architectural Antiques (OH)
Caravati, Louis J. (VA)
Castle Burlingame (NJ)
Cohen's Architectural Heritage (CAN)
Conservatory, The (MI)
Cosmopolitan International Antiques (NY)
Croton, Evelyn — Architectural Antiques (NY)
Florida Victoriani Architectural Antiques (FL)
Gargoyles, Ltd. (PA)
Great American Salvage (NY,VT)
Hanks Architectural Antiques (TX)
History Store (DE)
Housewreckers, N.B. & Salvage Co. (NJ)
Inglenook (NY)
Jerard Paul Jordan Gallery (CT)
Joe Ley Antiques, Inc. (KY)
Materials Unlimited (MI)
Neri, C./Antiques (PA)
New Boston Building-Wrecking Co., Inc. (MA)
Nostalgia, Inc. (GA)
Off The Wall (CA)
Old-Home Building & Restoration (CT)
Olde Bostonian Architectural Antiques (MA)
Olde Theatre Architectural Salvage Co. (MO)
Pelnik Wrecking Co., Inc. (NY)
Red Baron's Peachtree Antique Emporium (GA)
Rejuvenation House Parts Co. (OR)
Renovation Source, Inc., The (IL)
Salvage One (IL)
Sandy Springs Galleries (GA)
Second Chance (GA)
Spiess, Greg (IL)
Strip Shop (LA)
Structural Antiques (OK)
Sunrise Specialty & Salvage Co. (CA)
Sunset Antiques, Inc. (MI)
Thomas Antique Services (NC)
United House Wrecking Corp. (CT)
Walker, Dennis C. (OH)
Webster's Landing Architectural Antiques (NY)
Westlake Architectural Antiques (TX)
Wigen Restorations (NY)
Wilson, H. Weber, Antiquarian (MD)
Wrecking Bar of Atlanta (GA)
Wrecking Bar, Inc. (TX)
You Name It, Inc. (OH)

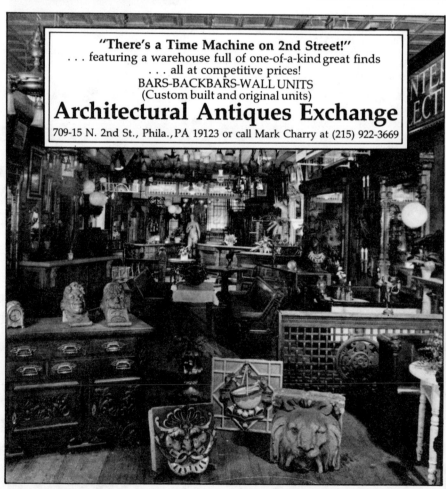
See Company Directory for Addresses & Phone Numbers

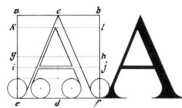

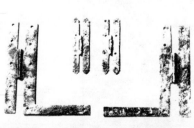

RECYCLED HOUSES, BARNS & OTHER STRUCTURES

Architectural Antique Warehouse, The (CAN)
Art Directions (MO)
Baker, A.W. Restorations, Inc. (MA)
Barn People, The (VT)
Belcher, Robert W. (GA)
Douglas Gest Restorations (VT)
Hulton, Roger L. (CAN)
Mountain Lumber Company (VA)
Old-Home Building & Restoration (CT)
Riverbend Timber Framing, Inc. (MI)
Vintage Lumber Co. (MD)
Wigen Restorations (NY)

**See Company Directory for
Addresses & Phone Numbers**

RENOVATION & RESTORATION SUPPLY STORES

(1) Walk-In Stores
(2) Mail-Order Suppliers

Architectural Antique Warehouse, The
  (CAN) 2
Architectural Archives (TX) 1
Architectural Emporium (IN) 1
Ball and Ball (PA) 2
Conservatory, The (MI) 1
Crawford's Old House Store (WI) 2
Emporium, The (TX) 1
Hood, R. and Co. (NH) 1
Inner Harbor Lumber & Hardware (MD) 1
Rejuvenation House Parts Co. (OR) 1,2
Remodelers & Renovators (ID) 1,2
Renovation Concepts, Inc. (MN) 1,2
Renovation Products (TX) 1
Renovation Source, Inc., The (IL) 1
Restoration Hardware (CA) 1,2
Restoration Works, Inc. (NY) 1,2
Squaw Alley, Inc. (IL) 1
Victorian Reproductions Enterprises, Inc.
  (MN) 2
Weaver, W. T. & Sons, Inc. (DC) 2

```
See Company Directory for
Addresses & Phone Numbers
```

period gingerbread, fretwork & gable treatments • period screen doors, porch swings & double facing glider • turnings, finials, posts & columns • plain & fancy wood stair parts cupboard & door trim kits & moldings • cupolas, weathervanes & fauna faucets • wood & brass house numbers & letters • cast table bases, park benches & lamp posts decorative wood & fibre carvings • wood, styrene & urethane moldings & brackets wood, brass & porcelain bath accessories & switchplates • gargoyles & cenotaphs steel ceiling & ceiling medallions

Send $2.00 for a complete catalogue.

RENOVATION PRODUCTS
5302 Junius
Dallas, Texas 75214
214—827-5111

REMODELERS & RENOVATORS:
SUPPLIES FOR VINTAGE HOUSES

● ——— ● ——— ●

RECAPTURE AND IMPROVE UPON THE PAST . . .

with our period brass bath and kitchen faucets and fittings, Victorian mouldings and wood products, gas/electric light fixtures, brass door hardware, fancy screen doors, copper weathervanes, columns and porch posts, mantels, stained and beveled glass, architectural antiques and a host of old-style and reproduction products for your preservation, building and decorating needs.

CATALOG $2.00   REFUNDABLE
1503 North 11th, Boise, ID 83702   (208) 377-5465

Your Source For Building Specialties.

Interior Woodwork	Plumbing Fixtures
Doors & Hardware	Lighting Fixtures
Wood Columns	Metal Ceilings
Exterior Trim	Brass Rail
And Much More

*New Retail/Wholesale Showroom
In Downtown Minneapolis*

Out of Town—Contact us for designer/
contractors catalog, home owners
discount catalog or free brochure:

A Business Whose Time Has "PAST"

Renovation Concepts

213 Washington Avenue North
Mpls., MN 55401   (612) 377-9526

Restoration Services

ANTIQUE REPAIR & RESTORATION

(1) Ceiling Fan Restoration
(2) Clock Repair & Parts
(3) Furniture Restoration
(4) Porcelain, Glass, & China Repair
(5) Stove Restoration
(6) Telephone Repair & Parts
(7) Textile Restoration

Aetna Stove Company (PA) 5
Agape Antiques (VT) 5
Alexandria Wood Joinery (NH) 3
Artistic Woodworking, Inc. (MI) 3
Beck, Nelson of Wash. Inc. (DC) 3
Billard's Old Telephones (CA) 6
Biltmore, Campbell, Smith Restorations, Inc. (NC) 7
Brass Fan Ceiling Fan Co. (TX) 1
Bryant Stove Works (ME) 5
Cambridge Textiles (NY) 7
Carriage Trade Antiques & Art Gallery (NC) 3
Country Roads, Inc. (MI) 3
D'Onofrio Restorative Studio (NY) 3
Durable Goods (MN) 5
Gaudio Custom Furniture (NY) 3
George Studios (NY) 4
Hess Repairs (NY) 4
Inglenook (NY) 3
Jim & Barb's Antique Stoves (WA) 5
Keystone (CA) 3
M — H Lamp & Fan Company (IL) 1
Merrimack Valley Textile Museum — Textile Conser. Cntr. (MA) 7
Ogren & Trigg Clock Service (MN) 2
Old World Restorations, Inc. (OH) 3,4
Poor Richard's Service Co. (NJ) 3
Restorations (NY) 7
Sawdust Room (MI) 3
Studio Workshop, Ltd. (CT)
Tec Specialties (GA) 2
Thomas Antique Services (NC) 3
Timesavers (IL) 2
Victorian Glass Works (CA) 3
Whitley Studios (PA) 3
Wiebold, Inc. (OH) 4
Wrisley, Robert T. (TN)

ARCHEOLOGICAL SURVEYS & INVESTIGATIONS

Archeological Research Consultants, Inc. (NJ)
Historic Preservation Alternatives, Inc. (NJ)

ARCHITECTURAL DESIGN & CONSULTING SERVICES

(1) Architectural Design—Restoration
(2) Consulting Services
(3) Historical Research
(4) Paint & Materials Analysis
(5) Lectures & Seminars

ARJ Assoc. — Reza Jahedi (MA) 1
Aachen Designers (FL) 1,2
Acquisition and Restoration Corp. (IN) ... 1,2
Arch Associates/ Stephen Guerrant AIA (IL)
.... 1
Archeological Research Consultants, Inc. (NJ)
.... 3
Architectural Accents (GA) 1
Architectural Reclamation, Inc. (OH) 1,2
Architectural Woodworking (CT) 2
Archive (NY) 1,2,3,5
Artistic License in San Francisco (CA) 4
Baker, A.W. Restorations, Inc. (MA) 2
Nancy Borden, Period Textiles (NH) 2
Breakfast Woodworks Louis Mackall &
    Partner (CT) 1
Brown, T. Robins (NY) 2,3
Bucher & Cope Architects (DC) 1,2,3,5
Carpenter and Smith Restorations (IL) 2
Clio Group, Inc. (PA) 2,3
Community Services Collaborative (CO)
.... 1,2,3,4
Consulting Services Group S.P.N.E.A. (MA)
.... 2,3,4
Cosmopolitan International Antiques (NY) . 2
Dierickx, Mary B. (NY) 2,3
Dodge, Adams, and Roy, Ltd. (NH) 1,2,3
Downstate Restorations (IL) 2
The Ehrenkrantz Group/Building
    Conservation Technology (DC) 2,3,4
Elmore, Chris/ Architectural Design (FL) 1
Enerdynamics (AK) 2
Enlightened Restorations (CT) 2,3
Ferris, Robert Donald, Architect, Inc. (CA)
.... 1,2
Gallier House Museum (LA) 5
Hart, Brian G./Architect (CAN) 1,3
Hasbrouck, W.R., Architect Historic
    Resources (IL) 1,2,3
Herman, Frederick, R.A., Architect (VA) 1,2,5
Hill, Allen Charles AIA (MA) 1,2,3,5
Historic Boulevard Services (IL) 2,5
Historic Preservation Alternatives, Inc. (NJ)
.... 1,2,3,5
History Store (DE) 3
Hobt, Murrel Dee, Architect (VA) 1,2,3
Holm, Alvin AIA Architect (PA) 1,2
Image Group, The (OH) 1,2
Interior Decorations (NH) 2,5
International Consultants, Inc. (PA) 2
Jennings, Gottfried, Cheek/ Preservationists
    (IA) 2,3
Jones Interior Design (TX) 2
Kaplan/Price Assoc. — Architects (NY) 1
Kruger Kruger Albenberg (MA) 1,2
Landmark Company (KS) 1
David M. LaPenta, Inc. (PA) 1
Mosca, Matthew (NY) 4
Munsell Color (MD) 4
Old House Inspection Co., Inc. (NY) 1
Pedersen, Arthur Hall — Design &
    Consulting Engineers (MO) 2
Perry, Edward K., Company (MA) 4
Piccone, James Corrado, & Associates (NY)
.... 1,2
Preservation Associates, Inc. (MD) 2,3
Preservation/Design Group, The (NY) .. 1,2,3,5
Preservation Development Group (CT) 1,2,3,5
Preservation Partnership (MA) 1,2,3,4,5
Preservation Resource Center of New
    Orleans (LA) 3

Preservation Resource Group (VA) 2,3,5
Renovation Source, Inc., The (IL) 1,2
Restoration A Specialty (OR) 2
Restoration Workshop Nat Trust For Historic
    Preservation (NY) 2
Restorations (NY) 5
Restorations Unlimited, Inc. (PA) 2,3
San Francisco Restorations, Inc. (CA) 2
Tomas Spiers & Associates (PA) 1,2,3
Stevens, John R., Associates (NY) 1
Stryker, Donald, Restorations (NJ) 2
Swofford, Don A., Architect (VA) 1,2
Szabo, George T., & Assoc., Inc. (CA) 1,3
T.A.G. Preservation Consultation (NY) 2
Tomblinson, Harburn, Yurk and Assoc., Inc.
    (MI) 1,3
Troyer, Le Roy and Associates (IN) 1
Victorian Interior Restoration (OH) 2
Welsh, Frank S. (PA) 4
Willard Restorations, Inc. (CT) 5
Wilson, H. Weber, Antiquarian (MD) 2,5
Winans, Paul/Designer-Builder (CA) 1
Wollon, James Thomas, Jr., A.I.A. (MD) 1,2,5

**See Company Directory for
Addresses & Phone Numbers**

CABINETMAKING & FINE WOODWORKING

Amherst Woodworking & Supply (MA)
Architectural Accents (GA)
Artisan Woodworkers (CA)
Artistic Woodworking, Inc. (MI)
Campbell, Marion (PA)
Carpenter and Smith Restorations (IL)
Congdon, Johns/Cabinetmaker (VT)
Crowfoot's Inc. (AZ)
Faucher, Evariste—Woodworker (GA)
Fine Woodworking Co. (MD)
Douglas Gest Restorations (VT)
Haas Wood & Ivory Works (CA)
Johnson Bros. Specialties (IL)
Kirk, M.A./Creative Designs (MI)
LaPointe, Chip, Cabinetmaker (NY)
Lea, James — Cabinetmaker (ME)
Leeke, John — Woodworker (ME)
Maine Architectural Millwork (ME)
Maurer & Shepherd, Joyners (CT)
Mead Associates Woodworking, Inc. (NY)
Millbranth, D.R. (NH)
Moore, E.T., Jr. Co. (VA)
Morningstar (MS)
Nutt, Craig, Fine Wood Works (AL)
Restorations Unlimited, Inc. (PA)
Rich Craft Custom Kitchens, Inc. (PA)
S H M Restorations (MN)
Schmidt, Edward P. — Cabinetmaker (PA)
Victorian Interior Restoration (OH)

CARPENTRY

Acquisition and Restoration Corp. (IN)
Anderson Reconstruction (MA)
Architectural Restoration (NY)
Beaumier Carpentry, Inc. (MD)
Eklund, Jon Restorations (NJ)
Fine Woodworking Co. (MD)
History Store (DE)
House Carpenters (MA)
Johnson, Walter H. (NY)
Joy Construction, Inc. (VA)
Knudsen, Mark (IA)
Oliver Organ Co. (NY)
Reed Illinois Corp. (IL)
Ross, Douglas — Woodworker (NY)
S H M Restorations (MN)
Seitz, Robert/Fine Woodworking (MA)
Stripper, The (KY)
Victorian Building & Repair (IL)
Women's Woodwork (MA)

CONTRACTING SERVICES—RESTORATION

Acquisition and Restoration Corp. (IN)
American Building Restoration (WI)
Anderson Building Restoration (OH)
Architectural Reclamation, Inc. (OH)
Baker, A.W. Restorations, Inc. (MA)
Beaumier Carpentry, Inc. (MD)
Brandt Bros. General Contractors (IN)
Canal Works Architectural Antiques (OH)
Carpenter and Smith Restorations (IL)
Castle Home Maintenance Co. Boston
    Victoriana (MA)
Dell Corp. (MD)
Dodge, Adams, and Roy, Ltd. (NH)
Downstate Restorations (IL)
Drill Construction Co., Inc. (NJ)
Eklund, Jon Restorations (NJ)
Elmore, Chris/ Architectural Design (FL)
Evergreene Painting Studios, Inc. (NY)
Great Northern Woodworks, Inc. (VT)
Heritage Home Designers (TX)
Historic Boulevard Services (IL)
Housejoiner, Ltd. (VT)
Huseman, Richard J. Co. (OH)
Johnson, Walter H. (NY)
Joy Construction, Inc. (VA)
Klinke & Lew Contractors (CO)
Knickerbocker Guild (CA)
David M. LaPenta, Inc. (PA)
Lesco Restorations, Inc. (GA)
Morningstar (MS)
Northern Design General Contractors (VT)
Preservation Associates, Inc. (MD)
Rambusch (NY)
Reed Illinois Corp. (IL)
Restoration A Specialty (OR)
Restoration Fraternity (PA)
Restoration Workshop Nat Trust For Historic
    Preservation (NY)
Restorations Unlimited, Inc. (PA)
River City Restorations (MO)
S H M Restorations (MN)
San Francisco Restorations, Inc. (CA)
Skyline Engineers, Inc. (MA)
Smolinsky, Ltd. (PA)
Stevens, John R., Associates (NY)
Stryker, Donald, Restorations (NJ)
Victorian Building & Repair (IL)
Victorian Interior Restoration (OH)
Warren, William J. & Son, Inc. (CO)
Westport Housewrights (MA)
Willard Restorations, Inc. (CT)
Winans, Paul/Designer-Builder (CA)
Women's Woodwork (MA)

FIREPLACE & CHIMNEY RESTORATION

Acquisition and Restoration Corp. (IN)
Durvin, Tom & Sons (VA)
Flue Works, Inc. (OH)
Douglas Gest Restorations (VT)
Haines Complete Building Service (IN)
Huskisson Masonry & Exterior Building
    Restoration Co. (KY)
Long, E. T., Inc. (VA)
Olde New England Masonry (CT)
Parsons, W.H., Jr. & Associates (CT)
Restoration Masonry (CO)
Welles Fireplace Company (NY)

HOUSE INSPECTION SERVICES

AMC Housemaster Home Inspection Svc.
    (NJ)
Acquisition and Restoration Corp. (IN)
Arch Associates/ Stephen Guerrant AIA (IL)
Baker, A.W. Restorations, Inc. (MA)
Building Inspection Services, Inc. (MD)
Carson, Dunlop & Associates, Ltd. (CAN)
Claxton Walker & Associates (MD)
Douglas Gest Restorations (VT)·
Guardian National House Inspection and
    Warranty Corp. (MA)
Haines Complete Building Service (IN)
Hart, Brian G./Architect (CAN)
Hill, Allen Charles AIA (MA)
Historic Preservation Alternatives, Inc. (NJ)
House Master of America (NJ)
Lieberman, Howard, P.E. (NY)
National Home Inspection Service of New
    England, Inc. (MA)
Oberndorfer & Assoc. (PA)
Old House Inspection Co., Inc. (NY)
Preservation Associates, Inc. (MD)
Preservation Partnership (MA)
Security Home Inspection, Inc. (NY)
Stryker, Donald, Restorations (NJ)
Warren, William J. & Son, Inc. (CO)
Women's Woodwork (MA)

**See Company Directory for
Addresses & Phone Numbers**

HOUSE MOVING

Baker, A.W. Restorations, Inc. (MA)
Barn People, The (VT)
Douglas Gest Restorations (VT)
Wigen Restorations (NY)
Willard Restorations, Inc. (CT)

LANDSCAPE GARDENING—PERIOD DESIGN

Blessing Historical Foundation (TX)
Gibbs, James W. — Landscape Architect (NY)
Philip M. White & Associates (NY)

LIGHTING FIXTURE RESTORATION & WIRING

The Antique Restoration Co. (NJ)
Authentic Lighting (NJ)
Bernard Plating Works (MA)
Boulder Stained Glass Studios (CO)
Century House Antiques (OH)
Chandelier Wharehouse (NY)
Conant Custom Brass (VT)
Dermit X. Corcoran Antique Services (NY)
Dotzel, Michael & Son Expert Metal Craftsman (NY)
Hexagram (CA)
Jefferson Art Lighting, Inc. (MI)
Jennings Lights of Yesterday (CA)
Kayne, Steve & Son Custom Forged Hardware (NC)
Littlewood, Craig (NJ)
M — H Lamp & Fan Company (IL)
Mattia, Louis (NY)
Menerey, E. W. (MI)
Moriarty's Lamps (CA)
Old Lamplighter Shop (NY)
Pyfer, E.W. (IL)
Roy Electric Co., Inc. (NY)
Squaw Alley, Inc. (IL)
Stanley Galleries (IL)
Victorian Reproductions Enterprises, Inc. (MN)
Village Lantern (MA)
Washington House of Reproductions (VA)
Yankee Craftsman (MA)

MASONRY REPAIR & CLEANING

Acquisition and Restoration Corp. (IN)
American Building Restoration (WI)
Anderson Building Restoration (OH)
Cathedral Stone Company (DC)
Downstate Restorations (IL)
Durvin, Tom & Sons (VA)
Evergreene Painting Studios, Inc. (NY)
Haines Complete Building Service (IN)
Huskisson Masonry & Exterior Building Restoration Co. (KY)
Lesco Restorations, Inc. (GA)
Mendel-Black Stone Restoration (CT)
Olde New England Masonry (CT)
Parsons, W.H., Jr. & Associates (CT)
R.D.C. Enterprises (OH)
Restoration Masonry (CO)
River City Restorations (MO)
Russell Restoration of Suffolk (NY)
Skyline Engineers, Inc. (MA)

METAL REPLATING

The Antique Restoration Co. (NJ)
Bernard Plating Works (MA)
Chandler — Royce (NY)
Conant Custom Brass (VT)
Dotzel, Michael & Son Expert Metal Craftsman (NY)
Estes-Simmons Silver Plating, Ltd. (GA)
Orum Silver Co., Inc. (CT)
Poor Richard's Service Co. (NJ)
Pyfer, E.W. (IL)

METALWORK REPAIRS

The Antique Restoration Co. (NJ)
Authentic Designs Inc. (VT)
Authentic Lighting (NJ)
Ball and Ball (PA)
Bernard Plating Works (MA)
Bronze et al (NY)
Dermit X. Corcoran Antique Services (NY)
Dotzel, Michael & Son Expert Metal
    Craftsman (NY)
Dura Strip of San Mateo (CA)
Experi-Metals (WI)
Howland, John — Metalsmith (CT)
Kayne, Steve & Son Custom Forged
    Hardware (NC)
Moriarty's Lamps (CA)
Orum Silver Co., Inc. (CT)
Retinning & Copper Repair (NY)

MIRROR RESILVERING

The Antique Restoration Co. (NJ)
Boomer Resilvering (CA)
Indiana Mirror Resilvering (IN)
Ring, J. Stained Glass, Inc. (MN)

MUSICAL INSTRUMENT RESTORATION

A Second Wind for Harmoniums (NY)

PAINT STRIPPING SERVICES

Alexandria Wood Joinery (NH)
American Building Restoration (WI)
Anderson Building Restoration (OH)
Architectural Restoration (NY)
Balzamo, Joseph (NJ)
Cosmetic Restoration by SPRAYCO (NY)
Dover Furniture Stripping (DE)
Downstate Restorations (IL)
Dura Strip of San Mateo (CA)
Eklund, Jon Restorations (NJ)
Great American Salvage (NY,VT)
Haines Complete Building Service (IN)
Johnson Bros. Specialties (IL)
Keystone (CA)
Poor Richard's Service Co. (NJ)
R.D.C. Enterprises (OH)
Stripper, The (KY)
Studio Workshop, Ltd. (CT)

PAINTING & DECORATING—PERIOD

(1) Decorating Contractor
(2) Gilding
(3) Glazing
(4) Graining
(5) Marbleizing
(6) Murals & Frescoes
(7) Stencilling
(8) Trompe l'oeil
(9) Wallpaper Hanging

ARJ Assoc. — Reza Jahedi (MA) *7*
Architectural Restoration (NY)
Archive (NY) *1,4*
Artistic License in San Francisco (CA)
    .... *1,2,3,4,5,7,9*
Biltmore, Campbell, Smith Restorations, Inc.
    (NC) *1,2,4,5,6,7,9*
Larry Boyce & Associates (CA) *2,3,6,7,9*
The Brass Stencil (CT) *7*
Buecherl, Helmut (NY) *2,3,4,5,6,7*
Canning, John (CT) *4,5*
Castle Home Maintenance Co. Boston
    Victoriana (MA) *1,7*
Country Stencilling (NY) *7*
Craftsmen Decorators (NY) *2,3,4,7*
Dee, John W. — Distinctive Decorating (MA)
    .... *1,9*
Evergreene Painting Studios, Inc. (NY)
    .... *2,4,5,6,8*
George Studios (NY) *2,5,6*
Grammar of Ornament (CO) *4,5,7*
Greenhalgh & Sons (MA) *1,7,9*
Hand-Stenciled Interiors (MA) *7*
Hopkins, Sara — Restoration Stenciling (OR)
    .... *7*
Knickerbocker Guild (CA)
National Guild of Professional Paperhangers,
    Inc. (NY) *9*
Perry, Edward K., Company (MA) *1,3,4,7,8*
Rambusch (NY) *1,2,4,5,6,7*
Reed Illinois Corp. (IL) *1*
Robson Worldwide Graining (VA) *2,4,5*
Silberman, Allen (NY) *7*
Wiggins, D.B. (NH) *5,6,7*
Willems Painting & Decorating (WI) *4,9*
Zetlin, Lorenz — Muralist (NY) *5,6,8*

PARQUET REPAIR & INSTALLATION

Nassau Flooring Corp. (NY)
New York Flooring (NY)
Sutherland Welles Ltd. (NC)

PHOTO RESTORATION

Artex Studio (NY)
Elbinger Laboratories, Inc. (MI)

PHOTOGRAPHY, ARCHITECTURAL

Byrd Mill Studio (VA)

PLASTERING, ORNAMENTAL

ARJ Assoc. — Reza Jahedi (MA)
Acquisition and Restoration Corp. (IN)
Casey Architectural Specialties (WI)
Castle Home Maintenance Co. Boston
   Victoriana (MA)
Felber, Inc. (PA)
Flaharty, David — Sculptor (PA)
Form and Texture — Architectural
   Ornamentation (CO)
Giannetti Studios (MD)
Kelly Plastering Co. (IL)
Mangione Plaster and Tile and Stucco (NY)
Olde New England Masonry (CT)
Ornamental Design Studios (NY)
Piazza, Michael — Ornamental Plasterer (NY)
Reed Illinois Corp. (IL)
Russell Restoration of Suffolk (NY)
J.P. Weaver Co. (CA)

PORCELAIN REFINISHING

Perma Ceram Enterprises, Inc. (NY)
Porcelain Restoration and Brass (NC)
Restore-A-Tub (KY)

ROOFERS, SPECIALTY

Alte, Jeff Roofing, Inc. (NJ)
C & H Roofing (SD)
Castle Roofing Co., Inc. (NY)
Haines Complete Building Service (IN)
Millen Roofing Co. (WI)
Raleigh, Inc. (IL)
Restorations Unlimited, Inc. (PA)
Skyline Engineers, Inc. (MA)
Wagner, Albert J., & Son (IL)
Westal Contracting (NY)

SANDSTONE (BROWNSTONE) REPAIR

Brooklyn Stone Renovating (NY)
Cathedral Stone Company (DC)
Evergreene Painting Studios, Inc. (NY)
Mendel-Black Stone Restoration (CT)
Parsons, W.H., Jr. & Associates (CT)

STAIRCASE REPAIR

American Stair Builder (NY)
Dean, James R. (NY)
Dixon Bros. Woodworking (MA)
Housejoiner, Ltd. (VT)

TERRA COTTA RESTORATION & CASTING

Architectural Terra Cotta and Tile, Ltd. (IL)
ART, Inc. (NJ)
Collyer Associates, Inc. (NY)
Gladding, McBean & Co. (CA)
Virtue, W.D., Co., Inc. (NJ)

TRAINING COURSES & WORKSHOPS

Association for Preservation Technology
  (CAN)
Campbell Center (IL)
Eastfield Village (NY)
Restoration Workshop Nat Trust For Historic
  Preservation (NY)
Winterthur Museum (DE)

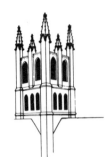

TURNINGS, CUSTOM

American Wood Column (NY)
Bartley's Mill — Victorian Woodwork (CA)
Cumberland Woodcraft Co., Inc. (PA)
Dixon Bros. Woodworking (MA)
Industrial Woodworking, Inc. (IL)
Johnson Bros. Specialties (IL)
Kaymar Wood Products, Inc. (WA)
Keystone (CA)
Knudsen, Mark (IA)
Leeke, John — Woodworker (ME)
Maine Architectural Millwork (ME)
Merit Moulding, Ltd. (NY)
Michael's Fine Colonial Products (NY)
Navedo Woodcraft, Inc. (NY)
Nelson-Johnson Wood Products, Inc. (MN)
Nutt, Craig, Fine Wood Works (AL)
**Pagliacco Turning & Milling Architectural
    Wood Turning (CA)**
Rich Woodturning and Stair Co. (FL)
Rosander's Wood Turning (UT)
Sawdust Room (MI)
Sheppard Millwork, Inc. (WA)
Sound Beginnings (NY)
Taft Wood Products Co. (OH)
Turncraft (OR)
Walbrook Mill & Lumber Co., Inc. (MD)
Woodstone Co. (VT)

WOOD CARVING

Braintree Woodworks (VA)
Dixon Bros. Woodworking (MA)
Knudsen, Mark (IA)
Lea, James — Cabinetmaker (ME)
Master Wood Carver (NJ)
Nutt, Craig, Fine Wood Works (AL)
Oak Leaves Woodcarving Studio (IA)
Shelley Signs (NY)
Wrisley, Robert T. (TN)

> **See Company Directory for
> Addresses & Phone Numbers**

> **You'll get better service
> when contacting companies
> if you mention
> The Old-House Journal
> Catalog**

THE COMPANY DIRECTORY

1874 House
8070 S.E. 13th Ave.   Dept. OHJ
Portland, OR 97202
(503) 233-1874
RS/O
Specialists in architectural fragments, antique
hardware for doors, cabinets, furniture, antique
Victorian lighting fixtures, antique plumbing
fixtures, antique sinks, replacements parts and
pieces for almost everything. Walk-in shopping
only. No literature.

● **1890 Iron Fence Co.**
P.O. Box 467   Dept. OHJ
Auburn, IN 46706
(219) 925-4264
MO
Manufacturers of an historic style of iron fence,
compatible with any style home built from the
Civil War through the 1920s. Installation
directions are geared to the handyman
homeowner. Descriptive brochure available. $1.

● **18th Century Hardware Co.**
131 East 3rd St.   Drawer OH
Derry, PA 15627
(412) 694-2708
RS/O MO
Reproduction hardware in brass, porcelain, and
black iron covering the Early American and
Victorian periods. Pulls, knobs, casters, hinges,
hooks, latches, door knockers, and other brass
accessories. Also, authentic hand-painted
cast-aluminum fire marks. Will duplicate and
repair hardware and locks. Catalog $4., by first
class mail (refundable with order).

19th Century Company
P.O. Box 599   Dept. OHJ
Rough & Ready, CA 95975
(916) 432-1040
MO RS/O
Manufacturer and distributor of hard-to-find parts
and hardware for antique furniture and vintage
homes. They carry a complete line of cast brass
including Victorian and Chippendale period items
through Art Deco and English hardware of the
early 20th century. They also offer desk
hardware, oak and walnut dowels and knobs,
and much more. Wholesale and retail. Illustrated
Catalog, $2.

21st Century Antiques
    Dept. OHJ
Hadley, MA 01035
(413) 549-6678
MO RS/O
A mail-order source for original 20th-century
decorative art-objects (Art-Deco, Arts & Crafts
Movement, etc.). Also a large selection of
reference books about the objects and the time
period. Replicas of some lines. Current catalog
and subscription for future catalogs, $4.

● **See Product Dis-
plays Index on page
199 for more details.**

● **AA-Abbingdon, Inc.**
2149-51 Utica Ave.   Dept. OHJ
Brooklyn, NY 11234
(212) 258-8333
RS/O MO
21 patterns of hard-to-find embossed tin panels,
and tin cornices in 10 patterns for metal ceiling
installation. Popular 50-100 years ago, metal
ceilings are an economical way to decorate in
period style. Free illustrated brochure.

A.A. Used Boiler Supply Co.
8720 Ditmas Avenue   Dept. OHJ
Brooklyn, NY 11236
(212) 385-2111
RS/O
Offering reconditioned gas and oil cast iron
boilers and sections. All types and sizes of cast
iron steam and hot water radiators. Many choices
of reconditioned gas and oil burners, controls,
coils, and oil tanks. All products are tested and
ready for immediate use. No literature; visit office
or call.

● **A-Ball Plumbing Supply**
1703 W. Burnside St.   Dept. OHJ
Portland, OR 97209
(503) 228-0026
RS/O MO
Various plumbing supplies and hardware,
including: Shower set-ups (brass or chrome),
high-tank toilets, faucets, waste & overflow in
brass, metal and tile cleaners, epoxy
tub-resurfacing kit, cast aluminum reproduction
grates, and old-fashioned soap dishes that hang
on footed tubs. Dealer inquiries welcome. Send
$2 for catalog. Mail orders arranged.

● **A.E.S. Firebacks**
334 Grindstone Hill Rd.   Dept. OHJ
North Stonington, CT 06359
(203) 535-2253
MO RS/O
Reproduction firebacks taken from original
designs. Placed in the rear of the fireplace, the
fireback protects masonry and radiates heat. Send
SASE for brochure.

A.J.P. Coppersmith
34 Broadway   Dept. OHJ
Wakefield, MA 01880
(617) 245-1216
MO DIST RS/O
Long-established company offers a complete line
of authentic Colonial lighting fixtures.
Chandeliers, sconces, post or wall lanterns are
hand-crafted with a choice of finishes: Copper
(antique or verdigris), Brass, Pewter-type
(lead-coated copper or terne). A distinctive
collection by three generations of craftsmen —
send $2.00 for catalog.

AMC Housemaster Home Inspection Svc.
18 Hamilton St.   Dept. OHJ
Bound Brook, NJ 08805
(201) 469-6050
RS/O
House inspections and warranty service working
in New Jersey. Free brochure.

A.R.D.
1 Fourth Place   Dept. OHJ
Brooklyn, NY 11231
(212) 624-5688
RS/O MO
Supplier of Victorian style kitchen cabinets, towel
warmers, brass sinks, period bathroom faucets
and accessories. Also, marble & granite, 12"by12"
tile. Information on kitchen cabinets $2.00, towel
warmers $.75, brass sinks $.50. Tile price sheet
free. A free information sheet lists discounts on
bathroom fittings and catalog costs. Please inform
us which product line you are interested in.

ARJ Assoc. — Reza Jahedi
29 Temple Pl.   Dept. OHJ
Boston, MA 02111
(617) 426-5057
RS/O MO
Custom design and restoration of ornamental
plasterwork for old and new buildings,
specializing in decorative cornices and moldings.
They execute specialist wall and surface effects
including: murals, stencilling, marbling, ragging
and gilding. Collection of traditional designs
hand painted on ceramic tile for bath, kitchen,
and fireplaces; also custom tile work. Free
catalogue and literature available.

● **A.S.L. Associates**
P.O. Box 6296   Dept. OHJ
San Mateo, CA 94403
(415) 344-5044
MO
Plans for building a gazebo. The set consists of
three 17" x 22" sheets, and includes full
construction details and a materials list. The
finished gazebo is 8 ft. in diameter and has an
inside height of 7. ft. 4 in. clear. Price — $10. No
literature.

Aachen Designers
308 NE Fifth Ave.   Dept. OHJ
Gainesville, FL 32601
(904) 372-5056
RS/O
Residential adaptive use and restoration:
comprehensive design services (schematic
through construction completion). Measured
drawings, programming, consulting. Special
expertise in kitchen design. Serving Southeast
and Indiana. No literature; will respond to
specific inquiries.

Abaroot Mfg., Co.
1853 W. Torrance Blvd.   Dept. OHJ
Torrance, CA 90501
(213) 320-8172
RS/O
Hand woodturning in Los Angeles since 1932.
Manufacture columns, newels, balusters, and
porch posts. Will work in hard or soft woods. No
literature.

Abatron, Inc.
141 Center Drive   Dept. OH
Gilberts, IL 60136
(312) 426-2200
MO
Manufactures epoxies and other materials for restoration, repair, coating, resurfacing, and maintenance. Wood consolidants, patching and resurfacing compounds for concrete, masonry and floors. Casting resins for moulds and patterns. Shrinkage-free fillers for wood, concrete and metal. Laminating resins for fiberglass. Structural restoration resins and adhesives. Also sealants and water-proof coatings. Dealer inquiries welcomed. Free brochure.

Accurate Weatherstripping Co., Inc.
725 South Fulton Ave.   Dept. OHJ
Mount Vernon, NY 10550
(914) 668-6042
MO
Integral weatherstripping in a variety of metals and sizes designed to fit casement or double-hung windows (wood & metal). Interlocking weatherstrip for doors, bronze & aluminum thresholds. Free catalog.

Ace Wire Brush Co.
30 Henry St.   Dept. OHJ
Brooklyn, NY 11201
(212) 624-8032
MO   DIST
All types of chimney brushes: wire, fibre, nylon. Free catalog.

Acme Stove Company
1011-7th St. N.W.   Dept. OHJ
Washington, DC 20001
(202) 628-8952
RS/O   MO
Major supplier of pre-fab fireplaces, wood-stoves, and woodburning accessories in the Mid-Atlantic area. Also chimney systems, efficient heat-circulating systems, fireplace accessories. Professional counselors will design complementary systems in townhouses and multifamily restorations. 9 locations; call or write for information.

Acorn Manufacturing Co., Inc.
PO Box 31, 457 School St.   Dept. OHJ
Mansfield, MA 02048
(617) 339-4500
MO   DIST
Selection of handcrafted reproduction Colonial hardware. Butterfly, strap, and H hinges. Cabinet, door, and shutter hardware. Catalog, $2.

Acquisition and Restoration Corp.
423 Massachusetts Avenue   Dept. OHJ
Indianapolis, IN 46204
(317) 637-1266
RS/O
Experienced general contractors, construction mgrs., consultants, and real estate developers in architectural restoration. Building inspection, historical research, financing and property-tax abatement consultation. 614 residential and commercial projects completed. No fee for initial correspondence. Restoration, renovation, and preservation projects undertaken throughout continental U.S.

Adams Company
100 E. 4th St.   Dept. OHJ
Dubuque, IA 52001
(319) 583-3591
DIST
Manufactures a line of fireplace furnishings of heavy-gauge steel, solid brass, and cast iron. Sold through distributors, but a free descriptive brochure is available with list of distributors.

Adams and Swett
380 Dorchester Ave.   Dept. OHJ
Boston, MA 02127
(617) 268-8000
RS/O   MO
Hand-braided and hooked rugs, 80%-90% wool, in 8 sizes. Special sizes (stairtreads, etc.) to order. Also cotton rag rugs in 4 colors. Brochure and price list -$.25.

Aetna Stove Company
S.E. Cor. 2nd & Arch Streets   Dept. OHJ
Philadelphia, PA 19106
(215) 627-2008
RS/O   MO
One of the oldest stove repair companies in the U.S., servicing and providing parts for gas stoves, coal ranges, etc. Large diversified stock of antique parts. Also supplies stove black, isinglass (mica windows). Please call or write for information. Prepaid shipments via UPS can be arranged.

Agape Antiques
Box 225   Dept. OHJ
Saxtons River, VT 05154
(802) 869-2273
RS/O
Period cast iron kitchen ranges and parlor stoves for sale. Restored to original condition and ready to use. Excellent selection of stoves dating from late 1700's to 1920's. Illustrated brochure available.

Ainsworth Development Corp.
Beckford   Dept. OHJ
Princess Anne, MD 21853
(301) 651-3219
MO
Manufactures turnbuckle stars for reinforcing masonry walls. Will design & supply tension member for determining tension being applied by turnbuckle. For literature, send stamped self-addressed envelope.

Air-Flo Window Contracting Corp.
194 Concord St.   Dept. OHJ
Brooklyn, NY 11201
(212) 875-8600
RS/O
Fabricates wood and metal storm and prime windows in 10 colors. Double-hung and casements available. Styles to suit old houses: windows conform to Landmark Commission standards. Can be glazed with Thermopane, Lexan, or Solar-Cool as well as single-pane glass. Free literature available on request, or call for more information.

Alcon Lightcraft Co.
1424 W. Alabama   Dept. OHJ
Houston, TX 77006
(713) 526-0680
RS/O   MO
Antique and reproduction early electric, gas and combination fixtures. Antique and reproduction lighting glassware replacements. Flyer available with stamped, self-addressed envelope.

Alexandria Wood Joinery
Plumer Hill Road   Dept. OHJ
Alexandria, NH 03222
(603) 744-8243
RS/O
Antique repair and restoration, furniture stripping and chair seating. Serving central New Hampshire. No literature.

Allentown Paint Mfg. Co., Inc.
E Allen & N Graham, Box 597   Dept. OHJ
Allentown, PA 18105
(215) 433-4273
RS/O   DIST   MO
Oldest ready-made paint company in U.S. (established 1855); offers a line of oil-based or latex exterior paints in colors appropriate for Colonial and Victorian era houses. Many colors and formulations date from the 1860s, with the exception of additives for easy application and color fastness. Literature available through local paint stores, or contact Allentown office for name of distributor.

Allied Resin Corp.
Weymouth Industrial Park   Dept. OHJ
East Weymouth, MA 02189
(617) 337-6070
MO
A mail-order source for epoxies. Will ship nation wide. Free literature.

Alte, Jeff Roofing, Inc.
PO Box 639   Dept. OHJ
Somerville, NJ 08876
(201) 526-2111
RS/O
General roofing contractors and roofing consultants serving Central and Northern New Jersey. Repair and reroofing of churches and older houses, including slate and cedar shingle work. Expertise and equipment to handle copper gutters, leaders, built-in gutters: their metal shop can fabricate gutters, ridge caps, etc. No literature; please call for appointment.

Amazon Vinegar & Pickling Works Drygoods
2218 E. 11th Street   Dept. OC
Davenport, IA 52803
(319) 322-6800
MO
A purveyor of items to create a 19th-century impression, 1750-1927. Emphasis on the hoop skirt and bustle era. Items include: Military accessories; period clothing & fabric for men, women, and children (patterns & ready-made); and books on clothing, history, period interiors, land-scaping and architecture. Victorian toys, cards & decorations for all holidays. 40-page catalog, $2.

Amerian Woodworking
1729 Little Orchard St.   Dept. OHJ
San Jose, CA 95125
(408) 294-2968
RS/O
Fireplace mantels, architectural paneling for walls and ceilings, and pre-fabricated wainscotting; bars and libraries comprise much of their work. Whenever possible, they pre-construct a system. For further information, please call or visit their showroom Monday thru Friday. Brochures are available for $1.50.

KEY TO ABBREVIATIONS

MO	**sells by Mail Order**
RS/O	**sells through Retail Store or Office**
DIST	**sells through Distributors**
ID	**sells only through Interior Designers or Architects**

American Boa, Inc. — Ventinox
PO Box 1743   Dept. OHJ
Albany, NY 12201
(518) 463-7284
DIST
Manufacturer's representative for the Ventinox stainless-steel chimney lining system, which is sold and installed by trained dealers nationwide. UL classified; type 321 stainless, continuously welded. Good installer servicing and guarantee. Also sell stove connector for safe installation of fireplace insert stoves. Free literature.

American Building Restoration
9720 So. 60th St.   Dept. OHJ
Franklin, WI 53132
(414) 761-2440
MO   DIST
Chemicals for paint stripping historical buildings. Sold to distributors and contractors. Also exterior restoration contractors. Interest free financing available — 6 months to 2 years. Works throughout the U.S. Slide presentation showing chemical systems and projects restored since 1970. Free color brochure.

American Comfort Systems, Inc.
24 East Parkway, Suite 7a   Dept. OHJ
Scarsdale, NY 10583
(914) 472-7171
RS/O
"Euroseal" metal weatherstripping installed to fit any shape or size window or door. Installation costs include any necessary reconditioning. Old home specialists. System guaranteed for 20 years. Serving NY and Conn. Free brochures and/or energy consultation available.

American Furniture Galleries
P.O. Box 60   Dept. OHJ
Montgomery, AL 36101
(800) 547-5240
DIST
Manufacturer of the two most widely known lines of Victorian reproduction furniture, Carlton McLendon and Capitol Victorian. All pieces are hand crafted from solid Honduras mahogany. Products are available at over 6,000 retail dealers throughout the U.S. & Canada. Brochures, $1.

American General Products
1735 Holmes Rd., PO Box 395   Dept. OHJ
Ypsilanti, MI 48197
(313) 483-1833
MO   DIST
Spiral and circular stairs. Spiral stairs are available in all wood, wood and steel designs, and all steel. All are available in a variety of styles, diameters and in any floor to floor height. Circular stairs are for interior use and shipped assembled; spirals are shipped knocked down. Literature available, $.50.

American Olean Tile Company
P.O. Box 271   Dept. OHJ
Lansdale, PA 19446
(215) 855-1111
DIST
A major tile manufacturer, makes the 1-inch square white ceramic mosaic floor tile and Bright White and Gloss Black glazed wall tiles used in early 20th century bathrooms. A terra-cotta quarry tile and a rough-textured tile are appropriate for rustic kitchens. Decorating Ideas Brochure No. 489 — $.50; Ceramic Mosaics Sheet 1352 — Free; Quarry Tile Sheet 1333 — Free; Primitive Encore Sheet 1383 — Free; Bright and Matte Sheet 1387 — Free; Quarry Naturals Sheet 1643 — Free.

American Ornamental Corporation
5013 Kelley St.   Dept. OHJ
Houston, TX 77026
(800) 231-3693
MO   DIST   RS/O
Manufacturers of steel spiral stairways. Free colored brochure. In Texas, phone (713) 635-2385.

American Stair Builder
9825 Linden Blvd.   Dept. OHJ
Ozone Park, NY 11417
(212) 843-1956
RS/O
Large selection of stair replacement parts. New stairs and will restore old staircases.

American Wood Column
913 Grand Street   Dept. OHJ
Brooklyn, NY 11211
(212) 782-3163
RS/O
Produces custom wooden exterior and interior columns, capitals, and bases. Also wood turnings, and mouldings of any description and ornamental work. Brochure available.

Amherst Woodworking & Supply
Box 575, Hubbard Avenue   Dept. OHJ
Northampton, MA 01060
(413) 584-3003
RS/O
Contract millwork and reproduction furniture to order. Sells hardwood lumber. Stock list available, send SASE.

Amsterdam Corporation
950 3rd Ave.   Dept. OHJ
New York, NY 10022
(212) 644-1350
DIST   RS/O
Large selection of imported hand-painted tiles including embossed and Delft tiles. A set of 3 brochures featuring Delft tiles are $3.00. Embossed tile brochures are $2.50.

Anderson Building Restoration
923 Marion Avenue   Dept. OHJ
Cincinnati, OH 45229
(513) 281-5258
RS/O
Exterior restoration contractors specializing in chemical paint removal and chemical cleaning of historic masonry structures. They provide expert tuck-pointing, caulking, epoxy consolidation, and painting. A member of The Association for Preservation Technology, the company takes great pride in using only the safest, most gentle methods. They work in the Ohio, Kentucky, and Southeastern Indiana areas. Free literature available.

Anderson Reconstruction
42 Boardman St.   Dept. OHJ
Newburyport, MA 01950
(617) 465-9622
RS/O
Works on houses built before 1850. White pine clapboards with graduated spacing, wooden downspouts, exterior and interior work. Replaces rotted corner posts, beams and sills with new or old wood. Wide pine floors and beaded sheathing. No literature.

Angelo Brothers Co.
10981 Decatur Rd.   Dept. OHJ
Philadelphia, PA 19154
(215) 632-9600
DIST
Primarily a wholesaler, this company has the largest selection of glass shades and globes for replacements on 19th century lighting fixtures. Angelo Master Catalog is $15. It can also be viewed at your local dealer.

Anglo-American Brass Co.
4146 Mitzi Drive Box 9792   Dept. OHJ
San Jose, CA 95157
(408) 246-0203
MO   RS/O
Authentic solid cast and stamped brass reproduction hardware for the restoration of furniture, built-in cupboards, etc. Included are bails, handle sets, knobs, drops, hinges, catches, lock sets, ice box, door knobs, and back-plates, kitchen hardware, coat hooks, etc. Since they are manufacturers, they can also custom-produce articles for builders, wholesalers or manufacturers. B/W catalog No. 113, $1.; Color catalog No. 119, $2.50.

Antares Forge and Metalworks
501 Eleventh St.   Dept. OHJ
Brooklyn, NY 11215
(212) 499-5299
RS/O
Design and forging of architectural and ornamental ironwork, domestic implements, fireplace equipment, etc. All work is custom. No literature.

Antiquaria
11 Whittier Rd.   Dept. OHJ
Lexington, MA 02173
(617) 862-9073
MO
Sell one-of-a-kind parlor sets, chairs, tables, divans, and other Victorian era furniture by mail. Victorian furniture catalog, $2.

Antique Bldrs. Hardware
10317 Meandering Way   Dept. OHJ
Fort Smith, AR 72903
(501) 452-4185
MO
Restored and operative old original builder's hardware, door locks, bells, bath accessories. Some parts may be new. Limited supply. Inventory changes constantly. Catalog — $2.00. Call or send SASE for more information.

Antique Color Supply, Inc.
PO Box 711   Dept. OHJ
Harvard, MA 01451
(617) 456-8036
MO
Finishing products for use on antique restorations, reproductions, & stencilling projects: authentic powdered milk paint, beeswax polish, antique dark paste wax, powdered paint stripper (that cuts through up to ten layers of old paint, including milk paint), and various wood stains. Free information.

Antique Hardware Co.
PO Box 1592   Dept. OHJ
Torrance, CA 90505
(213) 378-5990
MO
Manufactures a collection of authentic handcrafted reproduction antique hardware. Drawer pulls, Armoire pulls, tear drop pulls, knobs, hooks, ice box hardware, etc. Catalog, $2.00, refundable with purchase.

The Antique Restoration Co.
355 Bernard St.   Dept. OHJ
Trenton, NJ 08618
(609) 695-3644
RS/O
They specialize in quality restoration and repairs by dedicated craftsman, each a specialist in his field. Metal plating, mirror resilvering, glass bevelling, furniture refinishing, gold leafing. Also brass, copper, and silver polishing; bronze patinas and repairs; and light fixture repairs. No literature.

Antique Street Lamps
8412 S. Congress Ave.   Dept. OHJ
Austin, TX 78745
(512) 282-2650
RS/O
Manufactures old-fashioned street lamps in a
variety of styles and colors. Constructed of
high-strength thick fiberglass with Lexan globes.
Authentic reproductions of old cast-iron street
lamps used in early 1900s. Suitable for driveways,
entrances, townhouses, and offices. Free flyer
and price list.

● **Antique Trunk Supply Co.**
3706 W. 169th St.   Dept. HJ
Cleveland, OH 44111
(216) 941-8618
MO
Trunk repair parts, handles, nails, rivets, corners,
etc. Catalog, $.50. Instruction and repair manual,
$3. Price and identification guide to antique
trunks, $4.

Appropriate Technology Corp.
PO Box 975, Putney Rd.   Dept. OHJ
Brattleboro, VT 05301
(802) 257-4501
DIST
Manufactures Window Quilt, a five-layered,
quilted insulating window shade that can cut
household heat loss by as much as 79%. The
product is available through a national network
of over 1700 dealers. Window Quilt, including all
hardware, costs about $85 for the standard 2-1/2 x
4 window. Sizes available to fit any window and
sliding glass door. Available in 48 decorator
colors. Complete information package, including
dealer list, available on request.

Arch Associates/ Stephen Guerrant AIA
824 Prospect Avenue   Dept. OHJ
Winnetka, IL 60093
(312) 446-7810
RS/O
Chicago-area firm that specializes in restoration
and rehabilitation. Will provide measured
drawings and building surveys as well as full
architectural services. Maintains extensive
materials resource catalog file. Will also inspect
old houses on a fixed fee basis. No literature.

Archeological Research Consultants, Inc.
179 Park Avenue   Dept. OHJ
Midland Park, NJ 07432
(201) 652-3785
RS/O
Archeological and historical interpretation
services, including title examination, excavation
and artifact analysis. Services available anywhere
in the New York metropolitan area. No literature.

● **Architectural Accents**
2711 Piedmont Rd., NE   Dept. OHJ
Atlanta, GA 30305
(404) 266-8700
RS/O
Architectural antiques and design consultants.
Cabinetry, stained and bevelled glass, light
fixtures, decorative hardware, etc. for commercial
or residential applications. No literature. Call or
write with your needs.

**Architectural Antique & Salvage Co. of
Santa Barbara**
726 Anacapa St.   Dept. OHJ
Santa Barbara, CA 93101
(805) 965-2446
RS/O
A collection of unique windows and doors. Old
Californian wrought-iron gates & fences,
primitive Mexican doors, chain pull and unusual
flush toilets, pedestal and marble sinks, light
fixtures, gas stoves, and carved wood or marble
mantels, etc. No literature available, walk-in shop
only.

● **Architectural Antiques Exchange**
709-15 N. 2nd Street   Dept. OHJ
Philadelphia, PA 19123
(215) 922-3669
RS/O MO
Antique and recycled saloon fixtures and
restaurant decor including bars, backbars,
fretwork, ironwork doors, cabinets, counters and
carved wall units. Also antique and recycled
house parts; interior and exterior doors, fences
and gates, iron railings and window grills, wall
panelling, mantels, ceiling and wall fixtures, and
stained, bevelled, and etched glass. No literature;
call or drop in.

Architectural Antique Warehouse, The
P. O. Box 3065 Stn 'D'   Dept. OHJ
Ottawa, ONT, Canada K1P6H6
(613) 526-1818
MO RS/O
Antique architectural accessories, interior and
exterior. Antique plumbing & lighting, and
Colonial spiral staircases. Free literature — please
specify your interest.

Architectural Archives
10001 Westheimer, Suite 1490   Dept. OHJ
Houston, TX 77042
(713) 784-3296
RS/O
A large collection of restored architectural
antiques. Stained and beveled glass doors,
windows, entrances. Also restored brass
chandeliers & sconces; mantels; furniture;
decorative accessories; and bars. Free brochure.

● **Architectural Components**
PO Box 246   Dept. OHJ
Leverett, MA 01054
(413) 549-6230
MO RS/O
Produces and supplies 18th and 19th century
architectural millwork. Interior and exterior
doors; small pane window sashes; plank window
frames and a variety of reproduction mouldings
patterned after Connecticut Valley architecture.
Also custom work: panelled fireplace walls,
pediments, shutters, fan lights, French doors, etc.
Send $2.00 for brochure or call.

Architectural Emphasis, Inc.
2743 9th St.   Dept. OHJ
Berkeley, CA 94710
(415) 644-2737
RS/O MO DIST
Manufacturers of Victorian and Edwardian
bevelled glass windows, door panels, entryway
sets, arches, and accent pieces. Stock patterns
available for immediate shipment. Custom orders
welcome. Send for brochure; state whether
wholesale or retail. Also, bevelled glass supplies,
thermal paning, window frames, and inserts for
standard doors. Distributor inquiries welcome.

Architectural Emporium
1521 South Ninth Street   Dept. OHJ
Lafayette, IN 47905
(317) 474-3200
RS/O
Antique building supplies, and authentic
reproductions. Mantels, doors, posts and pillars,
light fixtures, bathroom and kitchen fixtures.
Supplies for restoration, preservation, remodeling
or new construction. The warehouse has a
constantly changing supply of salvaged building
parts, including some entire rooms. Photos sent
on specific request. Design service available.

● **Architectural Iron Company**
Box 674, Route 6 West   Dept. OHJ
Milford, PA 18337
(717) 296-7722
RS/O MO
A full service restoration company specializing in
19th-century cast and wrought iron work. They
make their own castings in their own foundry
and fabricate wrought work with historically
accurate techniques. They will also make custom
castings and fabrications for individuals or other
firms. In NY, call (212) 243-2664. Consulting
services and a free brochure are available.

Architectural Paneling, Inc.
979 Third Avenue, Suite 1518   Dept. OHJ
New York, NY 10022
(212) 371-9632
RS/O MO
Reproduces in carved wood English and French
paneling and mantels and built-in cabinets and
ceilings. Installations throughout the western
hemisphere. Fireplace carvings and mouldings
are also available. $5 for color brochure.

Architectural Reclamation, Inc.
312 S. River St.   Dept. OHJ
Franklin, OH 45005
(513) 746-8964
RS/O
Complete contracting services for restoration/
adaptive reuse of log, timber frame, balloon
frame, and masonry structures. Custom
woodworking; reuse of salvaged materials and
architectural antiques. Design and construction of
functional modern facilities compatible in style
with historic homes. Serving Southwestern OH.
No literature.

KEY TO ABBREVIATIONS

MO   sells by Mail Order

RS/O   sells through Retail
             Store or Office

DIST   sells through
             Distributors

ID   sells only through
             Interior Designers
             or Architects

● **See Product Dis-
plays Index on page
199 for more details.**

Architectural Restoration
1 Cottage Place   Dept. OHJ
New Rochelle, NY 10801
(914) 235-9442
RS/O
Restoration of interiors for townhouses, brownstones, and private homes. Services include woodstripping and repairs, varnishing and staining, carpentry and decorative painting. New York area only. Send $1 for brochure.

Architectural Sculpture
242 Lafayette Street   Dept. OHJ
New York, NY 10012
(212) 431-5873
RS/O   MO
Custom-order and in-stock cast plaster ornament — medallions, mouldings, brackets, capitols, plaques, sculptures, etc. Specializing in Neo classic and turn-of-the-century restoration ornament. They have replicated pieces for many landmark NYC interiors. Showroom hours M-F, 10-6. Catalog is $2.

Architectural Terra Cotta and Tile, Ltd.
727 S. Dearborn, Ste. 1012   Dept. OHJ
Chicago, IL 60605
(312) 786-0229
RS/O   MO
Custom manufactures and designs architectural ceramics: Terra cotta, encaustic tiles. Specializes in preservation and restoration. Write or call for more information, (312) 666-1181.

Architectural Woodworking
347 Flax Hill Rd.   Dept. OHJ
Norwalk, CT 06854
(203) 866-0943
RS/O   MO
Fine architectural woodwork. Cost estimates provided upon receipt of detailed material specifications. Consultation services available. No literature.

• Archive
50 West 29th St.   Dept. OHJ
New York, NY 10001
(212) 889-7855
RS/O
Specialists in the documentation of significant American architecture. Dossiers include plates of measured drawings, histories, and 35mm photography suitable for tax deductible donations to the Library of Congress. Also, illustrations of architectural subjects for use on identity programs and fund-raising/marketing materials. Free brochure.

Arden Forge
301 Brinton's Bridge Rd.   Dept. OHJ
West Chester, PA 19380
(215) 399-1530
MO   RS/O
Specializing in accurate reproductions of period iron work, hand-forged from original examples. Interior & exterior hardware, household accessories for kitchen, fireplace, etc. Also, Victorian hardware, and new-old hardware. Will also restore antique metalwork.

Armor Products
Box 290   Dept. OHJ
Deer Park, NY 11729
(516) 667-3328
MO   RS/O
Sells clock movements for restoring grandfather, mantel and banjo clocks. Also plans for those who wish to make their own. Other items include lamp parts, specialty hardware, butler tray and ice box hinges. Catalog, $1.

Arriaga, Nelson
418 Grand Avenue   Dept. OHJ
Brooklyn, NY 11238
(212) 783-1221
RS/O
Men's period accessories — Victorian shirts, collars and ties. Also Victorian and Edwardian coats, suits, dresses, complete ensembles for men and women — stock and custom made. Must visit shop for measurements.

• Art Directions
6120 Delmar Blvd.   Dept. OHJ
St. Louis, MO 63112
(314) 863-1895
RS/O   MO
12,000 sq. ft. of architectural antiques — stained and beveled glass windows and entrance ways; hundreds of light fixtures including large-and small-scale bronze, brass, crystal, gas, and electric; front and back bars; custom-built millwork; paneled rooms, columns, bronze work bank cages, architectural woodwork, mantels, trim, corbels. Comprehensive catalog, $3.

• ART, Inc.
315 N. Washington Ave.   Dept. OHJ
Moorestown, NJ 08057
(609) 866-0536
RS/O
Architectural Restoration Techniques specializes in the reproduction and restoration of exterior details and ornaments, including architectural sculpturing. Stone, terra cotta, wood, and cast iron. Free literature.

Artex Studio
6 Forest Ave.   Dept. OHJ
Glen Cove, NY 11542
(516) 676-0376
MO
Bring memories alive with our photo restoration service. Will do black & white or color. Also can convert black & white to color. Phone or write for information.

Artifacts, Inc.
702 Mt. Vernon Ave.   Dept. OHJ
Alexandria, VA 22301
(703) 548-6555
RS/O
Large stock of architectural salvage including doors, mantels, hardware, corbels, newels, balusters, railing, gingerbread, stained glass, and plumbing fixtures. No literature.

Artisan Woodworkers
21415 Broadway   Dept. OHJ
Sonoma, CA 95476
(707) 938-4796
RS/O
A group of artisans striving to produce high-quality furniture, cabinetry, and architectural details. No literature. Direct inquiries to John Ward.

Artistic Brass
4100 Ardmore Avenue   Dept. OHJ
South Gate, CA 90280
(213) 564-1100
DIST
Manufacturers of decorative, solid brass fittings for the lavatory, tub, shower, bidet, and bar. Matching accessories in Wedgwood, crystal, porcelain, onyx, gemstones, marble, and solid ash wood. Backed by a 5-year limited warranty on parts and finish, each fitting made of solid brass is polished, assembled, and tested by hand. A complete illustrated catalog is available for $5.00.

Artistic License in San Francisco
4902 California St.   Dept. OHJ
San Francisco, CA 94108
(415) 752-9855
RS/O
A Guild of Artisans specializing in Victorian restoration. They are trained in all areas of Victorian architectural & decorative art restoration/design. They'll give slide presentations to the general public specifically interested in the Victorian period. Free brochure. Can also call (415) 285-4544.

• Artistic Woodworking, Inc.
163 Grand Ave.   Dept. OHJ
Mt. Clemens, MI 48043
(313) 465-5700
MO   RS/O
Specialist in furniture and cabinetmaking. Will reproduce a piece from a drawing or photograph — Victorian, Rococo, Renaissance, and Eastlake styles. Also, furniture restoration. No literature.

Artistry in Veneers, Inc.
633 Montauk Ave.   Dept. OHJ
Brooklyn, NY 11208
(212) 272-6800
MO
More than 80 architectural grade species in lots as small as a single leaf. Also: Fancy Butts, burls, crotches and swirls. Also tools, cements, glues, instructional books. Catalog, $1.00.

A Second Wind for Harmoniums
256 Carroll Street   Dept. OHJ
Brooklyn, NY 11231
(212) 852-1437
RS/O
Restoration, appraisal, voicing, tuning & general rehabilitation of reed organs, melodeons, and harmoniums. In-home service available. Greater NY area, unless the job is extensive & merits travel. Monograph on reed organs available for $1.00. Prefers telephone consultation (a.m. & eves).

Association for Preservation Technology
Box 2487, Station D   Dept. OHJ
Ottawa, Ontario, Canada K1P 5W
(613) 238-1972
RS/O   MO
Prior to the yearly APT conference, two coinciding 3-day technical training seminars are held. Also "Home Restoration" seminars upon request. They have also started 4-day technical, professional development workshops on rehabilitating historic buildings. The workshops are held in the South, Midwest, West, Mid-Atlantic, and New England. Free information.

Astrup Company
2937 W. 25th St.   Dept. OHJ
Cleveland, OH 44113
(216) 696-2800
DIST
This 107 year old company makes fine fabric and the hardware for awnings. Window awnings not only keep a room cooler and save on air conditioning costs, but add an appropriate decorative feature to late 19th and turn-of-the-century houses. Write for free information.

Authentic Designs Inc.
The Mill Road   Dept. H
W. Rupert, VT 05776
(802) 394-7814
RS/O   MO
Handcrafted reproductions of colonial lanterns &
lighting fixtures for indoor and outdoor use. Also
colonial tinware, liners, pans, flower trays, boxes,
kitchen hoods, and a variety of custom made
items of brass, copper, galvanized, or tin. Send
photo, sketch or line drawing of the piece you're
interested in, and they will build it for you.

Authentic Lighting
558 Grand Avenue   Dept. OHJ
Englewood, NJ 07631
(201) 568-7429
MO   RS/O
Reproduction and restoration of all types of
lighting fixtures. Services include fixture cleaning,
rewiring, mounting of lamps, polishing. Also
metal polishing for beds, tables, fixtures, etc.
Crystal in stock. Reproduction sconces and
fixtures at reasonable prices. No literature; please
call or write with specific request.

Auto Hoe, Inc.
Lost Dauphin Dr. Box W121OH   Dept.
OHJ
De Pere, WI 54115
(414) 336-4753
MO
Besides the Auto Hoe, a tilling & hoeing machine
invented by the company's founder, they
manufacture and sell a no-nonsense set of wood
stove and fireplace tools. The tools are attractive
in their functional simplicity. Reasonable retail
cost: $21.95 for the full set, which includes a
brush. (Canada add $3. shipping.) Free flyer.

Avalon Forge
409 Gun Road   Dept. OHJ
Baltimore, MD 21227
(301) 242-8431
MO
Authentic replicas of 18th century goods for
living history and restorations. Emphasis on
military and primitive goods. Examples -
Hornware: snuffboxes, dippers, cups, combs.
Tinware: cups, canteens, plates. Leather:
cartridge boxes, handmade shoes, buckets. Tools:
pitchforks, axes, bill hooks, tomahawks.
Woodware: bowls, trenchers, spoons. Cookware:
cast iron pots, spiders. Printed matter: maps,
cards, books. Illustrated catalog $1.00.

KEY TO ABBREVIATIONS

MO   sells by **Mail Order**
RS/O   sells through **Retail
           Store or Office**
DIST   sells through
           Distributors
ID   sells only through
           **Interior Designers
           or Architects**

B

B & P Lamp Supply Co., Inc.
Route 3   Dept. OHJ
McMinnville, TN 37110
(615) 473-3016
DIST   RS/O
Manufactures and wholesalers of reproduction
lighting fixtures and parts. Selection includes
hand-blown and hand-decorated glass shades,
solid brass parts, and UL approved wiring
components. Also specialize in reproductions of
and parts for — "Gone with the wind", Handel,
Tiffany, Aladdin, and Emeraldlite fixtures.
Complete color catalog and price list for dealers
only $5., refundable.

Backlund Moravian Tile Works
46 Ocean Drive   Dept. OHJ
Key Largo, FL 33037
(305) 852-5865
MO   DIST
Over 300 hand-painted embossed tiles copied
from an interesting variety of sources: medieval
churches, Mexican and Yucatan codices, coats of
arms, etc. Custom work also, even to life size
mosaics made in the manner of a jig saw puzzle.
Illustrated 4 color catalog with wholesale and/or
retail price lists — $1.25.

Bailey Architectural Millwork
125 Slack Ave.   Dept. OHJ
Trenton, NJ 08648
(609) 392-5137
RS/O
Custom millwork including stair rail duplication.
No literature.

Baker, A.W. Restorations, Inc.
670 Drift Rd.   Dept. OHJ
Westport, MA 02790
(617) 636-8765
RS/O
Restoration consultants, contractors, and
documenters of 17th, 18th, 19th century
structures, they specialize in southern New
England historic architectural forms. Services
include moving, dismantling, re-construction and
on-site repairs, recycling and restoring. Available
are a variety of structural, decorative, and utility
house parts, and often very special whole
houses. Free brochure available; please call for
appointment.

Baker, Jim
PO Box 149   Dept. OHJ
Worthington, OH 43085
(614) 885-7040
RS/O
Hand-painted and custom designed fireboards.
Depicted scenes can reflect your particular
interest, your home, etc. Information provided
with SASE.

Baldwin Hardware Mfg. Corp.
841 Wyomissing Blvd. Box 82   Dept. OHJ
Reading, PA 19603
(215) 777-7811
DIST
Solid brass exterior locks suitable for Early
American houses. Interior latches, knobsets and
turn pieces for period houses. Lighting fixtures,
candlesticks, and accessories adapted from Early
American designs. Brass hardware line includes
knockers, hinges, knobs. Brochures are $.75 each:
rim locks, mortise locks, lever locks, lamps and
accessories, fine brass hardware. Please specify
brochure you require.

● Ball and Ball
463 W. Lincoln Hwy.   Dept. OHJ
Exton, PA 19341
(215) 363-7330
RS/O   MO
Vast selection of reproduction hardware for 18th
and 19th century houses. In addition to all types
of hardware for doors, windows and shutters,
the company also supplies security locks with a
period appearance, lighting fixtures, and will also
repair locks and repair or reproduce any item of
metal hardware. Call or write for free mini-
catalog or send $5 for complete 108-page catalog
— revised in 1983 (over 100 Victorian items now
included).

Balzamo, Joseph
103 N. Edward St.   Dept. OHJ
Sayreville, NJ 08872
(201) 721-2651
RS/O
Will strip paint from woodwork in the house; no
need for dismantling. No literature.

Bangkok Industries, Inc.
Gillingham & Worth Streets   Dept. OHJ
Philadelphia, PA 19124
(215) 537-5800
RS/O   MO   DIST
A wide variety of exotic hardwood flooring in
pre-finished and unfinished plank, strip and
parquet patterns—many of which can be used in
period houses. Of special interest are 2
ornamental border patterns. Custom colored
pre-finished parquet. Can be completely installed
in one day. Free consultation available.
Architectural grade paneling historically correct
for period dens, formal drawing rooms, etc. Free
illustrated brochures.

Bangor Cork Co., Inc.
William & D Streets   Dept. OHJ
Pen Argyl, PA 18072
(215) 863-9041
MO   DIST
True linoleum imported from Holland. Battleship
linoleum is offered in 9 colors, while
"Marmoleum" (designed to resemble Italian
Carrara marble) comes in a variety of colors. Free
literature.

Bank Architectural Antiques
1824 Felicity St.   Dept. OHJ
New Orleans, LA 70113
(504) 523-2702
RS/O
They offer a wide variety of original and
reproduction building materials. Always in stock
are bevelled and stained glass, brass hardware,
mantels, millwork, doors, shutters, brackets, and
columns. In addition they offer wood stripping
and carry reproduction shutters, French doors,
stair railings, interior and exterior spindles, and
newels. No literature.

Barap Specialties
835 Bellows Ave.   Dept. OHJ
Frankfort, MI 49635
(616) 352-9863
MO
Mail-order catalog supplies for cane, rush &
caning tools. Also, brass hardware, lamp parts,
finishing materials, turned wood parts and other
do-it-yourself supplies. Catalog, $1.

● See Product Dis-
plays Index on page
199 for more details.

Barclay Products Co.
424 N. Oakley Blvd.   Dept. OHJ
Chicago, IL 60612
(312) 243-1444
MO
Full line of quality Victorian and turn-of-century reproduction bathroom accessories. Includes faucet sets, towel racks, and soap dishes. Retail distributor of the Sterline shower conversions. Also special size shower curtains, and an old-style enameled cast-iron pedestal sink. Free catalog.

Barn People, The
P.O. Box 4   Dept. OHJ
South Woodstock, VT 05071
(802) 457-3943
RS/O MO
Offer 18th and 19th century Vermont barns, and frames of post and beam construction which have been dismantled, repaired/restored, shipped to any new site, and reassembled. Stock of salvaged building materials. Barn moving. Also related consulting services, such as feasibility and cost studies for restoration or relocation of barns in the Northeast. Portfolio (inventory, photo, etc.) is $10.00.

Barnard Chemical Co.
P.O. Box 1105   Dept. OHJ
Covina, CA 91722
(213) 331-1223
DIST
Manufactures fire retardant paints, coatings and varnishes. Coatings, for example, can add fire resistance to fine interior wood panel or exterior shakes and shingles. Will direct inquirers to nearest distributor or will fill orders direct from their warehouse when necessary. Free brochures.

Barnett, D. James — Blacksmith
81 N. Bank St.   Dept. OHJ
Marietta, PA 17547
MO
A blacksmith who makes items in the style of the early smiths: hardware, hinges, door latches, shutter hardware, fireplace equipment, trivets, toasters, andirons, nails. Catalog, $1.

Bartley's Mill — Victorian Woodwork
8515 San Leandro St.   Dept. OHJ
Oakland, CA 94621
(415) 569-5533
MO DIST RS/O
Wooden moulding and Victorian woodwork reproduction. Custom and stock items. 67-page catalog with 700 moulding cross-sections available for $15.98. Sales offices are located in Oakland, San Francisco, Honolulu, and Santa Clara.

Bassett & Vollum Wallpapers
217 N. Main St.   Dept. OHJ
Galena, IL 61036
(815) 777-2460
Specializes in reproductions of traditional border designs suitable for restoration. Borders, with matching sidewall papers, are available in widths from 1 to 21 inches. Folder describing their border patterns is available free. Available in stock colorings and/or as special orders.

Beaumier Carpentry, Inc.
5511 - 43rd Avenue   Dept. OHJ
Hyattsville, MD 20781
(301) 277-8594
RS/O
Designs, coordinates and executes the restoration and/or renovation of period rowhouses and single homes, in conjunction with the owner(s) and local authorities. Carpentry only, or a full spectrum of general contracting services is available in Washington, DC and Maryland. No literature.

Beauti-home
408 Airport Blvd.   Dept. OHJ
Watsonville, CA 95076
(408) 724-1066
RS/O MO
A custom shutter factory providing movable louvre shutters to fit any window or door. Different designs or styles with traditional or wide slats (up to 5-1/2 in. wide), horizontal or vertical. Shipped unfinished or finished. Inquiries answered promptly. Free literature.

Beck, Nelson, of Wash. Inc.
1048 Potomac NW   Dept. OHJ
Washington, DC 20007
(202) 333-4437
ID
Upholstered furniture restored and reupholstered. Period draperies - various types of poles, wood and metal. Custom finials for poles. Tab curtains, Austrian shades. Will supply fabrics or will use client's fabrics. Trade shop only - no literature.

Bedlam Brass
19-21 Fair Lawn Avenue   Dept. OH
Fair Lawn, NJ 07410
(201) 796-7200
RS/O MO DIST
Complete bar rail systems for commercial or residential use. Individual components can be purchased. Also, solid- brass furniture — reproductions of antique designs, but in today's sizes. Some antique fixtures, glass, etc. Bed and accessories catalog, $3. Bar & handrail catalog, free. Data sheet of parts for repairing antique brass or cast-iron beds, $1.

Bedpost, The
R.D. 1, Box 155   Dept. OHJ
Pen Argyl, PA 18072
(215) 588-3824
RS/O MO
Manufacturers of solid brass beds, and iron-and-brass beds in all sizes. Styling is copied from antique bed designs. Color catalogue is $2. A complete line of replacements parts for antique beds is also available. Replacement parts catalogue is $1.

Behlen, H. & Bros.
Rt. 30 North   Dept. OHJ
Amsterdam, NY 12010
(518) 843-1380
DIST
The largest stock of traditional and old world finishing supplies and products for hardwood finishing and paintings. Among the 90-year-old company's specialities: bronze powder and paste, lacquer tinting colors, wood fillers and glue, various lacquers, stains (including dry aniline) specialty waxes, hard-to-find brushes and tools, and varnish. Complete line of gilding supplies. Sold through distributors only.

Bel-Air Door Co.
P.O. Box 829   Dept. OHJ
Alhambra, CA 91802
(213) 283-3731
MO DIST
Handcrafted carved exterior wood doors (with designed panels and openings) in fir and mahogany, and a collection of bevelled, leaded, and etched glass. Several are suitable for Victorian, Tudor-style, Chippendale, and turn-of-the- century influenced houses. Security and fire-rated doors available. Standard door size: 30 in., 32 in., 36 in. x 80 in. x 1-3/4 in. Special sizes upon request. Illustrated brochures $1.50

Belcher, Robert W.
1753 Pleasant Grove Dr., NE   Dept. OHJ
Dalton, GA 30720
(404) 259-3482
RS/O
Has a supply of old weathered chestnut rails for zig-zag stacked rail fences. Supplies old barnboards, 55-gal. oak barrels and old yellow poplar and oak beams. Also has old hand hewn log houses, and consults on log house restoration. No literature; call for prices.

Bench Manufacturing Co.
PO Box 66, Essex St. Sta.   Dept. OHJ
Boston, MA 02112
(617) 436-3080
MO
Promenade benches in many styles, and planters, trash receptacles, gazebos, and custom-built small buildings. Ornamental cast-iron street light poles and fixtures. Please specify your interest for a free brochure.

Bendheim, S.A. Co., Inc.
122 Hudson St.   Dept. OHJ
New York, NY 10013
(212) 226-6370
RS/O
Supplier for replacement colonial-type window glass. Also imported and domestic stained glass, rondells, etc. No literature available.

Bendix Mouldings, Inc.
235 Pegasus Ave.   Dept. OHJ
Northvale, NJ 07647
(201) 767-8888
MO DIST
Supplies a diversified assortment of unfinished decorative wood mouldings, metal and plastic mouldings plus an extensive stock of pre-finished, authentic and carefully crafted picture frame mouldings. Also carved wood ornaments, pearl beadings, open fretwork, dentils, rosettes, crowns, cornices, functional hardware and scalloped plywood moulding. Illustrated catalog and price lists $1.00. Specify unfinished or pre-finished mouldings.

Benjamin Eastwood Co.
270 Marshall St.   Dept. OHJ
Paterson, NJ 07503
(201) 742-8700
MO RS/O
Custom castings in ductile & gray iron. Duplicates can be produced from an existing piece. They will do small jobs such as a few replacement finials for an iron fence. Will ship nationwide. Free brochure.

Benjamin Moore Co.
51 Chestnut Ridge Road   Dept. OHJ
Montvale, NJ 07645
(201) 573-9600
RS/O DIST
This major paint manufacturer has exterior and interior paints for early American houses — Historical Color Collection and Cameo Collection. There are free leaflets about these lines as well as these useful booklets — "Interior Wood Finishing", "Painting Walls, Ceilings and Trim" and "How To Paint The Outside of Your House."

● See Product Displays Index on page 199 for more details.

Bentley Bros.
918 Baxter Ave.   Dept. OHJ
Louisville, KY 40204
(502) 589-2939
MO RS/O
Direct importers of Crown high-relief wallcoverings, including Anaglypta, Supaglypta, and newly introduced period Lincrusta designs. Their store has a complete display of these products, including room settings. Catalog, $3.

Berea College Student Craft Industries
CPO No. 2347   Dept. OHJ
Berea, KY 40404
(606) 986-9341
RS/O MO
Reproductions of simple, classic period furniture - Empire armchairs, rope leg dining table, ladder back chairs, goose neck rocker. Also handcrafted decorative accessories and custom wrought iron work. Furniture catalog — $1.50.

Berkshire Porcelain Studios Ltd.
Deerfield Ave.   Dept. OHJ
Shelburne Falls, MA 01370
(413) 625-9447
MO DIST RS/O
Original paintings and designs on ceramic tile for custom bathrooms, kitchens, and murals. Glazes are applied to both imported bisque and standard glazed tile; they can decorate with a specialty tile of your choice or your own creation. Paintings and designs are permanent and are resistant to weather, fire, fading, and graffiti. Feel free to call for consultation. Flyer available.

Bernard Plating Works
660 Riverside Dr.   Dept. OHJ
Northampton, MA 01060
(413) 584-0659
RS/O MO
Silver, copper, nickel replating. Silver and pewter items cleaned and repaired. All types of brass and copper cleaned and polished; lamps rewired and refinished. Old fashioned hand-wiped tinning on copper and brass cookware (excluding teakettles). No literature; please write or call with specific inquiry.

Berridge Manufacturing Co.
1720 Maury   Dept. OHJ
Houston, TX 77026
(713) 223-4971
RS/O MO DIST
Manufactures metal roofing products, including Victorian classic and fish-scale metal shingles. Standing seam and batten seam metal roof systems are offered. These products are available in pre-finished galvanized steel, Galvalume, copper, and terne-coated stainless. Catalog free.

Betsy's Place
323 Arch St.   Dept. OHJ
Philadelphia, PA 19106
(215) 922-3536
MO RS/O
Six sundials, in traditional designs, made of brass (one model is solid bronze). Also, colonial reproductions: sconces, candlesticks, & chandeliers. Free literature.

Bevel Right Mfg.
3434 Route 9   Dept. OHJ
Freehold, NJ 07728
(201) 462-8462
RS/O MO
Can make bevelled tempered glass for front doors in the wide 1 in. and 1-1/4 in. bevels. No literature; call for latest prices.

Beveling Studio
15507 NE 90th   Dept. OHJ
Redmond, WA 98052
(206) 885-7274
MO RS/O
They manufacture bevelled windows and panels; also bevelled mirrors, to any size or shape. Windows and panels are reproduced to any designs for any period house or commercial building. All windows and panels are weather-proof. They also reproduce cut bevelled pieces and glue-chip bevelled glass. Stock & custom bevelled pieces are available. Price list, free.

Biagiotti, L.
229 7th Ave.   Dept. OHJ
New York, NY 10011
(212) 924-5088
RS/O MO
Manufactures mouldings for ceilings and walls, centers for chandeliers, columns, pilasters, capitals. Does sets for motion pictures and Broadway shows. Restored mouldings in City Hall. Restores frames and antiques. Can reproduce and ship mouldings from samples. No literature.

Bienenfeld Ind. Inc.
22 Harbor Park Dr., Box 22   Dept. OHJ
Roslyn, NY 11576
(516) 621-2500
DIST
Sells mouth-blown antique, Colonial, Cordele, Opalescent antique glass. Also other types in over 700 shades and colors. Sold only through distributors. For information about nearest distributor, call in NY (516) 621-0888; in Chicago, IL (312) 523-8400; in Houston, TX (713) 864-0193; in Wilmington, CA (213) 549-4329; in Mississuaga OT, Canada (416) 677-8600. For free brochure on varieties of stained glass, send SASE.

● **Biggs Company**
105 E. Grace St.   Dept. OHJ
Richmond, VA 23219
(804) 644-2891
RS/O MO
Reproductions of 18th century furniture. Several expensive lines are authentic historic reproductions licensed by Old Sturbridge Village, Independence National Historic Park and the Thomas Jefferson Memorial Foundation, Inc. 82 pg. catalog and price list — $5.

Billard's Old Telephones
21710C Regnart Rd.   Dept. OHJ
Cupertino, CA 95014
(408) 252-2104
MO
Old telephones and parts. Brass and oak sets. Old phones converted to modern use. Do-it-yourself kits available. Replica in oak of 1892 Kellogg crank phone, a working dial set. Their private museum also buys unusual telephones. Complete restoration parts catalog, $1., refundable on purchase.

Biltmore, Campbell, Smith Restorations, Inc.
One Biltmore Plaza   Dept. OHJ
Asheville, NC 28803
(704) 274-1776
RS/O
A company offering complete decorative restoration services: Stencilling, graining, gilding, and marbleizing. Will also clean and restore murals, textiles, and interior stonework. Other services include cloth & paper hanging, wood & stone carving, and stained glass repair. Free literature.

Binghamton Brick Co., Inc.
PO Box 1256   Dept. OHJ
Binghamton, NY 13902
(607) 772-0420
RS/O MO
Machine extruded brick designed to resemble old brick in traditional styles. Can also match your brick color, sample, and shape. Will ship nationwide. No literature.

Bird — X, Inc.
325 W. Huron St.   Dept. OHJ
Chicago, IL 60610
(312) 642-6871
MO
Supplier of complete line of bird-repelling products. Products include electronic ultrasonic bird repellers, bird lites, and chemical and steel needle roost inhibitors. Free brochures and consultation service available.

● **Bishop, Adele, Inc.**
Box 557   Dept. K-15
Manchester, VT 05254
(802) 362-3537
MO DIST
Stencil kits for walls, floorcloths, furniture, fabrics, etc., and a full line of supplies: instant-drying japan paints, fabric paint, brushes, and cutting knives. Specific directions supplied for all designs; also, the definitive book about stencilling, "The Art of Decorative Stencilling," $18.95 ppd. Complete color catalog, $2.50.

● **Bix Process Systems, Inc.**
PO Box 3091   Dept. OHJ
Bethel, CT 06801
(203) 743-3263
MO
Manufactures semi-paste and liquid paint removers. Also tung oil stains and varnishes. Sells portable units for on-site stripping of houses and furniture. Established business for 27 years. Complete illustrated catalog and discount price list, $1.

Black Wax — Pacific Engineering
P.O. Box 145   Dept. OHJ
Farmington, CT 06032
(203) 674-8913
MO
Black wax can often save stripping and refinishing of dirty, cracked and crazed wood surfaces. Company also manufactures Crystal Wax, a top-quality carnauba paste wax providing gloss and protection for fine furniture. Sienna paste wax is a blend of quality paste wax and brown pigment which prevents chalky effect left by some paste waxes. Free flyer.

Blaine Window Hardware, Inc.
1919 Blaine Dr.   Dept. OHJC84
Hagerstown, MD 21740
(301) 797-6500
MO
Large selection of contemporary replacement
hardware for windows, closet doors, sliding
doors, and patio doors. Hard-to-find and obsolete
hardware is a specialty. Custom design, casting,
and duplication available. End your search for
that special piece of hardware, send sample for
free identification and quotation. 32 page catalog
is offered for $2.50.

Blaschke Cabinet Glass
670 Lake Avenue   Dept. OHJ
Bristol, CT 06010
(203) 584-2566
RS/O
Curved china cabinet glass — all sizes in stock.
No literature; must call for appointment.

Blenko Glass Co., Inc.
P.O. Box 67   Dept. OHJ
Milton, WV 25541
(304) 743-9081
RS/O MO
Colored glass; Antique-style sheet glass for use in
restoration work for the windows in old houses.
Hurricane shades for use with candleholders.
Price list free.

Blessing Historical Foundation
Box 517   Dept. OHJ
Blessing, TX 77419
(512) 588-6332
MO
For fiber craftsmen and planters of ancient dye
gardens: A 'baker's dozen" of madder seeds will
be sent for a $5 tax-deductible donation to the
Foundation. Madder, rare in this country, is used
in textile printing and craftsmen's yarns, both
handspun and commercial. Directions for
growing included.

Blue Frog Enterprises
P.O. Box A   Dept. OHJ
Holy City, CA 95026
(408) 353-1754
MO
Plans for building a Victorian dumb-waiter, with
materials list and building instructions. Send
$20.00 to address above.

Blue Ridge Shingle Co.
    Dept. OHJ
Montebello, VA 24464
(804) 377-6635
RS/O
White oak shingles for roofing and siding.
Available in no. 1, no. 2, and no. 3 grades in 18
in. or 24 in. lengths. Free flyer.

Bombay Company, The
Box 79186, 5678 Bl. Mnd. Rd.   Dept. OHJ
Fort Worth, TX 76179
(817) 232-5650
MO
A selection of English and traditional antique
reproductions, wine, butler-, coffee-, end-, and
occasional-tables. Furnishings are mahogany
finished and solid rosewood; offered at a
affordable price. Color catalog, $1. Call toll free
(800) 535-6876.

●**See Product Dis-
plays Index on page
199 for more details.**

Bona Decorative Hardware
2227 Beechmont Ave.   Dept. OHJ
Cincinnati, OH 45230
(513) 232-4300
RS/O MO
Decorative hardware — mostly formal French and
English in style. Bathroom fittings and
accessories- several designs are appropriate for
period houses. Also black iron door & cabinet
hardware, brass rim locks, porcelain door knobs,
fireplace tools, and accessories. Also of interest
are their brass bar rail hardware and brass sliding
door pulls; faucets for footed tubs and brass
sinks. Illustrated catalog and price list, $3.

Boomer Resilvering
603 N. Court St.   Dept. OHJ
Visalia, CA 93291
(209) 734-2188
MO RS/O
Specialize in resilvering antique mirrors; cost
$6.50/sq. ft. Out-of-town customers can crate &
ship mirrors for resilvering. For local customers
we offer custom woodworking services including
replacement parts for furniture and re-veneering.
No literature.

Nancy Borden, Period Textiles
63 Penhallow St., PO Box 4381   Dept.
OHJ
Portsmouth, NH 03801
(603) 436-4284
MO RS/O
Period interior consultant specializing in custom
period bed hangings, window curtains, furniture
casings, and upholstering — using historically
accurate reproduction fabrics. Free brochure. Can
call shop (603) 431-8733.

Boren Clay Products Company
PO Box 368   Dept. OHJ
Pleasant Garden, NC 27313
(919) 674-2255
DIST RS/O
One of the largest manufacturers of clay face
brick in the U.S. They also have a retail store
which includes tile, fireplace accessories and
hardware items. Free color catalog.

Boseman Veneer & Supply Co.
Rt. 2, Box 2956   Dept. OHJ
Pearland, TX 77581
(713) 482-5730
MO RS/O
Stocks and distributes quality veneers and wood
finishing supplies. Good selection of crotches,
burls and quarter sawn veneer. Will accomodate
specific size requirements. Free catalog available.

Botti Studio of Architectural Arts
919 Grove St.   Dept. OHJ
Evanston, IL 60201
(312) 869-5933
RS/O
Designers, fabricators & installers of original
stained & faceted glass windows. Will do
extensive remodling and restoration throughout
the U.S. The firm has been continually in
business over 150 years. Free literature.

Boulder Stained Glass Studios
1920 Arapahoe Ave.   Dept. OHJ
Boulder, CO 80302
(303) 449-9030
MO RS/O
Designs and manufactures high-quality,
handcrafted reproductions of Victorian and Art
Nouveau window panels to fit any opening.
Colored and bevelled glass. Specialists in
reproducing etched glass — sandblasted or acid
etched finish. Replacement of bent, colored glass
panels in antique lampshades. Also appraisals &
expert repair of antique windows and
lampshades.

Bow House, Inc.
Randall Rd., PO Box 228   Dept. OHJ
Bolton, MA 01740
(617) 779-6464
MO
An architect-designed package that offers the
buyer an authentic reproduction of a bow-roof
Cape Cod house. The package supplies to the
builder those items necessary for the period
character of the house: roof and siding materials,
trim, windows, doors, hardware, stairs, glass,
etc; specifications working drawings, manual and
detail book. Illustrated brochure — $5.00. Also —
a belvedere or gazebo of classic and generous
proportions is available in kit form. Illustrated
brochure $2.

Larry Boyce & Associates
PO Box 421507   Dept. OHJ
San Francisco, CA 94142
(415) 626-2122
RS/O
An organization of artists trained in architectural
ornamental painting. They're most renowned for
elaborate Victorian ceiling stencilling, but they
also do gilding and leafing, secco-frescoing, in-fill
painting, glazing, and decoupage wallpapering.
Their work has been featured in major
publications such as Smithsonian Magazine, the
New York Times, and Historic Preservation. No
literature.

● **Bradbury & Bradbury Wallpapers**
PO Box 155   Dept. OHJ
Benicia, CA 94510
(707) 746-1900
MO DIST RS/O
Designers and handprinters of Victorian
wallpapers for private residences, house
museums, and commercial renovation. A small
firm willing to work directly with homeowners.
They produce reasonably-priced, hard-to-find
specialties: friezes, ceiling decorations,
multi-paper roomsets, and Morris papers. A
selected group of designs available by mail order.
Send $1.00 for illustrated brochure.

● **Bradford Consultants**
16 E. Homestead Ave.   Dept. OHJ
Collingswood, NJ 08108
(609) 854-1404
MO RS/O
Phoenix lightbulbs — the perfect bulbs for period
fixtures. "Edison" style: carbon loop bulbs —
1880 to 1918. "Mazda" style: zig-zag cage
filament in a straight side bulb — 1909 to 1930.
Also representing British made indoor and
outdoor Victorian lighting fixtures by Sugg, who
have been in the business since 1837. Free
brochures for all products.

Bradford Derustit Corp.
Box 151   Dept. OHJ
Clifton Park, NY 12065
(518) 371-5420
MO
B.P. Metal Cleaner: a biodegradable,
non-corrosive rust and oxide remover that does
not harm metal, finishes or normal skin. Liquid
or paste formulas. Also B-P No. 1 Brightner — a
metal cleaner for quick, economical removal of
heat stains, discoloration and tarnish from
stainless steel, chrome, nickel, copper or brass.
Free literature.

Braintree Woodworks
PO Box 425   Dept. OHJ
Lovingston, VA 22949
(804) 263-4827
MO
Specialize in architectural hand carving and
shaping. Most work is commissioned by
architects, interior decorators, and designers, but
will consider any carving from individuals. Also
carved signs. Free brochure.

Brandt Bros. General Contractors
2210 E. Southport Rd.   Dept. OHJ
Indianapolis, IN 46227
(317) 783-6633
RS/O
Primarily carpentry contractor but full
complement of sub-contractors available if
desired. Interior and exterior work. List of
renovation projects in Indianapolis area can be
furnished. No literature.

Brass & Copper Shop
2220 Cherokee   Dept. OHJ
St. Louis, MO 63118
(314) 776-8363
RS/O
Antique shop specializing in brass and copper
fixtures. Lighting, bath fixtures, door hardware,
glass globes, etc. Walk-in shop. No literature.

Brass & Iron Bed Co.
P.O. Box 453   Dept. OHJ
El Cerrito, CA 94530
(415) 526-5304
MO DIST
Authentic reproductions of turn-of-the-century
American cast iron and brass bedsteads and
daybeds. Solid handspun brass with a rail system
similar to the original, providing a very sturdy
bed. Four styles of beds are offered and three
daybeds. Daybeds are available with or without
trundle units. Four colors to choose from.
Catalog, $1.

Brass Bed Company of America
2801 East 11th St.   Dept. OHJ
Los Angeles, CA 90023
(213) 269-9495
DIST
Over 500 brass bed styles, cheval mirrors,
cradles, cribs, night stands, coat racks, entry hall
stand. Color illustrated catalog, $2.00.

Brass Connection, Inc.
3122 Magazine St.   Dept. OHJ
New Orleans, LA 70115
(504) 891-2794
MO RS/O
A large selection of combination brass & iron
beds. Catalog, $5.

Brass Fan Ceiling Fan Co.
1101 Stapleton   Dept. OHJ
Flower Mound, TX 75028
(214) 436-3052
RS/O MO
Repair and restoration of antique ceiling fans.
Company also carries Hunter and Old
Jacksonville ceiling fans and parts. No literature.

The Brass Knob
2309 18th St. N.W.   Dept. OHJ
Washington, DC 20009
(202) 332-3370
MO RS/O
Architectural antiques, specializing in brass
hardware; lighting fixtures; mantels; firebacks;
columns; doors; stained, etched, and leaded
glass; bathroom fixtures; corbel brackets;
ironwork; marble; tiles, and garden ornaments.

Brass Lion
P. O. Box 1135   Dept. OHJ
Tyler, TX 75710
(214) 561-1111
MO RS/O
Quality handmade reproduction of 17th and 18th
century brass chandeliers and sconces. The brass
is antiqued and hand polished. A complete
illustrated catalog is available for $3.

Brass Menagerie
524 St. Louis Street   Dept. OHJ
New Orleans, LA 70130
(504) 524-0921
RS/O
Solid brass hardware & locks of all periods,
antique & reproduction. Porcelain & wrought
iron hardware, rim locks, unusual hardware: bar
rails, solid brass drapery & curtain hardware,
fireplace hooks, chandeliers, wall brackets and
sconces. Bathroom fixtures & accessories of
American and European design, including period
toilets, with wall hung tanks, decorated sink
bowls and turn-of- century pedestal type sinks.
Send for free brochure.

The Brass Stencil
250 Long Bottom Rd.   Dept. OHJ
Southington, CT 06489
(203) 621-4021
RS/O
Custom stencilling in contemporary and
traditional designs. Walls, floors, fireboards, and
floorcloths. Lessons are offered. No literature.

● **Brasslight, Inc.**
90 Main Street   Dept. H
Nyack, NY 10960
(914) 353-0567
MO DIST
Solid brass desk lamps, wall sconces, and ceiling
fixtures. A variety of interchangeable glass shades
in green, brown, white, frosted, etc. Stylings
include Edwardian and late Victorian. Some
variations of style available on quantity
purchases. All lamps and fixtures are polished
and lacquered. Catalog, $1.

Brasslight Antique Lighting
719 S. 5th St.   Dept. OHJ
Milwaukee, WI 53204
(414) 383-0675
RS/O
Restores and sells Victorian, Mission, and early
20th century brass lighting fixtures. Walk-in shop
only. Call for appointment. All original antique
fixtures; no reproductions. No catalog, but write
or phone with specific needs.

Braun, J.G. Co.
7540 McCormick, PO Box 66   Dept. OHJ
Skokie, IL 60076
(312) 761-4600
MO DIST
Complete selection of architectural metal
extrusions & castings in aluminum, bronze and
steel. Featuring railing systems and component
parts. Catalog, $1.

**Breakfast Woodworks Louis Mackall &
Partner**
50 Maple St.   Dept. OHJ
Branford, CT 06405
(203) 488-8364
RS/O
Louis Mackall & Partner, and Breakfast
Woodworks are two companies that work
together to provide extensive architectural design
and woodworking services. Almost any wooden
element can be reproduced. Design expertise
allows for complete restoration or renovation
services. Specialize in passive solar retrofit and
additions. For more information, write or call.

Brewster's Lumberyard
211 Murphy Rd.   Dept. OHJ
Hartford, CT 06100
(203) 549-4800
RS/O MO
Source for white-cedar roof shingles, clear and
extra quality grade. Two yard locations: Milford,
CT and Hartford. Will send shingles anywhere,
but customer must call for particular shipping
charges and delivery specifics. No shingle
literature; free catalog of extensive lumberyard
stock for area residents.

Briar Hill Stone Co.
PO Box 398   Dept. OHJ
Glenmont, OH 44628
(216) 276-4011
MO
Quarriers of sandstone. Colors range from light
buff and gray through tans, browns, chocolates,
and reds. Sills, lintels, steps, balusters, and
coping. Free information brochure. Full-color,
32-page fireplace book, $2.

British-American Marketing Services, Ltd.
251 Welsh Pool Rd.   Dept. OHJ
Lionville, PA 19353
(215) 363-0400
MO
Solid teak benches with traditional
mortise-and-tenon construction. The 'Mendip'
and 'Warwick' are early 19th-century designs.
Brochures, $.50.

Broad-Axe Beam Co.
RD 2, Box 181-E   Dept. OHJ
West Brattleboro, VT 05301
(802) 257-0064
MO
Authentically produced hand-hewn beams of
white pine. Two types — structural and
decorative — in standard 8, 12, 14 and 16 ft.
lengths. Structural beams (7-1/2 in. square) $5.25
per linear ft.; decorative beams (3 1/2 x 7 1/2 in.),
$3.50 per linear ft. Custom hewing done.
Illustrated brochure and price list, $1.

Broadway Collection
601 W. 103rd   Dept. OHJ
Kansas City, MO 64114
(800) 255-6365
DIST MO RS/O
Solid brass, porcelain, crystal, and wood
bathroom fixtures/fittings. Standing lavatories;
door hardware (including rim locks), cabinet
hardware, and switch plates for Colonial &
Victorian style architecture. Also decorative
hardware of formal French/English derivation.
Brass bar rail. 90-page illustrated catalog, $5. Can
call (816) 942-8910.

You'll get better service
when contacting companies
if you mention
The Old-House Journal
Catalog

Bronze et al
Holbrook Road   Dept. OHJ
Briarcliff Manor, NY 10510
(914) 941-1015
MO   RS/O
Restoration and patina service for bronze, brass, copper, and other non-ferrous metals. Capacities range from repairs on art sculpture (fixing scratches, dents, holes, damaged patina, remounting, fabrication and replacement of missing parts) to replication of antique hardware including 're-patina' (hinges, knobs, drawer pulls, latches, railings, ornamentation). Free literature.

Brooklyn Stone Renovating
458 Baltic St.   Dept. OHJ
Brooklyn, NY 11217
(212) 875-8232
RS/O
Has expert masons who specialize in restoring brownstone stoops and facades. Will recreate carved ornament in brownstone stucco. Their services are in great demand, so you have to be persistent and prepared to wait awhile. No literature; call for appointment.

Brooklyn Tile Supply
184 4th Ave.   Dept. OHJ
Brooklyn, NY 11217
(212) 875-1789
RS/O
Carries small white hexagonal bathroom tiles, 6 x 3 white tile, American Olean tiles. No literature. Sells through store only.

Brown, Carol
    Dept. OHJ
Putney, VT 05346
(802) 387-5875
RS/O   MO
Simple, natural white wool single and double spreads from Ireland, suitable for curtains. Country style floor rugs, woolen bedspreads and throws in colors and patterns. Cotton spreads. Wall hangings, including a Bayeux Tapestry panel. Irish tweeds, fine cottons, handkerchief linen. Osnaburg, Liberty, Khadi, many other natural fiber fabrics. Individual, personal attention. Brochure on receipt of a business-size self-addressed stamped envelope.

Brown, T. Robins
12 First Avenue   Dept. OHJ
Nyack, NY 10960
(914) 358-5229
RS/O
Consultant in architectural history and historic preservation, restoration, and renovation. Services available in the Middle Atlantic states and Conn. National Register and historic Preservation Tax Incentives applications. Historic sites survey work. Historic research. Preparation of walking tours and other publications about an area's architecture. No literature.

Bruce Hardwood Floors
16803 Dallas Parkway   Dept. OHJ
Dallas, TX 75248
(214) 931-3000
DIST
World's largest manufacturer of hardwood flooring with more than 70 items to choose from including 3/4 in. solid oak plank, 3/4 in. solid oak parquet, 3/8 in. laminated oak plank, 3/8 in. laminated oak parquet, and 5/16 in. solid oak parquet. All products have a baked-in finish. Serves entire United States and Canada. Free information.

● **Brunschwig & Fils, Inc.**
410 E. 62nd Street   Dept. OHJ
New York, NY 10022
(212) 838-7878
ID
Museums, restoration and historical agencies use the fine reproductions of 18th and 19th century fabric, trimming and wallpaper made by this firm. A new collection inspired by the Brighton Pavillion, coordinates chintzes and wallpapers in the French chinoiserie tradition. Their products are sold only through interior designers.

Bryant Stove Works
R.F.D. 2, Box 2048   Dept. OHJ
Thorndike, ME 04986
(207) 568-3665
RS/O   MO
Family-owned business restores and then sells antique cast-iron cookstoves and parlor heaters. They specialize in old kitchen ranges. Search service finds rare stoves for museums and historic restorations. Large stock of antique parts. Also The Bryant Stove Museum is a collection of rare ornate stoves, many one-of-a-kind. Shipping can be arranged anywhere. Free flyers. Catalog, 24 pages, $10.

Bucher & Cope Architects
1536 16th Street NW   Dept. OHJ
Washington, DC 20036
(202) 387-0061
RS/O
Architectural and interior design for renovations and restorations of houses and commercial buildings. Serving the Washington/Baltimore metropolitan area. Specialists in economic feasibility studies for adaptive re-use, and structural analysis. Their Conn. Ave.—P St. Report is available for $3.50: It includes information on how to do an economic feasibility study yourself.

Buck Creek Bellows
PO Box 412   Dept. OHJ
Lovingston, VA 22949
MO
Company restores antique fireplace bellows for owners. They also make new bellows of hardwood, goatskin, and brass. Free brochure.

● **Buckingham-Virginia Slate Corporation**
Box 11002, 4110 Fitzhugh Ave.   Dept. OHJ
Richmond, VA 23230
(804) 355-4351
DIST
Excellent quality VA-region slate. Roofing slate available. Out-of-state shipping possible on orders. Samples and literature available upon request.

●See Product Displays Index on page 199 for more details.

● **Buecherl, Helmut**
548 Hudson St.   Dept. OHJ
New York, NY 10014
(212) 242-6558
RS/O
Master craftsman can re-create or duplicate any painted decoration from 18th or 19th century. Has executed work for several museums and many fine houses. Painted work includes: Marbleizing, graining, gilding, stenciling, glazing, striping, lacquered wall, murals. No literature; phone for appointment — evenings.

● **Building Conservation**
6326 W. Wisconsin Ave.   Dept. OHJ
Wauwatosa, WI 53213
MO
Plans are available for: garages or stables in the Italianate, Queen Anne, and Colonial Revival styles (12 versions); sheds in Eastlake, and Gothic (3 versions); Stick Style Gazebo; Gothic kennel, Victorian birdhouses and feeder. Featured are: plans for a "Solar Bay for Old Houses" and detailed patterns on "How to Victorianize the Modern Garage." Illustrated portfolio on heavy stock doubles as a calendar, $5.

Building Inspection Services, Inc.
12813 Prestwick Drive   Dept. OHJ
Oxon Hill, MD 20744
(301) 292-1299
RS/O
Prepurchase home inspections; renovating/rehabilitation consultants. Serving Washington, D.C., and the surrounding area. Members of the American Society of Home Inspectors. Please call for further information, prices, and brochure.

Building Materials Inc.
139 Front Street   Dept. OHJ
Fall River, MA 02722
(617) 675-7809
RS/O
Supplier of various masonry supplies specializing in brick, bluestone, cement blocks, asphalt roofing, adhesives, waterproofings, repair materials for masonry buildings. No literature.

Bullseyes Unltd.
129 Main St.   Dept. OHJ
W. Harwitz, MA 02671
Acrylic "bulls-eyes" for replacement pieces in doors, sidelights, and transoms. Free literature.

Burdoch Silk Lampshade Co.
3701 Orion Drive   Dept. OHJ
La Mesa, CA 92041
(714) 465-7291
MO
Embroidered, hand-sewn fabric shades in Victorian and turn-of-the-century, Art Deco styles. These highly decorative shades come in many colors including burgundy, light brown, peach, and dark green. Can be used on table or floor-lamp bases. Send stamped, self-addressed envelope plus $2. for color flyer.

Burt Millwork Corp
1010 Stanley Ave.   Dept. OHJ
Brooklyn, NY 11208
(212) 257-4601
RS/O
They manufacture wood windows and doors; also distribute other millwork products. Free list of products stocked & manufactured.

Butcher Polish Co.
120 Bartlett St., PO Box G   Dept. OHJ
Marlborough, MA 01752
(617) 481-5700
MO   DIST
Since 1880, Butcher's paste wax for wood floors, antiques, furniture and paneling has been a standard of quality. Butcher's also makes black stove polish, brick and hearth cleaner, and fireplace/stove glass cleaner. Free literature and price list. Booklet available: "More Handy Tips on Wood Care," $.50.

Butterfield Co.
360 W. 4th St.   Dept. OHJ
Colby, KS 67701
(913) 462-3251
MO   RS/O
Sandblast glass designs for transoms, sidelights, doors, and windows. In addition to stock period designs, this company will do custom designs.

● **ByGone Era Architectural Antiques**
4783 Peachtree Rd.   Dept. OHJ
Atlanta, GA 30341
(404) 458-3016
RS/O   MO
20,000 square feet of architectural antiques: lighting, stained and bevelled glass, staircases, doors, mantels, and columns. Specializing in bars, offices, restaurant furnishings. Always on hand: 500 stained glass windows, hundreds of doors and mantels, footed tubs, pedestal sinks, along with original fretwork and paneling. Stock constantly changing. Company will crate and ship. Call or write your needs.

Byrd Mill Studio
Rt. 5 Box 192   Dept. OHJ
Louisa, VA 23093
(703) 967-0516
MO   RS/O
Architectural photography - interior and exteriors. Photography of antique furniture & jewelry for insurance purposes or catalogues. No literature.

You'll get better service when contacting companies if you mention The Old-House Journal Catalog

C

C—E Morgan
PO Box 2446   Dept. OHJ
Oshkosh, WI 54903
(414) 235-7170
DIST
A major manufacturer of millwork, some of which can be adapted to period houses. Staircases and stair parts of birch and red oak, or hemlock. Pine and fir, panel and sash doors, stair systems, entrance systems, patio doors. Specify interest, send $.10 for each brochure.

● **C & H Roofing**
1713 South Cliff Ave.   Dept. OHJ
Sioux Falls, SD 57105
(605) 332-5060
MO   RS/O
In business for six years, this company specializes in custom cedar shake and shingle roofs. They also have experience in steam-bent cedar shingle roofs (imitative of the English cottage thatch style). Will travel for installation. References. Free information.

CW Design, Inc.
2325 Endicott St.   Dept. OHJ
St. Paul, MN 55114
(612) 644-0157
MO   RS/O
Acid etching on glass and mirrors using a standard design or submitting your own black and white artwork. Applications include windows, sidelights, doors, transoms, cabinet doors, bar or fireplace mirrors. A sample available for $2. Free brochure.

Cabot Stains
1 Union Street   Dept. OHJ
Boston, MA 02108
(617) 723-7740
DIST
The first company to manufacture wood stains, they make products primarily for exterior & interior wood surfaces . . . paneling, siding, clapboard, shingles and shakes. Free brochures and color cards.

Cain-Powers, Inc. Architectural Art Glass
Rt. 1, Box AAA   Dept. OHJ
Bremo Bluff, VA 23022
(804) 842-3984
MO   RS/O
Doors with bevelled glass inserts. Carved glass and stained glass — period designs such as Victorian or Art Nouveau, Art Deco, as well as contemporary. In-house custom design available. Literature available — color brochure, $3.

California Heritage Wood Products, Ltd.
4206 Sorrento Valley Blvd-Rm D   Dept. OHJ
San Diego, CA 92121
(619) 453-1400
RS/O
Furnish, manufacture, finish and install period moldings; including crown, chair rail, base, as well as fancy door and window heads. No literature.

Cambridge Textiles
Dept. OHJ
Cambridge, NY 12816
(518) 677-2624
RS/O   MO
Professional conservation, preservation, and restoration of textiles: American samplers, quilts, Coptic, archeological textiles, tapestries, rugs, silk pictures. Safe, spacious studios. By appointment or ship insured parcel post, registered mail, or UPS. Free protocol flyer.

Campbell Center
PO Box 66   Dept. OHJ
Mount Carroll, IL 61053
(815) 244-1173
RS/O
Courses are held each summer on a variety of restoration/preservation subjects. The courses are usually given by the leading expert(s) in the subject. Masonry, plastering, museum conservation are a sampling of what is offered. Write or call for the current schedule.

Campbell-Lamps
1108 Pottstown Pike, Dept. 25   Dept. OHJ
West Chester, PA 19380
(215) 696-8070
RS/O   MO
New gas and electric shades from original molds. Lamp chimneys, lantern globes, and misc. glass lamp parts. Wholesale and retail. Cased glass shades including Emeralite desk shades — student shades and gas and electric. Solid cast brass parts for gas and electric lights. Lighting catalog, $1. Distributor of Aladdin kerosene lamps and full line of replacement parts for most kerosene heaters. Aladdin catalog, $.75.

Campbell, Marion
39 Wall St.   Dept. OHJ
Bethlehem, PA 18018
(215) 865-2522
RS/O
Architectural woodwork and furniture in American period styles designed and built to order. Authentic details and finest materials are used to match or recreate old work. Projects include, but are not limited to, mantels, paneling, cornices, valances, doors and door ways, shutters, built-in cabinets, chests, desks, tables, stands, bookcases., etc. Finishing and installation. Appointment necessary. Brochure $.25.

● **Campbellsville Industries**
P. O. Box 278   Dept. OHJ
Campbellsville, KY 42718
(502) 465-8135
MO
Manufacturers of aluminum cupolas, domes, steeples, weathervanes, cornices, louvers, balustrades, and columns for exterior ornamental use. (Columns are load- bearing.) Aluminum balustrades and railings have been reproduced in exact detail for historic buildings — also a selection of standard components. (Balustrades are primarily for roofs.) Free brochure available — please specify your interest.

● **Canal Co.**
1612 14th St., N.W.   Dept. OHJ
Washington, DC 20009
(202) 234-6637
RS/O
Architectural antiques including fully restored lighting fixtures from the 1860's thru the 1930's; fireplace mantels; stained and leaded glass; interior and exterior doors; medicine cabinets; handrails, newel posts, and balusters; columns; brass door hardware; pedestal sinks; iron fencing & window guards. No literature.

Canal Works Architectural Antiques
28 North Patterson Blvd.   Dept. OHJ
Dayton, OH 45402
(513) 223-0278
RS/O
Architectural salvage. 20,000 sq. ft. showroom with large stock of interior parts, from ornate mantels to ulititarian doors. Specializing in fancy woodwork; also saloon/restaurant fittings, wrought iron and lighting fixtures. Contracting services offered for interior/ exterior design and custom woodwork. Bevelled and stained glass windows. Free brochure.

Cane & Basket Supply Company
1283 South Cochran Avenue   Dept. OJ
Los Angeles, CA 90019
(213) 939-9644
RS/O MO
Every supply necessary to re-cane, re-rush and
re-splint chair seats. Related tools and supplies.
Also furniture kits for a side chair and 3 stools.
Illustrated catalog with price list — $1.

Caning Shop
926 Gilman St.   Dept. OH
Berkeley, CA 94710
(415) 527-5010
MO
Cane webbing, chair cane, round and·flat reeds,
ash splints, Danish cord, rawhide, rattan,
instruction books. Authors of The Caner's
Handbook. Basketry supplies and books. Free
catalog.

Canning, John
132 Meeker Rd.   Dept. OHJ
Southington, CT 06489
(203) 621-2188
Mr. Canning is a painter/decorator well versed in
the art of fancy painting. His specialties include
marbleizing, wood graining, and tortoise shell
finishes.

Canterbury Designs, Inc.
PO Box 5730   Dept. OHJ
Sherman Oaks, CA 91413
(213) 936-7111
RS/O MO
Company has a line of streetscape and mall
furnishings — some pieces in period style. Of
special interest are 4-faced outdoor clocks; oak
and iron or aluminum benches; an 1890
hexagonal bench; and cast aluminum tree grates.
Equipment is high-quality and costly. (17-ft.
4-faced Victorian street clock is approximately
$18,000.00) Color catalog — free. Prices on
specific request.

Cape Cod Cupola Co., Inc.
78 State Road   Dept. OHJ
North Dartmouth, MA 02747
(617) 994-2119
RS/O MO DIST
Wooden cupolas in a variety of sizes and styles.
Over 200 weathervane designs in a choice of
finishes and sizes. Illustrated catalog and price
list — $1.00.

Caravati, Louis J.
1911 Porter St.   Dept. OHJ
Richmond, VA 23224
(804) 232-4175
RS/O
Salvaged house parts: Doors, window sash
frame, plumbing fixtures, etc. You name it . . .
they have it. Call or write with your needs.

● **Carlisle Restoration Lumber**
Rt. No. 123   Dept. OHJ
Stoddard, NH 03464
(603) 446-3937
RS/O MO
Restoration lumber dealer selling wide pine or
oak boards, ship-lapped boards, feather-edge
clapboards, and natural weathered (grey) board.
Free brochure — please specify your needs for a
price quote.

┌─────────────────────────┐
│ ●See Product Dis-   │
│ plays Index on page   │
│ 199 for more details.   │
└─────────────────────────┘

Carolina Leather House, Inc.
P.O. Box 5195   Dept. OH-1
Hickory, NC 28601
(704) 322-4478
RS/O MO
Fine hand-made leather furniture. Styles from
camel-back Queen Anne sofas and authentic
tufted Chesterfields, to comfortable club chairs,
and their Safari collection in suede. Top-grain
leather (50 colors), brass appointments, solid
mahogany legs and stretchers. A domestic source
for well- made leather furniture at reasonable
cost. Catalog $2.00.

Carpenter and Smith Restorations
504 Central Ct.   Dept. OHJ
Highland Park, IL 60035
(312) 433-7277
RS/O
A woodworking shop specializing in restoration
and custom woodworking. Commercial and
residential structural repair and design
consultant. Interior and exterior renovation —
large and small scale. Quality cabinetmaking
services — adaptations and reproductions.
Antique refurbishing with related leatherwork
and metalwork. Furniture restored, designed,
and built to order. No literature.

Carriage Trade Antiques & Art Gallery
802 Clark Street   Dept. OHJ
Greenville, NC 27834
(919) 757-1982
MO RS/O
Unique services for the collector: they will search
for you on a cost-plus basis. Their refinishing
department does all work by hand; also custom
restoration and relining of antique trunks.
Interior design consultation, and cataloging &
appraisal of household items of value. No
literature.

Carson, Dunlop & Associates, Ltd.
597 Parliament St., Ste. B-5   Dept. OHJ
Toronto, ON, Canada M4X1W3
(416) 964-9415
RS/O
Prepurchase home inspection services available in
the greater Toronto area. Written report includes
analyses of structure, heating, plumbing, wiring,
insulation, interior and exterior finishes. Budget
figures are also offered for recommended
improvements. Purchasers are invited to attend
inspection. Brochure available on request.

CasaBlanca Fan Co.
450 N. Baldwin Park Blvd.   Dept. OHJ
City of Industry, CA 91746
(800) 423-1821
DIST
Manufacturers of a full line of quality ceiling fans.
Sold through distributors nationwide. Write for
name of nearest retailer.

CasaBlanca Glass, Ltd.
1935 Delk Industrial Court   Dept. OHJ
Marietta, GA 30067
(404) 952-1281
RS/O MO
A design consulting service, also offering
beveled, stained, and etched glass work that has·
been used in restaurants, hotels, and fast food
chains in the U.S. and abroad. They can match
existing pieces, copy from photos, and design
new concepts. Beveled windows, $40, per sq. ft.;
beveled mirrors, $45. Frosted panels also
available. Write for free brochure.

Cascade Mill & Glass Works
21 Pkwy., Hwy 23, Box 316   Dept. OHJ
Ouray County, CO 81427
(303) 325-4780
MO
Collection of high-quality handcrafted entry,
interior, and screen doors. Available in a
selection of woods and styles. Custom orders
accepted. Catalog $2.00.

Casey Architectural Specialties
1124 East Lyon Street   Dept. OHJ
Milwaukee, WI 53202
(414) 765-9531
RS/O
Ornamental plasterer does stock and custom
mouldings; restoration, residential or commercial
work. Operates primarily in the Wisconsin area,
but can travel. Free flyer available.

Cassidy Bros. Forge
U.S. Route 1   Dept. O83
Rowley, MA 01969
(617) 948-7611
MO RS/O
Cassidy Bros. Forge is a manufacturer of standard
and custom-made forged reproduction hardware,
lighting devices, fireplace accessories and
architectural metalwork. Catalog, $1.

Castings Unlimited
PO Box 504   Dept. OHJ
Oneonta, NY 13820
(607) 263-5192
MO DIST
This foundry is strongly oriented toward making
fine quality replacement parts for antique and
uncommon stoves. Thin-wall stove plate accounts
for most of their work.

Castle Burlingame
R.D. 1, Box 352   Dept. OHJ
Basking Ridge, NJ 07920
(201) 647-3885
RS/O
Antique building materials of all types, but
specializes in antique wide-board flooring,
including installation, sanding & finishing. Three
booklets available: "Where to find and how to
select antique flooring"; "How to install antique
flooring — step by step"; "How to sand and
finish antique flooring." $4.99 each or all three for
$12.99.

**Castle Home Maintenance Co. Boston
Victoriana**
47 Cypress   Dept. OHJ
Brookline, MA 02146
(617) 731-1229
RS/O
Company carries on ordinary building
construction services; however, they specialize in
antique and Victorian restorations, coloring and
rehabilitation of Victorian exteriors, and interior
design of period rooms and ornamental artistry
(stencilling, plastering, etc.) Free brochure.

Castle Roofing Co., Inc.
107 W. 26th St., No. 2   Dept. OHJ
New York, NY 10001
(212) 989-2029
RS/O
Castle Roofing Co. works exclusively installing
slate and copper roofs. High quality, high tech.
Artistic, and challenging installations are our
forte. Free flyer.

Cathedral Stone Company
2505 Reed St., N.E.   Dept. OHJ
Washington, DC 20018
(202) 832-1135
RS/O
Suppliers of building stone (limestone and sandstone) for structural use as well as ornamental carving, lettering, etc. They supply for both restoration and additions and can duplicate existing or original features in stone. Also do on-site masonry repair and restoration. Free brochure available.

Cedar Gazebos, Inc.
10432 Lyndale Avenue   Dept. OHJ
Melrose Park, IL 60164
(312) 455-0928
MO
Pre-fabricated gazebo kits. Modular units are made of heartwood cedar; each wall and roof panel is handcrafted and comes pre-assembled. Three styles available: Pagoda (either 6- or 8-sided), South Seas Classic, and Midwestern Classic (both 6-, 8-, or 10-sided). Optional features: counter ledges, double entry door, and full lattice panels. Brochures and price list, $1.

Cedar Valley Shingle Systems
985 S. Sixth St.   Dept. OHJ
San Jose, CA 95112
(408) 998-8550
MO   RS/O
A source for red cedar shingles.

Ceilings, Walls & More, Inc.
Box 494, 124 Walnut St.   Dept. O
Jefferson, TX 75657
(214) 665-2221
RS/O   MO   DIST
Old tin ceiling panels reproduced in light-weight, hi-impact polymer materials. The 24 by 24 in. panels are easily installed in a suspended grid system or glued directly onto sheetrock or plaster ceilings. The decorative patterns are appropriate to any decor and especially to rooms of the Victorian period. Free literature and price list on request. Sample kits $7.50.

Center Lumber Company
85 Fulton Street, Box 2242   Dept. OHJ
Paterson, NJ 07509
(201) 742-8300
RS/O
Distributors of both domestic and imported hardwood, 1-in. thru 4-in. thicknesses. Special architectural millwork, including custom hardwood mouldings. Operate dry kilns. No literature.

Century Glass Inc. of Dallas
1417 N. Washington   Dept. OHJ
Dallas, TX 75204
(214) 823-7773
RS/O   MO
They will bevel 1/4'', 3/8'', 1/2'' and 3/4'' thick clear or colored plate glass. Widths of bevels range from 1/4'' to 1-1/2''. All bevels custom. Also offer glue chip design for mirrors, leaded-beveled installations, and sandblasted panels. Price list available for bevel work, including OG and double bevels.

Century House Antiques
46785 Rt. 18   Dept. OHJ
Wellington, OH 44090
(216) 647-4092
RS/O
Antique store specializing in antique lamps and lamp repair. Also a complete line of replacement parts, and metal stripping & buffing. Free literature.

Chandelier Wharehouse
40 Withers St.   Dept. OHJ
Brooklyn, NY 11211
(212) 388-6800
MO   RS/O
Large stock of period-style chandeliers, specializing in crystal chandeliers. Also restoration of antique fixtures, and distributor of Focal Point ceiling medallions. Catalog — $5.

Chandler — Royce
185 E. 122 St.   Dept. OHJ
New York, NY 10035
(212) 876-1242
RS/O   MO
Electro-plating shop. Will take small jobs. Copper, nickel, chrome, brass, antiquing and polishing. No literature.

Chapman Chemical Co.
PO Box 9158   Dept. OHJ
Memphis, TN 38109
(901) 396-5151
MO   DIST
A large selection of wood preservatives and water repellents such as Woodguard™. Also other specialty coatings. Free literature. Call toll free (800) 238-2523.

Charles Barone, Inc.
9505 W. Jefferson Blvd.   Dept. OHJ
Culver City, CA 90230
(213) 559-7211
DIST   RS/O
Traditional small-print & large scale wallpapers with correlated fabrics suitable for country & traditional houses. Also custom printing of fabric and wallpaper. Available through retail paint and wallpaper stores. No literature.

Charles St. Supply Co.
54 Charles St.   Dept. OHJ
Boston, MA 02114
(617) 367-9046
MO
This retail store has agreed to ship plaster washers to OHJ readers who can't find them locally. Price is $1.25 per dozen (ppd.), minimum order 3 dozen, or by the pound, approx. 23 dozen, $18.00 ppd. No literature.

Charleston Battery Bench, Inc.
191 King St.   Dept. OHJ
Charleston, SC 29401
(803) 722-3842
MO   RS/O
Their reproduction park bench has cast-iron sides and cypress slats painted a dark green. $135 each; two or more, $120 each.

Charmaster Products Inc.
2307 Hwy No. 2 West   Dept. OHJ
Grand Rapids, MN 55744
(218) 326-6786
MO   RS/O   DIST
Manufacturers of Charmaster combination wood/oil, wood/gas, wood/coal, or wood-only add-on furnaces for central heating. Available in 140,000 BTU to 300,000 BTU sizes. Uses unsplit wood. Provides economy of wood burning with security of oil gas back-up. U.L. approved models and ETLM (State of Maine) approval. Free literature.

Charolette Ford Trunks
Box 536   Dept. OH
Spearman, TX 79081
(806) 659-3027
MO
Antique trunk hardware and supplies. 32 pg. catalog, $1.00. ''How-to-Restore'' trunk book, $5.00, and ''History of Antique Trunks'', $2. ''Trunk Talk''—single issue $3., 4 issues/$10.

Chelsea Decorative Metal Co.
6115 Cheena Drive   Dept. OHJ
Houston, TX 77096
(713) 721-9200
MO   RS/O
Embossed metal for ceilings are stamped with the original dies that date back as far as the Civil War. There are eighteen designs and they come in 2' x 8' sheets. They are 26 gauge and have a silvery tin finish. Metal cornice comes in 4 ft. lengths, but the widths vary. Also, 2 ft. x 2 ft. plastic panels for suspended ceilings. Catalog free.

Chem-Clean Furniture Restoration Center
Historic Route 7A   Dept. OHJ
Arlington, VT 05250
(802) 375-2743
RS/O   MO
Wood finishing products for floors, stairs, fine furniture — paint and varnish removers, bleach, brush cleaner, satin finish polyurethane varnish. Brochure and price list — $.25.

Chemical Products Co., Inc.
P.O. Box 400   Dept. OHJ
Aberdeen, MD 21001
(301) 272-0100
DIST
Supplies chemicals in commercial quantities for professional vat strippers. Write for literature.

Cherry Creek Ent. Inc.
937 Santa Fe Drive   Dept. OHJ
Denver, CO 80204
(303) 892-1819
MO   RS/O   DIST
One of the largest manufacturers of machine bevelled parts, as well as fine quality hand bevelled pieces. Their modular bevels can be made into windows, skylights, door panels, etc. Also, custom design capabilities. Catalog, $2.

Chester Granite Co.
Algerie Road   Dept. OHJ
Blandford, MA 01008
(413) 269-4287
RS/O
Stone masons specializing in using traditional techniques and hand tools to produce architectural details such as door steps, pillars, quoins, window sills, and lintels. Available in granite, marble, or brownstone. They are also a source for quarried blue-gray granite. Work is done from architectural drawings or samples. No literature.

Chicago Faucet Co.
2100 South Nuclear Dr.   Dept. OHJ
Des Plaines, IL 60018
(312) 694-4400
DIST
Elegant brass faucets copied from turn-of-the-century designs with minor changes to meet modern plumbing codes. Sold through nationwide distributors. "The Renaissance Collection" brochure, $5.00.

Chilstone Garden Ornament
Sprivers Estate   Dept. OHJ
Horsmonden, Kent, UK
(089) 272-3553
RS/O MO DIST
Handsome garden ornaments — exact copies of 16th, 17th, and 18th century models — in cast stone. Urns, planters, benches, statuary, obelisks, pedestals, balls and bases, columns, balustrades — all by noted designers. Catalog — $6.00.

● **Chimney Relining International, Inc.**
P.O. Box 4035   Dept. OHJ
Manchester, NH 03108
(603) 668-5195
MO RS/O
Chimneys easily lined, new or old, straight or crooked using either of two new techniques: (1) Z-Flex™ flexible stainless steel chimney liners ideal for wood, oil or gas appliances. (2) Permaflu™ poured refractory liners, for all fuel use. Both tested by Arnold Greene Labs to U.L. Standard #103 and BOCA Evaluated (Report 82-23). Free literature.

Chromatic Paint Corp.
PO Box 105   Dept. OHJ
Garnerville, NY 10923
(914) 947-3210
DIST
Manufacturer of specialty paints such as Japan colors, sign paints, automotive finishes and industrial coatings. Free color card and information sheet.

● **Cirecast, Inc.**
380 7th St.   Dept. OHJ
San Francisco, CA 94103
(415) 863-8319
DIST
An outstanding collection of reproduction hardware, late 1870s to mid 1880s. Bronze doorknobs, hinges, escutcheons, keyholes, and sash lifts reproduced from original patterns using the lost-wax process. Other metals offered. Write for your nearest dealer.

● **City Barn Antiques**
362 Atlantic Ave.   Dept. OHJ
Brooklyn, NY 11217
(212) 855-8566
MO RS/O
A large selection of restored brass antique gas lighting fixtures with original etched glass shades. 1860 — 1910. No literature.

● **City Knickerbocker, Inc.**
781 Eighth Ave.   Dept. OHJ
New York, NY 10036
(212) 586-3939
RS/O
A large selection of 19th century lighting fixtures and lamps. Reproduction cased glass Emeralite Shades. Restores, rewires, adds antique or reproduction glass shades. Also, the "Tee" series — seven reproduction variations in the green glass shade type of fixture. "Tee" series brochure free.

● **City Lights**
2226 Massachusetts Ave.   Dept. OHJ
Cambridge, MA 02140
(617) 547-1490
RS/O MO
Dealer in fully restored antique lighting. Fixtures are repaired, rewired, cleaned, polished, and lacquered and have all antique glass shades. Fixtures displayed at shop. Photo sheet of typical fixtures available for $2. Will respond to specific requests with Polaroids, $1. each, refundable with purchase.

Clarksville Foundry & Machine Works
P.O. Box 786   Dept. OHJ
Clarksville, TN 37040
(615) 647-1538
RS/O
Gray iron foundry and machine shop in operation since 1854. They produce a wide range of rough and finished castings in volumes of one piece to several hundred. They have many old patterns, and can produce quality castings using a customer's sample as a pattern. Custom and jobbing work a specialty. No literature.

● **Classic Illumination**
431 Grove St.   Dept. OHJ
Oakland, CA 94607
(415) 465-7786
DIST
Manufacturers of authentic handcrafted solid brass Victorian and early-20th century lighting including the bronze griffin and craftsman collection. These U.L. listed electric and gas-style chandeliers, wall sconces and table lamps are available with a variety of shades, lengths and finishes (custom variations available). Free brochure upon request. Wholesale inquiries invited. Write for illustrated catalogue ($3.00) and nearest dealers.

Claxton Walker & Associates
10000 Falls Road   Dept. OHJ
Potomac, MD 20854
(301) 299-2755
RS/O
House inspection services in Washington, D.C., and surrounding Virginia and Maryland. Newly expanded service to Annapolis and Norfolk. Free brochure and price list of books and articles on home inspection and maintenance.

Clio Group, Inc.
3961 Baltimore Ave.   Dept. OHJ
Philadelphia, PA 19104
(215) 386-6276
RS/O
Consultants in architectural and land use history providing a full range of restoration and preservation services. Preparation of National Register Nomination forms; applications for Tax Certification; counseling for adaptive re-use projects. Specialists in archival, demographic and property research; interpretation of historic structures. Survey drawings. Free brochure.

Clocks, Etc.
3401-C Mt. Diablo Blvd.   Dept. OHJ
Lafayette, CA 94549
(415) 284-4720
RS/O MO
Restore, trade, buy and sell old and new clocks and watches. Nationwide clock locating service for specific antique timepieces. Photos available; please specify your wants or needs. Will ship anywhere. Brochures about new grandfather and wall clocks, $1.

Coalbrookdale Company
RD 1, Box 477   Dept. OHJ
Stowe, VT 05672
(802) 253-9727
MO DIST RS/O
British manufacturer of solid fuel appliances with high-quality iron casting and technical efficiency. Over two hundred years of experience and modern technology combined to produce multi-fuel stoves. Send for free literature on their complete line of products, including wood/coal burning stoves, cast iron furniture, and brassware.

Cohasset Colonials by Hagerty
643X Ship St.   Dept. OHJ
Cohasset, MA 02025
(617) 383-0110
MO RS/O
Manufactures and sells exact reproductions of early American furniture in kits. Assembly is easy and does not require special skills or tools. Stain, glue, hardware included. Choose from Shaker, Windsor, ladderback chairs. Also, canopy beds, tables, bureaus, mirrors. Catalog includes reproduction fabric, paints, lighting fixtures, brass, pewter. Color catalog, $1.

Cohen's Architectural Heritage
1804 Merivale Road   Dept. OHJ
Ottawa, OT, Canada K2G1E6
(613) 226-2979
RS/O
Architectural antiques and authentic period pieces. Stained glass windows and window sets in Victorian, Art Nouveau, and Art Deco styles. Complete restoration facility. Exterior and interior doors, gingerbread, mantels, stair parts, decorative plaster, bath fixtures, iron fences, light fixtures. Also, wood working facility for custom crafting. Will ship anywhere. 1 page flyer, $1.00.

Cole, Diane Jackson
9 Grove Street   Dept. OHJ
Kennebunk, ME 04043
(207) 985-7387
RS/O MO
Handwoven throws, lap robes, coverlets, blankets, and pillows in wools and mohairs, available in a variety of colors. Handwoven wool strip rugs with sturdy Irish linen warp, braided ends — custom colors. Fabric swatches and information about complete line, $5; or $2 each. Please specify.

Colefax and Fowler
39 Brook St.   Dept. OHJ
London, England, W1Y 1A
01-493-2231
MO RS/O
Twenty designs of Brussels and Wilton weave carpets. They are based on 18th- and 19th-century English patterns. The designs are in narrow widths (27 in.) and should be used with coordinating borders. Colors can be made to match customer swatches. Write for further details.

Collyer Associates, Inc.
30 East 33rd St.   Dept. OHJ
New York, NY 10016
(212) 684-0900
RS/O
Terra cotta restorations. Have done major projects such as the Woolworth Tower in NYC.

Colonial Casting Co., Inc.
443 South Colony St.   Dept. OHJ
Meriden, CT 06450
(203) 235-5189
MO DIST
Handcrafted pewter candlesticks and sconces in Early American and Queen Anne styles. Also; Plates, mugs, ash trays & goblets. Catalog and price list — $.50.

Colonial Charm
PO Box A-1111   Dept. OHJ
Findlay, OH 45840
(419) 424-0597
MO
A charming picket fence for your "old house"
This company offers a 20-page detailed
instruction guide to build your own. Colonial
thru Victorian styles, 22 full-sized patterns. $5.

Colonial Foundry & Mfg. Co.
57 Russell St., PO Box 8385   Dept. OHJ
New Haven, CT 06530
(203) 469-0408
MO DIST RS/O
A line of detailed cast-aluminum furniture. Each
piece is handcrafted from solid, full section
castings. A wide selection of paints and custom
materials. Also, street lamps and lanterns.
Catalog, $2.

Colonial Lock Company
172 Main St.   Dept. OHJ
Terryville, CT 06786
(203) 584-0311
MO
Box type rim locks based on the old-fashioned
style but with modern engineering. A maximum
dead bolt security lock. Send $.25 for catalog.

Colonial Tin Craft
7805 Railroad Ave.   Dept. OHJ
Cincinnati, OH 45243
(513) 561-3942
RS/O MO DIST
An array of folk art creations, plus Early
American, 18th century and Colonial lighting.
Chandeliers, lanterns, sconces, candleholders and
lamps. 40-page catalog available: $2.00

Colonial Weavers
Box 16   Dept. OHJ
Phippsburg Center, ME 04562
(207) 389-2033
MO RS/O
Handwoven reproductions of antique coverlets in
Colonial Overshot or summer & winter
techniques. Coverlets are woven to order in a
wide choice of traditional patterns and colors.
Drapery fabric woven to match coverlets or
tablecloths and runners. A reproduction of an
antique Maine coverlet was purchased by the
Renwick Gallery of the Smithsonian Institution
for their 'Crafts Multiples' show. Also tablecloths,
placemats. Catalog, $2.

**Colonial Williamsburg Foundation Craft
House**
PO Box C   Dept. OHJ
Williamsburg, VA 23187
(808) 229-1000
RS/O MO
WILLIAMSBURG Reproductions: More than 2,500
examples of fine home furnishings approved by
the Colonial Williamsburg Foundation as being
authentic reproductions, adaptations, and
interpretations of antiques at Williamsburg. The
286-page full color catalog and price list, $8.95
ppd, a must for those interested in seventeenth,
eighteenth, and early nineteenth-century
furnishing styles. Also, historic paint colors —
color card, $1.

● See Product Dis-
plays Index on page
199 for more details.

Combination Door Co.
P.O. Box 1076   Dept. JC
Fond du Lac, WI 54935
(414) 922-2050
DIST MO
Manufacturers (since 1912) of wood combination
storm and screen doors. Plain wood screen
doors, wood combination doors in many styles,
wood combination windows, wood basement and
garage windows, and wood patio storm doors
available through distributors and lumber dealers
in 18 states, and direct to consumers in those
states without distributors. Write for free
brochures and name of your distributor.

Community Services Collaborative
1315 Broadway   Dept. OHJ
Boulder, CO 80302
(303) 442-3601
RS/O
National practice with complete consulting and
architectural services for historic preservation and
restoration. Property surveys, interior/exterior
design, specifications, construction management,
and historic development research. Economic and
adaptive use studies and plans and full Tax Act
services. Consultant to National Park Service.
Historic materials laboratory; including paint,
mortar and plaster analysis. Literature available
on request.

Competition Chemicals, Inc.
P.O. Box 820   Dept. OHJ
Iowa Falls, IA 50126
(515) 648-5121
DIST
Importers of SIMICHROME POLISH for all
metals (brass, pewter, copper, etc.). Sold through
distributors/dealers. Literature available from
distributors/dealers or from main office at above
address.

Conant Custom Brass
270 Pine St.   Dept. OHJ
Burlington, VT 05401
(802) 658-4482
MO RS/O
They work with brass, bronze, and copper
offering a variety of services including polishing,
repair, restoration, chrome, nickel & silver
stripping, soldering, brazing, spinning, and
custom fabrication. They also buy and sell brass
antiques, specializing in fully restored lighting
fixtures. They can bring most brass items back to
their original condition. Free brochure.

Congdon, Johns/Cabinetmaker
RFD 1, Box 350   Dept. OHJ
Moretown, VT 05660
(802) 485-8927
RS/O MO
Fine cabinetwork in period styles. Authentic
reproductions, or original designs in appropriate
period fashion. All work done by hand; all solid
woods; fine brass hardware. Custom design
service built on a sound knowledge of 18th
century furniture. Prefers personal consultation
with customers, but will work through mail or by
phone if necessary. Photos and references to
serious inquiries. Catalog, $3.

Conklin Tin Plate & Metal Co.
P.O. Box 2662   Dept. OHJ
Atlanta, GA 30301
(404) 688-4510
RS/O MO
Manufactures metal roofing shingles, including
one pattern typical of late 19th century houses.
Available in galvanized steel, copper, aluminum
microzinc or terne. Also supplies galvanized
roofing sheets, gutters and leaders. Flyer "Metal
Shingles", $3.00.

Connecticut Cane & Reed Co.
PO Box 1276, 205 Hartford Rd.   Dept.
OHJ
Manchester, CT 06040
(203) 646-6586
MO RS/O
All types of chair seating available. Cane, rush,
and reed seating. Large stock/ prompt delivery.
Many patterns of pre-woven cane webbing in
stock. Brochure, $.50.

Conservatory, The
209 W. Michigan Ave.   Dept. OHJ
Marshall, MI 49068
(616) 781-4790
RS/O
Shop offers antique and contemporary products
for the older home, including selected
architectural artifacts, restored gas lighting
fixtures, Victorian hardware, marble sinks, and
leaded windows. Of special interest is the catalog
center, featuring the catalogs and brochures of
numerous fine companies. No literature.

Constantine, Albert and Son, Inc.
2050 Eastchester Rd.   Dept. OHJ
Bronx, NY 10461
(212) 792-1600
RS/O MO
Carries extensive selection of hardwoods and
veneers, tools, kits, furniture hardware, craft
books, and finishing materials. Illustrated
104-page catalog available for $1.00. Catalog and
set of 20 wood samples $2.00. $1.50 refundable
on first order with coupon in sample packet.

Consulting Services Group S.P.N.E.A.
141 Cambridge Street   Dept. OHJ
Boston, MA 02114
(617) 227-3956
RS/O
A consulting group of the Society for the
Preservation of New England Antiquities offering
expert advice to owners of older properties
concerned with the restoration, preservation and
conservation of their structures. Specialized
advice on historic paints, masonry and wood
conservation, and plaster repair. Physical and
documentary research into the history,
development and condition of historic properties.
Free brochure.

Consumer Supply Co.
1110 W. Lake   Dept. OHJ
Chicago, IL 60607
(312) 666-6080
MO RS/O
A large selection of used radiators and plumbing
fixtures in period styles. call or write with your
specifications. No literature.

KEY TO ABBREVIATIONS

MO   sells by Mail Order

RS/O   sells through Retail
Store or Office

DIST   sells through
Distributors

ID   sells only through
Interior Designers
or Architects

Continental Clay Company
PO Box 69   Dept. OHJ
Kittanning, PA 16201
(412) 543-2611
DIST   RS/O
Founded in 1896, Continental Clay Co. has been manufacturing brick and tile products continously from world renowned Kittanning, PA clay and shale. Traditional building products are made in a variety of colors and shapes in both glazed and unglazed brick and tile. They'll custom match sizes and colors for restoration projects. Free literature.

Contois Stained Glass Studio
Box 224-A, Rt. 2   Dept. OHJ
Hamlin, WV 25523
(304) 824-5651
MO
A selection of authentic "Tiffany Reproduction" and Victorian-styled stained glass lampshades. All lampshades are hand crafted with the skill and attention to detail displayed by turn of the century artisans. Will also do custom design work for lamps, windows, transoms, and doors. Color brochure, $2.00.

Cooper Stair Co.
1331 Leithton Road   Dept. OHJ
Mundelein, IL 60060
(312) 362-8900
DIST   RS/O   MO
Manufacturers of wood stairs: straight, circular, and spiral. Custom fitted with stock parts; or handrails, balusters, and newel posts may be manufactured to your architect's specifications in any wood. Installation instructions available. Available knocked-down, pre-assembled, or for professional installation. Also sculptured wood paneling. Brochures, $.25 each.

● **Copper House**
RFD 1, Rt. 4   Dept. OHJ
Epsom, NH 03234
(603) 736-9798
MO   RS/O
Handmade copper weathervanes and lanterns, for post, wall, or hanging. Authentic reproductions. A variety of styles and sizes are available. Flagpole balls and weathervane parts. Catalog $1.00.

Copper Sales, Inc.
2220 Florida Ave., South   Dept. OHJ
Minneapolis, MN 55426
(800) 328-0799
DIST
A mill distributor for copper and galvanized gutters. Selection includes half-round gutters and corrugated galvanized downspouts. Free information.

Coran — Sholes Industries
509 East 2nd Street   Dept. OHJ
South Boston, MA 02127
(617) 268-3780
RS/O   MO
Manufactures and distributes lead, glass, tools, equipment, pattern books to the stained glass artisan. A very complete line of Tiffany-style lamp kits. Illustrated catalog with price list — $3.00.

Dermit X. Corcoran Antique Services
Box 568 Montauk Hgwy.   Dept. OHJ
East Moriches, NY 11940
(516) 878-4988
RS/O
Specializing in the repair and restoration of ornamental and decorative metal items — lighting fixtures, brass beds, statuary, cast iron architectural features, weather vanes, American and European antiques. Custom work done on request. Inquiries welcomed. Flyer available.

Corner Legacy
17 Hilton St., PO Box 102   Dept. OHJ
Eureka Springs, AR 72632
(501) 253-7416
RS/O   MO
This small, family business specializes in fine corner cabinetry in limited production. They have a line of hand-crafted oak corner medicine chests, plus corner curio cabinets in various native hardwoods. Distribution is primarily through mail-order. Literature available, free.

Cornerstone Antiques
Box 477   Dept. OHJ
North Conway, NH 03860
(603) 356-5979
MO
100 different stencil designs in early American, Victorian, and contemporary. All stencils are pre-cut on durable Mylar. A starter kit is $5. Catalog, $1.

Cornucopia, Inc.
PO Box 44-J Westcott Road   Dept. OHJ
Harvard, MA 01451
(617) 456-3201
MO
Handmade and factory-built country primitive and Early American furniture. A nice variety of settees and rockers. The company also sells a furniture dressing for restoration of old pieces. Also, wool hand-braided rugs. Catalog, $2.

Cosmetic Restoration by SPRAYCO
1500 Straight Path   Dept. OHJ
Wyandanch, NY 11798
(516) 491-1616
RS/O
Large scale paint stripping services to restore wood and masonry buildings to their original surface. Specializes in old houses and churches. Literature free.

Cosmopolitan International Antiques
Box 314   Dept. OHJ
Larchmont, NY 10538
(914) 632-1571
MO   RS/O
Antique lighting fixtures, and Victorian, formal 18th & 19th century American & European furniture. Interior design & appraisal services available for the owners of turn-of-the-century, Neo-Classical and Colonial homes. Branch offices throughout NY, CONN & NJ. Please write or call with specific request.

Country Bed Shop
Box 222H   Dept. OHJ
Groton, MA 01450
(617) 448-6336
RS/O   MO
Custom-made furniture — hand-made in traditional American, country, and high styles from the 17th and 18th centuries. Numerous styles of beds including pencil-post and other tall posts with canopy frames, low post styles, folding beds, trundle beds, and cradles. Windsor chairs, chests, tables and cupboards. Illustrated 28 pg. catalog, $3. Pencil-post bed folder, $.50. Stamps OK.

Country Braid House
Clark Rd., RFD 2, Box 29   Dept. OHJ
Tilton, NH 03276
(603) 286-4511
RS/O   MO
Traditional New England Colonial braided rugs. Hand-laced all-wool rugs are made to order. They'll also make up custom kits for you to lace yourself. Free company brochure. Prices quoted on your requested size and style — or phone ahead to visit the shop.

Country Comfort Stove Works
Union Road   Dept. OHJ
Wales, MA 01081
(413) 245-7396
RS/O
Professional restorers of antique wood and coal burning kitchen ranges and parlor stoves. Totally restored stoves, will also do total or partial restoration of your stove. Can provide refractory liners for most stoves. Hours 6-9 pm weekdays, all day Sat. & Sun.

● **Country Curtains**
At The Red Lion Inn   Dept. OHJ
Stockbridge, MA 01262
(413) 243-1805
RS/O   MO
Curtains in cotton muslin, permanent-press and other fabrics, some with ruffles, others with fringe, braid or lace trim. Also bedspreads, dust ruffles, canopy covers and tablecloths. Tab curtains and wooden rods. Retail shops in Stockbridge, Salem, Braintree, and Sturbridge, MA. Free 56-page catalog includes illustrations and color photographs.

● **Country Floors, Inc.**
300 East 61st St.   Dept. OHJ
New York, NY 10021
(212) 758-7414
RS/O   MO   DIST
Handmade tiles for floors and walls, from Holland, France, Spain, Portugal, Italy, Israel, Mexico, & Finland. 60 page color catalog, $5. Regional representatives' names, and installation instructions available on request.

● **The Country Iron Foundry**
PO Box 600-OH   Dept. OHJ
Paoli, PA 19301
(215) 296-7122
Antique iron firebacks, hand-cast from original design which date back to Early American and European periods. Prices range from $75 to $400, depending on size. Illustrated and informative brochure available for $1.00. Showroom at 1792 E. Lancaster Pike, Paoli, displays firebacks.

Country Loft
South Shore Park   Dept. OHJ
Hingham, MA 02043
(617) 749-7766
MO
Furnishings and decorative accessories with an Early American flavor. Many attractive housewares appropriate for the country or Colonial home. Lifetime subscription to The Country Loft 48-page color catalog, with a minimum of 3 issues per year for just $5. (refundable with your first order).

Country Roads, Inc.
1122 South Bridge St.   Dept. OHJ
Belding, MI 48809
(616) 794-3550
MO   DIST   RS/O
This company restores old theater seats. Repair and refinishing of wood parts, metal refinishing, and reupholstering done on-site or in their shop. Their "Mobile Plant" — a renovation facility on wheels — goes anywhere to provide quick service for public buildings. Free brochure.

Country Stencilling
1537 York Street   Dept. J4
Lima, NY 14485
(716) 624-2985
MO
Wall and floor stencilling using authentic motifs and material (milk paint or oils, for added durability). They'll do custom designs, restore existing patterns, and travel to execute their craft. Stencilled curtains are another of their specialties. Brochure, $1.

Country Window, The
Box 382 Main St.   Dept. OHJ
Intercourse, PA 17534
(717) 768-8687
MO
Authentic reproductions of oil lamps from about 1890. Choice of electric or oil, and various hand-made cloth shades. Unique brass electric, and Williamsburg reproductions candlesticks are offered. Illustrated catalog with fabric samples, $1.00.

Couristan, Inc.
919 Third Avenue   Dept. OHJ
New York, NY 10022
(212) 371-4200
DIST
America's largest importer of Oriental design area rugs. Also supplies hand-knotted Orientals, contemporary rugs, as well as fine broadloom. Free brochure on hand-hooked rugs or full-color catalogues on Oriental design rugs — Gem $4; Ultramar $5; Kashimar $5; Omar $4.

Cowtan & Tout, Inc.
979 Third Avenue   Dept. OHJ
New York, NY 10022
ID
Domestic and imported glazed chintzes, wovens and silks; fine, handblocked wallpapers; wallcoverings with coordinating fabrics. Custom colorings available. Specialists in 18th and 19th century patterns. Many William Morris wallpapers.

Craftsman Lumber Co.
Main St.   Dept. OHJ
Groton, MA 01450
(617) 448-6336
RS/O MO
Specializing in kiln-dried, wide pine board flooring, 12 in. to 24 in. wide. Also, wide oak flooring, 4 in. to 9 in. wide, and Victorian wainscotting (custom-made). Custom-made panelling, flooring, moulding, and batten doors. Also Watco Danish oil products, and cut nails. Leaflet and price list — $.50. Stamps are OK.

Craftsmen Decorators
2611 Ocean Avenue   Dept. OHJ
Brooklyn, NY 11229
(212) 769-1024
RS/O
Specializes in graining, glazing, gilding, antiquing, stencilling and traditional decorating techniques. Restorations a particular specialty. No literature.

Crane Co.
500 Executive Blvd.   Dept. OHJ
Elmsford, NY 10523
DIST
A rolled-rim, acrylic bathtub with cast-brass claw feet. Available in two lengths: 5 ft. and 5-1/2 ft. Free literature.

● **Crawford's Old House Store**
301 McCall   Room 84
Waukesha, WI 53186
(414) 542-0685
MO
A wide variety of old-house items, including unusual reproduction door and window hardware, lighting and plumbing supplies, reproduction marble fireplace mantels, custom made wood storm, screen and replacement sash, all shapes in kits. Wood corner blocks, finials, fancy cut shingles, and corner beads. Specialty tools. Wood and brass refinishing kits. Reference books and furniture kits. Illustrated catalog, $1.75, refundable with purchase.

Creative Glass Works
3620 Spring Valley   Dept. OHJ
Bedford, TX 76021
(817) 498-0215
MO RS/O
Manufactures custom-made bevelled, etched, and leaded glass fixtures. Panel entrys (door lites, side lites, transoms), leaded glass (new and repair), custom bevelled glass (new, repair, zipper cut), hand-crafted sand etched glass (photo, process). No literature.

● **Creative Openings**
219 Prospect   Dept. OHJ
Bellingham, WA 98225
(206) 671-7435
RS/O MO
Hand-crafted hardwood screen doors, for Victorian or other style houses. Solid brass mesh screen. Your choice of oak, mahogany, ash. Bent laminations, hand-turned spindles. Brochure sent upon request; send $3 for design booklet.

Creatus
P.O. Box 6124   Dept. OHJ
Lancaster, PA 17603
MO
Personalized "House Blessing" Frakturs to record births, marriages, family tree, and special events. Authentic designs handlettered and printed in color on 9 x 12 natural parchment. Handcrafted frames in Fraktur style are available. Catalog, $1.

Croton, Evelyn — Architectural Antiques
51 Eastwood Lane   Dept. OHJ
Valley Steam, NY 11581
(516) 791-4703
MO RS/O
Antique architectural items such as marble and terra-cotta keystones, ornate iron registers and fence panels, iron and wood newel posts, balusters, door carvings, door surroundings, pilasters, fretwork, etc. Specializing in hand-carved corbels. Selling to dealers, architects, designers, and consultants only. Specific inquiries made on letterhead answered with photos, dimensions, prices.

Crowe Company
1136 Industrial Ave.   Dept. OHJ
Escondido, CA 92025
(619) 741-2069
MO RS/O
Custom and production woodturning and stairparts. Architectural millwork: mouldings, panelling, wainscotting, and mantels. Art glass: stained, leaded, bevelled, etched, and carved. Windows, doors, mirrors, skylights and lamps. Design service and installation are available. Brochure $.75.

Crowfoot's Inc.
Box 1297   Dept. OHJ
Pinetop, AZ 85935
(602) 367-5336
RS/O MO
Fine woodworking, cabinetmaking, turnings, furniture reproduction, Victorian and Early American. Works mainly in Southwest area. Will supply photos of work done to serious inquirers.

Crown Glass Co.
2556 15th St.   Dept. OHJ
Denver, CO 80211
(303) 455-7117
RS/O MO
Glass studio specializing in repair of antique leaded stained glass, and custom bevelling. No literature.

Crystal Mountain Prisms
PO Box 31   Dept. OHJ
Westfield, NY 14787
(716) 326-3676
MO RS/O
Prisms, pendants, bobeches, chains, pendelogues, plug drops, kite pendants, and prism pins are some of the items offered by this company. Send SASE for the complete list of sizes, shapes, and colors.

● **Cumberland General Store**
Route 3   Dept. OH-84
Crossville, TN 38555
(615) 484-8481
RS/O MO
"Complete outfitters: goods in endless variety for man and beast." From chamber pots to covered wagons — over 10,000 items, many available only here and all new goods. Of particular interest are the period kitchen utensils and implements, period bathtubs, and wood-burning cookstoves. The interesting, illustrated 250 pg. catalog makes fascinating browsing for $3. plus $.75 postage & handling.

● **Cumberland Woodcraft Co., Inc.**
PO Drawer 609   Dept. 105
Carlisle, PA 17013
(717) 243-0063
RS/O MO
Leading manufacturer of Victorian millwork faithfully duplicates the intricate designs of the Victorian era. Full line includes: architectural hand carvings, brackets, corbels, grilles, fretwork, turnings, plus special treatments. Also available: raised-panel ceiling treatments, bars, partitions, wainscotting. All crafted from solid oak or poplar. Unlimited quantities available. Complete 32-page, full-color catalog and price list, $3.50.

Curran, Patrick J.
30 No. Maple St.   Dept. OHJ
Florence, MA 01060
(413) 584-5761
MO RS/O
Custom stained, bevelled, and etched glass. Also, four styles and sizes of opalescent glass table lamps. Several lamp bases also offered. Send $1. for brochure.

Curry, Gerald — Cabinetmaker
Pound Hill Road   Dept. OHJ
Union, ME 04862
(207) 785-4633
MO
Small shop specializing 18th-century furniture reproductions. Design, construction, and materials are faithfully copied from the originals. Fine craftsmanship combined with years of study results in the museum-quality reproductions. An illustrated brochure is free.

Curvoflite
RFD 2. Box 145   Dept. OHJ
Kingston, NH 03848
(603) 642-3425
RS/O   MO
Solid oak spiral staircases and circular staircases
custom made to your specifications. Two basic
circular styles (Colonial and Contemporary) with
custom options. Also custom architectural
millwork: cabinetwork, raised panelling,
hand-turned balusters. Curvoflite staircase color
brochure — $1.00. Can also call (617) 889-0007.

Cushwa, Victor & Sons Brick Co.
MD RT 68   Dept. OHJ
Williamsport, MD 21795
(301) 223-7700
RS/O   DIST
Manufacturers and distributors of distinctive
"Calvert" machine-molded and custom
handmade molded brick. Specialize in matching
old brick and special brick designs for color,
texture, and size. Complete line of brick available
in numerous colors. Restoration work includes
Independence Hall and Betsy Ross House.
Brochure available for $2.00 prepaid.

Cusson Sash Company
128 Addison Road   Dept. OHJ
Glastonbury, CT 06033
(203) 633-4759
RS/O   MO
Manufactures a combination storm-screen
window with wooden sash. Double-hung, picture
windows, oriel-style. Storm/screen inserts are
interchangeable. Sized to order. Flyer and price
list, free.

Custom House
6 Kirby Rd.   Dept. OHJ
Cromwell, CT 06416
MO   RS/O
Silk lampshades: Custom designs and recovering
old frames. Hardback lampshades: hand made
from new or antique fabric. Also, pierced &
botanical lampshades. All shades made by a staff
of skilled craftsmen. Write your specific needs for
further details.

● **Custom Kitchen and Millwork**
2750 N. Bauer Rd., R 2   Dept. OHJ
St. Johns, MI 48879
(517) 593-2244
MO
Builders of custom kitchen and cabinets for 25
years. Also specialty millwork, such as Victorian
trim. Free catalog.

Custom Sign Co.
111 Potomac St.   Dept. OHJ
Boonsboro, MD 21713
(301) 432-5792
RS/O
Hand-lettered gold leaf numbers in period styles,
painted on your transom. Also, antique
reproduction signs. Free price list. Prefer
Washington DC suburbs or Frederick, MD
vicinity.

Cyrus Clark Co., Inc.
267 Fifth Avenue   Dept. OHJ
New York, NY 10016
(212) 684-5312
DIST
Their line of chintzes features some early 19th
century European patterns in an old-fashioned
glazed finish. Chintz is excellent for wall
covering, upholstery and draperies. Sold at
department stores and fabric shops, or write for
name of distributor nearest you. An instruction
booklet, "Everglaze Chintz Makes A Beautiful
Wallcovering" is free.

D

● **Daly's Wood Finishing Products**
1121 North 36th St.   Dept. OHJ
Seattle, WA 98103
(206) 633-4204
RS/O   MO   DIST
Manufacturing and marketing of wood finishing
products including brasswire brushes and a
wooden scraping tool; bleaches and stain
removers; BenMatte Danish finishing oil, clear
and stain; Floor Fin treatment. A complete guide
to wood finishing: 'Class Notes,' $2. Free
descriptive literature; free guidance in solving
wood finishing problems.

Dan Wilson & Company, Inc.
319 S. West St.   Dept. OHJ
Raleigh, NC 27603
(919) 821-5242
RS/O   MO   DIST
Custom-made garden furniture, handcrafted from
selected hardwoods. Chinese Chippendale
planters with removable galvanized liners,
Chippendale garden benches, tables and chairs.
Catalog, $2.

● **Dean, James R.**
15 Delaware Street   Dept. OHJ
Cooperstown, NY 13326
(607) 547-2262
RS/O   MO
Provides professional, individualized counselling
and custom stair and handrail work. All phases
of common, intricate, straight curved, new and
alteration work. Stair and railwork matched or
copied. All woods, all work special order only.
Material shipped anywhere F.O.B. Cooperstown,
N.Y. Planning, layout design and consulting
services available. Repair assistance information
available via phone/mail. $15.00 minimum fee for
services. Phone calls returned collect only. No
literature.

Decor International Wallcovering, Inc.
37-39 Crescent St.   Dept. OHJ
Long Island City, NY 11101
(212) 392-4990
MO
They offer an inexpensive Anaglypta substitute
called "Wall Sculpture." One pattern, Grandeur,
is an embossed paper that is appropriate for
19th-century houses. No literature; free samples.

Decorative Hardware Studio
160 King Street   Dept. OHJ
Chappaqua, NY 10514
(914) 238-5251
RS/O   MO
Fine decorative hardware and fittings. Crystal,
brass, porcelain accessories. Furniture hardware,
faucets, sinks, locksets, door hardware, etc.
Styles from Colonial to contemporary. Write for a
64-page catalog, $5, and more information.

Decorators Market, USA
PO Box 671   Dept. OHJ
New Braunfels, TX 78130
(512) 625-5654
MO
A source for reproduction Victorian, Art
Nouveau, and Colonial gift and decorative items.
Selection includes picture frames (brass & copper
lustre), brass candleholders, brass desk lamps,
and country gourmet ceramics. Free illustrated
brochure.

● **Decorators Supply Corp.**
3610-12 S. Morgan St., rear   Dept. OHJ
Chicago, IL 60609
(312) 847-6300
RS/O   MO
Thousands of composition and wood fibre
ornaments for woodwork, furniture and
architectural trim; hundreds of plaster ornaments,
composition capitals and brackets; 15 wood
mantels in Colonial, French and English styles. 4
illustrated catalogs and price lists. Plaster
Ornaments — $3.00, Capitals & Brackets — $3.00
Mantels — $2.00, Wood Fibre Carvings — $2.00,
Woodwork-Furniture Ornaments — $15.00.

Dee, John W. — Distinctive Decorating
342 Ames St.   Dept. OHJ
Lawrence, MA 01841
(617) 682-8647
RS/O
Interior & exterior painting. Wallcovering
installation. Home remodelling & repairs.
Paint-failure analysis & trouble shooting. Quality
restoration. Craftsmanship, integrity. Serving
greater Boston, North Shore, Southern NH. No
literature.

● **Deft Wood Finish Products**
PO Box 895   Dept. OHJ
Alliance, OH 44601
(216) 821-5500
MO   DIST   RS/O
Deft Clear Wood Finish; Defthane; Wood Armor;
Wood Stains, Spray Stains; Danish Oil. Free
brochure.

Delaware Quarries, Inc.
River Rd.   Dept. OHJ
Lumberville, PA 18933
(215) 297-5647
DIST   RS/O
Producers of an extensive line of building stone.
Specialists in the matching of stone from old,
unavailable sources. Custom fabrication of slate,
limestone, granite, marble and sandstone for a
variety of uses in the home. Genuine soapstone
warming plates for your wood stove. Free
building stone brochure.

Dell Corp.
912 Grandin Ave.   Dept. OHJ
Rockville, MD 20850
(301) 279-2612
DIST
The U.S. distributor for the Beta method. Epoxy
mortar with specially fabricated polyfiber
reinforcement rods for timber restoration. Skilled
craftsmen, needed for the process, are available
at distributors nationwide. Free information.

Dentelle de France
PO Box 255476   Dept. OHJ
Sacramento, CA 95865
MO
Importers of French lace in many traditional or
Victorian patterns including a peacock design.
Color brochure, $1.

Dentro Plumbing Specialties
63-16 Woodhaven Blvd.   Dept. OHJ
Rego Park, NY 11374
(212) 672-6882
RS/O   MO
Supplies modern or obsolete faucet & shower
stems or spindles only. Cannot supply porcelain
faucet handles or complete faucets. Must have
the old one for a sample. No diagrams or
sketches. Complete line of Case parts for tanks,
and original drainboards. No catalogs or other
literature available.

Depot Woodworking, Inc.
683 Pine St.   Dept. OHJ
Burlington, VT 05401
(802) 658-5670
MO   RS/O
The targest custom millhouse in Vermont, this
company has a stock selection of panelling,
wainscotting, and mouldings available in a
variety of hardwoods. They will also do custom
cutting to match an existing element. Profile
sheets and price list, $1.

Designer Resource
5160 Melrose Ave.   Dept. OHJ
Hollywood, CA 90038
(213) 465-9235
MO   RS/O
Complete selection of period and hard-to-find
architectural detail. Stock and custom designs in
columns, mantels, metal ceilings, composition
ornament, architectural plaster detail, carved,
embossed wood mouldings, metal mouldings,
plaster cornices, etc. Designer Resource sells to
designers, architects, and builders, but will sell to
the serious individual restoring a period home.
Extensive catalogs are available, please write or
call for list.

● **Devenco Louver Products**
2688 E. Ponce de Leon Ave.   Dept. OHJ
Decatur, GA 30030
(404) 378-4597
RS/O   MO
Specialists in Colonial wooden blinds, movable
louver and raised-panel shutters, all custom
manufactured to window specifications. Devenco
uses Ponderosa pine, and can stain or paint any
tone. Wood Finish by Minwax is used exclusively
for a finish. Mail orders accepted and shipment
arranged. Please write or telephone for specific
information and free color brochure.

Devoe & Raynolds Co.
4000 Dupont Circle   Dept. OHJ
Louisville, KY 40207
(502) 897-9861
DIST
Several years ago, Devoe was the first company
to issue a line of reproduction Victorian paints for
exteriors. Their ''Traditions'' line includes 48
exact reproductions of Devoe's line of 1885.
Acrylic-latex only. Contact office above if your
local paint store doesn't carry Devoe paints.

● **DeWeese Woodworking**
P.O. Box 576   Dept. OHJ
Philadelphia, MS 39350
(601) 656-4951
MO
Since 1976, DeWeese has grown to be the
country's foremost producer of oak commode
seats. They also offer other bathroom accessories:
towel bars, tissue roll holder, magazine rack,
toothbrush/tumbler holder, and our original towel
clip. They have a 30 day ''no hassle'' return
policy. Free color brochure.

● **Diedrich Chemicals-Restoration
Technologies, Inc.**
300 A East Oak Street   Dept. OHJC
Oak Creek, WI 53154
(414) 761-2591
DIST   MO   RS/O
Professional restoration chemicals for building
exteriors: masonry restorer-cleaner,
water-repellent preservative sealers. Paint
removers for both wood and masonry. Chemicals
sold ONLY to dealers/contractors around the
country. Film demonstrating products is
available. Write for free brochure and name of
your nearest dealer or contractor.

Dierickx, Mary B.
125 Cedar Street   Dept. OHJ
New York, NY 10006
(212) 227-1271
RS/O
Architectural preservation consultant providing
such preservation services as: restoration,
preservation & rehabilitation programs and
planning; maintenance programs; materials
conservation; architectural and historical research
and analysis; architectural surveys; feasibility
studies; photographic documentation; &
assistance with National Register nominations,
local landmark status & Tax Act certification. Free
brochure.

Dilworthtown Country Store
275 Brinton's Bridge Rd.   Dept. OHJ
West Chester, PA 19380
(215) 399-0560
MO   RS/O
Built in 1758 as a general store and saddlery, it is
believed to be one of the oldest continously
operated general stores in the country. They offer
American country gifts, accessories and folk art
along with antiques, herbs & dried flowers, 18th
century reproductions (including
Dummy-boards), and upholstered furniture from
Angel House Designs. Catalog, $1.

Dimension Lumber Co.
517 Stagg   Dept. OHJ
Brooklyn, NY 11237
(212) 497-7585
RS/O
Custom mouldings and millwork for wholesale
customers. Minimum order of 50 feet to
individuals, walk-in cash business only. No
literature.

Direct Safety Company
1607 W. 17th St., PO Box 26616   Dept.
OHJ
Tempe, AZ 85282
(602) 968-7009
MO
A large assortment of mail-order safety
equipment. Free catalog. You can call toll free
(800) 528-7405.

Dixon Bros. Woodworking
72 Northampton St.   Dept. OHJ
Boston, MA 02118
(617) 445-9884
RS/O
This custom millwork and cabinet shop can
produce most pieces required in the restortion of
old houses. They specialize in period entry doors,
paneling, interior shutters, mouldings, turnings,
and carving. Also kitchen cabinetry; straight and
curved handrailing and complete staircases.
Furniture specialties include an all-hardwood
rolltop desk. No literature.

Dodge, Adams, and Roy, Ltd.
Stoodley's Tavern, Hancock St.   Dept.
OHJ
Portsmouth, NH 03801
(603) 436-6424
RS/O
Architects and contractors specializing in
restoration and preservation of buildings. Survey
work, research, documentation, design are
aspects of their architectural services. Roofing,
interior and exterior woodwork, masonry, and
foundation work are contracting specialties.
They'll travel anywhere. Free brochure.

D'Onofrio Restorative Studio
81 Ulster Ave.   Dept. OHJ
Walden, NY 12586
(914) 778-7465
MO   RS/O
Restoration and conservation of furniture,
antiques, and wooden collectibles. Refinishing:
hand rubbed finishes; French polishing; repair,
rebuilding and replacement of damaged, loose or
missing parts. Woodturning, woodcarving,
veneering, inlaid work, gold leaf. Serving all 914
area code residents.

● **Dorothy's Ruffled Originals**
6721 Market Street   Dept. OHJ
Wilmington, NC 28405
(919) 791-1296
MO
Handmade ruffled curtains, specializing in
perma-press country curtain with a 7 in. ruffle.
Also complete line of ruffled accessories: dust
ruffles, pillow sham, coverlets, and lampshades.
Curtains can be made in any length. $4.00 for
36-page color brochure and samples.

Dorz Mfg. Co.
P.O. Box 456   Dept. OHJ
Bellevue, WA 98009
(206) 454-5472
MO   DIST
Manufacturer of built-in cabinet ironing boards.
Board swivels to save space. Doors to fit are
made of pine with raised panels, alder with
raised panels or flat birch plywood panels. Also
available are pads and covers that fit older
home's built-in ironing boards. Free literature.

**Dotzel, Michael & Son Expert Metal
Craftsman**
402 East 63rd Street   Dept. OHJ
New York, NY 10021
(212) 838-2890
RS/O
Restores, repairs, cleans brass, copper, pewter,
iron, lead, tole. Restores antiques to original
condition. Wires chandeliers and lamps.
Retinning, lacquering and silverplating. Also,
metal shades custom made. No literature.

Dover Furniture Stripping
505 S. Governors Ave.   Dept. OHJ
Dover, DE 19901
(302) 674-0220
RS/O   MO
A professional paint stripping service using dip
tanks - also offering supplies for restoring and
refinishing furniture, a full line of furniture parts
and solid brass hardware - also carries trunk
hardware, veneer, embossed wood, upholstery
supplies, caning tools. They also have a gift shop
that carries reproduction Early American and
Victorian furniture. Wholesale catalog available to
the trade, $1.

KEY TO ABBREVIATIONS

MO   sells by **Mail Order**

RS/O   sells through **Retail
Store or Office**

DIST   sells through
Distributors

ID   sells only through
**Interior Designers
or Architects**

• Dovetail, Inc.
PO Box 1569-102   Dept. OHJ
Lowell, MA 01853
(617) 454-2944
RS/O   MO
Traditional medallions, cornices, brackets, and complete ceiling designs that are strong, lightweight, and fire-resistant. All items designed with ease of installation in mind. Prompt efficient attitude combined with quality plaster castings and custom-drawn mouldings. Specialty work and consulting service available. Color catalogue: $3.

Downstate Restorations
2773 North Kenmore   Dept. OHJ
Chicago, IL 60614
(312) 929-5588
RS/O
Building restoration firm specializing in facade restoration. Extensive masonry cleaning and chemical paint removal experience. Ornamental cornice fabrication and repair — metal, fibre glass and plaster. Also painting, consulting, field testing, and research. Serving Illinois and the Midwest. Free company literature and client list.

Dremel/Div. of Emerson Electric
4915 21st St.   Dept. OHJ
Racine, WI 53406
(414) 554-1390
DIST
Manufactures compact electric power tools for fine work. High speed tools are ideal for woodcarving, shaping, routing, drilling, sanding and polishing most woods, metals and plastics. The Dremel line also includes a scroll and table saw, lathe, engraver, disc-belt sander and a full range of attachments and accessories. Also, hot melt glue guns, soldering irons, wood burning tools, book and patterns. Available at most hardware and hobby retail stores. Free brochure.

Drill Construction Co., Inc.
80 Main St.   Dept. OHJ
West Orange, NJ 07052
(201) 736-9350
RS/O
General contractors, specializing in renovation/restoration. No literature.

Driwood Moulding Company
P.O. Box 1729   Dept. OHJ
Florence, SC 29503
(803) 669-2478
RS/O   MO
They have been fabricating embossed hardwood period mouldings for over 50 years. Hundreds of historically authentic designs suitable for ceiling cornices, chair rails, door and window casings, bases, etc. They custom manufacture mantels, doors, and architectural millwork. Custom-made curved wood stairs. Mouldings normally shipped within two to three weeks of purchase order. Two catalogs of mouldings and millwork, $6 (cost credited against orders of $100 or more).

Drums Sash & Door Co., Inc.
P. O. Box 207   Dept. OHJ
Drums, PA 18222
(717) 788-1145
RS/O   MO
Architectural woodwork company supplying clear white pine custom window sash; stair treads, risers and mouldings; stock hardwood trim (casing, base, cove); wood screen/storm doors, custom interior & exterior doors. Also cabinet fronts in oak, birch, cherry, or poplar. Will supply window glass and other window parts. Catalog/price list: $2.00.

Dura Strip of San Mateo
726 S. Amphlett Blvd.   Dept. OHJ
San Mateo, CA 94402
(415) 343-3672
RS/O
Professional paint-stripping company using immersion process on all types of interior/exterior wood and metalwork: stained-glass windows, mouldings, registers, railings, gingerbread, doors, mantels, and pillars. Also metal de-rusting and etching. Specializing in antique repair-restoration-refinishing; and chair caning. Also reproduction oak tables and chairs. No literature.

Durable Goods
1808 Riverside Ave.   Dept. OHJ
Minneapolis, MN 55454
(612) 332-1868
RS/O
They service, sell, and restore antique wood heaters and ranges. Oak style heaters, made in U.S.A. 1870 to 1940, can be as efficient as any modern-style heater. They specialize in "Round Oak" heaters manufactured by the Beckwith Co., Dowagiac, Mich. No literature.

Duro Fiber Co.
239 Andover St.   Dept. OHJ
Wilmington, MA 01887
(617) 657-4205
RS/O   MO
Specialize in reproducing any architectural element in fiberglass — roofing tiles, cupolas, cornices, brackets, finials, etc. Wood or stone details can be reproduced in a material that isn't prone to deteriorate. All custom work, no literature.

Durvin, Tom & Sons
Rt. 6, Box 307   Dept. OHJ
Mechanicsville, VA 23111
(804) 746-3845
RS/O
Family-owned and operated brick contracting business. Services include fireplace and chimney restoration. Small, quality-oriented company with old-house experience. Greater Richmond area. Please phone for free estimate.

• Dutch Products & Supply Co.
166 Lincoln Ave.   Dept. OHJ
Yardley, PA 19067
(215) 493-4873
MO   DIST
The complete line — 26 patterns — of Royal Delft Tiles. Colonial chandeliers in solid brass and brass with Delft or Limoges parts. Also hanging brass oil lamps; wall sconces in brass/pewter. Brochure, $1.

Duvinage Corporation
P.O. Box 828   Dept. OHJ
Hagerstown, MD 21740
(301) 733-8255
MO
Manufactures complete lines of spiral and circular stairway systems for residential, commercial, and industrial applications; interior and exterior use. Circular and spiral stairs are custom built to specifications. Steel, aluminum, grating, cast iron, cast aluminum, and stainless steel. Treads covered in wood, carpet, rubber, terrazzo, marble, concrete or tile. Continuous rails of aluminum, steel or wood. Free brochure.

E

E & B Marine Supply
980 Gladys Court, PO Box 747   Dept. OHJ
Edison, NJ 08818
(201) 442-3940
MO
High-performance marine supplies are useful for restoration projects. Caulking compounds, exterior finishes, varnishes, rot-patching materials, epoxy fillers, and more. Mail and phone orders are filled promptly (within 48 hours). Major credit cards are accepted. Free discount catalog.

Eastern Marble Supply Co.
1833 Front St.   Dept. OHJ
Scotch Plains, NJ 07076
(201) 753-9171
MO   DIST
Suppliers of specialized stone adhesives.

Eastern Safety Equipment Co.
45-17 Pearson St.   Dept. OHJ
Long Island City, NY 11101
(212) 392-4100
DIST
A large selection of safety equipment including respirators for paint stripping and other hazardous fumes. They will not sell direct, however they will put you in contact with your local distributor. Free information.

Eastfield Village
Box 145 R.D.   Dept. OHJ
East Nassau, NY 12062
(518) 766-2422
RS/O
Dedicated to Historic Preservation and historical American trades, Eastfield's hands-on workshops employ traditional methods and tools. All of Eastfield's resources, including a study collection of 27 appropriately furnished and outfitted structures of the period 1787-1840, are available to workshop participants. Accommodations and the first-hand experience of early 19th-century living conditions is provided by the Village Tavern. Write or call for a free class schedule and details.

• Easy Time Wood Refinishing Products Corp.
PO Box 686   Dept. OHJ
Glen Ellyn, IL 60137
(312) 858-9630
MO   DIST   RS/O
Company sells a wood refinisher that removes varnish, lacquer, shellac, and light coats of paint, without sanding, scraping, or further preparation. No methylene chloride. Also tung oil penetrating sealer, lemon oil, and a lightweight electric heat gun for removing paint. Products distributed through antique and hardware stores, but they will also sell direct. Free brochures.

Econol Stairway Lift Corp.
2513 Center St.   Dept. OHJ
Cedar Falls, IA 50613
(319) 277-4777
MO   RS/O
Best known for their wheelchair elevators and stairlifts, this company also makes standard size dumbwaiters. Specify dumbwaiters for free information.

Eddy, Ian — Blacksmith
Sand Hill Rd. RFD 1 Box 213   Dept. OHJ
Putney, VT 05346
(802) 387-5991
MO DIST RS/O
A full-time blacksmith-craftsman traditionally
forging wrought iron functional objects. Special
orders, reproductions, and commission items
gladly accepted. Send SASE ($.37) for brochure.

**The Ehrenkrantz Group/Building
Conservation Technology**
1555 Connecticut Ave., N.W.   Dept. OHJ
Washington, DC 20036
(202) 387-8040
RS/O
Architectural firm specializing in technical
consulting and architectural design for
restoration/rehabilitation including condition
surveys, materials analysis and conservation,
maintenance programming, preparation of
historic structures reports, Tax Act certification
application and preparation of construction
documents and administration. Offices in
Washington, DC, New York, Nashville, and San
Francisco. Free brochure.

● **Eklund, Jon Restorations**
80 Gates Avenue   Dept. OHJ
Montclair, NJ 07042
(201) 746-7483
RS/O
On-site stripping and refinishing of interior
woodwork. Total restoration, interior/exterior, of
old houses and commercial buildings. Design,
construction of period- conforming additions or
extensions. Specializing in remodeling Victorian
and early 20th century kitchens and pantries.
Custom millwork, cabinets, doors, sashes.
Variation painting and stencilling, and leaded
and stained glass repairs. NY, NJ metro area. No
literature, call or write, free initial consultation.

● **Elbinger Laboratories, Inc.**
220 Albert St.   Dept. OHJ
East Lansing, MI 48823
(517) 332-1430
MO RS/O
Quality copying and restoration of heirloom and
historical photographs. Photos are copied on a
large-format negative and printed to meet or
exceed "archival" standards. Brochure, $2.00.

Elcanco
60 Chelmsford St.   Dept. OHJ
Chelmsford, MA 01824
(617) 256-9972
MO RS/O
Electric candles coated in natural beeswax are
available in two types. The Starlite burns at only
6 volts, while the Starlite uses conventional
voltage. Candles come in a variety of heights and
with plug-in or direct installation. Brochure and
price list available.

Electric Glass Co.
1 E. Mellen St.   Dept. OHJ
Hampton, VA 23663
(804) 722-6200
RS/O MO
They offer new beveled glass door and window
inserts, stained glass panels, new and old art
glass and Tiffany style shades. Beveled Glass
Catalog — $3.00.

Elk Valley Woodworking Company
Rt. 1, Box 88   Dept. OHJ
Carter, OK 73627
(405) 486-3337
MO RS/O
They specialize in redwood and cedar porch
columns and white pine, ash, oak, mahogany,
and walnut room columns and balusters. They
will also turn to your pattern or duplicate
columns for partial replacements. Many
decorative brackets are also available. Also
custom-built furniture: cabinets, tables, etc. Send
$2. for brochure.

Elliott Millwork Co.
640 E. Fairchild St.   Dept. OHJ
Danville, IL 61832
(217) 446-8443
RS/O
Manufacturers of architectural woodwork and
custom hardwood mouldings. A large line of
stock items, including wainscotting, chair rails,
and crown mouldings. Also manufactures
"Enduro" stile and rail 6-panel solid red oak
prefinished doors. Standard moulding for all
inside and outside mouldings. All of these
mouldings are custom manufactured. Free
literature.

Elmira Stove Works
22 Church St., W.   Dept. OHJ
Elmira, Ontario, Canada N3B1M3
(519) 669-5103
MO DIST RS/O
Wood- or coal-burning cast iron cookstoves.
Many are copies of turn-of-the-century designs.
Distributors throughout Canada and the United
States. Color brochure, $1.

Elmore, Chris/ Architectural Design
707 Simonton St.   Dept. OHJ
Key West, FL 33040
(305) 294-2014
RS/O
Restoration of old structures — both design and
execution. Working primarily in FL Keys, but will
travel for selected jobs throughout South.
Extensive background in the American Arts &
Crafts Movement: Will travel anywhere in U.S. to
work on Stickley, Wright, etc. houses. Complete
attention given to one job at a time. No literature:
call or write for referrals.

Elon, Inc.
198 Sawmill River Rd.   Dept. OHJ
Elmsford, NY 10523
(914) 592-3323
DIST RS/O
Source for Elon Carrillo® Mexican handmade
glazed and unglazed terra cotta tiles and
accessories. Mexican Ironware. Glazed tile from
Italy, Culinarios from Portugal, and handmade
French tiles. Palace Collection™ of hand-painted
English tile, plus panels, and trim. Catalog, $3.

Emperor Clock Co.
Emperor Industrial Park   Dept. OHJ
Fairhope, AL 36532
(205) 928-2316
MO
Manufactures a line of Grandfather clocks. Clocks
come in kit form or completely assembled. Each
kit is precision cut and pre-sanded for ease of
assembly. All hardware and step-by-step
instructions are included with each kit. Free
catalog.

Empire Stove & Furnace Co., Inc.
793-797 Broadway   Dept. OHJ
Albany, NY 12207
(518) 449-5189
RS/O MO
In addition to many wood and coal-burning
stoves, this shop (in business since 1901) carries
an extensive inventory of parts for old stoves,
ranges, furnaces & boilers, and accessories. There
are also patterns for many parts that aren't in
stock. No literature. For best results phone
number above or 449-2590.

Emporium, The
2515 Morse St.   Dept. OHJ
Houston, TX 77019
(713) 528-3808
RS/O MO
Walk-in store carries large stock of Victorian and
turn-of-century architectural embellishments,
such as tin ceilings, ceiling fans, mantels,
promenade benches, lamp posts, gingerbread, art
glass, doors, etc. Also, gingerbread by
mail-order. Corbels, fretwork, trim, and brackets
in pine. Illustrated 'gingerbread' brochure, $1.

Enerdynamics
PO Box 4-1831   Dept. OHJ
Anchorage, AK 99509
(907) 561-2477
MO RS/O
An energy management, design, consulting, and
auditing firm. Through use of a computerized
system they can provide a comprehensive and
accurate assessment of a homeowner's energy
use and make recommendations for cost effective
improvements. Will be happy to answer any
questions.

Energy Etcetera
PO Box 451   Dept. OH
Bayside, NY 11361
(212) 229-7319
MO
Mail order catalog specializing in wood, coal
stove and fireplace accessories, safety devices,
logging equipment and many unusual American
and European crafted gifts. Reproductions of
antique firebacks for fireplaces, as well as cast
iron and brass early American and
turn-of-the-century accessories. Also, energy
saving devices for electric and gas hot water
heaters, and oil burners. Illustrated catalog, $1.

Energy Marketing Corporation
PO Box 636   Dept. OHJ
Bennington, VT 05201
(802) 442-8513
MO DIST
Manufacturers of Home Heater Coal and
Wood-heating systems. Copper-coil domestic hot
water systems available for use with Home
Heater. Double glass door hearth and fireplace
stoves for viewing as well as heat. Home Heater
Coal/Wood Boiler also available. Free brochure.

● **See Product Dis-
plays Index on page
199 for more details.**

KEY TO ABBREVIATIONS

MO   *sells by Mail Order*

RS/O *sells through Retail
         Store or Office*

DIST *sells through
         Distributors*

ID   *sells only through
         Interior Designers
         or Architects*

Englander Millwork Corp.
2369 Lorillard Place   Dept. OHJ
Bronx, NY 10458
(212) 364-4240
MO   RS/O
Manufactures wood windows, doors and
mouldings to customer's specifications. Specialty:
round and curved windows. Will also duplicate
counter-balance, double-hung, and pulley wheel
window frames. Glass types available. No
literature.

Englewood Hardware Co.
25 No. Dean St.   Dept. OHJ
Englewood, NJ 07631
(201) 568-1937
RS/O
A restoration supply/hardware store, well-stocked
with reproduction faucets, door and furniture
hardware, fine brass fittings, ceiling and
ornament and cornice mouldings, etc. Walk-in
sales only; mail-order buyers contact Renaissance
Decorative Hardware, their subsidiary.

● **Enlightened Restorations**
51 Shadow Lane   Dept. OHJ
Wilton, CT 06897
(203) 834-1505
RS/O
Consulting services including house dating,
historical research, and the locating of capable
crafts people required for your house restoration.
Free brochure.

Entol Industries, Inc.
8180 NW 36th Ave.   Dept. OHJ
Miami, FL 33147
(305) 696-0900
MO   DIST
Art Carved® mouldings, medallions, and rosettes.
Made of lightweight urethane polymers and/or
fiberglass reinforced gypsum. Pieces can be
primed or pre-finished in white or wood grain
(custom finishes are also offered). Literature,
$.50.

Essex Forge
12 Old Dennison Rd.   Dept. OHJ
Essex, CT 06426
(203) 767-1808
MO   RS/O
Authentic hand-forged reproductions of early
American fireplace accessories; terne, copper and
iron chandeliers and sconces, copper and brass
exterior lanterns. Illustrated catalog — $2
(refunded with purchase).

Essex Tree Service
PO Box 158   Dept. OHJ
Stevenson, WA 98648
(509) 427-5345
MO
Red cedar shingles and shakes at a reasonable
cost — specialize in custom sizes. Stock shingles
are also available. Please call or write with
specifications; no literature.

Estes-Simmons Silver Plating, Ltd.
1168 Howell Mill Rd.   Dept. OHJ
Atlanta, GA 30318
(404) 875-9581
RS/O   MO
Silver, gold, pewter, brass, and copper are
skillfully repaired, plated, and polished.
Replacements for missing parts are hand made.
Free brochure.

Evergreen Slate Co.
68 East Potter Ave.   Dept. OHJ
Granville, NY 12832
(518) 642-2530
MO   RS/O
Producers of roofing slate in all colors and
thicknesses: Semi-Weathering Gray-Green, VT
Black & Gray-Black, Unfading Green, Red, Royal
Purple, Unfading Mottled Green & Purple, and
Rustics. Company also sells 'ESCO' Slate Cutters,
Slate Rippers, Slate Hammers, and Slate Hooks
for slate repairs. Write or call for free brochure.

Evergreene Painting Studios, Inc.
365 West 36th St.   Dept. OHJ
New York, NY 10018
(212) 239-1322
RS/O
Architectural construction and decorative painting
services. Int./ext. paint contracting. Interior &
exterior services include mural painting, trompe
l'oeil, frescoes, woodgraining & marbleizing, gold
leafing. Designed treatment of walls, ceilings,
floors. Free flyer.

Experi-Metals
524 W. Greenfield Avenue   Dept. OHJ
Milwaukee, WI 53204
(414) 384-2167
RS/O   MO
Individual craftsman does high-quality custom
castings in brass, bronze and related alloys.
Excellent reproduction work. Has done custom
duplication of hardware through the mail. No
literature — you must call or write.

KEY TO ABBREVIATIONS

MO   sells by **Mail Order**

RS/O   sells through **Retail Store or Office**

DIST   sells through **Distributors**

ID   sells only through **Interior Designers or Architects**

● **See Product Displays Index on page 199 for more details.**

You'll get better service when contacting companies if you mention The Old-House Journal Catalog

---

F

Facemakers, Inc.
140 Fifth St.   Dept. OHJ
Savanna, IL 61074
(815) 273-3944
RS/O   MO
Creates original paintings done to customer
specifications. Specializes in period portraits that
are done from clients' photographs. Customer
can have portrait done in almost any style and in
the appropriate costume of the period selected.
Paintings done in oils on stretched canvas. Prices
start at $1500. Also interior and exterior
restoration design service. Send $5.00 for
brochure.

Faire Harbour Ltd.
44 Captain Peirce Rd.   Dept. OHJ
Scituate, MA 02066
(617) 545-2465
RS/O   MO
Distributors of Aladdin kerosene mantle lamps
and manufacturers of several old-style kerosene
table and bracket lamps. These well-made brass
and brass-finish lamps with glass shades and
chimneys give a steady light equal to a 75 watt
bulb. Optional electric converter. Replacement
parts and supplies. Illustrated catalog and price
list — $2 by 1st class mail — refundable.
Minimum purchase, $5.

Faneuil Furniture Hardware
94-100 Peterborough St.   Dept. OHJ
Boston, MA 02215
(617) 262-7516
MO   RS/O
They stock extensive selections of pulls, handles,
knobs, ornaments, casters, grilles and allied items
for all periods of furniture design. A 138-page
catalog is available for $2.00.

The Farm Forge
6945 Fishburg Rd.   Dept. OHJ
Dayton, OH 45424
(513) 233-6751
MO   RS/O
Mr. Wood offers a complete selection of
reproduction and restoration hardware, lighting,
and architectural iron work, in traditional or
contemporary styles. Hand-Forged and custom
items. Catalog, $1.

Faucher, Evariste—Woodworker
300 Hunt Road   Dept. OHJ
Athens, GA 30606
(404) 548-6834
MO   RS/O
Master joiner, having worked in the industry for
over forty years. Usually restricts himself to
making items that others cannot or are not
generally willing to undertake. Will answer all
inquiries.

Feather River Wood and Glass Co.
PO Box 444, 1632 Midway   Dept. OHJ
Durham, CA 95938
(916) 895-0752
Doors with glass panels — singles, transoms,
sidelights, entryways. Wood panels with custom
mouldings, mantels, wainscottings. Illustrated
catalog, $4.

• Felber, Inc.
110 Ardmore Ave., Box 551   Dept. OHJ
Ardmore, PA 19003
(215) 642-4710
MO   RS/O
Felber, Inc. maintains a collection of 7,000 plus original antique ornamental castings. Ceiling medallions, cornices, cartouches, and niche shells are stocked. Their custom department can create new or restore period plaster mouldings and ornaments. Most castings will be reinforced with glass fibers and making them stronger and lighter than traditional ornamental plaster while maintaining the same intricate detail. Catalogue available, $2.00.

Fenton Art Glass Company
Caroline Ave.   Dept. OHJ
Williamstown, WV 26187
(304) 375-6122
RS/O   MO   DIST
Early American, handmade glassware and lamps, many of which are handpainted and signed by the artist. Also baskets, bells, vases, and figurines. Send $5. for complete 84 page color catalog and price guide.

FerGene Studio
4320 Washington Street   Dept. OHJ
Gary, IN 46408
(219) 884-1119
MO
Reproduction turn-of-century fireplace tiles. Face tiles 6 x 6. Hearth tile 6 x6, 6 x 3, 6 x 1-1/2 with some special sizes on request. Can color tiles, using modern commercial glazes, to complement other tiles, wallpaper or fabric. Patterns include: vine pattern, morning glory, scrolls, and medieval lady and knight. Flyer $1 (large self-addressed, stamped envelope, please).

Ferris, Robert Donald, Architect, Inc.
3776 Front St.   Dept. OHJ
San Diego, CA 92103
(714) 297-4659
RS/O
Architectural design services for interior and exterior restoration and rehabilitation of all types of buildings, including public buildings, commercial and residential. All types of construction, including adobe; adaptive re-use studies, feasibility reports and planning. Southern California and Hawaii. No literature.

Fichet Lock Co.
4 Osage Drive   Dept. OHJ
Huntington Station, NY 11746
(516) 673-1818
MO   DIST
Fichet is renowned for high security locks since 1825. High-security locking devices that can be adapted to old buildings/doors. Free literature.

Fine Woodworking Co.
4907 Quebec Street   Dept. OHJ-81
College Park, MD 20740
(301) 474-2456
RS/O
Small, quality-conscious company specializing in old-house restoration, custom cabinetwork, and custom millwork. Washington, D.C. metropolitan area. No literature.

• Finish Feeder Company
P.O. Box 60   Dept. J
Boyds, MD 20841
(301) 972-1474
RS/O   MO   DIST
A furniture polish based on an 18th century cabinetmakers' formula. For furniture, wood panelling and floors. Free literature.

Finishing Products
4611 Macklind Ave.   Dept. OHJ
St. Louis, MO 63109
(314) 481-0700
MO   RS/O
A full range of wood finishing materials including colored furniture lacquers, aniline dyes, bronzing powders, and Watco Danish Oils. Also, fibre replacement seats, brass reproduction hardware, Bendix decorative wood carvings, caning supplies, etc. Illustrated catalog, $2.

Finishing Touch
5636 College Avenue   Dept. OHJ
Oakland, CA 94618
(415) 652-4908
MO   RS/O
Manufacture and sales of genuine leather seats, available in six embossed designs, three shapes, six sizes and four colors. Sheet caning supplies and instructions available. Also, ''Howard's Restor-A- Finish'', for eliminating heat rings, water marks, and scratches in naturally finished wood. Catalog, $.50.

Finnaren & Haley, Inc.
2320 Haverford Road   Dept. OHJ
Ardmore, PA 19003
(215) 649-5000
RS/O   DIST
Interior and exterior paints in 30 colors of historic Philadelphia, 10 of which were authenticated through the cooperation of the National Park Service as used in historic Philadelphia buildings. F&H Color Card available upon request; send $.40 in stamps.

Fireplace Mantel Shop, Inc.
4217 Howard Ave.   Dept. OHJ
Kensington, MD 20895
(301) 942-7946
RS/O   MO
Architectural woodwork, specializing in decorative wood mantels, entrance sets, and cornices/mouldings. Also custom millwork, panels, doors. 22-page ''Wood Mouldings & Millwork'' catalog, $3.50.

Fischer & Jirouch Co.
4821 Superior Avenue   Dept. OHJ
Cleveland, OH 44103
(216) 361-3840
MO   RS/O
Ornaments of fiber-reinforced plaster. They also do restoration work, and can reproduce existing pieces if a good example is supplied. (For example, a foot of moulding in very good condition is needed to make a mould.) Complete catalog of 1500 items with prices and terms is $25.00. Photo-copies of single elements sent free on specific request.

Flaharty, David — Sculptor
79 Magazine Rd., R.D. 1   Dept. OHJ
Green Lane, PA 18054
(215) 234-8242
RS/O   MO
Specializes in the reproduction and restoration of architectural details and ornaments, especially in plaster and fiberglass. Among his clients are the State Department, the White House, the U.S. Capitol, Georgetown University, Metropolitan Museum of Art. No literature. Photos of work supplied for serious inquiries.

Flexi-Wall Systems
P.O. Box 88   Dept. OHJ
Liberty, SC 29657
(803) 855-0500
MO
They offer a patented, gypsum-impregnated flexible wallcovering, designed for problem wall surfaces (especially masonry). They have passed the rigid fire and toxicity tests required for use in New York City. An ideal finish for the thermal mass walls in the field of passive solar energy. ''Scotland Weave'' decorative finish. Complete test data, catalog information, and prices are available.

Floorcloths Incorporated
P.O. Box 812   Dept. OHJ
Severna Park, MD 21146
(301) 544-0858
RS/O   MO
Reproductions of 18th and 19th century painted canvas floorcoverings. Patterns are documented or adapted from original sources. Finest hand-painting and stencilling techniques. Their trained designers also work from designs supplied by the client. Prices start at $10.00 per square foot. Design portfolios available at $2.00 to cover postage and handling.

Florida Victoriani Architectural Antiques
901 W. Hwy. 46   Dept. OHJ
Sanford, FL 32771
(305) 321-5767
RS/O
Architectural antiques. Assorted stained, bevelled, leaded glass doors & windows; porch and stair railings, newel posts, columns, and capitals, mantels, backbars, pedestal sinks and tubs. Recycled building and plumbing materials. Can also call (904) 228-3404. Brochure available with SASE.

Flue Works, Inc.
86 Warren St.   Dept. OHJ
Columbus, OH 43215
(614) 291-6918
MO
A small construction company specializing in the building of Rumford fireplaces, and relining chimneys in old and historic homes. Also, a method of converting Victorian coal or gas fireplaces to woodburning without having to tear the chimney apart. Free brochure.

• Focal Point, Inc.
2005 Marietta Rd., N.W.   Dept. OHC4
Atlanta, GA 30318
(404) 351-0820
MO   DIST
Manufactures a handsome line of architecturally accurate ceiling medallions, cornice mouldings, niche caps, mantels, overdoor pieces, and more. Made of Endure-All™, a high-quality polymer, the product is resilient and lightweight. Factory-primed to receive paint or stain and is indistinguishable from wood or plaster. Easy to install. Available in 1983 is the American 19th Century Collection. Color catalog, $3.00.

Follansbee Steel
State St.   Dept. OHJ
Follansbee, WV 26037
(800) 624-6906
DIST
Manufactures terne roofing and terne-coated stainless for standing-seam metal roofs. One of the oldest types of metal roofing, terne is used on many historic buildings such as Monticello and the Smithsonian Institution. It's a a premium-quality long-lasting material. Free brochures: ''Terne Roofing'' and ''Terne-Coated-Stainless Roofing.''

Form and Texture — Architectural Ornamentation
12 So. Albion St.   Dept. OHJ
Denver, CO 80222
(303) 388-1324
RS/O
Restoration of ornamental plasterwork, interior and exterior. Also original designs, all periods. Sculptor and designer, Leo Middleman works primarily in Colorado, but will travel for larger projects. Experience in many well-received projects, residential and public buildings. Please write for references. No catalog. Custom work only.

Fourth Avenue Stove & Appliance Corp.
59 Fourth Ave.   Dept. OHJ
Brooklyn, NY 11217
(212) 622-0050
MO   RS/O
Coal and wood-burning stoves, including Franklin and pot-belly; parts for old stoves. Also sell ranges and heaters; parts for ranges and heaters, gas and electric. No literature; primarily a walk-in store, but mail orders are possible.

Fox Maple Tools
Box 160, The Snowville Road   Dept. OHJ
West Brownfield, ME 04010
(207) 935-3720
MO   RS/O
A source for an extensive variety of tools for timber framing and general woodworking. Their straight-forward catalog shows high quality tools useful to the owner-builder and craftsman. Also, Fox Maple Post & Beam builds traditionally framed houses and barns. Free Fox Maple Catalogs: Tools, Post & Beam, and Ashley Iles Tools Catalog. All catalogs are free.

Franklin Art Glass Studios
222 E. Sycamore St.   Dept. OHJ
Columbus, OH 43206
MO   RS/O
Stocks over 500 types of stained glass for restoration work. Samples of each available for $10. Also, lamp bases and parts, and stained glass tools. Please write with a specific inquiry. Free price list.

Frenzel Specialty Moulding Co.
4911 Ringer Rd.   Dept. OHJ
St. Louis, MO 63129
(314) 892-3292
MO
Any available moulding can be reproduced at a reasonable price. For an estimate, send a copy of existing moulding on piece of cardboard.

Friend, The
PO Box 421, Main St.   Dept. OHJ
Wiscasset, ME 04578
(207) 882-7806
MO   DIST   RS/O
Handmade tinware, antique finished, reproductions of old designs. Sconces, wall plaques, Christmas ornaments, and weather vanes. Catalog, $1.

Frog Tool Co., Ltd.
700 W. Jackson Blvd.   Dept. HJ1
Chicago, IL 60606
(312) 648-1270
MO   RS/O
An extensive collection of traditional and old-fashioned woodworking tools, including imported tools. Adzes, froes, broad axes, Myford lathes, wood moulding planes, wood finishing materials and wood carving chisels. Books, furniture plans, and many other unusual items. Catalog $2.50 for 3 year subscription refundable with purchase. Mail order catalog available — $2.50.

● **Fuller O'Brien Paints**
P.O. Box 864   Dept. OHJ
Brunswick, GA 31520
(912) 265-7650
DIST
Has a handsome collection of Early American and Traditional colors for both interior and exterior use. Free color chips include "Heritage" Color Collection, Whisper Whites and their Decorating Guide which has 136 different colors to choose from. The new palette of "Cape May" colors is $1.50.

● **Furniture Revival**
PO Box 994   Dept. OH3
Corvallis, OR 97339
(503) 754-6323
RS/O   MO   DIST
Wholesale/retail sales of furniture restoration specialities: solid brass; ice box and Hoosier cabinet hardware; roll top desk locks and replacement tambours; swivel mirror hinges; leather, wood, and fiber chair seats; chair cane; curved china-cabinet glass; trunk hardware; porcelain and brass castors, and wood replacement pieces. Catalog, $2.

Furniture Traditions, Inc.
PO Box 5067   Dept. HJ1
Hickory, NC 28603
(704) 324-0611
MO
Early American and traditional furniture. Finely crafted furniture collections ranging from country to formal English, French and American. 32-page catalog, $3.

Fypon, Inc.
Box 365, 22 W. Penna. Ave.   Dept. OHJ
Stewartstown, PA 17363
(717) 993-2593
DIST
High density polyurethane millwork that can be nailed, drilled, puttied, painted, and handled with regular carpenter tools. Four lines of entrance features, mouldings, specialty millwork, window features, and most recently, copper-finished bay window roofs. Designs are suitable for Colonial and Victorian style architecture. Free brochures upon request.

KEY TO ABBREVIATIONS

MO   sells by Mail Order
RS/O   sells through Retail Store or Office
DIST   sells through Distributors
ID   sells only through Interior Designers or Architects

● See Product Displays Index on page 199 for more details.

G

● **Gage, Wm. E., Designer of Homes**
7232 Boone Ave., N.   Dept. OHJ
Brooklyn Park, MN 55428
(612) 533-5026
MO   RS/O
Victorian, Tudor, or Colonial homes with conveniences necessary for today's living. Modern, energy efficient construction methods — plus the grace and charm of another era. Details of 100 homes, $10.

Gallier House Museum
1118-32 Royal Street   Dept. OHJ
New Orleans, LA 70116
(504) 523-6722
RS/O
Films on ornamental plasterwork, cast iron work, and marbling & graining are available for rental. Reproduction glass shades for 19th-century gasoliers. Please call for more information.

Gargoyles — New York
221 21st. Street   Dept. OHJ
Brooklyn, NY 11232
(212) 499-7494
MO   DIST
Fine reproductions of mirrors, architectural detail, gargoyles, and other objects. Many styles represented. Composition hydrastone is hand-finished in simulation of appropriate material, (porcelain — walnut — bronze-stone — etc.) Complete illustrated catalog is $2.

Gargoyles, Ltd.
512 South Third Street   Dept. OHJ
Philadelphia, PA 19147
(215) 629-1700
RS/O   MO
Architectural antique & reproductions, ironwork, fretwork, ceiling fans, tin ceilings, bars & backbars, leaded glass, mantels, Victorian wall units, complete store interiors, chandeliers, brackets, and anything they can find. Your best bet will be a visit to their warehouse/showroom, but please call & make an appointment if you come from out of town. Weekend hours by special appt.

Garrett Wade Company
161 Avenue of the Americas   Dept. OHJ
New York, NY 10013
(212) 807-1155
RS/O   MO
A comprehensive selection of quality hand woodworking and carving tools, many imported from Western Europe and Japan. Eight different wood-working benches and a complete line of Behlen finishing supplies, including stains, oils, waxes, and paint removers. Power tools include English lathes and INCA Swiss circular saws, bandsaws, jointer/planers. Extensive book list on working with wood. Illustrated catalog with price list, $3.

Gaston Wood Finishes, Inc.
3630 E. 10th St., PO Box 1246   Dept. OHJ
Bloomington, IN 47402
(812) 339-9111
MO
An excellent selection of traditional wood finishing supplies, reproduction furniture hardware, and veneer. Catalog $1.75.

Gates Moore
2 River Road, Silvermine   Dept. OHJ
Norwalk, CT 06850
(203) 847-3231
RS/O MO
Handmade reproductions of early American
lighting fixtures in a variety of finishes: old paint
effect, distressed tin, pewter, flat black. Will
make anything from drawings or sketch with
complete dimensions. Illustrated 29 pg. catalog
with price list — $2.

Gaudio Custom Furniture
21 Harrison Ave.   Dept. OHJ
Rockville Centre, NY 11570
(516) 766-1237
RS/O
Specializing in creations constructed with fine
veneer inlays of floral marquetry and geometric
parquetry. Also: antique reproduction and
restoration, bronze ormolu mounts, architectural
paneling. No literature.

Gazebo and Porchworks
3901 N. Meridian   Dept. OHJ
Puyallup, WA 98371
(206) 848-0502
MO RS/O
A small family business offering a wide selection
of gazebo, porch, and arbor kits. Kits have been
completely pre-assembled and numbered for
quick assembly. Designed to the customer's
specifications. Components can be purchased
separately along with a plan/instruction book.
Wide selection of turnings, corner brackets,
corbels, porch swings. Catalog, $2.

Gem Monogram & Cut Glass Corp.
623 Broadway   Dept. OHJ
New York, NY 10012
(212) 674-8962
MO RS/O
Chandeliers, antique & reproduction. Also crystal
prisms and pendants. No literature, specify your
requirements.

George Studios
45-04 97th Place   Dept. OHJ
Corona, NY 11368
(212) 271-2506
RS/O
Will restore wall murals or create one for you.
Will also restore or create hand-painted
decorations on porcelain, furniture, etc. Other
restorations skills — gold leafing, marblizing, and
faux finishes. No literature.

Gerlachs of Lecha
PO Box 213   Dept. OHJ
Emmaus, PA 18049
(215) 965-9181
MO RS/O
A large selection of Germanic traditional wooden,
wax, and blown-glass Christmas ornaments,
clip-metal candleholders, and Victorian
decorations. Reproduction Penn. German folk art
wares in tin, iron, slip-trailed and sgraffito
redware pottery, stoneware, etc. Fall-Winter or
Spring-Summer catalog, $1.25 each.

Douglas Gest Restorations
R.R. No. 2   Dept. OHJ
Randolph, VT 05060
(802) 728-9286
RS/O
Complete restoration services, specializing in
interior restoration — fine woodworking and
cabinetmaking. From time to time they have
antique houses available for purchase and
reconstruction on clients property. They also offer
a "locating service" for those interested in
acquiring an antique house suitable for
reconstruction on their property. No literature.

Giannetti Studios
3806 38th Street   Dept. OHJ
Brentwood, MD 20722
(301) 927-0033
RS/O MO DIST
Primarily engaged in the design, manufacture
and installation of ornamental plaster in the
Washington, DC metropolitan area. Some
restoration/preservation services. Brochure $3.00
(refundable on purchase).

Gibbons, John — Cabinetmaker
2070 Helena St.   Dept. OHJ
Madison, WI 53704
(608) 241-5364
RS/O MO
Cabinetmaker specializing in doors and windows.
Late Victorian and early 20th century panel doors
in 1-3/4-inch red oak with safety glass. Jambs
available. Sash in cherry, pine, or mahogany;
jambs and storm sash also. Custom sash and
door work for restorations welcomed. Free quotes
given from drawings or photos. Literature and
price list $1.00.

Gibbs, James W. — Landscape Architect
340 E. 93rd St., No.14C   Dept. OHJ
New York, NY 10028
(212) 722-7508
MO RS/O
Restoration design and financial packaging for
historic properties. Expertise in syndications,
certifications, historical research, and period
design architecture and gardens. All types of
urban garden design. Lecturers on gardening,
rehabilitation, community organizing, and fund
raising. Specialize in work with non-profits,
homeowners, and developers. Experience in
midwest and eastern/southern seaboards.
References price list, and brochure free.

Gifford, D.K.
230 Windshadow Ct.   Dept. OHJ
Roswell, GA 30075
(404) 993-3281
MO RS/O
Architectural paintings, commissioned works by a
painter who has had numerous shows all over
the East. Average price is $4,000. Paintings are
large panels done in Gifford's "Stereo-Line
Realism". Also limited-edition prints, $75.00, of
depots, Victorian houses, gazebos, etc. Free
brochure.

Giles & Kendall, Inc.
P.O. Box 188   Dept. OHJ
Huntsville, AL 35804
(205) 776-2979
DIST
4 x 8 ft. aromatic cedar closet panels to line
existing closets or for construction of free-
standing closets, entry hall and under-the-stair
closets. Cedar closet plans booklet & sample,
$.50.

Gill Imports
P.O. Box 73   Dept. OHJ
Ridgefield, CT 06877
(203) 438-7409
MO
Hand-made crewel fabric for upholstery, curtains,
bedspreads. Made in India of 100% wool
embroidery on natural cotton. From $13/yd. Send
$1 for swatch and catalog.

Gillinder Brothers, Inc.
Box 1007   Dept. OHJ
Port Jervis, NY 12771
(914) 856-5375
DIST
Manufacturers of glass parts for the lamp and
lighting industry. Products include cased glass
shades, clear & colored, gas shades, electric
shades, lamp bodies...Thousands of molds date
back to the 1800's. Sales are wholesale only. Their
catalog can be seen at many retail lighting fixture
stores. No literature available to retail customers.

Gingerbread House
PO Box 58355   Dept. OHJ
Raleigh, NC 27658
(919) 556-1401
MO RS/O
Victorian gingerbread: Brackets, valances,
balusters, headers, grilles, and a variety of other
fretwork hand-cut from sugar pine. Custom
designs and reproductions also offered. Catalog,
$1.

Gladding, McBean & Co.
PO Box 97   Dept. OHJ
Lincoln, CA 95648
(916) 645-3341
DIST
Produces architectural terra cotta: trim and all
decorative pieces for restorations. This company,
established in 1875, has supplied the terra cotta
for many extensive projects, such as the Hotel
Utah in Salt Lake City and the Prospect Park Boat
House in Brooklyn. Also, a full line of durable
clay roofing tiles, distributed nationally.
Company works through architects and other
preservation professionals only. Write or phone
for more information. Free roofing tile brochure.

**Glass & Aluminum Construction Services,
Inc.**
PO Box 7   Dept. OHJ
Marlow, NH 03456
(603) 835-2918
RS/O
A designer, fabricator, and installer of wood,
glass and aluminum windows, greenhouse, and
entry way systems. Specialize in refurbishing and
renovating older and historic structures — both
commercial and residential. Their primary market
is New England; no formal literature is available.

Glassmasters Guild
621 Avenue of the Americas   Dept. OHJ
New York, NY 10011
(212) 924-2868
RS/O MO
A stained glass craft center, with a gallery of
blown and leaded glass, which carries an
extensive selection of domestic and imported
glass, tools, supplies and books for hobbyist and
professional. Demonstrations held every Saturday
beginning at 11:00 A.M. Catalog costs $1.00,
which can be applied to any subsequent order of
$5.00 or more.

Glen - Gery Corporation
Draw S, Route 61   Dept. OHJ
Shoemakersville, PA 19555
(215) 562-3076
DIST
Manufacturers of a large array of molded colonial
brick that looks just like old brick. Free brochure
— "1776 Face Brick."

Goddard & Sons
P.O. Box 808   Dept. OHJ
Manitowoc, WI 54220
(414) 682-6153
DIST MO
Manufactures a collection of fine care products
for silver, jewelry, metal, fabric, and furniture
articles. An illustrated brochure is available at no
charge. Toll free (800) 558-7621.

Goldblatt Tool Co.
511 Osage   Dept. OHJ
Kansas City, KS 66110
(913) 621-3010
MO DIST
Well-established company manufactures a full line of trowel trades tools, including power trowelers and all accessories. Great for anyone who is getting into serious masonry or plastering work. Their "glitter gun" can be used for sand painting. Extensive updated catalog is free.

● **Golden Age Glassworks**
RD 3, Bellvale Rd.   Dept. OHJ
Warwick, NY 10990
(914) 986-1487
RS/O MO
Design and manufacture leaded and stained glass windows, lampshades, architectural pieces, skylights, room dividers, etc. Also museum quality Victorian (and other styles) reproductions and restorations. Extensive church and residential experience — in business over 10 years. Will work from your design or help you to create one. Free information; slides showing examples of work, $2/set.

Gold Leaf & Metallic Powders, Inc.
2 Barclay St.   Dept. OHJ
New York, NY 10007
(212) 267-4900
MO RS/O
Distributes a complete line of Genuine and Imitation Gold Leaf and other Leaf products such as 22K XX Deep Gold, Patent Gold, Lemon Gold, White Gold, Composition Gold Leaf, Aluminum Leaf, Copper Leaf, Variegated Leaf. Manufactures metallic pigments in bronze, copper and aluminum with a wide range of shades available in mesh sizes suitable for many applications. Product list and color card available — free.

● **Good Directions**
24 Ardmore Rd.   Dept. H
Stamford, CT 06902
(203) 348-1836
MO
All copper and solid brass weather vanes in 18 different styles. Also, sundials. Send $.50 for brochure.

● **Good Impressions Rubber Stamps**
1122 Avery Street   Dept. H
Parkersburg, WV 26101
(304) 422-1147
MO
Manufactures a collection of Victorian style rubber stamps and stamp pads. Hundreds of decorative word and picture stamps are offered through illustrated catalogue, $1.00. Prices range from $1.95 to $10.00, depending on size of stamp. They also offer period style advertising.

Good Stenciling
Box 387   Dept. OHJ
Dublin, NH 03444
(603) 563-8021
MO RS/O
Documented and original designs by Nancy Good Cayford are applied to canvas floor cloths — free hand and stenciled. Heavy canvas and oil base paints are used for durability. Finished with varnish for a long lasting, easy to clean carpet. Any color — any size available. Custom orders taken. Prices start at $4. sq./ft. Color catalog $2.

Gorsuch Foundry
120 E. Market St.   Dept. OHJ
Jeffersonville, IN 47130
(812) 283-3585
DIST ID
Authentic exterior cast iron & cast bronze ornament. Castings can be made from photograph, sample or artist rendering. Foundry will arrange for a local ironworks to install custom castings. No literature.

Gould-Mesereau Co., Inc.
21-16 44th Road   Dept. OHJ
Long Island City, NY 11101
(212) 361-8120
DIST
Manufactures a complete line of metal and real wood drapeware products, both utility and decorative in extensive variety of styles and finishes to complement every decor. "Sierra", Gould's all wood drapeware/ decorative products line, is available in traverse, pole sets and component parts. All accessories & installation aids. Consumer brochures for Sierra line available; catalogs available to the trade ONLY — both free.

Graham's Lighting Fixtures
550 So. Cooper   Dept. OHJ
Memphis, TN 38104
(901) 274-6780
MO RS/O DIST
A collection of antique lighting fixtures. They also produce reproductions and adaptations of 18th century and Victorian fixtures. Specific inquiries invited; no literature.

Grammar of Ornament
2626 Curtis Street   Dept. OHJ
Denver, CO 80205
(303) 295-2431
RS/O ID
Stencilers and interior ornamentists able to restore or re-create painted Victorian and other period interiors. In addition, they offer woodgraining and marbleizing services. No literature.

Grandpa Snazzy's Hardware
1832 S. Broadway   Dept. OHJ
Denver, CO 80210
(303) 935-3269
RS/O MO
An antique store which stocks reproduction hardware from 72 companies as well as antique hardware. They can match patterns of hinges, doorknobs, sash lifts, etc. Transom hardware and hard-to-find parts. Can also match furniture hardware. Mail order welcome. Send need. Catalogue in process.

Grant Hardware Company Div. of Grant Industries, Inc.
20 High St.   Dept. OHJ
West Nyack, NY 10994
(914) 358-4400
DIST
Manufactures a line of sliding and folding door hardware, including roller/sheaves suitable for replacements on old sliding doors. Condensed catalog available for $.50.

● **Great American Salvage**
3 Main Street   Dept. OHJ
Montpelier, VT 05602
(802) 223-7711
MO RS/O
Two showrooms comprising 32,000 sq. ft. of antique architectural components and artifacts. Specializing in stained, bevelled, and leaded glass. A vast selection of doors, columns, mantels, iron & stone work, pedestal sinks, and lighting fixtures. Also display cabinets, bars and back bars, theatre components, and numerous restoration materials. Other showroom: 34 Cooper Sq., NY, NY 10003. (212) 505-0070. Free flyer.

Great Northern Woodworks, Inc.
199 Church Street   Dept. OHJ
Burlington, VT 05401
(802) 862-1463
RS/O
This full service contracting firm specializes in quality restoration of 18th and 19th century buildings, both residential and commercial. Also available for home improvement, custom design/build, new construction additions, commercial establishment design and construction, custom case work: display and counters. All work includes one year free warranty inspection and a client list is available for references.

Greenfield Village and Henry Ford Museum
Box 1970   Dept. OHJ
Dearborn, MI 48121
(313) 271-1620
RS/O MO
Handsome reproductions of clocks, furniture, lamps, hooked rugs, wallpaper, fabrics and accessories from Greenfield Village and the Henry Ford Museum. Full line of early American paint colors. The furniture, chiefly Queen Anne, comes in kit form at considerable savings. Catalog $2.50, postpaid.

Greenhalgh & Sons
Farwell Road   Dept. OHJ
Tyngsborough, MA 01879
(617) 649-7887
RS/O
Interior and exterior painting, wallpapering, & stenciling. Specialists in the restoration of older homes. Stencils are traditional American patterns or are created to fit historical era of home. Interior design consulting available. Serving New England & Mass. In NH (603) 880-7887.

Greenland Studio, Inc., The
147 W. 22nd St.   Dept. OHJ
New York, NY 10011
(212) 255-2551
RS/O
Stained glass repaired and manufactured. Expert craftsmanship for new work and restoration of all kinds of leaded glass. Tiffany windows and lampshades, painted, etched, bevelled, carved, sandblasted. Museum-quality restoration practices. Conservator for several museum collections, including Metropolitan Museum of Art, the Cloisters, Church of St. Ann and the Holy Trinity, Brooklyn, NY. No literature.

Greensboro Art Foundry & Machine Co.
1201 Park Terrace   Dept. OHJ
Greensboro, NC 27403
(919) 299-0106
MO RS/O
Provides precise duplication services in brass, bronze, and iron for architectural hardware, components and sculpture. Shop uses sand and investment casting techniques. In house pattern shop, machine and welding facilities. Information sheets available.

Greg Monk Stained Glass
98-027 Hekaha St., Bldg. 3   Dept. OHJ
Aiea, HI 96701
(808) 488-9538
RS/O   MO
Stained glass windows designed and built by
Greg Monk, who has over ten years of experience
and has handled commissions from Guam to
New York. He can also assist in contacting other
glass artists in Hawaii. Custom-designed
windows; classes; supplies. No literature; please
write.

● **Greg's Antique Lighting**
12005 Wilshire Blvd.   Dept. OHJ
Los Angeles, CA 90025
(213) 478-5475
RS/O
Original antique lighting fixtures, 1850-1930.
Stock includes floor and table lamps, wall
sconces, and chandeliers. Specializes in
high-quality gas fixtures from the Victorian
period. Primarily supplying the Los Angeles area.
No literature.

Grilk Interiors
2200 E. 11th St.   Dept. OHJ
Davenport, IA 52803
(319) 323-2735
RS/O
Custom interior design studio. Historically correct
interiors or adaptive renovation. Dealers in
reproduction wallpaper, furniture, lighting,
carpets, Oriental rugs and all related items.
Period designs in window treatments custom
made. Drapery and upholstery fabrics. Complete
workroom services. Consultation available. Staff
of professional ASID Designers. Write for free
brochure.

**Guardian National House Inspection and
Warranty Corp.**
PO Box 115   Dept. OHJ
Orleans, MA 02653
(617) 255-6609
RS/O   DIST
Headquarters for the company. Services are
currently offered in twenty-two states. Company
provides in-depth engineering surveys of all
structural and mechanical components of an old
or newer house. A highly accepted guarantee is
available to back up their survey. Also, a
comprehensive program to train qualified
representatives is available. Free introductory
brochure.

● **Guerin, P.E. Inc.**
23 Jane Street   Dept. BD-1
New York, NY 10014
(212) 243-5270
RS/O   MO
Fabricators and importers of fine traditional brass
decorative hardware since 1857. Some Early
American and English designs, but the emphasis
is on period French hardware. Among the
splendid bathroom fittings, there are several
suitable for 19th and turn-of-the-century houses.
Over 50,000 models available for custom
manufacture. Specialists in careful reproduction
from owner's antique examples. Prices are not
cheap. 64 pg. (16 in color) illustrated catalog and
price list — $5.

Guild, The
2749 E. Anaheim St.   Dept. OHJ
Long Beach, CA 90804
(213) 434-1255
MO   RS/O
Roll top desk lock and key hole cover. Free
brochure upon request.

Gurian's
276 Fifth Ave.   Dept. OHJ
New York, NY 10001
(212) 689-9696
MO   RS/O
Hand-embroidered crewel fabric from India.
Multi-color wool on natural cotton. Also
ready-made bedspreads and table covers. Send
$1. for swatch and catalog.

● **Guthrie Hill Forge, Ltd.**
1233 W. Strasburg Rd.   Dept. OHJ
West Chester, PA 19380
(215) 436-6364
MO   RS/O
Hand forged reproductions of period hardware
from late 17th through 19th centuries. Two
grades and price ranges satisfy strict restoration
or new construction interests. Interior, exterior,
shutter and cabinet hardware, custom and in
stock. Retail and wholesale line of iron kitchen
wares and household goods. 24-page catalog of
hardware & household goods, $2., refund with
purchase.

KEY TO ABBREVIATIONS

MO sells by Mail Order

RS/O sells through Retail Store or Office

DIST sells through Distributors

ID sells only through Interior Designers or Architects

● See Product Displays Index on page 199 for more details.

You'll get better service when contacting companies if you mention The Old-House Journal Catalog

---

H

H & M Stair Builders, Inc.
4217 Howard Ave.   Dept. OHJ
Kensington, MD 20895
(301) 942-7946
MO   RS/O
Large selection of wood staircases and staircase
parts. Free brochure. Call for prices.

**H & R Johnson Tile Ltd./ Highgate Tile
Works**
Tunstall   Dept. OHJ
Stoke-on-Trent, Engl, ST64JX
DIST   MO
Founded prior to the 1840's, this company went
on to become the largest ceramic tile maker in
Victorian England. They now offer the Gladstone
Series, a collection of six Victorian reproduction
designs. For large restoration projects, the
company will consider custom duplication. Also,
traditional to mid-and late- Victorian style
encaustic floor tiles. Literature available.

● **Haas Wood & Ivory Works**
64 Clementina St.   Dept. OHJ
San Francisco, CA 94105
(415) 421-8273
RS/O   MO
They manufacture hand-turned or semi-automatic
ornamentation for both new construction and
restoration projects. Items include newels,
brackets, arches for windows and doors, scrolls,
balusters, handrails, mouldings, columns,
capitals, caps and hoods, finials. Custom cabinet
shop builds a wide variety of hand-constructed
and finished pieces for home or business. They
work from your plans and specifications, in any
type or combination of woods. Write for
brochure.

● **Habersham Plantation Corp.**
PO Box 1209   Dept. JR
Toccoa, GA 30577
(404) 886-1476
DIST   MO
Manufacturers of 17th and 18th century Colonial
reproductions. Furniture is handcrafted from
pine, oak, and cherry in the country manner.
Each piece is signed and dated. Includes tables,
beds, chairs, side boards, and a painted wedding
chest. Sold through 200 dealers throughout the
U.S. Large catalog, called "The Habersham
Workbook," shows complete collection, $10.00.

Haines Complete Building Service
2747 N. Emerson Ave.   Dept. OHJ
Indianapolis, IN 46218
(317) 547-5531
RS/O
One of the oldest and largest masonry restoration
companies in Indiana, family owned and
operated since 1936. Specialties include building
cleaning; tuckpointing, waterproofing, flashings,
slate roofing, caulking. They also do some
painting and remodeling, serving the complete
state of Indiana. They will give free technical
advice, inspections, and estimates. "Protection of
Masonry Surfaces", $1.

● **Hallelujah Redwood Products**
PO Box 669   Dept. OHJ
Mendocino, CA 95460
(707) 937-4410
RS/O   MO
Many stock patterns of sawn wood ornaments,
Victorian Gingerbread trim & decorative parts for
the house & porch: Applique & mouldings, porch
brackets, porch railings, posts & pickets, corbels,
baseboards, multi- pane windows, & French
doors. Also, custom work. New illustrated
catalog with price list — $2.

Hammerworks
75 Webster St.   Dept. OHJ
Worcester, MA 01603
(617) 755-3434
MO
Specialist in Colonial reproductions. Hand-forged door latches, hinges, locks, keys, fireplace cooking equipment. Also, a complete line of handmade copper & brass lanterns, chandeliers, tin & copper sconces. Custom work available. Catalogs: Lantern & Chandeliers, $2; Sconce, $1; Ironware, $1; Hardware, $1.

Hand-Stenciled Interiors
590 King Street   Dept. OHJ
Hanover, MA 02339
(617) 878-7596
MO
Personal, specialized stencilling service with hundreds of unpublished patterns available and custom stencil designs. Pre-cut patterns individually suited to customer's needs are sent with complete instructions; or professional stenciller will come to your home/business to complete the work. For information, send $1.; no catalog.

● **Hank, Dennis V.**
4040 Newberry Rd., Suite 950   Dept. OHJ
Gainesville, FL 32607
(904) 377-0438
MO RS/O
A millshop specializing in stock and custom size windows in Ponderosa pine; other woods by request. Also, custom wood storms & screens, and a replacement kit for double-hung sash. Also, custom moldings. Literature, $2.50.

Hanks Architectural Antiques
311 Colorado   Dept. OHJ
Austin, TX 78701
(512) 478-2101
RS/O
Architectural antiques: Doors, entryways, fireplaces, bevelled, etched, and stained glass, ironwork, panelling and panelled rooms, flooring, and garden furnishings. European architectural items. No literature.

Hardwood Craftsman, Inc.
121 Schelter Road   Dept. OHJ
Prairie View, IL 60069
(312) 634-3050
MO
Furniture kits. Solid woods. Cherry, birch and oak. Easy to assemble. Instructions included. Free catalog.

Harris Manufacturing Company
P.O. Box 300   Dept. OHJ
Johnson City, TN 37601
(615) 928-3122
DIST
This 80 year old company makes hardwood flooring in 22 parquet and plank patterns — many of which are suitable for period houses. Available in red oak, white oak, yellow pine, walnut, angelique teak, and maple. Plank available V-joint or square joint. Illustrated catalog and technical notes, $1.00 each.

● **See Product Displays Index on page 199 for more details.**

Hart, Brian G./Architect
4375 West River Road   Dept. OHJ
Delta, BC, Canada V4K1R9
(604) 946-8302
RS/O
Architectural services in the area of restoration, conservation, rehabilitation and adaptive re-use of historic buildings. Inspection services, feasibility studies, and building code analysis for existing buildings. Design Services for compatible additions to older buildings and sympathetic infill buildings for historic areas. Complete urban design services, historical research and inventories for heritage conservation areas. Primary involvement on the West Coast. No literature.

Hartco
PO Drawer A   Dept. OHJ
Oneida, TN 37841
(615) 569-8526
DIST
Prefinished solid-oak parquet flooring. Available in 3 finishes. Easy installation. Company also sells all mouldings needed for finishing, and floor-care products. Free brochure.

Hartmann-Sanders Column Co.
4340 Bankers Circle   Dept. OHJ
Atlanta, GA 30360
(404) 449-1561
MO RS/O
Architectural columns of clear heart redwood, or clear poplar. Pilasters and square columns as well as round columns in the Greek orders. Composition capitals; fiberglass bases, caps, and plinths. Finest quality materials, construction, detail (entasis, fluting). Load-bearing. Free color catalog.

Hasbrouck, W.R., Architect Historic Resources
711 South Dearborn St.   Dept. OHJ
Chicago, IL 60605
(312) 922-7211
RS/O
Architectural firm specializing in historic restorations and adaptive reuse. They prepare feasibility studies, programming, and furnish complete architectural service; the firm has acted as a consultant on numerous National Register properties. No literature.

Hayes Equipment Corp.
Box 526, 150 New Britain Ave.   Dept. OHJ
Unionville, CT 06085
(800) 243-8550
MO DIST
Efficient wood-heating stoves of heavy gauge steel plate. Specialists in fireplace stoves, and they also make freestanding stoves. Better'n Ben's stoves have been manufactured for over 30 years. Wood-heating, energy saving accessories also available. Also stowaway folding trailers; garden carts. Booklet, "Making Sense Out of Wood Stoves", free.

● **Heads Up**
2980 Blue Star "B"   Dept. OHJ
Anaheim, CA 92806
(714) 630-5402
MO RS/O
A complete line of solid oak bathroom furniture and accessories, including medicine cabinets, vanity cabinets, and reproduction high-tank pull-chain toilet. Send $1 for full brochure, can buy direct from factory.

Hearth & Home Co.
Box 371   Dept. OHJ
Brielle, NJ 08730
(201) 223-3218
MO
Chimney collars for woodburning stoves in solid brass, nickel over solid brass, and solid copper. Deeply stamped with a design that will enhance your stove by covering the unsightly chimney connection. Specify 6 or 8 in. stovepipe. Free brochure.

● **Hearth Realities**
246 Daniel Ave., S.E.   Dept. OHJ
Atlanta, GA 30317
(404) 373-7493
MO
The only U.S. manufacturer we've found of cast-iron hanging coal basket grates. Available in rounded, squared, and tiled. Also a selection of antique metal frames, grates, hearths, summer screens, etc. Free information.

Hearth Shield
PO Box 127   Dept. OHJ
Mercer Island, WA 98040
(800) 526-5971
DIST RS/O
Hearth Shield mats are installed on either walls or floors to prevent heat and fire damage caused by open hearth fireplaces and stoves. These UL-listed boards are made from decorative, heavy-gauge textured steel laminated to fire-resistant insulation core. Mat allows installation of fire-standing fireplace or stove anywhere in the home without fire hazard. Phone for free literature.

Hearthstone Tile Studio
10 St. John Place   Dept. OHJ
Port Washington, NY 11050
(516) 944-6964
RS/O
Handmade ceramic wall, floor, and fireplace tiles; murals. Custom size, design, color and handmade glazes. Call or write for appointment. No literature.

● **Heating Research**
Acworth Road   Dept. OHJ
Acworth, NH 03601
(603) 835-6109
MO RS/O
Antique stoves, wood and coal models, mostly from Europe. Dealer inquiries welcomed. Catalog, $3.

Heckler Bros.
464 Steubenville Pike   Dept. OHJ
Pittsburgh, PA 15205
(412) 922-6811
MO RS/O
They have acquired the original patterns for, and will repair/supply parts for the following: Williamson, Economy, Boomer, Leader, and Berger coal furnaces; and for Columbia and Economy coal boilers. Also supply and stock parts for thousands of coal furnaces, coal boilers, coal heating and coal cookstoves. Firebrick and grates for most coal furnaces. Please call or write with your specific request.

Heirloom Enterprises
PO Box 146   Dept. OHJ
Dundas, MN 55019
(507) 645-9341
DIST
Manufacturers of authentic early 20th-century chandeliers. These UL listed chandeliers are made of solid brass and are available with a variety of shades and styles. Also manufacturing solid brass furniture hardware and solid oak furniture, including library-style coffee tables and end tables. Free literature.

Heirloom Rugs
28 Harlem Street   Dept. OHJ
Rumford, RI 02916
(401) 438-5672
MO   DIST
Over 500 hand-drawn hooked rug patterns (on burlap base). Sizes range from chairseats to room-size. Company does not sell hooking materials or accessories. Illustrated catalog shows 297 of the patterns — $1.50.

Henderson Black & Greene, Inc.
PO Box 589   Dept. OHJ
Troy, AL 36081
(205) 566-5000
DIST
Manufactures stock millwork items as follows: Columns, turned posts, spindles, balusters, sidelights, mantels, ironing board cabinets and Colonial entrance features. Literature available on all items — please specify.

Henderson Lighting
PO Box 585   Dept. OHJ
Southbury, CT 06488
(203) 264-3037
MO
Recreations and adaptations of early American lanterns in brass and copper. Most are electrical. A classic cornucopia for Victorian entranceways is also available. Catalog, $2., refundable with first order.

Hendricks Tile Mfg. Co., Inc.
P.O. Box 34406   Dept. OHJ
Richmond, VA 23234
(804) 275-8926
RS/O   MO
Concrete and steel-reinforced roofing tiles in a variety of styles. Some styles resemble Colonial round butt and hand-split shakes, but are fire-proof and long lasting. Tiles are custom made in colors and textures selected for each specific job. Frost-proof and fireproof, Hendricks Tiles have been used in the Williamsburg and Old Salem restorations. Free color and application brochures.

Heritage Design
PO Box 103   Dept. OHJ
Monticello, IA 52310
(319) 465-5374
MO   DIST   RS/O
Furniture kits including a reproduction 1876 platform swing rocker, fern stand, quilt rack, and Roycroft-style serving table. Also finished furniture. All items handmade in kiln dried walnut, cherry, maple or oak with caned or upholstered seats. Literature is free.

Heritage Home Designers
810 N. Fulton, Suite 200   Dept. OHJ
Wharton, TX 77488
(409) 532-4197
MO
Four catalogues of Victorian house plans, $4 - $5. Also will do custom Victorian replicas. Call for details, 9-5 Mon.-Fri.

Heritage Lanterns
70A Main Street   Dept. OHJ
Yarmouth, ME 04096
(207) 846-3911
RS/O   MO
Wide selection of hand-crafted reproduction lanterns for interior or exterior use. Available in brass, copper or pewter. 52-page catalog, $2.

Heritage Rugs
P.O. Box 404, Lahaska   Dept. OHJ
Bucks County, PA 18931
(215)794-7229
MO   RS/O
Heritage Rugs has preserved the old craft of weaving early American rag rugs on their antique looms. These all wool rugs are custom made in sizes up to 15' wide and 25' long. Just send the colors you would like included (by enclosing paint, fabric or wallpaper samples). Each rug is numbered and registered as a Heritage original. Brochure available for $.50.

Heritage Studios
Rt. 3, Box 497D   Dept. OHJ
Boone, NC 28607
(704) 963-4943
MO
Frame restoration kit and supplies; for replacing missing design segments by the mould/cast process. A course is offered for people to increase their expertise. Free product information sheet.

Herman, Frederick, R.A., Architect
420 West Bute Street   Dept. OHJ
Norfolk, VA 23510
(804) 625-6575
RS/O
Restoration architect and historic preservation planner/consultant. Dr. Frederick Herman is available for lectures. No literature; please write or call for more information.

Hess Repairs
200 Park Ave., So.   Dept. OHJ
New York, NY 10003
(212) 260-2255
RS/O   MO
All types of repairs on fine antiques. Specializes in silver, glass, crystal, porcelain. Supplies missing parts and restores old dresser sets. No literature.

Hexagram
2247 Rohnerville Rd.   Dept. OHJ
Fortuna, CA 95540
(707) 725-6223
RS/O   MO
Specializing in antique lighting fixtures since 1968. Large selection of brass reproduction desk lamps, sconces, and chandeliers, both gas and electric. They will completely restore, wire, and polish any lighting fixture. Also a big selection of antique glass shades. Free photographs; please call or write. A brochure upon request.

● **Hexter, S. M. Company**
2800 Superior Ave.   Dept. OHJ
Cleveland, OH 44114
(216) 696-0146
DIST
This company manufactures Greenfield Village fabrics and wallcoverings: Designs are taken from documentary material found at the Henry Ford Museum, Greenfield Village in Dearborn, MI. Several of their books — including "Greenfield Village" and "The Countryside Collection" — are widely available at wallcovering distributors around the country. No literature.

Hi-Art East
6 N. Rhodes Center N.W.   Dept. OHJ
Atlanta, GA 30309
(404) 876-4740
MO   RS/O
Hi-Art East is the East Coast representative for the W.F. Norman Sheet Metal Manufacturing Co., makers of Hi-Art steel ceilings. A ceiling catalog is available for $3.00.

● **Hill, Allen Charles AIA**
25 Englewood Road   Dept. OHJ
Winchester, MA 01890
(617) 729-0748
RS/O
Consulting firm offering services in preservation & architecture: Architectural services for conservation, restoration and adaptive use; Surveys, inventories and preservation planning; Historical & architectural analysis, bldg documentation, & historic structures reports; National Register nominations; Technical consulting Assistance with grant applications; Lectures & workshops. Services range from brief consultations to extended architectural & preservation projects. Brochure available; specific inquiries answered.

● **Hilltop Slate Co.**
Rt. 22A   Dept. OHJ
Middle Granville, NY 12849
(518) 642-2270
MO   DIST   RS/O
NY—VT region slate in all colors and sizes. Specializing in roofing slate for restoration and new construction. Shipment arranged. Also structural slate and flagging. Free color brochure.

Historic Boulevard Services
1520 West Jackson Blvd.   Dept. OHJ
Chicago, IL 60607
(312) 829-5562
RS/O   MO
Restoration services, including structural engineering consultation, and general contracting. Will travel, consult, and speak nationally. "Turn-Key" masterbuilding is our specialty. Also have re-issued book on Masonry, Carpentry, and Joinery methods c. 1899; $20 postpaid. No literature available.

Historic Charleston Reproductions
105 Broad Street   Dept. OHJ
Charleston, SC 29402
(803) 723-8292
MO   RS/O
The sale of these reproductions of 18th — early 19th century pieces from historic Charleston generates royalties to further the preservation work of Historic Charleston Foundation. Charleston-made furniture, imported English pieces; porcelains; documentary fabrics; brass accessories; lamps, hand-made mirrors. Silver, glass, pewter; period paints by Devoe. 80-page color catalog $8.50.

Historic Preservation Alternatives, Inc.
15 Sussex Street   Dept. OHJ
Newton, NJ 07860
(201) 383-1283
RS/O
A multidisciplinary firm of planners, architects and historians specializing in preservation planning, historical research, National Register nominations, historic site surveys, adaptive reuse and restoration projects, grant proposals, building inspections, historic district ordinances and site interpretation. Brochure describing services provided free of charge on request.

Historic Windows
Box 1172   Dept. OHJ
Harrisonburg, VA 22801
(703) 434-5855
MO
Custom made Early American indoor shutters. Full or half in 3/4'' solid hardwoods. An excellent insulator for drafty windows. Small birch sample 8 in. x 12 in. is available for $15. (refundable). Send $1. for brochure.

Historical Replications, Inc.
P.O. Box 31198   Dept. OHJ-83E
Jackson, MS 39206
(601) 981-8743
MO
House plans in Victorian, traditional, and farmhouse styles. Modern, open floor plans with detailed historical facade. Portfolio, $10.

History Store
418 N. Union Street   Dept. OHJ
Wilmington, DE 19805
(302) 654-1727
RS/O
The History Store sells old architectural elements, lights, hardware, etc. Has store stock and computer inventory. Will do installations in old houses in the Wilmington area. Also, restoration carpentry, historical research, and professional guides for groups interested in history. Free literature.

Hoboken Wood Floors Corp.
100 Willow St., PO Box 510   Dept. OHJ
E. Rutherford, NJ 07073
(201) 933-9700
DIST
Manufacturers and wholesalers of hardwood floors in a variety of styles including random width plank, custom designed parquet, strip hardwood flooring, and vinyl- bonded wood veneers. Can also phone (212) 564-6818. A full-color 32 page brochure, $5.00.

Hobt, Murrel Dee, Architect
P.O. Box 322   Dept. OHJ
Williamsburg, VA 23185
(804) 220-0767
RS/O
Architectural services in the areas of historic restoration, conservation, rehabilitation and/or adaptive reuse of vintage buildings. Design of new buildings, structures or additions compatible with older buildings or historic districts. Designs for the reconstruction of period, replica buildings, commercial or residential. Historic surveys and inventories. No literature.

J.O. Holloway & Company
9208 N. Peninsular   Dept. OHJ
Portland, OR 97217
(503) 283-2172
RS/O
Quality duplications of unique ornamental building parts cast in polymers or glass reinforced concrete. Special attention to texture and detail make them indistinquishable from originals. Moulds made off original parts, from photos of originals, or from new designs. Interior or exterior use. Parts may be any size from medallions to pilasters. Call or write for free estimates.

Holm, Alvin AIA Architect
2014 Sansom St.   Dept. OHJ
Philadelphia, PA 19103
(215) 963-0747
RS/O
Architectural services for historic structures. Design and consultation, preservation, adaptive re-use, appropriate additions. Also historic structures reports, systems analysis, National Register nomination, etc. Registered in PA, NY, DE, and NJ. Serving individuals as well as organizations. Resume on request.

Home Fabric Mills, Inc.
PO Box 662, Route 202   Dept. OHJ
Belchertown, MA 01007
(413) 323-6321
MO   RS/O
Exclusive decorator fabrics at 'Mill-Store' prices. Their inventory includes velvets, upholstery, prints, antique satins, sheers, all-purpose, and thermal fabrics. Mail orders welcomed. Will custom-make drapes. Stores in Cheshire, Ct; Scotia, NY; and Belchertown, MA. Free brochure.

Homecraft Veneer
901 West Way   Dept. OHJ
Latrobe, PA 15650
(412) 537-8435
MO
Specialists in veneer and veneering supplies — domestic and imported veneers, tools, adhesives, wood finishes, brushes, sanding papers, saw blades, steel wood screws, dowels, dowel pins. 4 pg. illustrated instruction brochure, descriptive literature with price list — $1.00.

Homespun Weavers
530 State Ave.   Dept. OHJ
Emmaus, PA 18049
(215) 967-4550
MO   RS/O
Cotton homespun fabric handwoven in authentic Pennsylvania Dutch patterns. Suitable for tablecloths, drapes, bedspreads. Available by-the-yard or in custom-made tablecloths. 7 colors. Also available, 100% Cotton Kitchen Towels in 10 colors. Free color brochure with swatches.

Homestead Supply
PO Box 689   Dept. OHJ
Wilton, ME 04294
(207) 645-3709
MO   RS/O
Specialize in hard-to-find primitive and Colonial woodenware. Items are hand made using traditional techniques. Of special interest are several styles of shaving horses, hand carved tool handles, and hand-split shingles. Shingles can be split from wood other than cedar, i.e. hemlock. They'll travel to any site to produce (and install, if desired) shingles at a very reasonable charge. No literature, but inquiries are answered promptly and photos can be requested.

Hood, R. and Co.
RFD 3 College Rd.   Dept. OHJ
Meredith, NH 03253
(603) 279-8607
RS/O   MO
Early American decorating specialists, distributing Williamsburg line, Sturbridge reproductions, and other historic paints, wallpaper, fabrics, drapes, furniture, accessories, hardware, lighting fixtures, etc. Free brochure on Colonial hardware — send SASE.

Hope Co., Inc.
PO Box 1348   Dept. OHJ
Maryland Heights, MO 63043
(314) 432-5697
MO   DIST
Manufactures furniture refinishing and care products. 100% Tung Oil — no thinners added; Instant Furniture Refinisher; Tung Oil Varnish; Furniture Cleaner; Lemon Oil contains no wax or polish to build up; and new Hope's grill and stove black, a high-heat black finish for BBQ grills, woodburners, etc. Free brochure & literature on request.

Hopkins, Sara — Restoration Stenciling
3319 SW Water Ave.   Dept. OHJ
Portland, OR 97201
(503) 222-2903
RS/O
Restoration of Victorian wall, floor, and ceiling stenciling (especially ca. 1890 - 1910 Pacific Northwest). Professionally trained craftsperson, BFA, references. Personal service, including color matching, advice, original design consultation. Will travel. Inquiries welcomed, further information on request.

Horowitz Sign Supplies
166 Second Ave.   Dept. OHJ
New York, NY 10003
(212) 674-3284
RS/O   MO
Complete inventory of sign painter's supplies and tools, including pure gold-leaf. Helpful walk-in service for the trade or to individuals. Mail orders will be sent anywhere, but you must call for current prices and to arrange order. Raymond Le Blanc book on gilding techniques $13.50, plus parcel-post.

Horton Brasses
PO Box 120 Nooks Hill Rd.   Dept. OJ
Cromwell, CT 06416
(203) 635-4400
RS/O   MO
Manufacturers of reproduction brass furniture hardware for over 50 years. Their hardware covers periods from 1680 to 1920. Send $2.00 for catalog showing over 475 items.

House Carpenters
Box 217   Dept. OHJ
Shutesbury, MA 01072
(413) 256-8873
MO   RS/O
Custom-fabrication of 18th century millwork, including doors, windows, paneling, and flooring. The House Carpenters build 18th century timber framed houses throughout the Eastern U.S. All work is custom. Information on millwork is free. A brochure of timber framed house designs is available for $4.00.

See Product Displays Index on page 199 for more details.

House Master of America
421 W. Union Ave.   Dept. OHJ
Bound Brook, NJ 08805
(201) 469-6565
RS/O
Professional house inspection services through franchised agents in NY, NJ, Conn, Penn, Del, NC, Mass, and Texas. Inspection covers nine major structural, electrical, and mechanical elements. Inspection report and warranty on inspected elements. Free brochure. Outside NJ, call toll free (800) 526-3939.

House of Moulding
15202 Oxnard St.   Dept. OHJ
Van Nuys, CA 91411
(213) 781-5300
RS/O MO
An extensive selection of mouldings — softwood, hardwood, embossed, stairway parts, chair rails, cornices, bandsawn & carved corbels. Distributors for Focal Point architectural decorations. Illustrated catalog, $3.

● **House of Webster**
Box OH103   Dept. OHJ
Rogers, AR 72756
(501) 636-4640
MO
This established family business has a mail-order gift catalog. Of interest is a line of electric kitchen appliances (wall ovens, ranges) that are replicas of old-fashioned wood burners. Catalog is $.25.

Housejoiner, Ltd.
RD 1, Box 860   Dept. OHJ
Moretown, VT 05660
(802) 244-5095
RS/O
Consultation, design, and construction services for architectural restorations of period homes, adaptive use of "National Register" listed properties. Reconstruction and/or reproduction of original architectural detail is done to accurate specifications with planes and tools of the period. Brochure, $1.

Housewreckers, N.B. & Salvage Co.
396 Somerset St.   Dept. OHJ
New Brunswick, NJ 08901
(201) 247-1071
RS/O
This company has been salvaging old house-parts for over 50 years. Always a good supply of doors, windows, plumbing fixtures, interior and exterior moulding, posts and spindles, radiators, old brick and lumber, mantels, and so on. No literature.

● **Lyn Hovey Studio, Inc.**
266 Concord Avenue   Dept. OHJ
Cambridge, MA 02138
(617) 492-6566
MO RS/O
Stained and leaded glass lighting, windows, walls of glass, doors, and mirrors. Distinctive original designs in Early American, Victorian, and early 20th century styles. The studio features expertise in ancient painting techniques, acid etching, and glass bending as well as custom sashes, metal support bar systems, protective glazing, and restoration. Brochure, $1.00.

● **Howard Palmer, Inc.**
3341 Hancock St., Box 81724   Dept. OHJ
San Diego, CA 92138
(619) 297-1177
MO
A large selection of builder's hardware in various period styles including door hinges, door locks (reproduction and security), furniture hardware, door knobs, and bathroom accessories. Many items in solid brass. Also, brass gift accessories. Catalog, $1.

Howard Products, Inc.
411 W. Maple Ave.   Dept. OHJ
Monrovia, CA 91016
(213) 357-9545
MO DIST RS/O
They sell Restor-A-Finish, which can be used to restore naturally finished (but not painted) wood; it cleans and reamalgamates, rather than strips, the old finish. They also sell stripping chemicals of varying strengths. Free brochure: "How To Use Howard Finish Restorers."

Howard, David, Inc.
P.O. Box 295   Dept. OHJ
Alstead, NH 03602
(603) 835-6356
RS/O MO
Designs and builds old style braced post and beam houses in a variety of sizes and styles. Frame members are pre-fitted, numbered, and shipped to site. Their crew erects the structure. Windows, doors, siding, roofing, hardware, cabinets and stairs can be supplied. Also, imported English 15th & 16th century timber frames. Free introductory brochure. Detailed literature, $8.00.

Howland, John — Metalsmith
Elizabeth St.   Dept. OHJ
Kent, CT 06757
(203) 927-3064
MO RS/O
Restoration and repair of metal antiques. He will reproduce or manufacture missing parts, either from original or a sketch. Works in wrought iron, brass, copper, bronze, etc. Restores hardware, andirons, lamps, hinges, locks, brassware, etc. Can be reached by phone or mail Monday through Saturday. Estimates for work can be given upon visual inspection of the job. No literature.

Hubbardton Forge Corp.
RD H   Dept. OHJ
Fair Haven, VT 05743
(802) 273-2047
MO DIST RS/O
Hand wrought iron work including kitchen fixtures, panracks, lamps, chandeliers and sconces, and architectural iron work. Custom designed pieces are available. For file of 8 x 10 photo sheets, send $3.

S. & C. Huber, Accoutrements
82 Plants Dam Rd.   Dept. OHJ
East Lyme, CT 06333
(203) 739-0772
RS/O MO
Company produces hand crafted goods of 18th and early 19th century design on its small 1710 farm. They conduct lessons for such crafts as wool dyeing, soap making, candle dipping, paper making, rug braiding, etc. Among items for sale: Spinning wheels and fibers, handspun yarns and fabrics, weaving and textile tools, natural dyes, candles, candle making supplies, handmade soap, stencils and papermaking supplies. Craft books. Wooden treen ware. Charming catalog — $1.

Hudson Venetian Blind Service, Inc.
2000 Twilight Lane   Dept. OHJ
Richmond, VA 23235
(804) 276-5700
RS/O MO
Hudson has done reproductions for historical restorations. He custom builds Venetian blinds in 6 slat widths, from 1 inch to 2-3/8 inches. Wood blinds are a luxury item at approx. $12./sq. ft. But their beauty lasts over a lifetime. Free brochure; free paint-stain-tape samples; sample blinds are $40.00 plus freight.

Hulton, Roger L.
600 Oakwood Ave.   Dept. OHJ
Toronto, Ont., Canada M6E2X8
(416) 652-0234
RS/O
Specializes in finding, saving, and restoring hand-hewn log houses and barns. Will design a plan for the building's reconstruction, label the elements, dismantle the structure and deliver it to the new building site. Write or call with your needs.

Humphrey Products General Gaslight Co.
PO Box 2008   Dept. OHJ
Kalamazoo, MI 49003
(616) 381-5500
MO DIST
Exterior and interior gaslights, for use with propane gas. Also, tie-on and pre-formed gas mantles. Free brochure.

Hunrath , Wm. Co., Inc.
153 E. 57th St.   Dept. OHJ
New York, NY 10022
(212) 758-0780
RS/O
Shop carries a full line of decorative hardware in brass, bronze, iron. Furniture hardware, door knobs, etc. No literature.

Hunter Ceiling Fans
PO Box 14775   Dept. OHJ
Memphis, TN 38114
(901) 743-1360
DIST
Manufacturer of "Olde Tyme Ceiling Fan", little changed from models introduced in 1903. Hunter offers two sizes (36" and 52"), four motor finishes, and six choices of blades. Blades are mounted on hardwood irons, available in colors to match motors, which allows a multitude of combinations. Illustrated catalog $1.00. Brochure free.

Hurley Patentee Lighting
R.D. 7 - Box 98A   Dept. OHJ
Kingston, NY 12401
(914) 331-5414
RS/O MO
17th and 18th century lights reproduced from fixtures in museums and private collections. These unusual lights are authentic in appearance due to a special aging process. Over 150 tin, iron and brass bettys, candleholders, sconces, lanterns and chandeliers — electric or candle. A few non-lighting items — a bootscraper, iron firescreen and candle extinguishers. Illustrated catalog and price list — $2.

KEY TO ABBREVIATIONS

MO	**sells by Mail Order**
RS/O	**sells through Retail Store or Office**
DIST	**sells through Distributors**
ID	**sells only through Interior Designers or Architects**

Huseman, Richard J. Co.
2824 Stanton Avenue   Dept. OHJ
Cincinnati, OH 45206
(513) 861-7980
RS/O
Company has 45 years of experience in all phases of renovation and re-construction of some of the finest historical homes, churches and institutions in the Cincinnati area. They have their own cabinet shop for duplicating woodwork in every detail. No literature.

Huskisson Masonry & Exterior Building Restoration Co.
Box 949, 148 Jefferson St.   Dept. OHJ
Lexington, KY 40587
(606) 252-5011
RS/O
Contracting masonry restoration, renovation, reconstruction, and new masonry construction. Services available in Kentucky only. No literature.

Hyde Manufacturing Company
54 Eastford Road   Dept. OHJ
Southbridge, MA 01550
(617) 764-4344
DIST
A long established manufacturer of tools designed to prepare surfaces for painting, decorating and refinishing. Among the tools are — joint knives, paint, wood and wallpaper scrapers, putty knives, seam rollers, craft knives. Illustrated how-to book and catalog — $2.00.

● **Hydrochemical Techniques, Inc.**
P.O. Box 2078   Dept. OHJ
Hartford, CT 06145
(203) 527-6350
DIST
Hydroclean is a series of chemical cleaning systems for various kinds of masonry: brick, granite, sandstone, limestone & marble. It's available through restoration contractors nationwide. Free literature.

● **Hydrozo Coatings Co.**
P.O. Box 80879   Dept. OHJ
Lincoln, NE 68501
(402) 474-6981
MO DIST
Established manufacturer of clear, water-repellent exterior coatings. Masonry coatings, wood coatings protect surface without creating impermeable film. Also manufactures a sealer/preservative for wood that protects against rot and fungus, but contains safer zinc compounds — not mercury or chlorine compounds. Free literature.

I

Iberia Millwork
500 Jane Street   Dept. OHJ
New Iberia, LA 70560
(318) 365-5644
MO RS/O
New custom-made exterior wood rolling-slat shutter: hand stapled w/round crown copper coated staple. Shutters also appropriate for interior use as blinds. Standard fixed-slat shutters are available. Circle head shutters can also be fabricated. No literature; Photographs and scale drawings available free of charge for serious inquiries.

Ideal Millwork Co.
Box 889, 2400 Franklin Ave.   Dept. OHJ
Waco, TX 76703
(817) 754-4631
DIST
Ideal manufactures a wide variety of pine millwork products, including interior and exterior doors, casement and double hung windows, mantels and "built-in" ironing boards. For 92 years, they have manufactured the traditional panel, louvered and French door for both remodelling and new construction. Free catalogs and brochure.

Illinois Bronze Paint Co.
300 East Main Street   Dept. OHJ
Lake Zurich, IL 60047
(312) 438-8201
DIST
All purpose high gloss spray paints, epoxy spray paints, heat resistant paints, brush-on latex enamels, anti-rust enamels. Free literature.

Illustrious Lighting
1925 Fillmore St.   Dept. OHJ
San Francisco, CA 94115
(415) 922-3133
RS/O
Antique gas-electric chandeliers. Over 200 in shop restored & for sale. Reproductions also available. No literature, but letters will be answered with photos of available antique or reproduction fixtures.

Image Group, The
398 So. Grant Ave.   Dept. OHJ
Columbus, OH 43215
(614) 221-1016
RS/O
Architectural and interior design services in the area of building rehabilitation and restoration as well as specializing in "Theme" restaurant design. Offices across the country. No literature.

Impex Assoc. Ltd., Inc.
25 N. Dean St.   Dept. OHJ
Englewood, NJ 07631
(201) 568-2243
DIST
This company carries mostly furniture and door hardware in modern styles, some of the pieces are appropriate for old furniture and houses.

● **See Product Displays Index on page 199 for more details.**

Import Specialists, Inc.
82 Wall Street   Dept. OHJ
New York, NY 10005
(212) 709-9600
DIST
Importers and distributors of various kinds of natural fiber matting and rugs; i.e. sisal, coco, rice straw, seagrass, etc. An extensive selection of cotton rag rugs and dhurries. Distributed nationally to many large department stores and specialty stores like Bloomingdale's, Room & Board, Marshall Field's, etc. You can write for name of nearest retail store, but they do not sell outside of the trade.

Indiana Mirror Resilvering
3340 E. Lanam Rd.   Dept. OHJ
Bloomington, IN 47401
(812) 334-2276
MO RS/O
Antique mirrors carefully resilvered. Free price list and silvering information available.

Industrial Fabrics Association International
345 Cedar Bldg, Suite 450   Dept. OHJ
St. Paul, MN 55101
(612) 222-2508
MO
They offer a free directory of nationwide awning manufacturers.

Industrial Plastic Supply Co.
309 Canal Street   Dept. OHJ
New York, NY 10013
(212) 226-2010
RS/O MO
Sells mould-making compounds and casting materials for modern casting process. Stock includes polyester resin, fiberglass reinforcing strands, RTV rubber. Primarily a distributor with walk-in business, but they'll quote prices and arrange mail-order if necessary. How-to book also available: Plastics for Craftsmen, $7.45 ppd. No other literature.

Industrial Window Corp.
Box 716, Rt. 6   Dept. OHJ
Mahopac, NY 10541
(914) 628-4440
MO RS/O
This company sells and installs interior storm windows that reduce energy loss, through windows, by 30-50% — payback within two years. Windows can be round-topped or arched. Appropriate for landmark buildings. Also solar film, heat pump regulators, and insulation. Free brochure.

Industrial Woodworking, Inc.
1331 Leithton Rd.   Dept. OHJ
Mundelein, IL 60060
(312) 367-9080
DIST RS/O
Industrial Woodworking, Inc., is a full service mill featuring stock as well as custom interior woodwork and mouldings. Stair parts brochure, $.25, moulding catalog, $1.25, and panelling brochure, $.25.

Inglenook
523 Hudson Street   Dept. OHJ
New York, NY 10014
(212) 675-0890
MO RS/O
An antiques shop specializing in American furniture and decorations of the 19th century. Also sell architectural details such as stained glass windows, fretwork and mantel pieces. Since they do not deal in new manufactured merchandise, there is no catalogue; however, photographs furnished upon request. Extensive restoration experience.

Inner Harbor Lumber & Hardware
900 Fleet St.   Dept. OHJ
Baltimore, MD 21202
(301) 837-0202
RS/O
Renovation products center in downtown
Baltimore & Northern Baltimore (4345 York Rd.,
(301) 532-2710). Stock includes structural as well
as decorative materials. Bricks, framing lumber,
flooring, treated lumber, gutters, plumbing &
electrical, decorative hardware, Diedrich
chemicals, and shutters. Custom orders on
replacement window sash. No literature.

Interior Decorations
48-52 Lincoln Street   Dept. OHJ
Exeter, NH 03833
(603) 778-0406
RS/O
17th — 18th — 19th century interior restoration
throughout New England by decorator Jane Kent
Rockwell. Specializing in period draperies,
documentary fabrics, wallcoverings and carpets.
Lectures given. No literature.

International Building Components
Box 51   Dept. OHJ
Glenwood, NY 14069
(716) 592-2953
DIST
Cupolas, carved wooden mantels, china cabinets,
ironing board cabinets, wood doors, and spiral
and circular stair components. Sold through
distributors. Product literature is free — please
specify your interest.

International Consultants, Inc.
227 South Ninth St.   Dept. OHJ
Philadelphia, PA 19107
(215) 923-8888
RS/O
Company is versed in project management, cost
estimating and CPM scheduling. Has performed
design and project management services for
many historic restoration projects in the
Mid-Atlantic and New England states. Brochure
free.

International Terra Cotta, Inc.
690 N. Robertson Blvd.   Dept. OHJ
Los Angeles, CA 90069
(213) 657-3752
MO   RS/O
A complete line of European terra cotta urns and
planters in classical styles. Also available:
sandstone fountains and statues. Free brochure
— specify retail or wholesale price list.

International Wood Products
9630 Aero Drive   Dept. OH
San Diego, CA 92123
(619) 565-1122
DIST
Solid, carved hardwood doors (interior &
exterior) in mahogany, oak, or Ponderosa pine.
Also sidelights and panels. All are available with
optional bevelled, crystalline glue chipped,
etched, sand carved or leaded glass inserts. Also,
custom designs. Color brochure, $2.

Iron Anvil Forge
4043 S. I-25   Dept. OHJ
Castle Rock, CO 80104
(303) 688-9428
MO   RS/O
Handforged iron products. Extensive use of forge
welding, riveting, collaring, and tenons. No arc
or gas welding used. Interior/exterior,
architectural and ornamental ironware produced
the old way. Free information and estimates.

Iron Craft, Inc.
2 Pleasant St., PO Box 108   Dept. OHJ
Freedom, NH 03836
MO   DIST
Cast and wrought iron accessories, including
cooking equipment, fireplace tools and grates,
dutch oven doors, Colonial hardware, and lamp
brackets. They also carry isinglass (stove mica),
bellows, oil lamps, and maintenance supplies
such as stove polish, furnace cement, and
chimney brushes. Mail-order catalog is $1.00.

Iron Horse Antiques, Inc.
R.D. No. 2   Dept. OHJ
Poultney, VT 05764
(802) 287-4050
RS/O   MO
Specializes in old and antique tools. Also carries
books dealing with restoration, tools, crafts, etc.
"The Fine Tool Journal", illustrated, is published
10 times a year, $10.00 per year. Current issue,
$1.50. Brochure/booklist, free.

Iron-A-Way, Inc.
220 W. Jackson   Dept. OHJ
Morton, IL 61550
(309) 266-7232
DIST   RS/O
Manufacturers of built-in ironing centers. Several
models; many safety features. Free literature.

● **Island City Wood Working Co.**
1801 Mechanic St.   Dept. OHJ
Galveston, TX 77550
(409) 765-5727
MO   RS/O
Vintage mouldings, made-to-order cypress
shutters, windows and doors. Reproduction of
Victorian style interior and exterior trim our
specialty, from drawings or samples. Custom
millwork since 1908. Call or write for description
and quotations on specific items.

Itinerant Artist
Box 222   Dept. OHJ
Falls Church, VA 22046
(703) 241-8371
DIST   RS/O
Over 300 durable plastic stencils for walls, floors,
fabric, furniture, glass, tile, and tin. Patterns
include New England Reproduction,
Pennsylvania Dutch, Classic, Colonial Virginia,
Victorian, and Contemporary. Accent and
recreation. Stencil plastic paper available; also
doll house kits. Stencils are easily cut and applied
using latex or oil house paint. Catalog of reduced
patterns with instructions, $6.

KEY TO ABBREVIATIONS

MO   **sells by Mail Order**

RS/O   **sells through Retail Store or Office**

DIST   **sells through Distributors**

ID   **sells only through Interior Designers or Architects**

J

JGR Enterprises, Inc.
PO Box 32, Rt. 522   Dept. OHJ
Ft. Littleton, PA 17223
(717) 987-3640
MO   DIST
Manufacturers and suppliers of contemporary
sliding and folding door hardware. An alternate
source for replacement parts when reproduction
hardware and fittings are available. Also, a
selection of antique sliding door hardware. Free
"Kennaframe" catalog.

● **JMR Products**
PO Box 442   Dept. JC
St. Helena, CA 94574
(707) 942-4551
MO
Reproduction Victorian-style screen doors made
from #1 clear-heart redwood and decorated with
hardwood turnings and filagrees, etc. $174.95 for
standard sizes. Send $.50 for detailed brochure.
Dealer and wholesale information available.

Jack's Upholstery & Caning Supplies
52 Shell Ct.   Dept. OHJ
Oswego, IL 60543
(312) 554-1045
MO
A complete line of supplies and tools for
upholstry and caning — strand or sheet cane,
rush, & splint. Also, instruction books. Catalog,
$1.50.

● **Jackson Bros.**
3465 Nebo Rd.   Dept. OHJ
Boulder, CO 80302
(303) 442-5498
MO   RS/O
Manufacturers of hardwood storm windows and
screens. All custom-made to order. No literature.

Jackson, Wm. H. Co.
3 E. 47th St.   Dept. OHJ
New York, NY 10017
(212) 753-9400
RS/O   MO
Manufactures and retails a full line of fine
fireplace equipment, carved wood mantels,
andirons, fire tools, grates, fenders, hand-painted
tiles, delft tiles, etc. Company established 1827.
Their lava gas fire simulates real coal and fits
most grates. Also: a full line of antique fireplace
equipment, including marble mantels, fenders,
fire tools, delft tiles, etc. For a brochure send
self-addressed business size envelope.

Jacobsen, Charles W., Inc.
401 S. Salina St.   Dept. OHJ
Syracuse, NY 13202
(315) 471-6522
RS/O   MO
3000 or more handmade Oriental rugs — new,
used, semi-antique and antique — in many sizes
are in stock at all times. The company, whose
president is a recognized authority in the field,
keeps its prices below the market level by acting
as direct importers or contractors on new rugs
and by volume of retail and mail order sales. Free
and very complete, helpful and informative
literature and descriptive lists.

Janovic/Plaza, Inc.
1150 Third Avenue   Dept. OHJ
New York, NY 10021
(212) 772-1400
RS/O   MO
Store has probably the largest stock of specialty painting and decorating supplies in the U.S. Will also service mail orders. No literature.

Jaxon Co., Inc.
Box 618, 118 N. Orange Ave.   Dept. OHJ
Eufaula, AL 36027
(205) 687-8031
MO   RS/O
Representatives of Jaxon Co. are available to assist customers plan and implement historical & civic markers, signage & monument programs. Range of products is from metal castings (bronze or aluminum) to sculpted marble and granite. Call or write for further information.

Jefferson Art Lighting, Inc.
4371 Lima Center Rd.   Dept. OHJ
Ann Arbor, MI 48103
(313) 428-7361
MO   RS/O
Design and manufacture original lamps, and custom lighting, from photographs or blueprints. Repair and reproduce antique fixtures. Large selection of antique, new, and imported shades. In house white metal and bronze casting. Sole U.S. producer of engraved porcelain lithophane panels and porcelain shades. Complete catalogue of architectural plaster ornaments, 158 pages for $25, plus $1.50 postage.

Jenifer House
    Dept. OJ
Great Barrington, MA 01230
(413) 528-1500
MO   RS/O
Their 96-page catalog offers fine gifts, decorative accessories, dinnerware, flatware, rugs, lamps, furniture, etc. Also Early American hardware and authentic reproduction of Early American furniture.

Jennings, Gottfried, Cheek/ Preservationists
Box 1890   Dept. OHJ
Ames, IA 50010
(515) 292-7192
RS/O
Provides historic preservation services, including architectural, archeological, and historic surveys; cultural resource analysis; preservation planning; preservation implementation through public policy and private initiative; neighborhood conservation planning; public education including volunteer training; preparation of National Register forms and certification applications; rehabilitation guidelines; interior or exterior design consultation; townscape design. Send SASE for free literature.

Jennings Lights of Yesterday
1523 San Pablo Ave.   Dept. OHJ
Berkeley, CA 94702
(415) 526-1008
RS/O   MO
Original restored chandeliers and wall sconces from the 1800's to 1920's. They also make reproduction brass chandeliers and wall sconces; brass towel bars and tissue holders. Also pull-chain toilets, oak seats, and brass plumbing fixtures. No literature available.

● **Jerard Paul Jordan Gallery**
PO 71, Slade Acres   Dept. OHJ
Ashford, CT 06278
(203) 429-7954
MO   RS/O
Jerard Paul Jordan Gallery is a distributor of 18th century building materials including such items as panelling, sheathing, beams, windows, brick, H & HL hinges, butterfly hinges, strap hinges, barn siding, doors, mantels, latches for both the interior and exterior. No literature.

Jim & Barb's Antique Stoves
E 4007 Lyons   Dept. OHJ
Spokane, WA 99207
(509) 489-4938
MO   RS/O
The largest selection of antique wood cook stoves and heaters in the Inland Empire. Stoves are completely renickeled and restored to original condition. Will buy, collect, sell and restore old stoves, also some parts for sale. Pictures & prices sent on request.

JoEl Enterprises
PO Box 1834   Dept. OHJ
West Palm Beach, FL 33402
(305) 627-0419
MO
Restored authentic antique lighting, 1890-1930s. Most are solid brass with antique glass shades. Sales only, no restoration services available. Catalog $2., credited to first order.

Johnson Bros. Specialties
1030 S. Cedar   Dept. OHJ
New Lenox, IL 60451
(815) 485-4262
RS/O
A full service finishing/restoration shop. Paint stripping, staining & finishing, and custom repairs. Also, custom furniture making. No literature.

Johnson Paint Co.
355 Newbury St.   Dept. OHJ
Boston, MA 02115
(617) 536-4838
RS/O   MO
A specialty paint distributor catering to the Boston restoration market. They will ship hard-to-find calcimine paint on receipt of a written order and payment (no COD's). Minimum order 25 lbs. of powder (makes between 12-15 qts). Please call for current prices & shipping charges before ordering.

Johnson, R.L. Interiors
312 South Fifth East   Dept. OHJ
Missoula, MT 59801
(406) 543-5414
MO   RS/O
Competitively-priced suppliers of leading reproduction and quality wallcoverings, fabrics, trims, and carpets. Delivery 2-3 weeks from order date. Quotations given at no charge. Free cuttings available when customer sends color sample and indicates desired material. Call for prices; no literature available.

Johnson, Walter H.
Rich Hill Rd.   Dept. OHJ
Shushan, NY 12873
(518) 854-7826
RS/O
Restoration of old houses, and new (reproduction) construction such as salt boxes and gambrels. They make trim, doors, cupboards, fireplace walls, and so on. Serving Washington and Saratoga Counties, and Western Vermont. No literature.

Jones Interior Design
4232 Mc Cart   Dept. OHJ
Ft. Worth, TX 76115
(817) 921-3351
RS/O
An interior design firm specializing in preserving the period feeling of old homes. They will match paints and restore wallpapers where possible. No literature.

Jotul U.S.A., Inc.
343 Forest Ave., PO Box 1157   Dept. OHJ
Portland, ME 04104
(207) 775-0757
DIST
United States subsidiary of A/S Jotul, Oslo, Norway, manufacturer of Jotul cast-iron wood and coal burning stoves and combi-fires. All models UL-listed; wood, coal, wood/coal combination and high efficiency stoves. Porcelain enamelled stoves available in red and green. Free brochures and flyers on request.

Joy Construction, Inc.
4803 Courthouse Rd.   Dept. OHJ
Fredericksburg, VA 22401
(703) 898-4139
RS/O
General contractors in restoration and renovations of old buildings, in the Fredericksburg, VA area for over 12 years. Recent buildings have included Chatham Manor and Little Whim. All aspects of carpentry and painting, both interior and exterior. Cost estimates provided upon request with detailed material specifications. No literature.

● See Product Displays Index on page 199 for more details.

K

Kane-Gonic Brick Corp.
Winter St.   Dept. OHJ
Gonic, NH 03867
(603) 332-2861
RS/O   MO
Manufacture authentic Harvard water-struck brick. Hand-, and machine-moulded in many sizes and shapes. Can do custom shapes and colors. Numerous restoration projects including South Street Seaport. Will ship nationwide. No brochure.

Kaplan/Price Assoc. — Architects
808 Union St.   Dept. OHJ
Brooklyn, NY 11215
(212) 789-8537
RS/O
Architectural firm specializing in brownstones, townhouses, restoration and adaptive re-use of old buildings and commercial interiors. Metropolitan NYC area. No literature.

Kaymar Wood Products, Inc.
4603 35th S.W.   Dept. OHJ
Seattle, WA 98126
(206) 932-3584
MO   RS/O
Kaymar Wood Products was established in 1947 as a manufacturer of wood products for the marine-shipping trade. Since that time they have expanded to custom wood turning, millwork, unfinished hardwood stools, and the retail sale of 70-80 exotic hardwoods, plus producing many unusual items. Free hardwood price list.

Kayne, Steve & Son Custom Forged Hardware
Route 4, Box 275 A   Dept. OHJ
Candler, NC 28715
(704) 667-8868
RS/O   MO
Custom forged to specifications — hinges, latches, bolts, shutter dogs, fireplace tools, cranes, andirons, dutch-oven doors, hearth accessories, brackets, candlelighting fixtures, drawer/door hardware and accessories. Stock cast brass/bronze interior/exterior hardware, hinges, thumb latches, icebox hardware, door knockers. Repairs and restorations. Hand Forged Hardware catalog including fireplace tools—$2; Cast Brass/Bronze hardware catalog— $2; both $3.50. Basics of blacksmithing booklet—$2.

Keddee Woodworkers
PO Box 148   Dept. OHJ
East Greenwich, RI 02818
(401) 943-1694
MO   RS/O
Manufacturer of architectural restoration sash and mill work. Will match windows, doors, pediments, mouldings, turnings, brackets, "Gingerbread", carvings, etc. to samples or drawings. Also, will reproduce synthetic marble, casting, etc. Free literature.

Kelly Plastering Co.
15322 S. Drexel Ave., Box 275   Dept. OHJ
So. Holland, IL 60473
(312) 339-3810
RS/O
Plain and ornamental plasterwork in the Chicago area. Please call — no literature.

● Kenmore Industries
44 Kilby St.   Dept. OHJ
Boston, MA 02109
(617) 523-4008
MO   RS/O
A stock line of decorative and historical over-door pieces, and a variety of fanlights (half-round and elliptical). Georgian, Federal, Victorian, and Revival designs. Color brochure, $3.

Kenneth Lynch & Sons, Inc.
Box 488   Dept. OHJ
Wilton, CT 06897
(203) 762-8363
MO
Metal cornice parts, ornamental gutters & leaders, weather vanes . . . thousands of stamped metal designs made from original dies. Work done in copper, lead, zinc, etc. Cast stone garden ornament. Sun dials, park benches, & bldg. ornaments of all kinds. Custom hammerwork. Architectural Sheet Metal Ornament catalog 7474—$3.50. Garden Ornament book 2076—$7.50. Other architectural handbooks available. Free flyer — Oriel Windows.

Kentucky Ornamental Iron
1047 Goodwin Dr.   Dept. OHJ
Lexington, KY 40505
(606) 255-7791
MO   RS/O
Metal fabricators: fireplace tools, fences & gates, cast aluminum ornaments such as an eagle (with 4 ft. wing span). Individual castings. No literature.

Kentucky Wood Floors, Inc.
4200 Reservoir Avenue   Dept. OHJ
Louisville, KY 40213
(502) 451-6024
DIST
Full line of hardwood flooring, from classic designs to plank and parquet, both prefinished and unfinished. Directed toward the architect, designer, and upper-end consumer. Contemporary designs as well as reproductions of European classics, Colonial America's hand-scraped plank and Jefferson's Monticello parquet. Literature, $1.

Keystone
P.O. Box 3292   Dept. OHJ
San Diego, CA 92103
(619) 297-3130
RS/O
Restoration service for San Diego area. Stripping, repairing, and refinishing of furniture and architectural details, such as doors and mouldings, window frames, mantels. Custom wood-turning work done. Booklet, "A Guide to Furniture Restoration" is available by mail for $2.

Kimball Furniture Company
1549 Royal Street   Dept. OHJ
Jasper, IN 47546
(812) 482-1600
DIST
Manufacturers of authentic 19th century Victorian reproductions. Company uses hand-carved solid Honduras mahogany, Italian marble, and Belgian fabrics for detailed reproductions. Products include sofas, chairs, tables, complete dining room, and bedroom suites. A free color brochure is available.

King Energy Corp.
2121 Morris Avenue   Dept. OHJ
Union, NJ 07083
(201) 688-7676
RS/O
Exclusive distributor & manufactor of an interior magnetic window system for New Jersey, 5 boroughs of New York, Long Island, & Westchester. Magnetite® with an acrylic window is custom made for any shape or size window. Free brochure.

● King's Chandelier Co.
Highway 14, PO Box 671   Dept. OHJ-1
Eden, NC 27288
(919) 623-6188
RS/O   MO
A huge collection of chandeliers, sconces and candelabra — each assembled from imported and domestic parts that are designed and maintained by the company. There are brass and crystal reproductions of Victorian styles, and elegant formal 18th century crystal ones, including Strass crystal. Also early American brass and pewter ones. 96-page illustrated catlogue — $2.

● Kings River Casting
139 Wood Duck Dr.   Dept. OHJ
Sanger, CA 93657
(209) 875-8250
MO   RS/O
Cast aluminum benches, with solid oak slats, in several models including a hanging swing. Catalog, $1.

● Kingsway
4723 Chromium Drive   Dept. OHJ
Colorado Springs, CO 80918
(303) 599-4512
MO   RS/O
They sell Victorian restoration materials: gingerbread brackets and fretwork, stair parts, door and window casings, brass hardware for doors and bathrooms, panelling, wainscotting, wood shingles, front doors, plaster and composition ornaments, mouldings, and wood fiber carvings. Catalog, $2.50 plus $.50 postage.

Kirk, M.A./Creative Designs
4777 Powell Rd.   Dept. OHJ
Okemos, MI 48864
(517) 349-6110
RS/O
Fine cabinetry and custom reproduction of period pieces. Will work closely with architect or client to provide design consultation and custom fabrication. Free brochure.

Kittinger Company
1883 Elmwood Avenue   Dept. OHJ
Buffalo, NY 14207
(716) 876-1000
DIST
Kittinger traditional furniture including Williamsburg and Historic Newport Furniture Reproductions may be seen at Kittinger showrooms, and is sold through accredited furniture dealers and interior designers. 180-page catalog: "Library of 18th-Century English and American Designs", $8.

Klinke & Lew Contractors
1304 Greene Street   Dept. OHJ
Silverton, CO 81433
(303) 387-5713
RS/O   MO
Specializing in Victorian construction and restoration. Distributors for W.F. Norman Co. pressed tin ceilings in Western Colorado. No literature.

Klise Manufacturing Company
601 Maryland Ave.   Dept. OHJ
Grand Rapids, MI 49505
(616) 459-4283
MO   DIST
Furniture and cabinet trim. Manufactures
decorative carved-wood mouldings and
ornaments. Bamboo, ropes, dentils, classical
patterns, carved and plain rosettes. Metal
furniture grilles of formed or woven wire, brass
plated and antiqued. Send two $.20 stamps for
Accent Mouldings literature and prices: two
stamps for metal-grille catalog.

Knickerbocker Guild
623 N. Catalina Ave.   Dept. OHJ
Pasadena, CA 91106
(213) 792-6528
RS/O
A painting and decorating company specializing
in authentic restoration work. Restoration
consultants, crafts persons who strip, stain, not
to mention paint & repair. Free brochure.

Knudsen, Mark
1100 E. County Line Rd.   Dept. OHJ
Des Moines, IA 50315
(515) 285-6112
RS/O
Wood carver and turner who offers a full range of
custom woodworking services. Duplication of
moulding, ornament, and gingerbread; fancy
joinery; stair parts, porch posts, doors, and
windows; repair and reproduction of fine period
furniture. Please contact for specific information.

Kool-O-Matic Corp.
PO Box 310   Dept. OHJ
Niles, MI 49120
(616) 683-2600
DIST
This manufacturer of residential ventilating
equipment even makes an attic fan concealed in
an Early American cupola. Also roof, gable and
'Energy Saving' whole house ventilators,
complete with solid state speed controls and
timer features. For complete information send
$.25.

Koppers Co.
1900 Koppers Bldg.   Dept. OHJ
Pittsburgh, PA 15219
(412) 227-2000
DIST
Manufactures fire-retardant red cedar shakes and
shingles. Also produces "Wolmanized"
pressure-treated lumber for outdoor use. This
process gives long-term termite and rot resistance
to economical, plentiful types of wood. "How to
Build a Deck," $1.00; "How to Build a Fence,"
$1.00.

Kraatz/Russell Glass
RFD 1, Potato Hill Road   Dept. OHJ
Canaan, NH 03741
(603) 523-4289
MO   RS/O
Manufactures hand-blown, wavy bulls-eye
window panes with pontil mark in center,
appropriate for side lights and transoms in Early
American restorations and reproductions. Panes
are cut to customer's specifications; sizes from 5
in. x 5 in. to 10 in. x 10 in. Also makes
diamond-pane leaded casement windows for 17th
century buildings.

Peter Kramer/Cabinetmaker
Gay St., PO Box 232   Dept. OHJ
Washington, VA 22747
(703) 675-3625
MO   RS/O
Handcrafted early American country furniture
inspired by life in an imagined community of the
early 1700s. Illustrated portfolio and price list —
$2.75

John Kruesel's General Merchandise
22 3rd St., S.W.   Dept. OHJ
Rochester, MN 55901
(507) 289-8049
RS/O
Has been in the business of collecting early
lighting and plumbing fixtures since he was 8 yrs.
old. Will consult, sell, purchase — everything is
original. No literature.

● **G. Krug & Son, Inc.**
415 W. Saratoga St.   Dept. OHJ
Baltimore, MD 21201
(301) 752-3166
RS/O
Specializing in custom restoration of ornamental
ironwork such as gates, fences, tables, etc. Work
done to customer's drawings or photographs.
Fancy blacksmithing work also done. This is the
oldest continuously operating iron shop in the
country: since 1810. No catalog or regular
mail-order procedure.

Kruger Kruger Albenberg
2 Central Square   Dept. OHJ
Cambridge, MA 02139
(617) 661-3812
RS/O
Architects, engineers, builders serving the New
York Metropolitan area and New England. Office
also at 24 Beverly Rd., West Orange, NJ 07052,
(201) 325-8040. Services include determination of
replacement cost of construction, investigation of
construction problems, construction documents
for and construction management of repairs and
changes. No literature; telephone inquiries
welcomed.

Kyp-Go, Inc.
20 N. 17th St., PO Box 247   Dept. OHJ
St. Charles, IL 60174
(312) 584-8181
DIST
Manufacturer of true carbon filament light bulbs.
Offered in a 8-, or 16-candle power bulb, with a 2
year warranty. The "Victorian Light Bulb"
information sheet is free.

L

Lachin, Albert & Assoc., Inc.
618 Piety Street   Dept. OHJ
New Orleans, LA 70117
(504) 948-3533
MO   RS/O
Architectural sculptors specializing in ornamental
plaster and cement work. Ceiling medallions
(ornate, 18-60-in.), mouldings, columns and
capitals, domes, finials, etc. Reinforced plaster or
stone. Custom work. Cement products shop:
Columns, finials, fountains, and balustrades. Free
flyer.

LaForte Design
PO Box 744   Dept. OHJ
Northampton, MA 01060
(413) 584-3540
MO
The Canvas Roll-Up Shade is made of 100%
cotton duck, with hardwood dowels, and
attractive hardware. Can be used in place of
conventional curtains and shades. Comes
pre-assembled in a variety of sizes. Brochure $1.

Lake Shore Markers
P.O. Box 59   Dept. OHJ
Erie, PA 16512
(800) 458-0463
MO
Makes historical markers, date plates, and
plaques out of cast aluminum. Also custom
ornamental aluminum work. Weatherproof vinyl
coatings in many colors can be applied to
plaques. Catalog No. 182 free.

Lamb, J & R Studios
30 Joyce Drive   Dept. OHJ
Spring Valley, NY 10977
(914) 352-3777
RS/O   MO
Established in 1857, they do large-scale
restoration, repair, and new work in leaded and
stained glass, mosaic, stone, metal, wood, and
general decoration. Also install protective
covering on stained glass windows. Additional
office Philmont, NY (518) 672-7267. Free
brochures.

Lancaster Paint & Glass Co.
235 N. Prince St., Box 201   Dept. OHJ
Lancaster, PA 17603
(717) 299-7321
MO
This company, in existence since 1884, offers a
large selection of metal graining combs and a
combination graining tool. Free information.

Landmark Company
Box 1408   Dept. OHJ
Manhattan, KS 66502
(913) 776-6010
RS/O   MO
Architectural restoration, rehabilitation, and
design services for all types of public,
commercial, and residential buildings. Energy
conservation, measured drawings, feasibility
studies, and building surveys. Specialize in
adaptive re-use & new uses for historic buildings.
Brochure, resume, and list of completed projects
available on request.

Langhorne Carpet Co.
PO Box 175   Dept. OHJ
Penndel, PA 19047
(215) 757-5155
MO RS/O
Wilton weave carpets in a variety of Victorian patterns. Period reproductions are their specialty.

David M. LaPenta, Inc.
157 North Third Street   Dept. OHJ
Philadelphia, PA 19106
(215) 627-2782
RS/O
Architectural and general contracting services for the renovation and restoration of old buildings for residential and commercial use in the Philadelphia area. No literature.

LaPointe, Chip, Cabinetmaker
419 Grand Avenue   Dept. OHJ
Brooklyn, NY 11238
(212) 857-8594
MO RS/O
Custom cabinetmaking specializing in integrating new cabinetry with old or original designs. Designs made to be compatible with the feel of the home. Also custom doors, shutters, mantels, panelling, spindles etc. can be made to specification. No literature.

Larcomb & Wicht
10686 Larcombe Rd.   Dept. OHJ
Marysville, OH 43040
(614) 666-1781
MO RS/O
A curved arm table lamp is offered with a selection of free blown, art glass shades. Reminiscent of the "Aurene/Favrile" type of glass, these shades can also be purchased separately. Custom work is considered. Free brochure.

LaRoche Stained Glass
441-443 Fulton Street   Dept. OHJ
Medford, MA 02155
(617) 395-5047
RS/O
Specializing in stained glass restoration and new design. Free brochure.

J.C. Lauber Co.
504 E. LaSalle Ave.   Dept. OHJ
South Bend, IN 46617
(219) 234-4174
RS/O
Founded in 1890, this company will fabricate almost anything in any type of sheet metal — gutters, cornices, finials, steeples, and mouldings. Will also do slate and clay roofing. Specialize in custom and one-of-a-kind work. Free brochure.

Laura Copenhauer Industries, Inc.
PO Box 149   Dept. OHJ
Marion, VA 24354
(703) 783-4663
MO RS/O
Quality handmade quilts, coverlets, and hand-tied canopies. Every detail of the original process is carefully followed to produce exquisite products in traditional designs. Black and white brochure, $.50.

Lauria, Tony
RD 2, Box 253B   Dept. OHJ
Landenberg, PA 19350
(215) 268-3441
MO
Authentic new battleship linoleum in six solid colors (beige, terra cotta, dark green, gray, brown, and black). It's one-eighth inch thick, burlap-backed and priced at $3/sq. ft. Available in widths up to 6 ft. No literature but they will send samples.

● **Lavoie, John F.**
P.O. Box 15   Dept. OHJ
Springfield, VT 05156
(802) 886-8253
RS/O MO
Manufacturers of historical windows: Rounds, ovals, fanlights, transoms. Frames are clear pine; double-strength glazing. Brochure $2.00.

● **Lawler Machine & Foundry**
PO Box 2977   Dept. OHJ
Birmingham, AL 35212
(205) 595-0596
MO DIST
Complete line of ornamental metal castings and accessory items (gray iron & aluminum). Designs from Vintage to Modern. Sold as component parts to metalworking shops who fabricate, assemble, and finish for the homeowner. Casting catalog, $4.

Lea, James — Cabinetmaker
Harkness House   Dept. OHJ
Rockport, ME 04856
(207) 236-3632
MO RS/O
Handcrafted reproductions of 18th century American master cabinetmakers' furniture and Windsor chairs. Prices compare favorably with commercial reproduction furniture. Illustrated catalog and price list — $3.

LEE JOFA
979 Third Ave.   Dept. OHJ
New York, NY 10022
(212) 889-3900
ID
For 100 years, they have provided authentic documentary fabrics, Indian crewel embroideries & authentic Tartan plaids. Also, they offer largest single collection of English chintzes & linens which meticulously duplicate the ancient hand-block printing technique. Leading source to museums, restorations & historical agencies, they maintain an ongoing collection of documentary fabrics & wall coverings derived from authentic designs at the Museum of the American China Trade, Milton, MA. No literature.

● **Lee Valley Tools, Ltd.**
2680 Queensview Dr.   Dept. OHJ
Ottawa, Ontario, Canada K2B8J9
(613) 596-0350
MO RS/O
An impressive selection of antique hardware: Early American to Victorian — all restored and working order. Also, a complete selection of woodworking tools including chisels, saws, axes, drawknives, planes, etc. Antique hardware catalog, $1; Tool catalog, $2.

Lee Woodwork Systems
466 Harvey's Bridge Rd.   Dept. OHJ
Unionville, PA 19375
(215) 486-0346
MO RS/O
Colonial beaded tongue and groove wainscot system, including baseboard, 32 in. vertical beaded boards, chair rail. Various hardwoods & clear poplar. Also random-width tongue and groove hardwood flooring: 13/16-inch, hardwoods, end-grain plugs or Tremont nails. Brochure not yet availble, so send all dimensions, including elevations, and accessory needs for fixed price quote and photo. Shipment anywhere.

Leeke, John — Woodworker
RR1, Box 847   Dept. OHJ
Sanford, ME 04073
(207) 324-9597
MO RS/O
Custom woodworking that includes new furniture and cabinet work as well as historic house restoration (doors, raised panelling, stairwork, sash & mouldings for interior & exterior). Turning & carving (even by mail order) are specialities and include architectural column restoration & reproduction. Consulting to homeowners, carpenters, & wood-workers on restoration of architectural woodwork, and columns. Information sheet, $1.

Legacy Pine Ltd.
P.O. Box 52614   Dept. OHJ
Atlanta, GA 30355
(404) 233-0067
RS/O MO
Kiln-dried, remilled heart pine tongue-and-groove flooring, architectural millwork, mouldings, custom doors, beams, "V" joint panelling, wall panelling systems, staircase parts, and other custom items fabricated from drawings submitted by architect or designer. Color brochure, $2.

Lehigh Portland Cement Co.
PO Box 1882   Dept. OHJ
Allentown, PA 18105
(215) 776-2600
MO DIST
Produces Atlas colored masonry Portland cements available in twelve colors, plus white. All masonry cements meet ASTM specifications. Write for free color chart.

Lehman Hardware & Appliances
PO Box 41J   Dept. OHJ
Kidron, OH 44636
(216) 857-5441
MO RS/O
Old-fashioned but still useful appliances from the Amish/Mennonite community. Includes wood-coal-electric stoves; quality tools. Full catalog — $2.

● See Product Displays Index on page 199 for more details.

Leichtung, Inc.
4944 Commerce Parkway   Dept. OHJ
Cleveland, OH 44128
(216) 831-6191
MO RS/O
U.S. distributor of Lervad (Denmark) workbenches, Bracht (Germany) chisels, Sarjent (England) woodthreading tools plus a treasury of fine, difficult-to-find tools from all over the continent. 1982 catalog (98 pages) from all over the continent. Free 1983 catalog (98 pages).

Lemee's Fireplace Equipment
815 Bedford St.   Dept. OHJ
Bridgewater, MA 02324
(617) 697-2672
RS/O MO
Handmade bellows & fireplace accessories & equipment. Also: iron hardware, brass bowls, candlesticks & doorknocker, cast iron banks & doorstops, black doorknockers, cast iron firebacks, copper kettles & buckets, black bath accessories, black & brass eagles, lighting fixtures in brass, copper & black, post lanterns, fireplace cranes, andirons & screens. Plant hooks, black kettles, hooks & umbrella stands. Illustrated catalog & price list of fireplace equipment — $1. refundable with first order.

Lenape Products, Inc.
Pennington Ind. Ctr., Rt. 31   Dept. OHJ
Pennington, NJ 08534
(609) 737-0206
MO DIST
One of the leading manufacturers of porcelain "clip-on" bath accessories. Available in white (and 9 other colors) the selection includes a corner soap dish, towel bars, hooks, drawer pulls, etc. Catalog, $2.

Lena's Antique Bathroom Fixtures
PO Box 1022   Dept. OHJ
Bethel Island, CA 94511
(415) 634-5933
MO RS/O
An extensive selection of antique plumbing fixtures and bathroom accessories. Tubs, toilets, sinks, etc. 90% of the merchandise has been reconditioned and restored, but they also have products for the do-it-yourselfer. No literature, but write with your specific needs and they'll send photos.

● **Leo, Brian**
7520 Stevens Ave., So.   Dept. OHJ
Richfield, MN 55423
(612) 861-1473
MO
Door and window hardware executed in bronze or brass. Hinges, knobs, escutcheon plates, handles, and letter drops. Also, hard to find shutter hinges in steel. All reproduced from 19th century originals. Four sizes of hinges, many sizes and styles of doorplates, and large handles suitable for commercial use. Careful and prompt replicating of your most difficult hardware originals. Brochure, $2., refunded with purchase.

Lesco, Inc.
3409 W. Harry, Box 12209   Dept. OHJ
Wichita, KS 67277
(316) 943-3284
MO
Builders hardware of all kinds, including cast-iron hinges. Builders tools of all kinds. No literature.

Lesco Restorations, Inc.
PO Box 13313   Dept. OHJ
Atlanta, GA 30324
(404) 873-2156
RS/O
Exterior waterproofing and restoration contractor of masonry buildings. Services include stone and brick repointing, all types of caulking, concrete repair, shelf angle repair, coatings, roof repairs, exterior building cleaning, brick replacement/repair, needle caulking, window replacement and other related waterproofing. Are prepared to submit written budget estimates and set up repair programs. No literature.

Leslie Brothers Lumber Company
Box 566   Dept. OHJ
Cowen, WV 26206
(304) 226-3844
MO RS/O DIST
Solid hardwood tongue-and-grooved panelling, flooring, & mouldings. In oak, maple, ash, cherry, walnut, bass, beech, birch, or poplar. Also, will produce or match decorative mouldings for renovation work and pressure-treated hardwoods for exterior work. Prices are very reasonable. Samples, $6, deductible from 1st order. Free brochure.

Lewis, John N.
156 Scarboro Drive   Dept. OHJ
York, PA 17403
(717) 848-8461
MO RS/O
Antique barometers bought and sold. Mechanical repair and complete restoration for those looking for professional craftsmanship. Unable to ship finished product by way of common carrier — barometers have to be picked up by owner due to the elusiveness of the mercury. No problem with shipping aneroid barometers. No literature.

● **Joe Ley Antiques, Inc.**
615 East Market St.   Dept. OHJ
Louisville, KY 40202
(502) 583-4014
RS/O
Six buildings stocked with architectural antiques. Hard-to-find items including mantels, columns, newels. Specializing in light fixtures, restaurant items, doors, garden ornaments, brass hardware, and iron fences/gates. No literature.

Leyva's Ornamental Staff & Stone
917 Westminster Ave.   Dept. OHJ
Alhambra, CA 91803
(213) 289-4364
RS/O
Restoration or recreation of architectural details in cast-stone or plaster. Columns, balusters, cornice moulding, etc. Also works in fiberglass. A sample isn't necessary, can duplicate from fragments or photos. No literature.

Lieberman, Howard, P.E.
434 White Plains Rd.   Dept. OHJ
Eastchester, NY 10709
(914) 779-3773
RS/O
Prepurchase building inspection and consulting, engineering services. No literature.

Life Industries
205 Sweet Hollow Road   Dept. OHJ
Old Bethpage, NY 11804
(516) 454-0055
MO
Manufactures "Fix-Rot", a two-part liquid epoxy that restores the strength of rotted wood. Available on a mail order basis. 4 oz kit — $7.50, 16 oz kit — 18.95. Include $1.50 for shipping and handling.

● **Light Fantastic**
8414 Greenwood Ave., N.   Dept. OHJ
Seattle, WA 98103
(206) 783-0103
MO RS/O
Period lampshades made of silk, satin, and a variety of other fine materials. Stock and custom shades. Catalog, $3.

Lisa — Victoria Brass Beds
17106 So. Crater Rd. - 7   Dept. OHJ
Petersburg, VA 23805
(804) 862-1491
MO
Reasonably priced, custom-made solid brass beds with the emphasis on Victorian styles. Available only by mail-order. Color catalog, $4, refundable with order.

Litchfield House
On-The-Green   Dept. OHJ
Sharon, CT 06069
(203) 355-0375
MO RS/O DIST
Exclusive importer of English porcelain china door fixtures, and cabinet, wardrobe knobs from Manchester, England. Door knobs, push plates and florets (keyhole covers) available individually or in complete sets in range of antique designs and colors. Complete fittings to U.S. specifications included for simple installations. Send for free illustrated color brochure.

Littlefield Lumber Co., Inc.
299 Vaughn St.   Dept. OHJ
Portsmouth, NH 03801
(603) 436-3211
MO RS/O
Variety of woods including eastern white pine, southern pine, and other foreign & native hardwoods. All wood can be planed and cut to your specifications. Doors, windows, shingles, flooring, and other millwork. No literature.

Littlejohn's
PO Box 1144   Dept. OHJ
Monroe, NC 28110
(704) 283-8843
MO
English antique reproductions, many hand-crafted pieces include plant stand and candlestand table. Free flyers available.

Littlewood, Craig
PO Box 402   Dept. OHJ
Palmyra, NJ 08065
(609) 829-4615
MO RS/O
Restoration of period lighting fixtures for museums and private collectors. The American Lighting (1825 — 1900) Consultant to American Wing of the Metropolitan Museum, Mr. Littlewood lectures and demonstrates working lamps of the period. Also, an office in Provincetown, MA: (617) 487-1966. No literature.

● **London Venturers Company**
2 Dock Square   Dept. OHJ
Rockport, MA 01966
(617) 546-7161
RS/O MO
Specializing in original gas, oil, and early electric lighting fixtures: chandeliers, hall lights, wall sconces and table lamps. Also quality reproductions of gas, oil, and early electric lighting. Illustrated catalog, $2.

Long, E. T., Inc.
21st & Bainbridge Sts.   Dept. OHJ
Richmond, VA 23225
(804) 232-1231
MO   RS/O
Cast-iron wood burning stoves and old stove parts (custom casting is offered for parts that are no longer available). Also offer stove installation, fireplace restoration and flue relining. Free information sheet.

Loose, Thomas — Blacksmith/ Whitesmith
R.D. 2, Box 124   Dept. OHJ
Leesport, PA 19533
(215) 926-4849
MO   RS/O
Hand-wrought items for home and hearth, finely decorated with brass and copper inlay. Kitchen and fireplace utensils and lighting devices. Hardware and other items for old home restoration made to your specifications. Brochure available; please enclose a stamp with your request.

Louis Baldinger & Sons
248 Flushing Ave.   Dept. OHJ
Brooklyn, NY 11205
(212) 875-1400
DIST   RS/O
Large selection of prisms. Also custom chandeliers and recreating of period fixtures, i.e., NY State Capitols. Free literature.

Lovelia Enterprises, Inc.
Box 1845, Grand Cen. Sta.   Dept. OHJ
New York, NY 10017
(212) 490-0930
MO   RS/O
Importers of machine woven tapestries from France, Belgium and Italy in sizes 10 inches to 10 feet. Gobelin and Aubusson tapestries are woven on old looms from original jacquards in either wool or 100% cotton. Some are copies of masterpieces with the signature of the original artist. 20-page color catalog, plus 4 illustrated pages on new uses for tapestries, $4.00.

Ludowici-Celadon Co.
P.O. Box 69   Dept. OHJ
New Lexington, OH 43764
(614) 342-1995
MO   RS/O
Manufactures wide range of handsome ceramic roofing tiles. Free product data sheets on each style, which include: Barrel mission style, Spanish and various interlocking roof tiles, also flat ceramic shingle tile.

Luigi Crystal
7332 Frankford Ave.   Dept. OHJ
Philadelphia, PA 19136
(215) 338-2978
MO
Painted glass Victorian table lamps, cut crystal chandeliers, hurricane lamps, sconces. Reasonably priced. Imported crystal prisms. Illustrated catalog & price list — $1.00.

Lundberg Studios
P.O. Box C   Dept. OHJ
Davenport, CA 95017
(408) 423-2532
MO   DIST   RS/O
They offer a variety of art glass, including Tiffany-style surface decorated paper-weights and vases. They specialize in lamps and shades imitating Tiffany and Steuben shades. Over 20 different shades in Art Nouveau style available. Metal lamp bases and replacement parts also available. They will buy or trade for original Tiffany lamp bases. Quantity discounts offered to distributors. Individuals can order from $3 color catalog.

Lyemance International
P.O. Box 6651   Dept. OHJ
Louisville, KY 40206
(502) 896-2441
DIST
Top-sealing fireplace damper saves energy; reduces heat loss by controlling down drafts when fireplace is not in use. Seals out birds and insects, keeps out rain, sleet and snow and saves on air conditioning costs. The damper is shut by means of a stainless-steel cable that extends down the flue to the firebox, where it is secured to a bracket on the side firebox wall. Installed on chimney tops. Brochure free.

KEY TO ABBREVIATIONS

MO   sells by Mail Order
RS/O   sells through Retail Store or Office
DIST   sells through Distributors
ID   sells only through Interior Designers or Architects

You'll get better service when contacting companies if you mention The Old-House Journal Catalog

---

● See Product Displays Index on page 199 for more details.

M

M — H Lamp & Fan Company
7231-1/2 N. Sheridan Road   Dept. OHJ
Chicago, IL 60626
(312) 743-2225
MO   RS/O
They manufacture solid brass, hand-made, Victorian reproduction light fixtures. Also specialize in complete restoration of antique desk and ceiling fans, and antique light fixtures. They have a limited supply of restored fans, inquiries welcome. Catalog, $1.

M.R.S Industries, Inc.
115 Fernwood Dr.   Dept. OHJ
Rocky Hill, CT 06067
(203) 563-4082
RS/O   MO
Work gloves for all applications. Eye, ear and respiratory protection. Protective clothing and rubber foot wear. Industrial catalog — $1.

● **Mad River Wood Works**
P.O. Box 163   Dept. OHJ
Arcata, CA 95521
(707) 826-0629
MO   DIST   RS/O
Manufacturers of Victorian millwork in redwood and select hardwoods. Several patterns of ornamental shingles, turnings, door and window sash, mouldings, old-style screen door replicas, corbels, brackets, balusters and railing, and ornamental pickets. Custom work is also accepted. Catalog, $2.

Maggiem & Co.
1117 Elm Dr.   Dept. OHJ
St. Louis, MO 63119
(314) 962-7778
MO
Offers a high-tank toilet hand made from white oak, with a copper liner, & solid brass pipes. The price, $675, includes a wash-down bowl and oak set. Call or write for further details.

Magnolia Hall
726 Andover Dr.   Dept. OH9
Atlanta, GA 30327
(404) 256-4747
MO
Well-built, solid mahogany, hand-carved Victorian reproduction furniture. Some brass and oak pieces. Collection of highly-carved Louis XIV French sofas, chairs. Also lamps, clocks, mirrors, footstools. Large selection of whatnot stands and wall curio cabinets. 80-page illustrated catalog and fabric samples — $1.00.

● **Maine Architectural Millwork**
Front Street   Dept. OHJ
South Berwick, ME 03908
(207) 384-9541
RS/O   MO
Established artisans located in historic New England. Production of custom millwork (mantels, paneled walls, doors, Palladian windows, etc.) and mouldings a specialty. Duplication of porch parts, balusters, doors, brackets, turnings, and window sash. Restoration services for the aging home, repair and reproduction of architectural antiques. No fee for prices supplied on request; literature, $5.

Malleable Iron Range Co.
715 N. Spring St.   Dept. OHJ
Beaver Dam, WI 53916
(414) 887-8131
MO RS/O
An old-time stove manufacturer, this company can still furnish some Monarch parts back to 1896.

Mangione Plaster and Tile and Stucco
21 John St.   Dept. OHJ
Saugerties, NY 12477
(914) 246-9863
RS/O
Specializes in the restoration of ornamental plasterwork. Will also reproduce plaster domes and mouldings. Serving New York/Connecticut area. No literature.

Mannington Mills, Inc.
PO Box 30   Dept. OHJ
Salem, NJ 08079
(609) 935-3000
DIST
Inexpensive floor coverings with several patterns reminiscent of turn-of-the-century linoleum. "Thrift-tex" is an asphalt-saturated felt. "Manolux" is a printed vinyl. They're temporary floorings, not recommended for high traffic areas, but they chould be used as an appropriate period flooring. Free pattern chart.

Manor Art Glass Studio
20 Ridge Road   Dept. OHJ
Douglaston, NY 11363
(212) 631-8029
RS/O MO
Professionally trained craftsmen will restore your antique stained glass windows to their original strength and beauty, either in your home or at their studio. Will create new windows to blend with the period architecture of your home. Slides available on specific request.

Mansion Industries, Inc.
14711 E. Clark, Box 220   Dept. OHJ
Industry, CA 91746
(213) 968-9501
DIST
Hemlock stairparts in traditional styles: newel posts, balusters, and railings. Installation instructions, architectural tracing details, reference wall charts, audio-visual training films — all available on request. Contact Customer Service Dept. for direct assistance.

Marsh Stream Enterprise
RFD 2, Box 490   Dept. OHJ
Brooks, ME 04921
(207) 722-3575
MO
Nine stencils of original 'Knees' from a turn-of-the-century woodworking mill enable you to make your own gingerbread. Popular designs used on porches, eaves, and gables, ranging in size from 18-in. x 30-in. to 6-in. x 10-in. $6.50 for complete set, including instructions.

Marshall Imports
713 South Main   Dept. 15
Mansfield, OH 44907
(419) 756-3814
MO
Sole United States importer of Antiquax, the pure wax polish used by museums. Gives a soft mellow sheen, will not fingerprint, produces a deep patina on both antique and contemporary finishes. Ideal for kitchen cupboards. Sold through better stores or by mail. A brochure describing Antiquax products is available at no charge.

Marshalltown Trowel Co.
PO Box 738   Dept. OHJ
Marshalltown, IA 50158
(515) 754-6116
DIST
Trowels and other tools for working with cement, brick, concrete block, dry wall and plaster. Free illustrated catalog. A useful 24 pg. booklet "Troweling Tips and Techniques" is available for $1.00.

Martha M. House Furniture
1022 So. Decatur Street   Dept. OHJ
Montgomery, AL 36104
(205) 264-3558
RS/O MO
A large mail-order source for Victorian reproduction furniture. Hand-carved solid mahogany pieces; tables with wood or Carrara marble tops. Sofas, chairs, bedroom and dining furniture. Large choice of covers and finishes. "Southern Heirlooms" catalog, $2.

● **Marvin Windows**
   Dept. OHJ
Warroad, MN 56763
(800) 346-5128
DIST
Wood windows and patio doors for replacement and remodelling. Available in standard, retro, and custom sizes. Single, double, and triple glazing and wood storms. All units are weather stripped, and may be ordered bare wood, primed or prefinished. Options include authentic divided lites, or grids. Custom shapes and sizes include round and arched windows. Free brochure. In Minn., (800) 552-1167.

Mason & Sullivan Co.
586 Higgins Crowell Rd.   Dept. 4512
W. Yarmouth, MA 02673
(617) 778-1056
MO RS/O
Reproduction clock kits, copies of clocks by Aaron Willard and other great American clock craftsmen. Also movements, dials, assembled clocks, specialty tools, and books. 32 page color catalog, $1.

Masonry Specialty Co.
4430 Gibsonia Rd.   Dept. OHJ
Gibsonia, PA 15044
(412) 443-7080
MO DIST
Manufactor/distributor of top quality tools and equipment for the construction trades. Including tools for brick masonry, cement finishing, drywall, tilesetting, and plastering. Free catalog illustrating over 1900 items.

Master Wood Carver
103 Corrine Dr.   Dept. OHJ
Pennington, NJ 08534
(609) 737-9364
MO RS/O
Handcrafts authentic Colonial reproduction pieces in solid wood. Each item is signed and numbered. Antique restoration and repair expertly done. Custom pieces from drawings or pictures. Please call for appointment or send $.50 for introductory brochure.

Master's Stained and Etched Glass Studio
729 West 16th St., No. B-1   Dept. OHJ
Costa Mesa, CA 92627
(714) 548-4951
RS/O MO
Painted, leaded, etched and bevelled glass. Residential and commercial commissions. Antique windows. Free brochure.

Masters Picture Frame Co.
PO Box 1181   Dept. OHJ
Southgate, MI 48195
(313) 282-0545
MO
Period style picture hangers, $3.50 each ppd. Also, moulding hooks, $3.00 ppd for a dozen.

Materials Unlimited
2 W. Michigan Ave.   Dept. OHJ
Ypsilanti, MI 48197
(313) 483-6980
RS/O
The largest collection of restored architectural antiques in the midwest. Three floors of display. Stained & beveled glass doors, windows, entrances; restored brass chandeliers & sconces; mantels; furniture; hardware; decorative accessories; front & back bars. Custom services include: beveling, leaded glass repair, refinishing, modification to specification, custom design & fabrication of stained or beveled panels, and front & back bars. Free brochure.

Mattia, Louis
980 2nd Ave.   Dept. OHJ
New York, NY 10022
(212) 753-2176
RS/O
This little store is full of turn-of-century lighting fixtures. Mattia restores, rewires, adds antique or reproduction glass shades. Hundreds of wall sconces — wired or for candles. Cannot handle mail orders. No literature.

● **Maurer & Shepherd, Joyners**
122 Naubuc Ave.   Dept. OHJ
Glastonbury, CT 06033
(203) 633-2383
RS/O MO
Handcrafted custom-made interior and exterior 18th century architectural trim. Finely-detailed Colonial doors and windows, shutters, wainscot and wall panelling, carved details, pediments, etc. Wide pine flooring, half-lapped. Pegged mortise and tenon joints — authentic work. Free brochure.

Max-Cast, Inc.
RFD 3, Box 230 B   Dept. OHJ
Iowa City, IA 52240
(319) 351-0708
RS/O
A custom foundry willing to do small runs of appliance and architectural castings in brass, bronze, aluminum, and grey iron. Stove parts a specialty. No literature.

Mayer, Michael, Co.
PO Box 1522   Dept. OHJ
San Marcos, CA 92069
MO
Solid oak toilet seats, with brass hinges. Feature built-in wood spline for added durability, 100% water proof. Complete with hardware. Reasonably priced at $38 ppd ($39 ppd for elongated size). Free literature.

Mazza Frame and Furniture Co., Inc.
35-10 Tenth Street   Dept. OHJ
Long Island City, NY 11106
(212) 721-9287
RS/O MO
Manufacturers of hardwood furniture frames in period styles. Mail orders shipped throughout the U.S. and overseas. Firm sells primarily to decorators and upholstery shops. Can handle variations of standard designs, and custom work. Free brochure; prices and specific photos on request.

Mazzeo's Chimney Sweep Suppliers
RDF 1, Box 1245   Dept. OHJ
Rockland, ME 04841
(207) 596-6296
MO   DIST   RS/O
A major supplier to masons, contractors, and chimney sweeps of tools, such as "Acu-set", a tile lining tool used to fit older chimneys with new clay tiles. They will supply homeowners with all the necessary tools for cleaning their chimney — brushes, chimney rods, etc. Free information.

McAvoy Antique Lighting
1901 Lafayette Avenue   Dept. OHJ
St. Louis, MO 63104
(314) 773-9136
RS/O   MO
Large stock of restored antique lighting fixtures available. Ornate gas and electric fixtures, oil lights, circa 1910 chain fixtures, and many wall sconces. Design and rebuilding of fixtures on specific order. Shipping pre-arranged by customer's request. Sample sheet — send SASE. Photos of specific items are $1 each. Please: Always call for an appointment.

McCloskey Varnish Co.
7600 State Road   Dept. OHJ
Philadelphia, PA 19136
(215) 624-4400
DIST   RS/O
Manufactures a complete line of wood finishing and refinishing products, stains, sealers, floor varnishes, rubbing varnishes, and polyurethanes. Free literature.

McGivern, Barbara — Artist
3545 Oakshire Drive   Dept. OHJ
Oak Creek, WI 53154
(414) 762-0849
MO   RS/O
Will do pen & ink drawing, $10, or full color watercolor, $25, of a home, scene, historic building, etc. Send photo (returnable) and check.

Mead Associates Woodworking, Inc.
63 Tiffany Place   Dept. OHJ
Brooklyn, NY 11231
(212) 855-3884
RS/O
Custom cabinetmaking and architectural woodworking. Expert at details in keeping with the restoration of older houses. We make kitchens, library units, offices, commercial interiors and furniture. We also custom make doors of all types and styles including completely weatherized doors and entrances. We prefer to work from drawings and we will consult. Cabinetmakers to the Old House Journal. No literature, references available; call for appointment.

The Mechanick's Workbench
PO Box 544   Dept. O
Marion, MA 02738
(617) 748-1680
MO
They specialize in fine quality, antique woodworking tools for craftsmen and collectors. Their catalogues have the reputation of being the best in the field and are published 2 or 3 times a year — all different offerings in each. Catalog, $8.

● **See Product Dis-plays Index on page 199 for more details.**

Meierjohan — Wengler, Inc.
10330 Wayne Ave.   Dept. OHJ
Cincinnati, OH 45215
(513) 771-6074
MO
Firm has been making cast tablets and markers for over 50 years. Available in a variety of stock shapes or special sizes. Emblems, symbols or crests can be incorporated to create a special one-of-a-kind design. Choice of material: Bronze, aluminum or silver-bronze. Can also do lost-wax casting. Free catalog.

Mel-Nor Marketing
303 Gulfbank   Dept. OHJ
Houston, TX 77037
(713) 445-3485
MO
A large selection of Victorian-styled park benches made of cast aluminum and a choice of fir or oak slats. Custom sizes & colors are offered. Also, porch swings, mail-box, and street lamps. Free catalog.

Melotte-Morse Studios
3 Old State Capitol Plaza S.   Dept. OHJ
Springfield, IL 62701
(217) 789-9515
RS/O
Melotte-Morse Studios designs, fabricates and renovates stained glass art for ecclesiastical, commercial, and individual clients. A division of Melotte-Morse, Architects and Planners, the Studio also works extensively with existing antique glass works, performing corrective maintenance and restorative repairs or renovations. The studio has refurbished entire stained glass collections for churches as well as individual panels for residential reinstallation. Brochure is free.

Memphis Hardwood Flooring Co.
P.O. Box 7253   Dept. OHJ
Memphis, TN 38107
(901) 526-7306
DIST
Hardwood flooring available through distributors. Colorful 12-page catalog available $.50 postpaid.

KEY TO ABBREVIATIONS

MO   sells by Mail Order
RS/O   sells through Retail Store or Office
DIST   sells through Distributors
ID   sells only through Interior Designers or Architects

You'll get better service when contacting companies if you mention The Old-House Journal Catalog

---

Mendel-Black Stone Restoration
33 Westward Rd.   Dept. OHJ
Woodbridge, CT 06525
(203) 389-0205
RS/O
Stonecarvers specializing in traditional stone recarving and "dutchman" techniques as an alternative to patching. Will also custom recreate masonry replacements, i.e., columns, lintels in poured concrete. Custom carving and sculptural works in brownstone, limestone, marble. Will travel to do installations.

Menerey, E. W.
4079 Five Mile Road   Dept. OHJ
Traverse City, MI 49684
(616) 938-2743
MO   RS/O
Porcelain painting. Antique lamps a specialty: Lamp shades painted to match founts, or founts to match shades. New lamps painted to order. A painted lampshade costs from $35 to $150 or more, depending on the degree of detail. Extra charge for enamel and/or gold. (No wiring please.) Lessons given. No literature.

Merit Metal Products Corp.
242 Valley Rd.   Dept. OHJ
Warrington, PA 18976
(215) 343-2500
MO   DIST
Manufactures a complete line of authentic solid brass door, furniture and cabinet hardware. Specializing in fine traditional, colonial and Victorian designs. Locks, latches, knobs, pulls, handles, hinges, hooks, door stops, & window hardware. Free color brochure.

Merit Moulding, Ltd.
95-35 150th St.   Dept. OHJ
Jamaica, NY 11435
(212) 523-2200
RS/O
Manufacturer of custom wood mouldings — short runs a specialty. Also, oak mouldings and trim. No literature.

**Merrimack Valley Textile Museum —
Textile Conser. Cntr.**
800 Massachusetts Ave.   Dept. OHJ
North Andover, MA 01845
(617) 686-0191
MO   RS/O
A center specializing in the conservation of textiles; services include stablizing, mounting, cleaning, and analyzing fabrics. Conservation workshops are arranged for groups. Free brochure.

Merritt's Antiques, Inc.
Route 2   Dept. OHJ
Douglassville, PA 19518
(215) 689-9541
MO   RS/O
Large selection of metal and wood clock parts including hands, pulleys, keys, dials, movements, and pendulums. Also, a nice selection of wall, shelf, and grandfather clocks (antique, reproduction, and kits). Parts catalog, $1.50; Clock catalog, $1. Call toll-free (800) 345-4101.

Mexico House
Box 970   Dept. OHJ
Del Mar, CA 92014
(714) 481-6099
MO   RS/O
A good source for chandeliers, candleabra and lighting fixtures suitable for Spanish Colonial houses. Also custom design work for Spanish Colonial fittings: Window grilles, rails, outdoor furniture, fireplace screens and tools. Catalog $1. (refundable with purchase).

Meyer, Kenneth Co.
327 6th Ave.   Dept. OHJ
San Francisco, CA 94118
(415) 752-2865
ID
Manufacturers of custom-made trimmings,
fringes, tassels, tiebacks for Interior Decorators.
No literature.

● **Michael's Fine Colonial Products**
Rte 44, RD1, Box 179A   Dept. OHJ
Salt Point, NY 12578
(914) 677-3960
MO
Custom-made millwork appropriate for 19th
century as well as Colonial houses: Divided light
sash; circle head sash; Gothic, triangle, and
segment windows; raised panel blinds & shutters;
stock and custom stair parts; doors. Mouldings to
pattern. Free flyer with large SASE.

Mid-State Tile Company
PO Box 1777   Dept. OHJ
Lexington, NC 27292
(704) 249-3931
DIST
Quarry pavers are available in 4-in x 8-in, 6-in
sq., 8-in sq., and 8-in hex. Five natural colors and
matching trim will give you an authentic look in
any application. Tough enough for exterior use in
areas below the freeze line. Brochures, $.50 each.

Midwest Spiral Stair Company, Inc.
263 N. West Ave.   Dept. OHJ
Elmhurst, IL 60126
(312) 941-3395
MO   RS/O
A complete selection of spiral stairs in both metal
and wood, shipped anywhere in the U.S. Flyer
available.

Miles Lumber Co, Inc.
Railroad Avenue   Dept. OHJ
Arlington, VT 05250
(802) 375-2525
RS/O
Custom millwork from shop drawings or
architect's drawings. No stock items; no
literature.

Mill River Hammerworks
65 Canal St.   Dept. OHJ
Turners Falls, MA 01376
(413) 863-8388
MO   RS/O
Museum experienced metal craftsman offers
repair and reproduction services in iron, copper,
brass, pewter, and tin. Hardware, lighting
devices, kitchen and fireplace accessories, etc.
Hand-forged, cast, spun, or fabricated as needed.
Also, exterior architectural hardware, gates,
railings, and grilles. Difficult or unusual antique
repair or reproduction a specialty. Free brochure.

Millbranth, D.R.
PO Box 1174   Dept. OHJ
Hillsboro, NH 03244
(603) 464-5244
RS/O   MO
Custom handcrafted, 18th century furniture
reproductions and adaptations. Quality antique
restoration services. Inquiries to be accompanied
by SASE.

Millen Roofing Co.
2247 N. 31 St.   Dept. OHJ
Milwaukee, WI 53208
(414) 442-1424
MO   RS/O
Tile and slate roofing. Large supply of old types
of roofing tile and weathered slate for restoration
work. Tools, equipment, copper nails, copper
clips and fasteners, brass snow guards also
available. Does consulting, design, specifications,
and inspections. No literature.

Howard Miller Clock Co.
860 Byron Road   Dept. OHJ
Zeeland, MI 49464
(616) 772-9131
DIST   ID
Reproductions and adaptations of antique wall,
mantel, and grandfather clocks using the finest of
woods, movements, and craftsmanship. Sold
through fine furniture distributors. Literature free
to the trade.

● **Millham, Newton — Blacksmith**
672 Drift Road   Dept. OHJ
Westport, MA 02790
(617) 636-5437
RS/O   MO
Offers a wide selection of 17th, 18th and early
19th century architectural house hardware:
latches, spring latches, H and strap hinges, bolts,
shutter dogs. Household ironware includes:
cooking utensils, hearth items, early
candleholders, candlestands, rush lights pipe
tongs, etc. Illustrated catalog and price list $1.00.

Millwork Supply Company
2225 1st Ave. South   Dept. OHJ
Seattle, WA 98134
(206) 622-1450
MO   RS/O
In business at this location for 58 years. They are
manufacturers and distributors for stock and
custom; wood doors, windows, frames,
mouldings, mantels, and stair parts. Free stock
moulding sheet.

Mine Safety Appliance Corp.
1100 Globe Ave.   Dept. OHJ
Mountainside, NJ 07092
(201) 232-3490
MO
Manufactures the Comfo II Respirator Mask for
filtering toxic particles — recommended for
people stripping lead-based paints indoors.
Please call for current prices and information on
proper cartridges.

Minwax Company, Inc.
102 Chestnut Ridge Plaza   Dept. HC
Montvale, NJ 07645
(201) 391-0253
DIST
Easy-to-use stains and woodfinishing products
for durable, attractive finishes from a 75-year old
company. Free literature & color card. Also free:
"Tips on Wood Finishing", a 22 page booklet
providing do-it-yourselfers with information
ranging from how to apply a preservative stain to
a house exterior to preparing antiques for
refinishing.

Mirror Patented Stove Pipe Co.
11 Britton Drive, Box A   Dept. OHJ
Bloomfield, CT 06002
(203) 243-8358
DIST
A manufacturer of No. 304, 24-gauge stainless
steel pipe for chimney relining. No literature, but
will put you in contact with a distributor in your
area.

Mittermeir, Frank Inc.
3577 E. Tremont Ave., Box 2   Dept. OHJ
Bronx, NY 10465
(212) 828-3843
MO
Imported and domestic quality tools for
woodcarvers, sculptors, engravers, ceramists, and
potters. Of special interest are their tools for
ornamental plasterwork. They also sell a number
of books on sculpture, wood carving, and related
arts. Free catalog.

Modern Technical Tools & Supply Co.
211 Nevada St.   Dept. OHJ
Hicksville, NY 11801
(516) 931-7875
MO
A wide selection of clock movement materials for
serving modern and antique clocks. Repair parts
and obsolete movements, as well as precision
tools and supplies. Catalog, $3.50, refundable
upon purchase.

Mohawk Electric Supply Co., Inc.
36 Hudson Street   Dept. OHJ
New York, NY 10013
(212) 227-0466
MO   RS/O
Old-fashioned push-button electric light switches.
No catalog. Can ship COD via UPS. Telephone
for details and prices.

Mohawk Industries, Inc.
PO Box 71   Dept. OHJ
Adams, MA 01220
(413) 743-3648
DIST
Coal and woodburning heating stove.
Manufacturer of the UL listed "Tempwood" II &
V, the "Tempview" UL Combi-Stove and the
"Tempcoal" II top loader, plus accessories such as
Fireplace Damper Panel, Flue Adaptor, log rack,
shovel & poker, hot water panel, utility shelf,
brass decorator kit. Wood/coal Energy brochure,
plus full color literature - $1.

Monier
1091 North Batavia   Dept. OHJ
Orange, CA·92667
(714) 538-8822
DIST
Concrete roofing tiles in imitation of terra-cotta
'S' tiles, shake roof tiles, and slate roof tiles. Free
information.

Monroe Coldren and Sons
723 East Virginia Ave.   Dept. OHJ
West Chester, PA 19380
(215) 692-5651
MO   RS/O
Original antique hardware. Specialize in the 18th
and 19th century. For large installations, they'll
travel to your site to determine your needs and
for installation instructions. Custom-order
reproduction hardware, as well as original doors,
mantels, and shutters. No literature.

J.H. Monteath Co.
2500 Park Ave.   Dept. OHJ
Bronx, NY 10451
(212) 292-9333
MO   DIST
A major supplier of foreign and domestic
hardwoods — throughout the U.S. Also, a
limited selection of mouldings, and veneers. The
minimum order is $500. Free literature.

Moore, E.T., Jr. Co.
119 E. 2nd St.   Dept. OHJ
Richmond, VA 23224
(804) 231-1823
MO RS/O
Large selection of custom and stock heart pine products; Mantels, columns, flooring, mouldings, and panelling. Also hand-hewn beams, and custom furniture & cabinets. Free literature.

Morgan & Company
443 Metropolitan Ave.   Dept. OHJ
Brooklyn, NY 11211
(212) 387-2196
RS/O
Company will bend glass. Can make bent glass to repair tops of leaded glass shades, curio cabinets and china closets. No literature; walk-in shop only.

Morgan Bockius Studios, Inc.
1412 York Road   Dept. OHJ
Warminster, PA 18974
(215) 674-1930
RS/O MO
Stained, painted, and leaded glass, period and custom designs. Their artists design and craft Victorian and contemporary adaptations for any architectural situation. Coats of arms, and other decorative work available including mirrors, beveled glass, etched and carved panels on clear and tinted glass. Custom designed lamps; repairs to old fixtures including glass bending and painting, and metal work. Call for more information or driving directions. Free brochure.

Morgan Woodworking Supplies
1123 Bardstown Rd.   Dept. OO3K1
Louisville, KY 40204
(502) 456-2545
MO RS/O
Hardwood lumber, inlays, veneers, chair cane, embossed replacement seats for chairs, early American furniture plans, period hardware, colonial nails, upholstery supplies, Shaker pegs, dowels and coffee grinder mechanism. Catalog, $.50.

Moriarty's Lamps
512 Brinkerhoff Avenue   Dept. OHJ
Santa Barbara, CA 93101
(805) 966-1124
RS/O
Sells old chandeliers, wall sconces, kerosene lamps, old electric and gas-electric fixtures, old shades. Also metal refinishing and old lamp parts. Also refinishes old doorknobs, window latches, plumbing fixtures, etc. Inquiries answered; no literature.

Morningstar
PO Box 162   Dept. OHJ
Clermont Harbor, MS 39551
(504) 831-2926
RS/O MO
Company handles all phases of old house restoration, including custom cabinets and fine woodworking. Serves mainly the Mississippi Gulf Coast to the New Orleans area. Mail-order sales welcomed; free estimates and bids. No literature.

● **Mosca, Matthew**
Box 960, Bowling Green Sta.   Dept. OHJ
New York, NY 10274
(516) 431-3592
RS/O
Historic paint specialist. Microscopic techniques and chemical testing are used to determine the original composition and color of paints and other architectural finishes. Has done work on Mt. Vernon and National Trust properties. Can analyze samples taken by architect or homeowner. Complete interior design capability available utilizing research for restorations and historically compatible rehabilitations. Before taking samples, write describing your needs and objectives.

Moser Brothers, Inc.
3rd & Green Sts.   Dept. OHJ
Bridgeport, PA 19405
(215) 272-1052
RS/O
Quality screen/storm doors and windows in wood. Old styles, choice of patterns and wood species, including Brazilian mahogany. Standard or custom designs, all sized on order. Removable screen or safety-glass panel held in place by bronze tabs. Also: fine kitchen cabinetwork. Specialist in restoration. Please call; no literature.

Moultrie Manufacturing Company
PO Drawer 1179   Dept. OHJ
Moultrie, GA 31768
(912) 985-1312
MO RS/O
Ornamental columns, gates, and fences of cast aluminum. Old South Reproductions catalog shows selection of period-style fence panels and gates; also aluminum furniture, fountains, urns, plaques, etc. Catalog is $1.00. Can also call (800) 841-8674.

● **Mountain Lumber Company**
1327 Carlton Ave., Box 285   Dept. OHJ
Charlottesville, VA 22901
(804) 295-1922
MO RS/O
Specialist in: random-width and wide plank old, longleaf heart pine flooring; wormy chestnut, heart pine, and mahogany panelling. Handhewn and rough-sawn beams. Custom millwork: cabinets, doors, mouldings, & trim. All lumber kiln-dried. Free brochure.

Mr. Slate - Smid Incorporated
    Dept. OHJ
Sudbury, VT 05733
(802) 247-8809
RS/O
Quality salvaged roofing slate for repair work, restorations, and new construction. Inventory includes most colors and sizes. Antique/salvage slate tiles, 'Vermont Cobble Slate', for flooring, hearths, and countertops. Also new slate from the quarries of the East Coast. Color brochure and sample, $2.

Munsell Color
2441 North Calvert St.   Dept. OHJ
Baltimore, MD 21218
(301) 243-2171
MO RS/O
The Munsell color notation system is a professional reference resource. In restoring an old house to its original appearance, color samples would be collected and checked against the Munsell Book of Colors. The painter or decorator would then be given the appropriate color codes and could mix the paints accurately. There are two basic books — glossy finish $615.00, and matte finish, $440.00. Free full-color brochure.

Muralo Company
148 E. Fifth St.   Dept. OHJ
Bayonne, NJ 07002
(201) 437-0770
DIST
Besides being the inventor (and major manufacturer) of Spackle, this old company may be the only remaining maker of old-fashioned calcimine paint. Also makes a full line of latex paints, wallpaper adhesives, texture and sand finish, Georgetown colors in latex house paint, 100 percent pure linseed oil house paint, and fire-retardant paint. No literature — please write for name of distributor.

Museum of the City of New York
Fifth Ave. at 103rd St.   Dept. OHJ
New York, NY 10029
(212) 534-1672
MO
Large selection of reproduction Edwardian (1901-1910) Christmas decorations. Catalog, $1.

KEY TO ABBREVIATIONS

MO   sells by Mail Order

RS/O   sells through Retail Store or Office

DIST   sells through Distributors

ID   sells only through Interior Designers or Architects

●See Product Displays Index on page 199 for more details.

You'll get better service when contacting companies if you mention The Old-House Journal Catalog

N

Nassau Flooring Corp.
P.O. 351, 242 Drexel Ave.   Dept. OHJ
Westbury, NY 11590
(516) 334-2327
RS/O   MO
Will reproduce old parquet patterns as well as
install new flooring and repair worn floors. No
literature.

Nast, Vivian
49 Willow St., 3B   Dept. OHJ
Brooklyn, NY 11201
(212) 596-5280
RS/O
Expert designer and colorist does commission
work in stained and leaded glass. Also works in
etched glass, both sand blasting and acid-etched.
Will reproduce work from existing originals, or
will create original designs in period styles.
Makes etched patterns in flashed glass. Also fine
art portraits of your historic building. Please call
or write for further deatils.

**National Guild of Professional
Paperhangers, Inc.**
PO Box 574   Dept. OHJ
Farmingdale, NY 11735
RS/O
This nationwide organization will put you in
contact with your local chapter of professional
paperhangers. They also publish a bi-monthly
newsletter. Free general information.

**National Home Inspection Service of New
England, Inc.**
2 Calvin Rd.   Dept. OHJ
Watertown, MA 02172
(617) 923-2300
RS/O
Complete structural and mechanical pre-purchase
home inspections anywhere in New England.
After the inspection, a complete written report of
the condition of the property is issued to you.
Maintenance and restoration advice is also
provided if desired. All inspectors are members
of the American Society of Home Inspectors and
subscribe to its Standards and Code of Ethical
Conduct. No literature available.

● **National SUPAFLU Systems, Inc.**
Route 30A, PO Box 289   Dept. OHJ
Central Bridge, NY 12035
(518) 868-4585
RS/O   DIST
A unique system of relining chimneys, with
poured refactory cement especially effective for
chimneys with bends, offsets, or multi-flues. Free
literature.

Native American Hardwood Ltd.
RD 1, Box 6484   Dept. OHJ
West Valley, NY 14171
(716) 942-6631
RS/O   MO
American hardwoods including walnut,
butternut, cherry, and birdseye maple always in
stock. Specializing in wide and thick stock, stock
for flooring, panelling, and woodwork; both
cabinet and economy grade. No minimum on
orders — will ship. Listing $.50.

Native Wood Products, Inc.
Drawer Box 469   Dept. OHJ
Brooklyn, CT 06234
(203) 774-7700
MO   RS/O
Blueprint, material list, and instruction sheet for
building a post and beam carriage shed, $10.00.
Also, complete lumber package to customers in
New England, NY, and PA. Many sizes and
styles of post and beam buildings available,
including houses. Information and prices
available upon request. Also available, colonial
reproduction wood products including beaded
clapboard, wainscot paneling, and hand-forged
hardware.

● **Navedo Woodcraft, Inc.**
179 E. 119th St.   Dept. OHJ
New York, NY 10035
(212) 722-4431
MO   RS/O
An old line custom cabinetmaking shop. They
fabricate furniture, doors, trims, and shutters as
per drawings/ specifications. Millwork, including
mouldings, custom duplicated in oak, poplar,
and pine. No literature, call or write with
specifics.

Nelson-Johnson Wood Products, Inc.
4326 Lyndale Ave., No.   Dept. OHJ
Minneapolis, MN 55412
(612) 529-2771
MO   RS/O
Custom wood turning: 6 in. to 10 ft. in length, 1
in. to 12 in. dia. All woods, 1-100 piece limit.
Stock items include decorative wood ornaments,
hardwood and pine mouldings, wood finials, and
turned posts & spindles. Free catalogs: Wood
Carvings & Mouldings, Wood Turnings, and
Wood Carving Tools.

Neri, C./Antiques
313 South Street   Dept. OHJ
Philadelphia, PA 19147
(215) 923-6669
RS/O
Fine antique furniture and mantels; the largest
selections of American antique lighting fixtures in
the country. Catalog, $5.

● **New Boston Building-Wrecking Co., Inc.**
84 Arsenal Street   Dept. OHJ
Watertown, MA 02172
(617) 924-9090
RS/O
Dealers in original architectural finishwork for
quality restoration or contemporary application in
the home or commercial space. Inventory from
17th through 19th centuries includes millwork,
mantels stained/bevelled glass, doors, plumbing/
lighting fixtures, columns, corbels, wrought iron
and decorative accessories. Call for appointment.
No literature.

New England Brassworks
220 Riverside Avenue   Dept. OHJ
Bristol, CT 06010
(203) 582-6100
MO   DIST
Manufactures and distributes solid brass
hardware and decorative accessories including
towel bars, toilet paper holders, shower curtain
rods, kick plates, door knockers, and
candlesticks, wall sconces, & candelabras. Also
produces a wide range of custom brass hardware
for architects and designers. An illustrated
brochure is available for $.50.

● **New Victorians of Arizona, Inc.**
PO Box 32505   Dept. OJ
Phoenix, AZ 85064
(602) 956-0755
MO
A catalog of 15 floor plans, 900 to 6000 sq. ft. All
with Victorian exteriors. Some are adapted from
designs of famous Victorian architects; interior
plans are contemporary. For do-it-yourself
owners with energy-saving construction. Custom
plans and revisions are available. Catalog, $6.

New York Carved Arts Co.
115 Grand Street   Dept. OHJ
New York, NY 10013
(212) 966-5924
RS/O
Creates etched glass panels by the sand-blasting
process. Will do custom work. No literature;
walk-in shop only.

● **New York Flooring**
979 3rd Ave., Rm. 825   Dept. OHJ
New York, NY 10022
(212) 427-6262
RS/O
Since 1911, this company has been offering
quality wood floor refinishing and restoration.
Also, new installations and custom stencilling.
Free literature.

New York Marble Works, Inc.
1399 Park Ave.   Dept. OHJ
New York, NY 10029
(212) 534-2242
MO   RS/O
Manufacturers of marble vanities, sinktops,
fireplaces, hearthstones, pedestals, steps,
saddles, table & furniture tops, and marble and
granite floor tiles. They also repair, restore, and
repolish marble. Free literature.

Newby, Simon
P.O. Box C414   Dept. OHJ
Westport, MA 02790
(617) 636-5010
MO   RS/O
Offers a selected line of hand-produced
architectural exterior and interior finish
woodwork for the 17th and 18th century homes
on a custom basis: entrance ways, raised panel
doors, wainscotting, chimney breasts, shutters,
etc. Also custom reproduction of 17th and 18th
century furniture. Specific inquiries welcomed.
Illustrated brochure, $2.

Newe Daisterre Glas
13431 Cedar Rd.   Dept. OHJ
Cleveland, OH 44118
(216) 371-7500
MO   RS/O
Custom art glass studio who works in stained
and bevelled glass for commercial and residential
markets. Will do etching, sandblasting, slumped
glass, and painting on glass. Will do on-location
restoration of lead windows; restoration of
stained & bevelled glass in studio. Free illustrated
brochure.

Newell Workshop
19 Blaine Ave.   Dept. OHJ
Hinsdale, IL 60521
(312) 323-7367
MO
Restoration materials for chairs — cane webbing,
rush seating material, flat weaving material, hand
caning kits. Free catalog with price list.

Newstamp Lighting Co.
227 Bay Rd.   Dept. OH-84
North Easton, MA 02356
(617) 238-7071
RS/O MO
Large selection of Early American lanterns,
sconces, and chandeliers. Catalog is $2.00,
refundable. Also distributor of Hunter Olde Tyme
Ceiling Fans.

Nixalite of America
417 25th Street   Dept. OHJ
Moline, IL 61265
(309) 797-8771
MO
Architectural bird control by Nixalite. Esthetically
correct — inconspicuous- humane. Stainless steel,
porcupine-like strips protect architectural
intracacies, gutters, eaves, ledges, etc., from pest
birds! See OHJ, June 1981, for details on this first
class bird control. Brochure, $.10, phone calls
welcomed.

Norcross Galleries
95 S. Peachtree St.   Dept. OHJ
Norcross, GA 30071
(404) 448-1932
MO RS/O
Aluminum lamps, benches, tables, fountains,
urns, and other accessories — many of which are
cast from original turn-of-the-century molds.
Street lamps a specialty. Catalog, $2.

Nord, E.A. Company
P.O. Box 1187   Dept. OHJ
Everett, WA 98206
DIST
The world's largest manufacturer of stile and rail
wood doors, many of which are suitable for
period houses. Also, stock wood columns; 9
spindle designs; turned posts; fancy stair parts;
exterior louver blinds; spindle, louver, and panel
bifold doors; and hemlock screen doors. Stained
and leaded glass inserts available. Full-color,
68-page catalog, $2.50.

Norman, W.F., Corporation
P.O. Box 323   Dept. OHJ
Nevada, MO 64772
(417) 667-5552
MO DIST
This company is again producing an 81-year old
line of metal ceiling, wainscotting, wall panels,
cornices, mouldings and metal Spanish Tile
roofing. Patterns come in many architectural
styles: Greek, Gothic, Rococo, Colonial Revival.
Unique patterns; made from original dies. Write
for: Ceiling Catalog No. 350 — $3.00. Also, (800)
641-4038.

Norman's of Salisbury
PO Drawer 799   Dept. OHJ
Salisbury, NC 28144
(704) 636-7900
DIST
Large selection of bed canopies and coverlets
with an inventory of approximately 900 fabrics to
choose from. Coverlets, canopies, dust ruffles,
pillow shams, table covers, and shades. Write for
the nearest dealer.

North Coast Chemical Co.
6300 17th Ave. So.   Dept. OHJ
Seattle, WA 98108
(206) 763-1340
MO DIST
Free data sheets available on: S-E-G professional
paint remover, Durofilm gym finish and
penetrating seal, Northco Masonry Cleaner,
Rustphoil metal treatment compound, Northco
rust remover, lemon oil & cleaners, Barnacle Milk
additive to improve adhesion and workability of
portland cement.

North Pacific Joinery
76 West Fourth Street   Dept. OHJ
Eureka, CA 95501
(707) 443-5788
MO RS/O
Custom fabrication of millwork, turnings, and
trim: Newels, balusters, handrails, mantels,
windows, doors, wainscot, scrollwork. Design
service available. Catalog, $3, or call or write with
your specific request.

Northern Design General Contractors
138 Main Street   Dept. OHJ
Montpelier, VT 05602
(802) 223-3484
RS/O
Serves the state of Vermont, specializing in
energy conservation oriented renovation and
restoration of old buildings. Architectural
services. Franchised Lord and Burnham
greenhouse dealer. Offering residential and
commercial greenhouses and solariums.
Literature available.

Nostalgia, Inc.
307 Stiles Ave.   Dept. OHJ
Savannah, GA 31401
(912) 236-8176
RS/O MO
Architectural antiques of all kinds. Demands for
certain items prompted them to develop a
selection of reproductions: dolphin downspouts,
brass hardware, summer fireplace covers, and
balcony brackets. Also, Hodkin & Jones
(Sheffield, England) 'Simply Elegant' decorative
plasterwork. Brochures — Simply Elegant, $1.50;
Dolphin Downspouts, $.50; and Pedestal Sinks,
$.50.

Novelty Trimming Works, Inc.
317 St. Paul's Ave.   Dept. OHJ
Jersey City, NJ 07306
(201) 656-2414
MO
Mail-order source for inexpensive Victorian-style
picture-hangers with tassels. In natural off-white
or gold. (Not silk.) Packed in boxes of 6 only, at
$1.50 each hanger. Postage is $2.50 per order.

**•See Product Dis-
plays Index on page
199 for more details.**

Nowell's, Inc.
Box 164   Dept. OHJ
Sausalito, CA 94966
(415) 332-4933
RS/O MO DIST
Victorian reproduction brass lighting fixtures,
made by hand. Aladdin Lamps, parts and
shades. Brass oil lamps both table and hanging.
Complete line of Victorian glass shades and lamp
parts. Fixture catalog $3.50, refundable with
purchase.

NuBrite Chemical Co., Inc.
1 Hill Street   Dept. OHJ
Taunton, MA 02780
(617) 824-4124
DIST
One of the few companies offering 'true'
linseed-oil paints. Available in sixteen house
paint colors and four primer colors. Also, quality
interior paints and stains. Distribution at the
moment is limited to the New England area. Free
information is available by written request.

Nutt, Craig, Fine Wood Works
2014 Fifth St.   Dept. OHJ
Northport, AL 35476
(205) 752-6535
RS/O MO
Fine cabinet-making and joinery; wood carving.
Museum-quality furniture: reproductions,
adaptations, and custom designs. Southern
American furniture is a specialty. Mostly custom
work. Small showroom with ready-to-sell items.
Send $.25 for brochure and current price list.

Nye's Foundry Ltd.
503 Powell St., E.   Dept. OHJ
Vancouver, BC, Canada V6A1G8
(604) 254-4121
RS/O
A small foundry offering prompt service on
specialty parts. They are cast in fine-grained
Olivine molding sand, using the old part as a
pattern, when possible. Gray & ductile iron,
aluminum alloys. Pattern making and machine
shop service available.

**You'll get better service
when contacting companies
if you mention
The Old-House Journal
Catalog**

O

Oak Leaves Woodcarving Studio
RR 6, The Woods, No. 12   Dept. OHJ
Iowa City, IA 52240
(319) 351-0014
MO RS/O
A service providing wood carvings of all kinds, with particular attention paid to figure and ornamental architectural carving, signs, doors, plaques, free standing and hanging sculpture. Free brochure.

Oak Post Reproductions
303 North Main St.   Dept. OHJ
Adairsville, GA 30103
(404) 773-7674
RS/O
Builders of solid oak furniture. Curved-glass china cabinets, book cases, round tables, dry sinks, corner cabinets, roll-top desks, ice boxes, etc. Literature, catalog $.50.

Oberndorfer & Assoc.
1979 Quarry Rd.   Dept. OHJ
Yardley, PA 19067
(215) 968-6463
RS/O
A house inspection company serving the Princeton-Bucks County and Philadelphia areas with complete structural, mechanical and electrical inspection of property. Free brochure.

● **Ocean View Lighting and Home Accessories**
1810 Fourth St.   Dept. OHJ
Berkeley, CA 94710
(415) 841-2937
RS/O MO
Retail sellers of fine antique and reproduction lighting fixtures, & table lamps. Handle Classic Illumination products. Replacement glass shades. Brochures on Classic Illumination products and mail order price list available for $1.

Off The Wall
950 Glenneyre St.   Dept. OHJ
Laguna Beach, CA 92651
(714) 497-4000
RS/O
Architectural antiques gathered from California to the midwest, England and France. Specialties: bathroom fittings, mantels, and fireplaces. Free literature.

Ogren & Trigg Clock Service
2616 Colfax Ave So.   Dept. OHJ
Minneapolis, MN 55408
(612) 377-2290
RS/O MO
Company specializes in the repair and restoration of antique clocks. No literature.

Ohman, C.A.
455 Court Street   Dept. OHJ
Brooklyn, NY 11231
(212) 624-2772
RS/O MO
Supplies and installs metal ceilings in the New York metropolitan area. Shipping and literature available.

Old And Elegant Distributing
10203 Main St. Lane   Dept. OHJ
Bellevue, WA 98004
(206) 455-4660
RS/O MO DIST
Manufactures and distributors of period style (old & new) cabinet, door, and plumbing hardware. Also, parts for old lighting fixtures. A large collection of weathervanes. Free information sheet; catalog, $3.

Old Carolina Brick Co.
Rt. 9, Box 77 Majolica Rd.   Dept. OHJ
Salisbury, NC 28144
(704) 636-8850
RS/O DIST
Company produces hand-moulded bricks, architectural brick shapes, and arches in 8 color ranges. A complete line of patio pavers is available including 8″ x 8″ Dutch pavers, 4″ x 8″ pavers, and hexagonal pavers. Can match existing handmade brick: send sample and indicate desired quantity. Illustrated brochure — $1.00.

● **Old Colony Crafts**
PO Box 155   Dept. O
Liberty, ME 04949
MO RS/O
Plans for entrance door frames, fireplace mantels and surrounds, bookcases with or without cabinets, open corner cupboard, interior cornice mouldings, Colonial wash stand, stereo cabinet, & a two-car salt box garage. Units are easily built from simplified plans and instructions by registered architect. Brochure, $.50.

Old Colony Curtains
P.O. Box 759   Dept. OHJ
Westfield, NJ 07090
(201) 233-3883
RS/O MO
A comprehensive selection of colonial and country style curtains, Bates woven spreads, bedroom ensembles, dust ruffles, and accessories. They specialize in multiple width priscillas, and hard-to-find sizes. Most merchandise shipped within 24 hours. New thermal-backed curtains and stencilled curtains. Catalog — $1.

Old-Fashioned Milk Paint Co.
Box 222H   Dept. OHJ
Groton, MA 01450
(617) 448-6336
RS/O MO DIST
Genuine milk paint, homemade in the traditional way, gives an authentic look to period furniture, old houses, weathered signs, cupboards, and stencilling. In powdered form, it is available in 8 colors by pints, quarts or gallons. Distributors for Watco/Dennis products which include Watco Danish Oil for furniture, woodwork, floors and exterior use. Brochure and color card, $.60. (Stamps okay.)

Old-Home Building & Restoration
P.O. Box 308   Dept. OHJ
West Suffield, CT 06093
(203) 668-0374
RS/O
Antique building materials including, but not limited to: chestnut & wide pine flooring, chestnut beams, planks & timbers, hand hewn beams, post & beam barn and house frames for re-assembly, weathered barn siding in silver, gold, brown & colors, roofing slate, hardware, doors & farm implements. They also use these materials in restoration and true reproduction to your specifications. Design & drafting services available. No literature.

● **Old House Inspection Co., Inc.**
140 Berkeley Place   Dept. OHJ
Brooklyn, NY 11217
(212) 857-3647
RS/O
House inspection service by licensed registered architect. Specializes in brownstones, old houses and cooperative apts. in the New York City metropolitan area. Member of "American Society of Home Inspectors" and "American Institute of Architects". No literature.

● **Old-House Journal**
69-A Seventh Ave.   Dept. OHJ
Brooklyn, NY 11217
(212) 636-4514
MO
Sells the Heavy-Duty Master Heat Gun. Ideal for stripping paint when large areas are involved. Saves mess and expense of chemical removers. Won't scorch wood or vaporize lead pigments as a propane torch will. Heat bubbles up — which can then be lifted with a scraper. Minor cleanup with chemical remover usually required. Price of $72.95 includes same-day shipping via United Parcel Service. Free flyer.

Old Lamplighter Shop
At the Musical Museum   Dept. OHJ
Deansboro, NY 13328
(315) 841-8774
RS/O MO
Specialists in the restoration and repair of Victorian and turn-of-the-century lamps and lighting fixtures. They also sell restored lamps and lighting fixtures of these periods. Also a small stock of restored melodeons dating from 1850 — 1860. The Musical Museum workshop repairs melodeons, grind and pump organs, etc. Free brochure.

● **Old'N Ornate Wooden Reproductions**
969 West 3rd Avenue   Dept. OHJ
Eugene, OR 97402
(503) 345-7636
MO RS/O
A small company dedicated to handcrafting fine, ornate wooden screen and storm doors. Over 30 styles in Douglas fir with various options & hardware. Custom orders including over- and under-sized doors, and arched doorways. Brochure, $1.

Old Stone Mill Corp.
Route 8, PO Box 307   Dept. OHJ
Adams, MA 01220
DIST
Hand-printed wallpaper manufacturer. Also, contract printing. Please write with specific request for more information.

Old Wagon Factory
PO Box 1085 , Dept. OHJ
Clarksville, VA 23927
(804) 374-5717
MO
Handcrafted chippendale-style combination storm and screen doors in all sizes. Also, new Victorian design. $1 for brochure of designs.

Old World Moulding & Finishing Co., Inc.
115 Allen Boulevard   Dept. OHJ
Farmingdale, NY 11735
(516) 293-1789
RS/O MO
Hardwood embossed mouldings, cornices, baseboards, mantels and a modular system of panelling suitable for a variety of period styles. Custom work also. Color catalog and price list - $2.00.

● See Product Displays Index on page 199 for more details.

Old World Restorations, Inc.
705 Wooster Pike, Rt. 50   Dept. OHJ
Terrace Park, OH 45174
(513) 831-2724
MO RS/O
An art conservation lab specializing in paintings, frames, porcelain, gold leaf, ivory, stained glass, china, glass, sculpture, pottery, wood, stone, and antiques. All forms of art restoration from the cleaning of an oil painting to the fabrication of missing porcelain. Free estimate and literature. Nationwide service.

Old World Sewing Pattern Co.
Rt. 2, Box 103   Dept. OHJ
Cold Spring, MN 56320
MO
Patterns for accurate recreation of 19th-century fashions. Complete sewing instructions and historical information included — male and female. Patterns, $9.95 ea; Catalog, $.75.

● **Olde Bostonian Architectural Antiques**
135 Buttonwood St.   Dept. OHJ
Dorchester, MA 02125
(617) 282-9300
RS/O
Has a wide collection of old doors, fireplace mantels, columns, floor registers, stained glass, brackets, newel posts, wainscotting, balusters, electric lighting and brass work. They specialize in mouldings. No literature; call or visit.

Olde New England Masonry
334 Grindstone Hill Rd.   Dept. OHJ
North Stonington, CT 06359
(203) 535-2253
RS/O
Company specializes in chimney repair, plastering, fireplaces, exterior stonework and bakeovens. No literature; call for appointment.

Olde Theatre Architectural Salvage Co.
1309 Westport Rd.   Dept. OHJ
Kansas City, MO 64111
(816) 931-0987
RS/O
Large selection of antique and recycled house parts. Free brochure.

Olde Village Smithery
PO Box 1815, 61 Finlay Rd.   Dept. OHJ
Orleans, MA 02653
(617) 255-4466
MO RS/O
Traditional crafted period lighting fixtures in brass, tin, and copper: primitive Colonial, 18th century, and Pennsylvania Dutch designs. They offer chandeliers, sconces, lanterns, postlights, candlesticks, and beeswax candles. Catalog available, $2.50.

Oliver Organ Co.
633 Bergen St.   Dept. OHJ
Brooklyn, NY 11238
(212) 783-2145
RS/O
Custom woodworking, specializing in matching or reproducing antique doors, room panelling, decorative woodwork, and veneering. Also, they will supply missing stair parts. Installation available in NY metro area. Call or send plans for quotes or estimates.

Oliver, Bradley C.
Box 41   Dept. OHJ
Mountainhome, PA 18342
(717) 629-1828
RS/O MO
Dealer in antique iron fences, urns, furniture, etc. Write with a description of what you require. No literature, but inquiries will be answered. They can ship anywhere.

Omnia Industries, Inc.
49 Park St., PO Box 263   Dept. OHJ
Montclair, NJ 07042
(201) 746-4300
DIST
Offers a collection of solid brass door hardware, including knob and lever latchsets, hinges, bolts, door knockers, coat hooks, pushplates, and door pulls. Also high security lock products of CISA-Italy. Complete catalog furnished at no charge to the trade only. Free 4-page brochure sent to the consumer upon written request.

Orlandini Studios Ltd. Decorative Plaster Supply Co.
633 W. Virginia St.   Dept. OHJ
Milwaukee, WI 53204
(414) 272-3657
MO RS/O
Ornamental plaster: will consult, design, model, mold, cast, install any type of ornament. Residential, commercial, and church statuary. Original designs, stock, or duplicate. Will supply cement ornament or duplicate terra-cotta in cast cement. Prices quoted from your samples, photos, drawings: include dimensions and SASE. Visits by appointment no literature.

● **Ornamental Design Studios**
1715 President Street   Dept. OHJ
Brooklyn, NY 11213
(212) 774-2695
RS/O
Restoration of plaster ornamentation including mouldings, medallions, and bas relief. Muddled ornaments restored, missing elements reproduced. Installation of stock and custom ornamentation. No literature, but all inquiries answered.

Orum Silver Co., Inc.
Box 805, 51 S. Vine St.   Dept. OHJ
Meriden, CT 06450
(203) 237-3037
MO RS/O
Plating shop: silver, 24k gold, nickel, and copper. Also, refinishing of copper, brass, and pewter. Restoration of old silver and antiques such as tea sets and lamps. Free literature or call.

Osborne, C. S. & Co.
125 Jersey St.   Dept. OHJ
Harrison, NJ 07029
(201) 483-3232
DIST
Manufactures a complete line of upholstering hand tools, including certain do-it-yourself kits with instruction books. Free upholstery tool brochure and name of nearest distributor available on receipt of self-addressed, stamped envelope.

Ostrom Studios
532 SE Belmont St.   Dept. OHJ
Portland, OR 97214
(503) 233-6847
RS/O
Designs and produces period acid etched, sandblasted and gluechip glass, mirrors and signs. Reproduction of broken panels. Many old style patterns available. All work custom made, no premade panels in stock. No literature.

O'Sullivan Co.
156 S. Minges Road   Dept. OHJ
Battle Creek, MI 49017
(616) 964-1226
MO DIST
Manufactures O'Sullivans Liquid Wax Furniture Polish - an 18th century formula that is designed for wood panelling, board floors, kitchen cabinets as well as furniture. Dries to a soft luster without buffing. Cleans and polishes. Erases light scratches and white rings. Free descriptive folder and mail order form.

P

● **P & G New and Used Plumbing Supply**
155 Harrison Ave.   Dept. OHJ
Brooklyn, NY 11206
(212) 384-6310
RS/O
Shop has a selection of old-fashioned used bathroom and plumbing fixtures, radiators etc. No literature — walk-in shop only.

● **PRG**
5619 Southampton Drive   Dept. OHJ
Springfield, VA 22151
(703) 323-1407
MO
Specialized tools and instruments to home owners and professionals for the restoration and care of buildings. These conservator's tools include moisture meters, profile gauge, temperature and humidity gauges, microscopes, lights and more. Also, books for instruction and reference on all aspects of historic preservation, building science and maintenance. New Products bulletin, illustrated catalogue and booklist available free.

● **Pagliacco Turning & Milling Architectural Wood Turning**
    Dept. OHJ
Woodacre, CA 94973
(415) 488-4333
MO RS/O
Produces custom & stock balusters, newel posts, porch posts, columns & pilasters (Victorian, Colonial, Post Modern, Greek & Roman columns offered plain or fluted with true entasis). Will duplicate turnings from drawing or photo. Also finials, capitals, circular frames, arches, brackets, corbels, railings, & cornices. Suppliers to the trade of first-growth, decay-resistant, clear-heart, dry Redwood beams & timbers. Free brochure.

Paints N Papers
107 Brook St.   Dept. OHJ
Sanford, ME 04073
(207) 324-9705
MO RS/O
This company offers linseed oil base primers and
exterior paints. In traditional and custom colors.
Free literature.

Paramount Exterminating Co.
460 9th Avenue   Dept. OHJ
New York, NY 10018
(212) 594-9230
RS/O
Exterminating company providing termite
inspections, termite control treatment, and
general pest control services in the New York
Metropolitan area, Rockland & Westchester. Free
brochure.

Parsons, W.H., Jr. & Associates
119-D House St.   Dept. OHJ
Glastonbury, CT 06033
(203) 633-6972
RS/O
Consulting in historic preservation projects
involving masonry. Preparation of National
Register applications. Paint & graffiti removed.
Also, chimney relining. Free literature.

● **Past Patterns**
2017 Eastern S.E.   Dept. OHJ
Grand Rapids, MI 49507
(616) 245-9456
MO
Meticulous patterns of fashion rages between the
gilded and Supersonic ages. Turn-of-the-century
catalog with standard sizes 10 through 16 (and a
few 18 and 20) — $10. Brown Paper Copies
catalog — $8.50. Duplicates of original patterns
from 1900 to 1950 in one size only. Patterns of
corsets (1857, 1880, and 1902) can be purchased
as patterns, complete kits, or ready made.

Pasvalco
400 Demarest Ave.   Dept. OHJ
Closter, NJ 07624
(800) 222-2133
MO RS/O
Re-claimed Connecticut brownstone (a deep red
brown) from demolished buildings and inactive
quarries. All types of natural stone.

Patchmakers
920 Broadway   Dept. OHJ
New York, NY 10010
(212) 673-1164
MO DIST
"Almost-ready-to-wear" pre-cut clothing kits
which include pre-cut, washable fabric,
coordinated lace and trimmings, bindings,
buttons, etc. Along with detailed instructions.
Many of the delicate designs are direct
adaptations of Victorian fashions. A free brochure
describes these reasonably priced kits.

Patterson, Flynn, & Martin, Inc.
950 Third Ave.   Dept. OHJ
New York, NY 10022
(212) 751-6414
RS/O
High quality carpets—although they aren't
'authentic' reproductions they certainly have a
period feeling.

● **Paxton Hardware Ltd.**
7818 Bradshaw Rd.   Dept. OHJ
Upper Falls, MD 21156
(301) 592-8505
MO RS/O
Comprehensive catalog showing a large selection
of solid brass period, Victorian and contemporary
hardware. Furniture locks, mirror screws, table
slides, chair-caning supplies, porcelain knobs,
etc. Also a wide variety of lamp parts, chimneys,
and glass shades. Catalog $2.50 1st class, $1.t0
3rd class.

**Pedersen, Arthur Hall — Design &
Consulting Engineers**
34 North Gore   Dept. OHJ
Webster Groves, MO 63119
(314) 962-4176
RS/O MO
Solar, structural, architectural, and mechanical
engineers specializing in solar greenhouses and
other passive and active solar system design
services for retrofit, add-on, energy conservation,
restoration, or new construction. No literature.

Peerless Imported Rugs
3028 N. Lincoln Avenue   Dept. OHJ
Chicago, IL 60657
(312) 472-4848
MO
Rugs and tapestries by mail. Showroom open 7
days a week. They pay shipping charges.
Questions welcome. Call toll-free: 800-621-6573.
Full money-back guarantee. Free color catalog
and price list.

Peg Hall Studios
111 Clapp Road   Dept. OHJ
Scituate, MA 02066
(617) 545-3605
MO
Patterns and design books for decorating period
furniture and accessories. Catalog and price list,
$.25.

Pelnik Wrecking Co., Inc.
1749 Erie Blvd., E.   Dept. OHJ
Syracuse, NY 13210
(315) 472-1031
RS/O
Wreckers with 50-years' experience in sensitive
salvaging. Bevelled and stained glass a specialty.
Mantels, newel posts, railings, entryways,
corbels, tin ceilings, brass rails, cast iron
elements, columns, marble sinks, old brick and
timber, terra-cotta friezes. Further services for
restaurant designers and architects. Photos on
request.

Pemaquid Floorcloths
    Dept. OHJ
Pemaquid, ME 04558
(207) 529-5633
MO
Canvas floorcloths in two sizes and stencilled in a
variety of patterns representative of the late
1700s. Will also do custom orders. Send $2.00 for
color brochure, refundable upon order. Also,
(207) 677-2659.

Pemko Co.
Box 3780   Dept. OHJ
Ventura, CA 93006
(805) 642-2600
DIST
Commercial, residential and do-it-yourself
aluminum integral weatherstripping, and related
products. Free catalog.

Pennsylvania Barnboard Company
729-1/2 S. Main St., Box 639   Dept. OHJ
Bangor, PA 18013
(215) 588-2838
MO RS/O
The Pennsylvania Barnboard Company
dismantles 100 — 200 year old eastern
Pennsylvania barns. They offer authentic
weathered siding, hand-hewn oak columns and
beams, and related antique hardware for
decorative building purposes. An inventory of
yellow pine flooring is also maintained and a
wide range of custom milling services is available.
Free brochure and price list.

Pennsylvania Firebacks, Inc.
1011 E. Washington Lane   Dept. OH
Philadelphia, PA 19138
(215) 843-6162
MO DIST
Manufactures a collection of cast-iron firebacks
for the rear of the fireplace. A fireback radiates
heat from the fire and protects back wall from
deterioration. Ten original designs in Colonial
and contemporary motifs. New extra large
fireback can be personalized with name and/or
special year. Complete illustrated catalog
available for $2.

Period Furniture Hardware Co., Inc.
Box 314, Charles St. Station   Dept. OHJ
Boston, MA 02114
(617) 227-0758
RS/O MO
A selection of high-quality period accessories
with the emphasis on solid brass. Items include a
wide selection of furniture and builders
hardware, hand-crafted weathervanes, lighting
fixtures, fireplace accessories, and bathroom
fittings. Catalog, $4.

● **Period Lighting Fixtures**
1 West Main Street   Dept. OJ-4
Chester, CT 06412
(203) 526-3690
MO RS/O
Handmade 17th & 18th century early American
lighting fixtures, chandeliers, wall sconces and
lanterns. Finishes vary from hand rubbed pewter,
naturally aged tin, and old glazed colors for
interior fixtures, to exterior post and
wall-mounted lanterns in oxidized copper. Their
catalog is also a reference source on the origin,
selection and installation of early lighting.
Catalog & price list, $2.00.

● **Period Pine**
P.O. Box 77052   Dept. OHJ
Atlanta, GA 30357
(404) 876-4740
RS/O MO
They salvage Southern Yellow Heart Pine from
the demolition of turn-of-the-century warehouses
and cotton mills, and recycle the salvaged
material into flooring, paneling, beams, and
mouldings. Free brochure and moulding
cut-sheet available.

Perkasie Industries Corp.
50 East Spruce Street   Dept. OHJ
Perkasie, PA 18944
(215) 257-6581
MO
Thermatrol storm window kit is designed for the
do-it-yourselfer. Surface mounts to the window
frame on the interior side. Provides a thermal
barrier by using lightweight acrylic framing and
glazing, coupled with gasketing. Thermatrol is
applicable to most window designs and can be
designed so that it stores within itself for summer
ventilation. Free literature.

Perkowitz Window Fashions
135 Green Bay Rd.   Dept. OHJ
Wilmette, IL 60091
(312) 251-7700
RS/O MO
A major supplier of louvered shutters carries a full line of stock shutters and custom sizes. Shutters are pine and can be ordered unfinished or with standard colors and stains, or matched to your sample. Catalog & price list, $1.

Perma Ceram Enterprises, Inc.
65 Smithtown Blvd.   Dept. OHJ
Smithtown, NY 11787
(516) 724-1205
DIST
Largest in-home bathroom resurfacing company in the country. Exclusive formula to resurface bathtubs, sinks, and tile. Applied only by authorized factory trained technicians. Available in all decorator colors. Work done in your house. Fully guaranteed. For a local Perma Ceram dealer: (800) 645-5039. Free brochure.

Perry, Edward K., Company
322 Newbury St.   Dept. OHJ
Boston, MA 02115
(617) 536-7873
A 4th-generation family business specializing in fine interior and exterior painting of historic structures and homes. Responsible for original painting in many McKim, Mead, and White, and H.H. Richardson buildings. Also involved with color selection and painting at Colonial Williamsburg, Old Sturbridge Village, Tryon Palace and Winterthur. Special decorative techniques include gilding, graining, glazing, encaustics, marbleizing, tromphe l'oeil, and stencilling. Free brochure.

Peterson, Robert H., Co.
530 N. Baldwin Park Blvd.   Dept. OHJ
City of Industry, CA 91744
(213) 960-5085
DIST
Manufacturers of a complete line of Real-Fyre radiant gas logs, cast iron shaker grates, and log grates for woodburning fireplaces. Hallmark handcrafted fireplace accessories, including solid brass firesets, woodholder, hearth fenders, andirons, and standing screens. Fire Magic built-in gas and charcoal barbecues and accessories. Free catalogs and price sheets available upon request.

Pfanstiel Hardware Co.
Route 52   Dept. OHJ
Jeffersonville, NY 12748
(914) 482-4445
MO
Manufactures and imports an extensive line of decorative hardware, primarily brass and bronze. Styles are French, Renaissance Revival, Rococo, and Georgian. Among their unusual items are decorative finials and finial-tipped hinges. Handsome 96 page catalog — $7.50.

• **Philadelphia Resins Corp.**
Box 454, 20 Commerce Dr.   Dept. OHJ
Montgomeryville, PA 18936
(215) 855-8450
MO DIST
Their "Woodfast" is an epoxy resin which can be used to repair rotted and damaged wood. Can be pressure injected, poured, or made into a putty consistency. Free literature.

Philip M. White & Associates
Box 47   Dept. OHJ
Mecklenburg, NY 14863
(607) 387-6370
RS/O MO
Founded in 1934, this company specializes in design and restoration of 19th and early 20th century gardens. Also, appraisal and damage estimate work for tax & insurance purposes. Services by a licensed landscape architect. Please call; free literature.

Phoenix Studio, Inc.
374 Fore St.   Dept. OHJ
Portland, ME 04101
(207) 774-4154
MO RS/O
A design and stained glass studio. Specialize in restoration of all leaded work, and can furnish excellent references. They are also a retail outlet for related supplies (glass tools, etc.) and maintain a gallery in Portland. Classes are offered. Free information sheet.

Piazza, Michael — Ornamental Plasterer
540 80th Street   Dept. OHJ
Brooklyn, NY 11209
(212) 745-6111
RS/O
From four generations of European craftsmen, Michael Piazza continues the traditional methods of design and restoration of ornamental plaster. Work is run and modelled in position, and he can use heirloom ornamental moulds of the 19th century. Lectures in the history, development, and skill of the craft. No literature.

Piccone, James Corrado, & Associates
56 Linden Avenue   Dept. OHJ
Ossining, NY 10562
(914) 762-5334
RS/O
Comprehensive firm covering all phases of historic preservation and restoration services. Organization specializes in a one day architectural consultation for effective project initiation including maximizing tax benefits as per 1981 Preservation law. Professional standards maintained for 12 years; serving the continental U.S.

Pike Stained Glass Studios, Inc.
180 St. Paul Street   Dept. OHJ
Rochester, NY 14604
(716) 546-7570
RS/O
Founded in 1908 by William J. Pike, and continued by James J. O'Hara, his nephew, Pike Stained Glass Studio, Inc. is currently under the direction of Mr. O'Hara and his daughter, Valerie. Both father and daughter design, fabricate, install and repair windows for churches, businesses and homes. Storm protection is also available. Call or write for estimates. Free brochure.

●See Product Displays Index on page 199 for more details.

Pine & Palette Studio
20 Ventura Drive   Dept. OHJ
Danielson, CT 06239
(203) 774-5058
MO RS/O
Fireplace bellows hand-crafted with authentic Early American designs, on hardwood. Genuine brass fittings and leather gussetts. Will also do bellow repair. Satisfaction guaranteed. Brochure, $.50.

Piscatagua Architectural Woodwork, Co.
RFD 2, Bagdad Rd.   Dept. OHJ
Durham, NH 03824
(603) 868-2663
MO DIST RS/O
Ten stock hand-run 18th-century style mouldings for use in quality restorations, reconstructions, and reproductions. On a custom basis, they produce interior & exterior doors, panelling, shutters, sash, etc., as well as any 18th-century moulding. All of their work is hand done. Send a large SASE for information.

Plexacraft Metals Co.
5406 San Fernando Rd.   Dept. OHJ
Glendale, CA 91203
(213) 246-8201
MO DIST
A manufacturer of modern lucite hardware, they also produce hand-cast solid brass knobs & pulls in traditional styles. Catalog, $3.50. Also, white porcelain knobs. Free flyer.

Pocahontas Hardware & Glass
Box 127   Dept. OHJ
Pocahontas, IL 62275
(618) 669-2880
RS/O MO
Etched glass especially suited for windows, doors, transoms and cabinets. Patterns are exact reproductions of old glass. They also produce three stock doors (five panel, oval, or three panel) of solid sugar pine. Wood carving is added on request. Doors have etched glass inserts. Custom made doors can be ordered. Illustrated brochure is $2.

Pollitt, E., AIA
Vista Drive   Dept. OHJ
Easton, CT 06612
(203) 268-5955
MO
A collection of Colonial period house plans, measured and drawn from originals. Exteriors are faithfully reproduced; interiors are updated. Specifications make use of stock building materials. Full plans are $70.00 each. Two portfolios available: Old Colonial Houses, 32 reproduction houses; Old Cape Cod Houses, 24 reproductions and adaptations. Each $5.00.

Pompei Stained Glass
455 High St. (Rt. 60)   Dept. OHJ
Medford, MA 02155
(617) 395-8867
RS/O   MO
Custom design & fabrication of period leaded and
stained glass shades and window panels of all
types, including fan lights, side lights, transoms,
cabinet doors, mantel mirrors & signs & logos.
Beveled, etched and sand-blasted glass. Repair
and restoration of leaded windows and shades.
Glass slumping, resizing, "secularization", and
installation services. Catalog & price list, $1.

Poor Richard's Service Co.
101-103 Walnut Street   Dept. OHJ
Montclair, NJ 07042
(201) 783-5333
RS/O
Furniture stripping, refinishing and repair, metal
polishing and plating; reupholstery work; cane
and rush work and supplies. Walk-in shop.
Furniture touch-ups and polishing done in the
home. No literature.

Porcelain Restoration and Brass
1007 W. Morehead St.   Dept. OHJ
Charlotte, NC 28208
(704) 372-9039
RS/O   MO
Porcelain resurfacing in the home. Not an epoxy,
but a curothane — polyvinyl butyral primer with
multiple glaze coats. Specialists in pedestal sinks,
footed tubs, original water closets. They make
available original plumbing fixtures and
reproduction brass hardware for fixtures. Also
brass-polishing available and wood washstands
with corian lavatory bowls. Catalog, $3.50.

● **Porcelli, Ernest**
333 Flatbush Ave.   Dept. OHJ
Brooklyn, NY 11217
(212) 857-6888
RS/O
Original creations in stained and leaded glass.
Will also do custom work. Also will do stained &
leaded glass repair. Free estimates with stamped
self-addressed envelope. Send dimensions. No
literature.

Potlatch Corp. — Townsend Unit
P.O. Box 916   Dept. OHJ
Stuttgart, AR 72160
(501) 673-1606
DIST
Prefinished hardwoods in 18 wood finishes.
Random widths and lengths. Free 8 pg. brochure.

Poxywood, Inc.
PO Box 4241   Dept. OHJ
Martinsville, VA 24115
(703) 638-6284
MO
Two-part epoxy system available in pine, oak, or
universal colors. It only has a two-month shelf
life, but you can buy small quantities at a
reasonable cost. Free literature.

Pratt & Lambert
75 Tonawanda Street   Dept. OHJ
Buffalo, NY 14207
(716) 873-6000
DIST
A manufacturer of paints, chemical coatings, and
adhesives with its origin in 1849. Pratt & Lambert
is recognized as a color leader and recently was
authorized by the Henry Ford Museum and
Greenfield Village in Michigan to produce a
special series of interior and exterior paints "Early
American Colours from Greenfield Village."
These paints duplicate shades of the 18th and
19th centuries. Color card, $.50.

Pratt's House of Wicker
1 West Main Street   Dept. OHJ
Adamstown, PA 19501
(215) 484-2094
RS/O   MO
This company has several antique pieces for sale,
but they deal primarily in new wicker. The
emphasis is on Victorian reproductions. Their
speciality, wicker porch furniture, is displayed on
the large wrap-around porch of their 1845 home.
Catalog, $5.

Preservation Associates, Inc.
PO Box 100   Dept. OHJ
Sharpsburg, MD 21782
(301) 791-7880
RS/O
Nationwide building-restoration and rehab
consultation: research services to individuals,
organizations, and agencies. Full consulting
services; preparation of state and National
Register nominations. Introductory brochure
available on request.

Preservation/Design Group, The
388 Broadway   Dept. OHJ
Albany, NY 12207
(518) 463-4077
RS/O
Highly-qualified group of individuals deals with a
full range of preservation/architectural services.
Extensive experience and capabilities. "A Primer
of Historic Preservation Services", $2.00.

Preservation Development Group
96 Main St.   Dept. OHJ
Stamford, CT 06901
(203) 324-9317
RS/O
A planning & design firm specializing in the
restoration of historic structures & communities.
Planning, research, & design for government
agencies & private developers. National Register
nominations & tax act certifications. Will also
locate appropriate interior & exterior elements, &
designs compatible additions to historic
buildings. Renee Kahn, Director.

Preservation Partnership
345 Union St.   Dept. OHJ
New Bedford, MA 02740
(617) 996-3383
RS/O
A preservation firm whose architectural and
planning services include surveys, historic
structures reports, and the inspection,
conservation, rehabilitation, restoration, and
adaptive reuse of existing buildings. Some 300
completed projects range from private homes to
scores of house museums. Conservation of
institutional and public cultural property and
certified rehabilitation are specialties. Free
brochure.

**Preservation Resource Center of New
Orleans**
604 Julia Street   Dept. OHJ
New Orleans, LA 70130
(504) 581-7032
RS/O
Promotion of preservation through publications,
projects, programs, historical research,
consultation, facade servitude donations and
architectural tours. Monthly meetings are held to
discuss issues. "Preservation in Print", a 16-20
page newspaper, is published monthly.
Membership in the PRC is $15 annually. A
Warehouse District Planning Study is $17.50.

Preservation Resource Group
5619 Southampton Dr.   Dept. OHJ
Springfield, VA 22151
(703) 323-1407
RS/O
Assists agencies, organizations and individuals in
development of their historic preservation
programs and personnel. Lectures and
workshops for owners of old houses are
conducted for groups on request. No literature,
but will provide sample programs.

Preway, Inc.
1430 2nd Street, North   Dept. OHJ
Wisconsin Rapids, WI 54494
(715) 423-1100
DIST
Energy-efficient built-in and free-standing
fireplaces. Manufacturers of "Energy-Mizer"
fireplaces. All built-in units are rated
zero-clearance to combustibles and are UL listed.
Choices of hearth opening sizes available, plus
accessories. Also, easy to install masonry
fireplace insert. Color pamphlet illustrates
fireplaces and insert, and describes all available
accessories.

● **Progress Lighting**
G St. & Erie Ave.   Dept. OHJ
Philadelphia, PA 19134
(215) 289-1200
DIST
A selection of documented American Victorian
lighting fixture reproductions: Classical Revival,
Rococo Revival, Colonial Revival, Art Nouveau.
Authenticated by Dr. Roger Moss. All electrified;
most of solid brass. Also matching wall, hall, and
streetlight adaptations. Quality production by the
world's largest manufacturer of home lighting
fixtures. Also ceiling fans. Full color catalog, $1.

● **ProSoCo, Inc.**
P.O. Box 1578   Dept. OHJ
Kansas City, KS 66117
(913) 281-2700
DIST   RS/O
Manufacturers of Sure Klean masonry cleaning
and sealing materials. For restoring brick, stone
and other masonry surfaces. Chemicals do not
harm the masonry surface and are less costly
than sandblasting. Free brochures.

Puget Sound Shake Brokers
12301 218th Pl. SE Suite 711   Dept. OHJ
Snohomish, WA 98290
(206) 668-6642
MO   RS/O
Fancy butt red cedar shingles 5" x 18", 9 cuts:
octagonal, arrow, square, fish scale, diagonal,
half cove, diamond, round, hexagonal. Shipped
to customer direct from distributor. Prepayment
required. Eastern time differential no problem;
call and leave message. Sample shingle and
literature $1.00. Refundable first order.

Purcell, Francis J., II
88 North Main Street   Dept. OHJ
New Hope, PA 18938
(215) 862-9100
RS/O
Antique American fireplace mantels dating from
1750 to 1850. Large collection of over 100 formal
and folk art mantels. 70 examples are cleaned of
paint and have hand rubbed finishes. Majority of
mantels priced between one and three thousand
dollars. No literature — collection seen by
appointment only.

Putnam Rolling Ladder Co., Inc.
32 Howard St.   Dept. GPM-T
New York, NY 10013
(212) 226-5147
RS/O MO
Of special interest is their rolling library ladder —
made-to-order from oak and finished to
customer's specifications. Hardware for rolling
ladder available in four finishes including chrome
and brass plated and polished. They make an oak
pulpit ladder, "office ladders", stools, and library
carts. Also full line of wood, aluminum, and
fiberglass step, straight and extension ladders,
and aluminum scaffolds. Catalog No. 650, $1.

Pyfer, E.W.
218 North Foley Ave.   Dept. OHJ
Freeport, IL 61032
(815) 232-8968
MO RS/O
Lamp repair and rewiring: chandeliers restored,
oil and gas lamps converted, replacement of
missing lamp parts. Brass plating service. Chair
recaning (rush, reed, and splint). Also sells
caning supplies and instruction books. Free
description of services — please call for
appointment before visiting.

Q

QRB Industries
3139 US 31 North   Dept. OHJ
Niles, MI 49120
(616) 683-7908
MO
A chemical paint stripper which doesn't
immediately burn your skin and has only a trace
of fumes. Also, it doesn't raise the grain of the
wood so only minimal sanding would ever be
required. Free 60 min. tape on wood refinishing.
Free information. Also, phone (616) 471-3887.

● **Quaker City Manufacturing Co.**
701 Chester Pike   Dept. OHJ
Sharon Hill, PA 19079
(215) 727-5144
DIST
WINDOW FIXER Replacement Window Channels
can be used with standard wood sash to give
snug fit and prevent heat loss. Available through
most lumber yards, home centers and major
hardware stores. Free literature.

Quaker Lace Co.
24 West 40th Street   Dept. OHJ
New York, NY 10018
(212) 221-0480
DIST
Quaker Lace Company is a manufacturer of lace
tablecloths & placemats, curtains, and bed
coverlets. Many of the patterns are made on the
famed Nottingham Lace machines. Free
brochures available with listing of major retail
department stores carrying Quaker Lace
products.

Quality Woodworks, Inc.
PO Box 1117   Dept. OHJ
Jasper, FL 32052
(904) 792-2939
MO RS/O
Quality panelling and millwork including custom
cabinets, exposed beams, mantels and timbers,
beaded ceiling and Heart Pine plank flooring,
furniture, and decorative panels. A sampling of
their sidings, beaded ceiling, and pine flooring is
$5. Free brochure.

R

● **R.D.C. Enterprises**
166 Merry Robin Rd.   Dept. OHJ
Troy, OH 45373
(513) 339-1981
RS/O
A stone mason with a special interest in the
restoration and preservation of old houses. Will
also do chemical stripping and general
contracting.

Ragland Stained Glass
116 No. Main Street   Dept. OHJ
Kokomo, IN 46901
(317) 452-2438
RS/O
Designs and builds stained glass windows and
shades. Company also repairs and restores
stained glass, along with custom glass beveling.
Serving the Midwest. No literature.

Raleigh, Inc.
2022 Nebraska Rd.   Dept. OHJ
Rockford, IL 61108
(815) 229-0688
MO RS/O
Concrete tiles designed to resemble wood shakes,
clay tiles, and slate shingles. Offered in eleven
colors with a 50-year guarantee. Roof restoration/
repair is available with their large selection of
salvaged concrete, slate, and clay tiles. Free
brochure.

Rambusch
40 West 13th St.   Dept. OHJ
New York, NY 10011
(212) 675-0400
ID
Company specializes in major restoration projects
for museums, churches and public buildings. Has
a large staff of skilled craftsmen in such areas as
painting and decorating, lighting and stained
glass. Free brochure: "Restorations By
Rambusch." Through Interior Designers and
Architects only.

RAM's Forge
3678 Taneytown Road   Dept. OHJ
Gettysburg, PA 17325
(717) 359-7675
MO RS/O
Colonial and contemporary hand-forged wrought
iron work. Specializing in fireplace equipment;
also, gates, window grilles, lighting, hardware,
boot scrapers, kitchen pot racks, and weather
vanes in hand-wrought iron. Each piece custom
forged for its particular application, using
traditional designs and forging techniques. Write
giving your specific need in colonial ironware. No
literature.

Ram's Head Forge
RR 34A, Fish St.   Dept. OHJ
Fryeburg, ME 04037
(207) 697-2011
MO RS/O
Hand-forged hardware in standard reproduction
designs, also some unusual patterns in strap
hinges. Cranes, fireplace tools, & cooking
utensils. Will do custom and restoration work.
Free catalog.

●**See Product Dis-
plays Index on page
199 for more details.**

Rastetter Woolen Mill
Star Route 62 & 39E.   Dept. OHJ
Millersburg, OH 44654
(216) 674-2103
MO RS/O
5th generation manufacturers, wholesalers, and
retailers of hand-woven rag rugs, including throw
rugs, stair runners, and treads, area rugs, &
wall-to-wall carpet. Availble in 100% cotton;
wool; cotton/rayon rug yarn; or various
synthetics. Custom work and reasonable prices
are their specialty. Brochure, $1.

● **Readybuilt Products, Co.**
Box 4425, 1701 McHenry St.   Dept. OHJ
Baltimore, MD 21223
(301) 233-5833
MO RS/O
More than 25 different styles of hand-crafted
ready to install wood mantels for built in
masonry fireplaces or factory-built metal units.
Most mantels have wood openings 50" wide x
30" high and can be modified at additional cost.
A Booklet, 'Wood Mantel Pieces" shows styles
and a diagram for taking measurements - $2.00.

Red Baron's Peachtree Antique Emporium
3264 Peachtree Road   Dept. OHJ
Atlanta, GA 30328
(404) 237-9338
RS/O
Always a large inventory of American
architectural antiques and collectibles.
Specializing in stained and bevelled glass
windows and doors. Walk-in shop throughout
the year, with periodic auctions. Catalog
available.

Red Devil, Inc.
2400 Vauxhall Rd.   Dept. OHJ
Union, NJ 07083
(201) 688-6900
DIST
Wide line of home maintenance and decorating
products, including wood & paint scrapers; putty
& taping knives; glaziers tools; spackling
compounds; and caulks & sealants. Available at
most hardware, paint, and home center stores.

Reed Illinois Corp.
930 W. Division   Dept. OHJ
Chicago, IL 60622
(312) 943-8100
RS/O
A full service general contracting firm (founded
in 1893) specializing in restoration. Offering
quality construction in carpentry, cabinetry, brick
and stone masonry, and plain or ornamental
plastering (including Scagliola). No literature.

The Reggio Register Co.
P.O. Box 511   Dept. OJ-3
Ayer, MA 01432
(617) 772-3493
MO
Manufacturers of a complete line of quality, decorative, cast-iron and solid brass floor registers and grilles from the turn-of-the-century period. Suitable for use with either natural convection or forced-hot-air heating systems. A complete detailed catalog is available for $1.

● **Rejuvenation House Parts Co.**
901 N. Skidmore   Dept. OHJ
Portland, OR 97217
(503) 249-0774
RS/O MO
Manufacturers of reasonably priced solid brass Victorian and turn-of-the-century light fixtures. All are authentic and meticulous recreations of the originals. Their mail order catalogue, $2, includes light fixtures, cast-iron roof cresting, and anaglypta. The retail store has 10,000 sq. ft. of antique plumbing and lighting fixtures, doors, millwork, hardware, etc.

● **Remodelers & Renovators**
1503 North 11th   Dept. OHJ
Boise, ID 83702
(208) 377-5465
MO RS/O
Suppliers of quality building, finishing & decorating products for renovators. Old-style faucets, fittings, pedestal sinks in ceramic or wood, brass sinks; Victorian mouldings, fretwork & millwork;; reproduction gas/electric lighting; porch & garden furniture; Victorian reproduction cast aluminum spiral staircase; & Steptoe cast iron stair- case; brass hardware; tin ceiling; anaglypta wall covering; old-style entrance doors & screen doors; large inventory hard-to-find items, including architectural antiques. Catalog, $2.

● **Renaissance Decorative Hardware Co.**
PO Box 332   Dept. OHJ
Leonia, NJ 07605
(201) 568-1403
MO
Renaissance Decorative Hardware Co. is an importer of solid brass door, cabinet and furniture hardware. The door hardware includes pulls, knobs, and lever handles. The knobs and lever handles are intended for older homes utilizing mortise mechanisms. Catalog—$2.50.

● **Renaissance Marketing, Inc.**
PO Box 360   Dept. OHJ
Lake Orion, MI 48035
(313) 693-1109
MO RS/O
A source for high-quality reproduction Tiffany table lamps. Also, imported French cameo lamps and antique styled bronze and brass lamp bases. Brochures: Lamps de Vianne, $2; The Renaissance Collection, $1.

● **Renovation Concepts, Inc.**
213 Washington Ave., North   Dept. OHJ
Minneapolis, MN 55401
(612) 377-9526
RS/O MO
Unique and decorative materials for building renovation, 'theme' bars and restuarants and condominimums. Materials available include: mouldings, tin ceilings, brass rail & fittings, plumbing hardware, hardwood panelled doors, lighting fixtures, door locksets and trim, wood columns, and many more products. Trade Catalog $10. Free brochure.

● **Renovation Products**
5302 Junius   Dept. OHJ
Dallas, TX 75214
(214) 827-5111
MO RS/O
Restoration/renovation products source. Common items such as doors & mouldings, turnings in stock. Showroom and retail store with special-order service for a variety of other materials: custom made and stock screen doors, gingerbread, fretwork, Victorian design porch swings, park benches, lamp posts, entry doors, gargoyles, newels, mantels, metal ceilings, window sash, cupolas. Design consultation available to customers. Catalog, $2.

Renovation Source, Inc., The
3512 N. Southport Ave.   Dept. OHJ
Chicago, IL 60657
(312) 327-1250
MO RS/O
Firm provides both architectural consulting/design services, and restoration/renovation products. Architectural services from site consultation to a complete set of construction drawings. Supplier of salvaged architectural trim, newly reproduced decorative materials, and restoration aids. Also represent growing number of old-house products manufacturers. Catalog, $1.50.

● **Reproduction Distributors, Inc.**
Box 638   Dept. OHJ
Joliet, IL 60434
MO
Colonial reproduction brass rim locks and hinges. Replicas of those used at Williamsburg, VA. Some internal adaptations have been made to meet modern requirements. A Colonial Williamsburg® registered certificate is enclosed with each lock. Send $.40 in stamps for brochure.

Restoration A Specialty
6127 N.E. Rodney   Dept. OHJ
Portland, OR 97211
(503) 283-3200
RS/O MO
Restoration contracting/interior design services for authentic individual home restoration. Individualized custom design for period homes. Serving Pacific NW. Literature available for individualized work.

Restoration Fraternity
PO Box 234   Dept. OHJ
Lima, PA 19060
(215) 565-6885
RS/O
Contractors specializing in authentic restoration, repairs, and replacements, including new work. Custom doors, sash, breakfronts, mantels, panelled walls, and wainscot for early period work. Send specifications for consultation or free estimates on millwork. No literature.

● **Restoration Hardware**
438 Second St.   Dept. OHJ
Eureka, CA 95501
(707) 443-3152
RS/O MO
Mail order and walk-in store for restoration materials: door hardware, bath fittings, lighting, millwork, cabinet hardware, etc. Specializing in Victorian house parts. Manufacture Victorian mouldings, mantels, and the only Victorian wood doorstop available. Complete catalog, $3 (refundable).

Restoration Masonry
1141 Adams Street   Dept. OHJ
Denver, CO 80206
(303) 377-6566
RS/O
All types of old house masonry restoration and repair: Tile work, stucco, ornamental brickwork, fireplaces, consultation. No literature.

Restoration Works, Inc.
412-1/2 Virginia Street   Dept. OHJ
Buffalo, NY 14201
(716) 882-5000
MO RS/O
Importers, manufacturers, and distributors of high-quality hardware and plumbing, ceiling medallions and trims. Wide range of brass, porcelain, glass and iron. Catalog, $2.

Restoration Workshop Nat Trust For Historic Preservation
635 South Broadway   Dept. OHJ
Tarrytown, NY 10591
(914) 631-6696
Preservation/restoration construction and maintenance services provided on a contractual basis, contact the Director, Restoration Workshop. If travel and living expenses are reimbursed they can serve nationwide. Also: paid apprenticeships available to those committed to a career in the preservation trade. Brochure available on request.

Restorations
382 Eleventh Street   Dept. OHJ
Brooklyn, NY 11215
(212) 788-7909
RS/O MO
Quality restoration of antique lace curtains, hooked rugs, quilts, samplers and household textiles. Consulting services and lectures available on textile conservation, and American rugs and carpets from the 17th century to present. Textile restoration supplies available. Free price list on request.

Restorations Unlimited, Inc.
24 West Main St.   Dept. OHJ
Elizabethville, PA 17023
(717) 362-3477
RS/O
Full restoration contracting and interior period design services, including: Analysis of remodeled old houses for reconstruction of original layout; Design and execution of period and creative interiors; Custom cabinets, furnishings, and woodwork; Procurement of architectural antiques. Authorized dealers of Rich Craft custom cabinets. Literature available on Rich Craft $1.00. Period & modern kitchen design and installation services. Company literature $.25.

● **Restore-A-Tub**
PO Box 7681   Dept. OHJ
Louisville, KY 40207
(502) 452-6022
MO RS/O
Specialists in early 1900 bathrooms, restoring bathtubs including antique clawfoot tubs, pedestal sinks. They carry solid brass and chrome plumbing fixtures for all types of sinks and tubs, marble tubwalls, as well as custom-made shower doors, pull chain toilets, and handmade oak medicine cabinets. Free information.

● **See Product Displays Index on page 199 for more details.**

Retinning & Copper Repair
525 West 26th St.   Dept. OHJ
New York, NY 10001
(212) 244-4896
MO RS/O
Specializes in hot-dip tinning and finishing of copper cookware, bakery equipment and refrigerator racks. Repairs on all copper, brass and tin items. Cleaning and buffing included in services. Goods accepted at shop in person or via UPS. Estimates available by phone or mail. A selection of copperware available on sale at shop. No literature.

• **Rheinschild, S. Chris**
2220 Carlton Way   Dept. OHJ
Santa Barbara, CA 93109
(805) 962-8598
MO RS/O
This company has for ten years produced quality reproductions for old house kitchens and bathrooms. Oak pull-chain toilets, low-tank toilets, oak bath sinks, and copper kitchen sinks. Also, period style faucets. New this year, cast-iron drinking fountain, oak medicine cabinet, and decorated basins. They have limited toilet parts and offer custom work. Brochure, $1.35.

• **Rich Craft Custom Kitchens, Inc.**
141 West Penn Avenue   Dept. OHJ
Robesonia, PA 19551
(215) 693-5871
DIST
Manufacturers of a variety of kitchen cabinet work. A few are period-inspired. There are 100 door styles, available in 8 different woods. Cabinets produced to buyer's specifications, so you may want to purchase them through Rich Craft distributors (designers, architects) who will help plan your kitchen. Send $1.00 for catalog.

Rich Woodturning and Stair Co.
98 N.W. 29th St.   Dept. OHJ
Miami, FL 33127
(305) 573-9142
MO RS/O
Hand turnings from small bobbins to large porch columns. Their stair dept. produces fine curved and spiral stairs. Four generations of woodturners—stairbuilders assure every architectural detail will be perfect. Woodturning catalog, $5; stair parts catalog, $1.50.

Richardson, Matthew Coppersmith
Box 69   Dept. OHJ
Greenfield, MA 01302
(413) 773-9242
MO
Craftsman producing contemporary interpretations of the traditional metalsmith's art. Copper and brass windvanes, garden ornament, fountains, interior & exterior lighting, original wall art. Pieces are compatible with a broad range of historical styles. Range hoods a specialty. Custom work is considered. Catalog, $2.50.

Richmond Doors
P.O. Box 65   Dept. OHJ
Manchester, NH 03105
(603) 487-3347
MO DIST
Manufacturers of quality custom built, odd size and reproduction solid panel doors in sugar pine, oak, mahogany and a variety of other hardwoods. Interior/exterior. All mortise and tenon. Specialize in early New England designs developed from existing 18th century doors. Will quote from blue prints, sketch or clear photo. Commercial restoration work welcomed. Literature $1.00.

Rising & Nelson Slate Co.
    Dept. OHJ
West Pawlet, VT 05775
(802) 645-0150
MO
Vermont Colored Roofing Slate available in all colors, sizes, thicknesses, designs to match and restore old roofs. Also slate flagstone. Brochure with descriptive and technical information available free.

Ritter & Son Hardware
PO Box 578, (38401 Hwy 1)   Dept. OHJ
Gualala, CA 95445
(707) 884-3363
MO
Solid brass, bronze, and porcelain hardware. They feature a large array of Victorian door and window hardware for buildings; knobs, hooks, pulls, and icebox fittings for antiques and cabinets; garden embellishments, such as animal faucets and wind chimes. Catalog $2, refundable with purchase. Call (800) 358-9120, in CA (800) 862-4948.

River City Restorations
200 South 7th   Dept. OHJ
Hannibal, MO 63401
(314) 248-0733
RS/O
Serves N.E. Missouri, West Central Illinois, and Southern Iowa. Specializing in non-abrasive cleaning, paintstripping, repointing. Other services include exterior/interior restoration and rehabilitation of private residences and commercial properties. Contracting business helps clients with design, estimates, and priorities. Answers to all inquiries. Free brochure available.

Riverbend Timber Framing, Inc.
PO Box 26   Dept. OHJ
Blissfield, MI 49228
(517) 486-4566
RS/O
Using traditional heavy timber framing, this company can design and create a traditional or contemporary house with large open space and passive solar design. Also a resource center for the owner-builder and those interested in learning more about this type of construction. Free brochure.

Riverton Corporation
    Dept. OHJ
Riverton, VA 22651
(703) 635-4131
MO DIST
A major manufacturer of masonry cement. Will match any mortar color from stock selection or create a custom color (and composition). Technical assistance is offered. Free literature. Can phone toll free (800) 336-2490, in VA (800) 572-2480.

Roberts, Lee & Lynne
PO 141   Dept. OHJ
Fair Haven, NJ 07701
(201) 842-1863
RS/O
Dealers in restored gas & electric lighting, 1860-1930. Solid brass chandeliers and wall sconces with original glass shades. Also original brass bath accessories. Sold at antique shows (write for list), and by appointment. Will also travel to serious groups and firms. No catalogue.

• **Robinson Iron Corporation**
Robinson Road   Dept. OHJ
Alexander City, AL 35010
(205) 329-8484
RS/O
Authentic 19th century cast iron for the home and garden including: flowing fountains, urns and vases, planters, statuary, fence posts, hitching posts, street lamp standards, garden furniture, and traditional railroad benches. Historic restoration and custom casting services also available. Send $3.00 to receive complete brochure.

• **Robinson Lumber Company**
Suite 202, 512 S. Peters St.   Dept. OHJ
New Orleans, LA 70130
(504) 523-6377
MO RS/O
Family owned lumber company started in 1893, offering long leaf heart pine flooring, beaded ceiling, wainscotting and timbers. Can custom cut to customer's specifications. Free brochure with price list. Samples available at cost.

Robson Worldwide Graining
4308 Argonne Dr.   Dept. OHJ
Fairfax, VA 22032
(703) 978-5331
RS/O
Fifth-generation international grainer and marbler apprenticed for 15 years in England. Has worked throughout Europe, the Middle East, and America. Simulation of any wood, marble, or glazed finish. Has worked in Buckingham Palace, Mount Vernon, and the Philadelphia Athenaeum, as well as private residences worldwide. Please call for prices and a personal viewing of styles and colors available.

Rocker Shop of Marietta, GA
1421 White Circle NW, Box 12   Dept. OHJ
Marietta, GA 30061
(404) 427-2618
RS/O MO
The Brumby rocker made of solid red oak with cane seat and back. A smaller, armless rocker is part of the line, as are a child's rocker and an oak slat porch swing (4, 5, and 6 feet lengths available). Also 2 country-style dining chairs, 2 stools, a lap desk, and small round and oval tables (coordinating). Free catalog and price list.

You'll get better service when contacting companies if you mention The Old-House Journal Catalog

Rohlf's Stained & Leaded Glass
783 South 3rd Ave.   Dept. OHJ
Mount Vernon, NY 10550
(212) 823-4545
RS/O   MO
Since 1920 this company has been designing and
making stained (i.e. painted not merely colored)
and leaded glass windows for the religious
community. They also provide an extensive
leaded glass selection to the furniture industry.
Not for the budget-minded home owner. A repair
and restoration service for glass and windows.
Free literature.

● **Roland Spivak's Custom Lighting,
Pendulum Shop**
424 South Street   Dept. OHJ
Philadelphia, PA 19147
(215) 925-4014
RS/O   MO
Handmade Victorian, turn-of-the-century, Art
Nouveau, and Art Deco chandeliers, sconces, and
floor and table lamps. Not exact reproductions,
but rather styled to the Period. Will custom make
and design fixtures to meet special needs. All
fixtures are solid brass. Also reproduction
pendulum clocks with one-year guarantee.
Walk-in shop. Catalog for lighting only, $1.

Rollerwall, Inc.
PO Box 757   Dept. OHJ
Silver Springs, MD 20901
(301) 649-4422
MO
Sells the design paint roller. A wallpaper effect
can be obtained by the use of a 6-in. rubber roller
with a design embossed on its surface. Can also
be used on fabric and furniture. Over 100
patterns including wood grain and marble.
Illustrated brochure — free.

Roman Marble Co.
120 W. Kinzie   Dept. OHJ
Chicago, IL 60610
(312) 337-2217
RS/O   MO
Company sells imported antique marble mantels.
Restoration and installation of marble mantels.
Also — custom marble pieces, pedestals and
statuary of marble, from Italy and France.
Shipment can occasionally be arranged. Literature
available — please come in or telephone.

Rosander's Wood Turning
1001 East 4060 South   Dept. OHJ
Salt Lake City, UT 84117
(801) 266-1639
RS/O
Will duplicate any wood turning. Items can range
from 1 in. to 18 ft. in length, and 1-24 inches in
circumference. No literature.

Ross, Douglas — Woodworker
P.O. Box 480   Dept. OHJ
Brooklyn, NY 11215
(212) 499-5152
RS/O
Custom cabinetwork and furniture; restoration
and finish carpentry. Free estimate; portfolio and
references available, no literature.

● **Roy Electric Co., Inc.**
1054 Coney Island Avenue   Dept. OHJ
Brooklyn, NY 11230
(212) 339-6311
RS/O   MO
Large selection of gas and electric fixtures,
sconces, brackets, pendants, table and pole
lamps, Emeralites, bases and fixture parts, glass
shades. Antique Victorian and turn-of-century
brass beds and brass & iron beds. Also
reproductions of gas and electric fixtures and
lamps, custom brass beds and brass accessories.
They restore, repair, cast, bend, plate, polish,
lacquer, and extend old brass beds to Queen/King
size. Catalog and price list, and pictures available
for $3.00.

Royal River Bricks Co., Inc.
PO Box 458   Dept. OHJ
Gray, ME 04039
(207) 657-4498
RS/O
Many sizes and shapes of handmade, waterstruck
bricks fired in a period kiln. The results are bricks
available in blacks, deep purples, and a wide
range of reds. Used in numerous restoration
projects: Strawberry Banke, parts of Faneuil Hall,
the the Henry Wadsworth Longfellow House.
Free information.

Royal Windyne Limited
1022 W. Franklin St.   Dept. OH-4
Richmond, VA 23220
(804) 358-1899
MO
Hand-built reproductions of 19th century ceiling
fans. Nostalgic fans save energy by cooling in
summer and circulating warm air in winter.
Solid-brass appointments and hand-rubbed
furniture-finish dark walnut or golden oak blades
made of one-piece solid wood. Available with or
without lights. Please allow 3-5 weeks for crafting
of your order. Illustrated catalog, $1.00.

● **Rue de France**
77 Thames St.   Dept. OH
Newport, RI 02840
(401) 846-0317
MO   RS/O
A mail-order source of fine, French lace in
traditional patterns. Can be purchased by the
yard or as ready-made curtains and tablecloths.
Catalog, $2.

● **Rumplestiltskin Designs**
8967 David Ave.   Dept. OHJ
Los Angeles, CA 90034
(213) 839-4747
MO
A source for hard-to-find, beaded lampshade
fringe. Different patterns and colors are available.
Also, replacement panels with embroidered
designs for recovering an old shade. Send $1 and
SASE for photos and current price list.

● **RUSCO**
RD 2   Dept. OHJ
Cochranton, PA 16314
(814) 724-4200
DIST
Tubular steel-framed storm windows which are
flush-mounted. Can be adjusted to fit even
out-of-square windows, and are offered in a large
variety of traditional colors. Free literature.

Russell & Company Victorian Bathrooms
23400 Peralta, Unit E   Dept. OHJ
Laguna Hills, CA 92653
(714) 770-5391
MO
Oak bathroom accessories at a reasonable cost.
Also, vanities, and high-tank toilets. Brochure,
$1.

● **Russell Restoration of Suffolk**
Rte. 1, Box 243A   Dept. OHJ
Mattituck, NY 11952
(516) 765-2481
MO   RS/O
Quality restoration of ornamental plaster and lath
plaster (flat work): cornice mouldings, ceilings,
medallions, and brackets. Also custom niches,
columns, light domes and other architectural
details. From one foot of moulding to an entire
room reconstructed. Any period or style from
Colonial to Rocco to Art Deco. Also restoration of
masonry, and re-pointing in original materials.
Will travel. Brochure, $.75.

W.N. Russell and Co.
34-60 Albertson Ave.   Dept. OHJ
Westmont, NJ 08108
(609) 858-1057
RS/O   MO
Specialize in cast stone, including capitals (Doric
& Composite), mouldings, gargoyles, arches, and
cornices. Custom work and some stock items.
Free brochure.

Rustic Home Hardware
R.D. 3   Dept. OHJ
Hanover, PA 17331
(717) 632-0088
MO
A small specialty welding shop offering wrought
iron fireplace equipment, early American
hardware, and accessories. Catalog, $2.

Rutland Products
P.O. Box 340   Dept. OHJ
Rutland, VT 05701
(802) 775-5519
DIST
Home repair products — glazing compounds,
caulks, sealants, adhesives, putty, grout, spackle,
metal roofpaint, clearwood finish, roof cement,
coating and patching compounds, furnace
cement, stove lining compound. Free catalogs.

KEY TO ABBREVIATIONS

MO   sells by Mail Order

RS/O   sells through Retail
Store or Office

DIST   sells through
Distributors

ID   sells only through
Interior Designers
or Architects

**You'll get better service
when contacting companies
if you mention
The Old-House Journal
Catalog**

S

S H M Restorations
887 Ashland Ave.   Dept. OHJ
St. Paul, MN 55104
(612) 291-7117
RS/O
Carpentry, general contracting, cabinetmaking, and fine woodworking. They specialize in restoration of Victorian houses and commercial structures. Design services for Victorian recreation and architecturally compatible remodeling. Reproduce moldings, spindle work, etc. Dealers for many restoration products. No literature available.

S & W Framing Supplies, Inc.
120 Broadway   Dept. OHJ
Garden City Park, NY 11040
(800) 645-3399
MO RS/O
Major distributor of framing supplies and machinery, serving the picture framing trade and art galleries. Their picture rail hangers, sold in gold with gold buttons and rope, were recommended by an OHJ subscriber. Free illustrated catalog.

● St. Louis Antique Lighting Co.
25 N. Sarah   Dept. OHJ
St. Louis, MO 63108
(314) 535-2770
MO RS/O DIST
Antique and authentic handcrafted brass reproduction ceiling fixtures, sconces and lamps. Gas, electric and combination fixtures from 1880 to 1930. ''Mission Oak'' ceiling fixture now available. Will also manufacture to your design specifications. Catalogue, $3.00.

● Saltbox
2229 Marietta Pike   Dept. OHJ
Lancaster, PA 17603
(717) 392-5649
RS/O MO DIST
American period lighting fixtures: Extensive collection of lanterns, post lights, and chandeliers handcrafted of tin, copper, brass and pewter. The Period Collection is designed for traditional, Early American and Colonial homes in primitive, country or formal styles. Stores also in Lexington, Ky, Green Bay, WI, and Greensboro, NC. Illustrated brochure showing 25 of over 250 pieces — $1.00.

Salvage One
1524 S. Peoria   Dept. OHJ
Chicago, IL 60608
(312) 733-0098
RS/O MO
Enormous selection of architectural artifacts, housed in multi-storey warehouse. Can supply complete room interiors for restorations, or period decor in restaurants, etc. In-stock items available for prop rentals. Walk-in store only, open to the public. No literature.

**●See Product Dis-
plays Index on page
199 for more details.**

● San Francisco Restorations, Inc.
175 Bluxome, 2nd Floor   Dept. OHJ
San Francisco, CA 94107
(415) 896-1910
RS/O
Restoration contractor specializing in the Victorian Era. Their work ranges from residential kitchens, baths and additions, to commercial rehab for stores and office buildings. The emphasis focuses on practical cost effective restoration using as many stock components as possible. Also, a full cabinet shop capable of reproducing most ornate millwork. Works primarily in the San Francisco Bay area, but will do design and consulting work elsewhere. No literature.

San Francisco Victoriana
2245 Palou Avenue   Dept. OHJ
San Francisco, CA 94124
(415) 648-0313
RS/O MO
Manufactures and supplies stock reproduction Victorian and traditional wood mouldings, ceiling cornices, and fireplace surrounds; also reproductions of fibrous plaster ceiling centerpieces, cornices, and brackets. Supplies embossed anaglypta wallcoverings; embossed wall and frieze border papers; bronze door and window hardware in matched patterns; and cast iron spiral staircases. Custom duplications from plaster or wood samples. Product catalog, $3; Hardware catalog, $1.

Sanders, David & Co.
115 Bowery   Dept. OHJ
New York, NY 10002
(212) 334-9898
RS/O
Large selection of brass & bronze hardware including wheels and tracks for sliding doors. No literature; walk-in store only.

Sandy Springs Galleries
233 Hilderbrand Dr., N.E.   Dept. OHJ
Atlanta, GA 30328
(404) 252-3244
RS/O
Specializes in old lighting fixtures and sconces, many of which were originally gas or kerosene, in brass, wood, and wrought iron, all rewired to meet the National Code. They also have 5000 square feet of European and American furniture, mirrors. No literature.

Sarah Bustle Antiques, Ltd.
1701 Central St.   Dept. OHJ
Evanston, IL 60201
(312) 869-7290
RS/O
They specialize in restored brass, copper, and iron lighting fixtures. Including ceiling lights, wall sconces, desk lamps and floor lamps, dating from 1850 to 1920. All fixtures are complete with antique light shades. Also old hardware in stock. No supplies or literature.

Sawdust Room
P.O. Box 327, 1856 S. Sierra   Dept. OHJ
Stevensville, MI 49127
(616) 429-5338
MO RS/O
Early American wood products made and repaired: canopy beds, spinning wheels, custom wood products. Cylindrical lathe duplications. Will replace missing wooden parts: chair rungs, rockers, spokes, Shaker clothes racks, etc. Will answer serious inquiries if you enclose a stamped, self-addressed envelope.

● Scalamandre, Inc.
950 Third Avenue   Dept. OHJ
New York, NY 10022
(212) 980-3888
ID
For over 50 years this company has been making superb period fabrics. The authenticity of their fabrics, wallpapers, carpets and trimmings is acknowledged by museums. Scalamandre has been involved in the restorations at Monticello, San Simeon, and Sturbridge. A research library and consulting services are available to those persons involved in the restoration of public buildings. Free brochure.

Schmidt, Edward P. — Cabinetmaker
205 N. Easton Rd.   Dept. OHJ
Glenside, PA 19038
(215) 886-8774
RS/O
Cabinetmaker will do reproduction work: furniture, doors, brackets, turnings, bookcases, wall units, and built-ins; in primitive, country, Early American, Colonial, Victorian, and contemporary styles. Pieces available in hardwoods, softwoods, and exotic species. Will also duplicate wood pieces for the rehabilitation of antique furniture and woodwork. References available. No literature, but inquiries will be answered.

Schumacher
939 3rd Avenue   Dept. OHJ
New York, NY 10022
(212) 644-5943
DIST ID
Schumacher has a large line of period and traditional fabrics and wallcoverings available at decorating shops and department stores. The documentary patterns have the historical information printed on back of the samples. They also have a fine line of damasks and brocades and Victorian prints, but these are decorator only. No literature.

Schwartz's Forge & Metalworks
P.O. Box 205   Dept. OHJ
Deansboro, NY 13328
(315) 841-4477
RS/O MO
Designs and executes architectural ironwork in a variety of styles, for use as gates, railings, grilles, furnishings etc. Traditional blacksmithing techniques used on all work. Custom design work. Will work with architect. Representative portfolio available for $3.50.

● Schwerd Manufacturing Co.
3215 McClure Avenue   Dept. OHJ
Pittsburgh, PA 15212
(412) 766-6322
MO RS/O
Aesthetically pleasing, mathematically correct wooden columns. Available in Tuscan, Greek, and Roman orders, fluted or plain; round, square, or octagon shapes. Can manufacture columns to stock designs, or to your specifications. Ornamental caps: Scamozzi, Ionic, Doric, Temple of the Winds, Erechtheum, Roman Corinthian. Also — wooden lamp posts and lanterns. Specify interest for free brochure.

● Sculpture Associates, Ltd.
40 East 19th Street   Dept. OHJ
New York, NY 10003
(212) 777-2400
MO RS/O
Fine imported tools, including rasps and carving tools. Also offer a complete line of woods, and clays. Casting materials such as plasters, plastics, rubbers, and liquid metals are available. Many tools are good for scraping paint out of difficult places. Also has marble polishes and buffers. Send $2 for catalog.

Sculpture House
38 East 30th St.   Dept. OHJ
New York, NY 10016
(212) 679-7474
MO   DIST
Manufacturers of handmade tools, and suppliers of material for all forms of three dimensional art. Tools are available for working in plaster, ceramics, wood, and stone. Complete catalogue with prices available for $2.00.

Sculptured Tiles
8 Bridge Street   Dept. OHJ
Florida, NY 10921
(914) 651-7331
MO   RS/O
Handcarved and handpainted tiles in the spirit of the Arts & Crafts movement. Also, molded tiles and custom designs. Price list and photos with SASE.

Second Chance
972 Magnolia St.   Dept. OHJ
Macon, GA 31201
(912) 742-7874
RS/O   MO
Specializes in hard-to-find restoration items. Inventory includes brass hardware, plumbing fixtures, fireplace tile, and old stained and beveled glass. A large collection of corbels, gingerbread, columns, entrance frames, heavily carved doors, mantels and antique staircase parts. Serves the middle Georgia area. No literature, but photographs can be supplied on request with a stamped, self-addressed envelope.

Security Home Inspection, Inc.
5906 Avenue T   Dept. OHJ
Brooklyn, NY 11234
(212) 763-5589
RS/O
Old house inspection in the New York metro area. No literature.

Sedgwick House
101 North 10th St.   Dept. OHJ
Noblesville, IN 46060
(317) 773-7372
MO
A wonderful selection of period inspired frames for photographs and paintings/drawings. Finishes include: antique gold, walnut, oak, gold, and silver. Free literature.

● **Sedgwick Machine Works, Inc.**
PO Box 630   Dept. OHJ
Poughkeepsie, NY 12602
(914) 454-5400
DIST
The oldest company in the dumbwaiter business, Sedgwick manufactures both electric and hand-powered dumbwaiters. Also manufactures a line of residence elevators. Free catalog.

Seitz, Robert/Fine Woodworking
Farwell Rd.   Dept. OHJ
Tyngsboro, MA 01879
(617) 649-7707
RS/O
Architectural work in the Boston and southern New Hampshire area. Both on site carpentry and the use of a well-equipped shop for millwork are available. Send $1.00 for brochure; or send sketch, photo, etc., for consultation and estimate.

Shades of the Past
PO Box 502   Dept. OHJ
Corte Madera, CA 94925
(415) 459-6999
MO
A collection of Victorian, Deco, & Traditional silk lampshades & fine quality bases. Each shade is original, hand sewn & custom designed. Only the finest quality materials are used. A special custom service is also available for the customer who wants a shade restored, or a unique one-of-a-kind piece. Color brochure, $3.

Shadovitz Bros. Distributors, Inc.
1565 Bergen Street   Dept. OHJ
Brooklyn, NY 11213
(212) 774-9100
DIST   MO
For their 80th Anniversary celebration, they are offering a series of specialized catalogs for a nominal charge: Glazing ($1.00); Stained, Etched, Bevelled Decorative Glass ($1.00); Picture Framing ($1.00); Security Glazing ($1.00); Old Home Glazing ($3.00); Gift Ideas ($1.00); Interior Design ($3.00); Solar Efficiency ($3.00). Add $1.50 postage and handling per request. Literature indexes for "Do It Yourselfers" and "Architects" are free (send SASE).

● **Shaker Workshops**
PO Box 1028   Dept. OHJ
Concord, MA 01742
(617) 646-8985
MO   RS/O
Reproduction Shaker furniture kits, oval boxes, baskets, pegs & pegrail, lighting fixtures & rag rugs. Of special interest are the Shawl-Back and Tape-Back Rockers, in child and adult sizes, identical to those made by the Mt. Lebanon, NY Shakers. Replacement chair tape also available in authentic Shaker colors. Showroom is at Old Schwamb Mill, Mill Lane, Arlington, Mass. Catalog and tape samples, $.50.

● **Shakertown Corporation**
P.O. Box 400   Dept. OH
Winlock, WA 98596
(206) 785-3501
MO   RS/O   DIST
A major manufacturer of shakes and shingles has red cedar shingles in 9 specialty patterns appropriate for Queen Anne and shingle-style houses. Fancy-butt shingles are 18 in. long and 5 in. wide, and are available for prompt shipment. Shakertown also manufactures 8' and 4' lengths of wood shingle & shakes panels. Free illustrated brochure, catalog $4.

● **Shanker—Glendale Steel Corp.**
70-32 83rd St.   Dept. OHJ
Glendale, Queens, NY 11385
(212) 326-1100
MO
Company is a major manufacturer of pressed steel ceilings. Catalog, price list and brochure on how to put material up are available free.

● **See Product Displays Index on page 199 for more details.**

Shaw Marble & Tile Co., Inc.
5012 S. 38th St.   Dept. OHJ
St. Louis, MO 63116
(314) 481-5860
RS/O
Supply and/or install all types of marble. Custom cut to individual needs, from small bases to fireplaces, bathrooms, office lobbies, etc. Furnish and install ceramic and quarry tile work. No literature.

Shelley Signs
Box 94   Dept. OHJ
West Danby, NY 14896
(607) 564-3527
MO
Signs (carved/painted) designed & executed in a traditional American vein. Custom carving work, including door panels, shells, scrolls. Handcarved wooden placques. Please send SASE and request for a representative slide or photo.

Shenandoah Manufacturing Co.
P.O. Box 839   Dept. OHJ
Harrisonburg, VA 22801
(703) 434-3838
DIST
Wood and/or coal stoves and furnaces; thermostatically regulated, utilitarian in design. Fireplace insert that will increase the efficiency of a fireplace. Also — add-on furnaces, to be used alone or added to an existing forced-air heating system. Free literature.

Sheppard Millwork, Inc.
21020 70th Ave. W.   Dept. OHJ
Edmonds, WA 98020
(206) 771-4645
RS/O
A custom woodworking shop. They make custom & stock doors, mouldings, sashes, turnings, etc. Can also purchase stock doors. Will do a wide variety of mouldings as they can grind their own knives and turnings are done by hand to match the existing work in a house.

Shingle Mill, Inc.
73 Stuart Street   Dept. OHJ
Gardner, MA 01440
(617) 632-3015
MO   DIST   RS/O
Manufactures wooden shingles used in restoration work, for roofing and exterior siding. Also, a wide variety of special architectural shapes. Where it is within their range of capability, they'll cut to order any special size or shape you may desire. If unable to duplicate your order exactly, they'll send a sample of the closest possible alternative. Free brochure.

Sierra Trading Co.
1836 Old Ione Rd.   Dept. OHJ
Martell, CA 95654
(209) 223-0886
MO   RS/O
Manufacturers of turn-of-the-century style lamps. Mostly desk lamps with brass, emeralite-style, or Tiffany-style shades. Catalog, $1.

Sign of the Crab
8101 Elder Creek Rd.   Dept. 132
Sacramento, CA 95824
(916) 383-2722
RS/O   DIST
Manufacturer of brass hardware, plumbing fixtures, lamps, clocks, antique re-creations and nauticals. Wholesale catalog and price list to dealers. Call or write for name of distributor nearest you.

Silberman, Allen
18 Homer Avenue   Dept. OHJ
Cortland, NY 13045
(607) 756-2632
RS/O
Decorative painter specializing in stencilling. Has patterns available, can create new stencils or restore old ones. Has restored the Victorian stencilling in the 1890 House in Cortland, NY. Will travel; also will consult and/or train local craftsmen in the art of stencilling. Also conducts stencilling workshops. No literature; call or write specifying interest.

Silver Dollar Trading Co.
1446 So. Broadway   Dept. OHJ
Denver, CO 80210
(303) 733-0500
RS/O   MO
This company carries Victorian reproduction spiral staircases, street lights, mailboxes, light fixtures, fountains, benches, and stained glass. Free catalog.

● **Silverton Victorian Millworks**
P.O. Box 877-35   Dept. OHJ
Silverton, CO 81433
(303) 387-5716
MO
Offer a variety of custom Victorian and Colonial mouldings, as well as the standard patterns. They also have window and door rosettes available in many combinations. The millwork is available in pine or oak. They welcome any inquiries concerning custom milling. For custom mouldings, send a detailed drawing or sample for prompt quotation. Catalog — $3.50.

● **The Sink Factory**
2140 San Pablo Ave.   Dept. OHJ
Berkeley, CA 94702
(415) 548-3967
MO   RS/O
Manufacturers of hand-crafted porcelain, specializing in pedestal sinks and floral vanity basins. Victorian design fluted base pedestal sink, and 1920's smooth pedestal sink. Bathroom accessories. Custom orders welcomed. Catalog, $3. (Formerly Stringer's Environmental Restoration & Design.)

● **Sky Lodge Farm**
Box 62   Dept. OHJ
Shutesbury, MA 01072
(413) 253-3182
MO
Producers of Early American clapboards with quartersawn squared edges. Also, 18th & 19th century building materials, and bricks. Send for free brochure.

Skyline Engineers, Inc.
58 East St.   Dept. OHJ
Fitchburg, MA 01420
(617) 342-5333
RS/O
Specialists in steeple restoration, gold-leafing, and the preservation of historic buildings. Nationwide services include: sandblasting, chemical restoration, repointing, carpentry, painting, roofing (slate and copper), masonry, bird-proofing, lightning protection, and waterproofing. Projects include: six state capitol buildings, Georgetown University, Holy Cross College, the "clustered spires of Frederick, Md."; Faneuil Hall; Old State House, Boston, Mass, and Old North Church. Call toll free (800) 343-8847 for free estimate and brochure.

Smith-Cornell Homestead, Inc.
P.O. Box 666   Dept. OHJ
Auburn, IN 46706
(219) 925-1172
MO
Manufactures cast bronze and Italian marble plaques for National Register, Historic American Buildings Survey, and Certified Historic Structure properties. Also makes custom plaques with image permanently embedded into anodized aluminum plate in bronze or pewter finish. May be mounted inside or outside. Special rates for not-for-profit groups. Free brochure or quotation.

Smith, F.E., Castings, Inc.
PO Box 2126   Dept. OHJ
Kingsford, MI 49801
(906) 774-4956
RS/O
Smith specializes in small orders from loose patterns. They have made some parts for antique stoves and want to do more. Will make new patterns for deteriorated parts. Also, decorative figures for iron fencing. No literature, write with specific needs.

Smithy, The
    Dept. OHJ
Wolcott, VT 05680
(802) 472-6508
MO   RS/O
Hand-forged iron executed in the centuries-old manner, with forge, hammer, and anvil. Diversified work includes hardware necessary in restoration of old houses and construction of new reproductions: hinges, door latches, fireplace equipment, kitchen items, lighting fixtures, weathervanes, etc. Write for free brochure.

Smithy Hearth Products
174 Cedar St., PO Box 551   Dept. OHJ
Branford, CT 06405
(203) 488-7225
MO   DIST
Custom-built fireplace screens, using black enamel wire mesh cloth, hand-clinched to a steel frame, furnished with two brass support handles. Smith also manufactures wrought iron log holders, child guards and mitten dryers. Free brochure.

Smolinsky, Ltd.
203 Fawn Hill Road   Dept. OHJ
Broomall, PA 19008
(215) 353-2893
RS/O
Services southeastern Pennsylvania, southern New Jersey and Delaware with restoration contracting services. No literaure.

Somerset Door & Column Co.
P.O. Box 328   Dept. OHJ
Somerset, PA 15501
(814) 445-9608
MO   DIST   RS/O
Company has been manufacturing wood columns since 1906. Composition capitals also available. Column sizes from 6-in. bottom diameter to 40-in. diameter by 40 ft. long. They can also provide custom millwork such as stair parts, sash, moulding, panelling, and doors to customer's specifications. Columns brochure is free.

● **Sound Beginnings**
40 E. 21st St.   Dept. OHJ
New York, NY 10010
(212) 741-2456
MO   RS/O
Custom and reproduction turnings of all types. Wood of any type. No literature.

● **South Coast Shingle Co.**
2220 E. South Street   Dept. OHJ
Long Beach, CA 90805
(213) 634-7100
RS/O   MO
Manufactures fancy butt red cedar shingles. Also distributes cedar shakes and shingles for roofing and siding. Free flyer — please specify.

Southeastern Art Glass Studio
100 Avondale Road   Dept. OHJ
Avondale Estates, GA 30002
(404) 294-4296
RS/O   MO   DIST
Leaded and beveled glass panel sets in several period styles. Handcrafted sidelights, doors, and transoms. Also custom designs. Brochure available.

● **Southern Heritage Metal Amenities, Ltd.**
PO Box 2782   Dept. OHJ-3
Birmingham, AL 35202
(205) 251-1596
MO
Over 300 designs of Classic, Victorian and Southern inspired outdoor and dining furniture, landscape items and decor items cast in aluminum and iron. Custom casting, consultation, design, fabrication and erection services. 68-page color catalog, $5. (refundable with 1st order).

● **Southington Specialty Wood Co.**
100 West Main St.   Dept. OHJ
Plantsville, CT 06479
(203) 621-6787
RS/O
Deal strictly with wood products, expertly milled to pattern for random width floor planning in oak, ash, cherry, maple, and whatever else suits your fancy. Specialize in wide (8-in. to 14-in.) kiln-dried oak, cherry, & pine. Delivery available based on quantity and distance. Free brochure and price list.

Spanish Pueblo Doors
PO Box 2517   Dept. OHJ
Santa Fe, NM 87501
(505) 473-0464
MO   RS/O
Exterior and interior doors of select hardwoods, Ponderosa pine, Phillipine mahogany, red alder, red oak, or other woods. All custom milled to your size specifications in standard or custom designs. Custom furniture. Free literature.

Specialized Repair Service
2406 West Bryn Mawr Ave.   Dept. OHJ
Chicago, IL 60659
(312) 784-2800
MO   RS/O
Missing hardware and castings in yellow brass, red brass, or bronze are made to match existing hardware. Other services include welding, machining, and silver brazing. No literature, write for a price quote.

KEY TO ABBREVIATIONS

MO   sells by **Mail Order**

RS/O   sells through **Retail Store or Office**

DIST   sells through **Distributors**

ID   sells only through **Interior Designers or Architects**

Spencer, William, Inc.
Creek Road   Dept. OHJ
Rancocas Woods, NJ 08060
(609) 235-1830
RS/O   MO
Manufacturers of solid brass chandeliers and
sconces made according to blueprints dating from
1897. Fine materials and workmanship. Custom
work and refinishing of metals an added service.
60-page lighting fixture catalog available for $2.

Tomas Spiers & Associates
PO Box 3742   Dept. OHJ
Harrisburg, PA 17105
(717) 763-7396
RS/O
Architectural/Engineering firm specializing in
preservation consultation and professional
services including restoration rehabilitation and
adaptive use, preparation of historic structure
reports, condition surveys, research, state and
national register nominations and grant-in-aid
applications, in Pennsylvania and surrounding
states. No literature.

Spiess, Greg
216 East Washington   Dept. OHJ
Joliet, IL 60433
(815) 722-5639
RS/O
Antique architectural ornamentation. Interior and
exterior ornamental wood, mantels a specialty.
Stained, leaded and bevelled glass; Antique and
custom fabrication. Custom bevelling. Also
handles antique tavern back bars. Good general
architectural selection. No literature.

Spiral Manufacturing, Inc.
17251 Jefferson Hwy.   Dept. OHJ
Baton Rouge, LA 70816
(504) 293-8336
MO   RS/O
Wood, steel, aluminum and cast aluminum spiral
stairs in diameters from 48 in. up to 96 in.
Available in kit form for do-it-yourselfers or
contractors. For additional information and a free
catalog call (800) 535-9956.

Spring City Electrical Mfg. Co
Drawer A, Hall & Main Sts.   Dept. OHJ
Spring City, PA 19475
(215) 948-4000
MO
Manufactures cast-iron ornamental lamp posts
and bollards, and bronze fountains. Lamp posts
are suitable for street use. Free brochure.

Squaw Alley, Inc.
401 S. Main Street   Dept. OHJ
Naperville, IL 60540
(312) 357-0200
MO   RS/O
A restoration supply source, specializing in sale
and restoration of oil lamps (including Aladdins),
gas and early electric fixtures. Also lamp repair
parts, lampshades, antique and reproduction
hardware (very large stock), caning supplies, and
cleaning/refinishing products. Serves mainly
Chicago area but hardware can be shipped
anywhere. Catalog, $3.00.

● **Stained Panes**
PO Box 15   Dept. OHJ
Fairfield, CT 06430
(203) 259-6351
MO   RS/O
Stained glass patterns and complete custom
stained-glass window designs. Design catalog,
$3.50 ppd.

Stair-Pak Products Co.
Rt. 22, Box 334   Dept. OHJ
Union, NJ 07083
(201) 688-8000
MO   DIST   RS/O
Manufactures all-wood spiral stairways for both
interior and exterior use. Interior units come in
oak or a poplar/particle board combination;
exterior units come in Philippine mahogany with
brass hardware. Standard interior styles are
Colonial, Mediterranean, and Contemporary;
other styles as special orders. Also conventional
wooden stairways to customer specifications and
pre-assembled stair rail systems. Free brochures.

Stamford Wallpaper Co., Inc.
153 Greenwich Ave.   Dept. OHJ
Stamford, CT 06904
(203) 323-1123
RS/O   DIST
Documented lines of reproduction wallpapers.
Two lines of textures available which could
accompany any pattern. No literature.

Standard Heating Parts, Inc.
4615 Belden Avenue   Dept. OHJ
Chicago, IL 60639
(312) 227-4546
MO   RS/O
Stoker parts. Write for free brochure.

Standard Trimming Co.
1114 First Ave. (61st St.)   Dept. OHJ
New York, NY 10021
(212) 755-3034
RS/O
Manufacturers of trimmings and crystal drapery
hardware. Antique tassels, fringes and tiebacks.
Special cords and ropes. No literature.

● **Stanley Galleries**
2118 N. Clark Street   Dept. OHJ
Chicago, IL 60614
(312) 281-1614
MO   RS/O
They specialize in restoring and selling American
antique lighting from 1850 to 1925. All fixtures are
thoroughly researched so that antique shades can
be matched with them. Only old glass is used,
not reproductions. All fixtures are taken apart,
stripped, rewired, and relacquered. Walk-in store
has large selection; mail orders also taken. Call or
write about specific fixtures; a Polaroid photo will
be sent on request.

● **Staples, H. F. & Co., Inc.**
Webb Drive, Box 956   Dept. OHJ
Merrimack, NH 03054
(603) 889-8600
MO   DIST
Founded in 1897 as the manufacturer of carnauba
paste waxes for wood floors and furniture,
Staples now manufactures several products for
the do-it-yourselfer and professional. These
products include "Dry Strip" powdered paint
remover, paste waxes, "Miracle Wood",
"Decto-Stick", ladder mitts, William's stove
polish, and Patina Rub. Free literature.

Stark Carpet Corp.
979 Third Ave.   Dept. OHJ
New York, NY 10022
(212) 752-9000
ID
Documented carpets for historical restorations.
Also a stock line of historical Wilton carpets;
machine-made and handmade rugs from over 20
countries, including Portuguese needlepoints,
Romanian kilims, and orientals. Please inquire on
your letterhead.

● **Stencil House**
RFD 9, Box 287   Dept. OHJ
Concord, NH 03301
(603) 225-9121
MO
Over 80 designs printed on "Mylar". Cut & uncut
stencils ranging from $3.00 to $30.00. Designs
include Shaker Tree of Life, Moses Eaton patterns
— strawberries & pineapples. Send $1. for
brochure.

Stencil School
Box 94   Dept. OHJ
Shrewsbury, MA 01545
MO
Hand-stenciled country accessories and stencils
printed on mylar. Country gifts including:
potholders, placemats, aprons, woodenware and
more. Stencil designs including country village,
schoolhouse, rooster, etc. Brochure $1.

Stencil Store
PO Box 21076   Dept. OHJ
Columbus, OH 43221
MO   RS/O
Full size "MYLAR" stencils, ranging in price from
$2 to $12. All stencil designs from original
patterns. Furniture stencils and supplies.
Brochure, $1. "Welcome Friends" stencil
workbook. 32 designs printed on one side of
durable manilla paper. Instructions included.
$19.95 plus $1.50 postage.

● **W. P. Stephens Lumber Co.**
145 Church St.   Dept. OHJ
Marietta, GA 30061
(404) 428-1531
MO   RS/O
Since 1925, this company's architectural millwork
includes custom mouldings, sidings, flooring,
panelling, doors, shutters, mantels, and cabinet
work. Stock lumber includes oak, honduras
mahogany, cherry, birch, black walnut, poplar,
clear yellow pine, and virgin long leaf heart pine.
Stock moulding catalog, $1. Can match customer
profiles.

● **Steptoe and Wife Antiques Ltd.**
3626 Victoria Park Ave.   Dept. OHJ
Willowdale, ON, Canada M2H3B2
(416) 497-2989
MO   RS/O   DIST
Reproduction Victorian style cast-iron spiral &
straight staircases. Knock-down for shipping and
on-site assembly — modular units for any
elevation. They also distribute W.F. Norman
sheet metal ceiling panels, plaster cornices &
medallions, brass & steel railing systems and
"Converto"™ showers. Complete product
catalogue, $2.

Sterline Manufacturing Corp.
410 N. Oakley Blvd.   Dept. OHJ
Chicago, IL 60612
(312) 226-1555
DIST
"CONVERTO" Shower systems for adding a
shower to old bathtubs. Includes tub and shower
faucet, rectangular, corner, and straight shower
rods. Available in chrome-plated brass and
polished brass. A free brochure is available.

Donald C. Stetson, Sr., Enterprises
Calvin Coombs Rd.   Dept. OHJ
Colrain, MA 01340
(413) 624-5512
MO   RS/O
Hand crafted wrought iron items ranging from
candle holders to fire place accessories, etc. Also,
various types of hooks, handmade nails, etc.

Stevens, John R., Associates
1 Sinclair Drive   Dept. OHJ
Greenlawn, NY 11740
(516) 420-5295
RS/O
Specializing in the restoration of buildings from the 17th century to the mid 19th century and restoration of antique street railway rolling stock. New York metropolitan region and New Haven, Connecticut area. No literature.

● **Stewart Manufacturing Company**
511 Enterprise Drive   Dept. OHJ
Covington, KY 41017
(606) 331-9000
MO   DIST   RS/O
They manufacture ornamental iron fence and gates. Each design is custom made, with the ability to match various old designs manufactured after 1886. No cost or obligation for an estimate. A complete, illustrated catalog is available upon request.

● **Strafford Forge**
Box 148   Dept. OHJ
So. Strafford, VT 05070
(802) 765-4455
MO   RS/O
A small company producing accurate reproductions of 17th, 18th, and early 19th-century hardware. All items are hand forged and finished to ensure an authentic representation of pieces of the period. In addition to stock items illustrated in the catalogue, they welcome your inquiries concerning custom work such as house hardware, gates, railings, and sign brackets. Catalog, $2.

Strip Shop
2201 Tchoupitoulas Street   Dept. OHJ
New Orleans, LA 70130
(504) 522-7524
RS/O
Architectural antiques - doors, mantels, shutters, stained and bevelled glass. A quality selection of oval bevelled entrance doors. Also brass, porcelain, and other hardware to complement doors. All material is stripped and ready to be refinished. Large stripping service to handle all needs. No literature.

Stripper, The
407 Scott St.   Dept. OHJ
Covington, KY 41011
(606) 491-1292
RS/O   MO
Custom paint-stripping services. Complete repair service; custom duplication of missing pieces. Hand-rubbed refinishing. Also design, consultation, and appraisal service. Architectural restoration for vintage homes, including custom woodworking. Free brochure.

● **Strobel Millwork**
P.O. Box 84, Route 7   Dept. OHJ
Cornwall Bridge, CT 06754
(203) 672-6727
RS/O   MO
Stock and custom architectural millwork. Company specializes in the exact duplication of all styles of wood windows, doors, and entrance frames, particularly Italianate or Renaissance styles. Full line of interior trims. New this year: stock size fanlight windows with etched glass accents. Brochure, $2.

● **See Product Dis-
plays Index on page
199 for more details.**

Structural Antiques
3006 Classen Blvd.   Dept. OHJ
Oklahoma City, OK 73106
(405) 528-7734
RS/O   MO
Over 8,000 sq. ft. of inventory consisting exclusively of American antique architectural elements. They offer a large selection of original stamped tin ceilings, mantels, doors, stained glass windows, brass light fixtures, columns, staircase parts, and other items. Also, decorating and design ideas and installation of architectural elements. No literature, but will answer all inquiries.

Structural Slate Company
222 East Main Street   Dept. OHJ
Pen Argyl, PA 18072
(215) 863-4141
RS/O   DIST
A primary source of structural slate products for flooring, stair treads, and accent trim; slate tile for slate roofs. Free brochure.

Stryker, Donald, Restorations
154 Commercial Ave.   Dept. OHJ
New Brunswick, NJ 08901
(201) 828-7022
MO   RS/O
Provides interior and exterior restoration services for residential and small-scale commercial buildings, with special emphasis on 19th century residential structures. Also offer "Historic Property Analysis" that describes present condition, immediate repairs needed, maintainance cycles, suggested restoration plans, and restoration resources available. Free literature.

Studio Design, Inc., t/a Rainbow Art Glass
49 Shark River Rd.   Dept. OHJ
Neptune, NJ 07753
(201) 922-1090
MO   RS/O
One of the largest dealers of stained glass kits and supplies. Kits come with pre-cut glass pieces, mold, pattern, and all supplies necessary. Large selection of lamps, clocks, mirrors, wall & window decor, terrariums, and suncatchers. Also available: mold and patterns only for those who enjoy cutting their own glass. Catalog, $3.

Studio Workshop, Ltd.
22 Bushy Hill Rd.   Dept. OHJ
Simsbury, CT 06070
(203) 658-6374
MO   RS/O
Studio Workshop does restoration work on both antique furniture and stained glass. They will do extensive repair & refinishing using either hand rubbed oil, or lacquer finishes. They do custom designs in stained glass, specializing in turn-of-the-century and Victorian windows, as well as repair of antique windows. No literature.

● **Stulb Paint & Chem. Co., Inc.**
P.O. Box 297   Dept. OHJ
Norristown, PA 19404
(215) 272-6660
MO   DIST   RS/O
Manufacturers of authentic 18th and 19th century paint colors for furniture, walls, woodwork — interior and exterior. Oil-based, lead-free. Also, polyurethane paste stain and clear paste varnish, for use inside or outside. Exclusive maker of Old Sturbridge Village colors. Send $1. for color cards and literature.

Such Happiness, Inc.
P.O. Box 32   Dept. OHJ
Fitchburg, MA 01420
(603) 878-1031
MO   RS/O
Custom designed and restored stained glass windows and leaded, bevelled, and etched panels. Decorative, Victorian, and contemporary designs. For homes, restaurants, public spaces, etc. Delivery and installation available anywhere. Call or write for estimates and literature. Their stained glass gallery, features restored Victorian windows & panels.

'**Summitville Tiles, Inc.**
PO Box 73   Dept. OHJ
Summitville, OH 43962
(216) 223-1511
DIST
A manufacturer of unglazed and glazed ceramic tile for use on floors and walls. Also a collection of tile imports from European countries. They manufacture a complete line of cementicious grouts, mortars, and epoxies for installing ceramic tile. Catalog, $2.

● **Sun Designs**
PO Box 206   Dept. OHJ
Delafield, WI 53018
(414) 567-4255
MO
Study-plan books for a variety of structures. Includes Gazebos & other garden structures — 55 designs from 8' to 30', 13 strombellas, 7 arbors, & 18 bird feeders. Includes mini-plans: 1 gazebo and 2 birdfeeders. $7.95. Outhouse: 25 designs (can be converted to sauna, playhouse, garden shed, etc.) — $7.95. Bridges and Cupolas, $8.50. Construction plans available for all designs. All PPD.

Sunburst Stained Glass Co.
119 State St.   Dept. OHJ
Newburgh, IN 47630
(812) 853-0460
MO   RS/O
Design, construction, restoration, and repair of stained, etched, and bevelled glass windows. Will travel for on-site work when appropriate. Services range from complete releading to minor repair to creating a new-old window. Furniture restoration and cabinet making is also offered. Brochure, $.50.

KEY TO ABBREVIATIONS

MO   **sells by Mail Order**

RS/O   **sells through Retail
           Store or Office**

DIST   **sells through
           Distributors**

ID   **sells only through
           Interior Designers
           or Architects**

**You'll get better service
when contacting companies
if you mention
The Old-House Journal
Catalog**

Sunflower Studio
2851 Road B-1/2   Dept. OHJ
Grand Junction, CO 81503
(303) 242-3883
MO   DIST
Handwoven in Early American tradition,
complete line of 38 fabrics in 34 historically
accurate colors. Includes pure linens, checks,
plain cotton calicoes, linsey-woolseys, wool
flannels, broadcloths, and serges. Hand-woven
carpeting includes ingrain, Venetian, and jerga.
Fabrics are entirely handmade in our own
workrooms. Custom fabrics, colors, and historical
clothing are a specialty. Color-illustrated
catalogue, $2.50.

● **Sunrise Specialty & Salvage Co.**
2210 San Pablo Ave.   Dept. COHJ
Berkeley, CA 94702
(415) 845-4751
MO   RS/O
Supplier of complete selection of bath fixtures
and faucets for the older house. Specializes in
brass and china shower systems for claw foot
tubs. Also oak and brass toilet, tanks, both pull
chain and low-tank types. Oak toilet seats.
16-page color catalog and price list, $2.

● **Sunset Antiques, Inc.**
PO Box 378   Dept. OHJ
Lake Orion, MI 48035
(313) 693-4770
MO   RS/O
Antique stained and bevelled glass windows,
doors, sidelights. Architectural salvage including
mantels, back & front bars. Also known as
Williams Art Glass Studios, Inc.: Restoration and
custom designing of stained, bevelled, etched, or
glue chip glass. Photo catalog available. Request
details.

Sunshine Architectural Woodworks
Rt. 2, Box 434   Dept. O
Fayetteville, AR 72701
(501) 521-4329
MO
Solid-hardwood, raised-panel, fireplace mantels;
interior shutters; wainscotting; wall panels. Stock
sizes and custom-made. Detailed color catalog,
$3.

● **Superior Clay Corporation**
P.O. Box 352   Dept. OHJ
Uhrichsville, OH 44683
(800) 848-6166
MO   RS/O   DIST
Manufacturers of clay flue linings and clay
chimney tops. The clay chimney tops come in
various sizes & styles. In Ohio, phone (800)
282-6103. Free brochure.

● **Supradur Mfg. Corp.**
122 E. 42 St.   Dept. OHJ
New York, NY 10168
(212) 697-1160
DIST
Manufacturer of mineral-fiber (asbestos-cement)
roofing shingles: an acceptable substitute for slate
when replacement becomes necessary.
Supra-Slate line closely approximates color and
size of real thing. Also available — Dutch Lap,
Twin Lap, American Traditional, and Hexagonal
asbestos shingles appropriate for early 20th
century houses. Free literature.

● **Surrey Shoppe Interiors**
665 Centre St.   Dept. OHJ
Brockton, MA 02402
(617) 588-2525
MO
Hard-to-find sizes in shower curtains and rods.
Wide selection of colors, widths, lengths in
polyester/cotton. Also clear plastic liners and
heavy-gauge clear vinyl. Catalog of rods that
convert tubs into showers, $1.

● **Sutherland Welles Ltd.**
403 Weaver St.   Dept. OHJ
Carrboro, NC 27510
(919) 967-1972
RS/O   MO   DIST
Tung Oil finishing, restoring and maintenance
products for wood, concrete, and masonry.
Easy-to-use for both exterior and interior surfaces
including walls, floors, paneling, cabinets, fine
furniture. Custom stain, paint, finish, and
varnish. Consultation for custom finishing. Send
for Tung Oil catalog, $3.00.

Swan Brass Beds
1955 East 16th Street   Dept. OHJ
Los Angeles, CA 90021
(800) 421-0141
DIST
Solid brass beds, etageres, wrought iron baker
racks, solid brass desks, planters, coat trees.
Many other reproductions including 19th century
wood carousel horses. Through retail outlets
only. No literature but to find nearest distributor,
call toll-free number.

● **Swift & Sons, Inc.**
10 Love Lane, PO Box 150   Dept. OHJ
Hartford, CT 06141
(203) 522-1181
MO   RS/O   DIST
A primary supplier of gold leaf, roll gold and
silver leaf. How-to booklet, free.

Swiss Foundry, Inc.
518 S. Gilmor St.   Dept. OHJ
Baltimore, MD 21223
(301) 233-2000
RS/O
A foundry specializing in custom castings. Can
reproduce large orders or as few as one. Sand
castings in grey iron, aluminum, or bronze. No
literature.

Swofford, Don A., Architect
1843 Seminole Tr.   Dept. OHJ
Charlottesville, VA 22901
(804) 973-3155
RS/O
Architectural firm specializing in restoration,
adaptative renovation, compatible new design,
and maintenance -consulting. Reconstruction or
new design of period buildings, both residential
and commercial. Planning surveys and
inventories. Passive solar heating retrofits.
References and full written proposals available.

Szabo, George T., & Assoc., Inc.
3425 Kenyon St., Suite 202   Dept. OHJ
San Diego, CA 92110
(619) 224-3676
MO
Provides consultation and architectural services
on a national and world-wide basis, for
restoration, rehabilitation, and reconstruction
projects. Only the safest and most proven
preservation techniques and practices are
recommended and utilized for historical masonry,
stone, wood, metal, and glass materials.
Feasibility studies, structural and code analysis,
historical research and other investigative
services. Free information will be mailed to
serious inquiries.

●**See Product Dis-
plays Index on page
199 for more details.**

T

T.A.G. Preservation Consultation
226 88th St.   Dept. OHJ
Brooklyn, NY 11209
(212) 748-4934
RS/O
Preservation consultation services, such as
preparation of preservation plans, National
Register nominations; walking tours and
publications; and design services with an
emphasis on adaptive re-use. Serving NY
metropolitan area, including N. NJ and S. CT. No
literature.

Taft Wood Products Co.
6520 Carnegie Ave.   Dept. OHJ
Cleveland, OH 44103
(216) 881-8937
RS/O
Custom wood mouldings and turned posts &
spindles. Can custom make almost anything to
your specifications. No literature.

TALAS
213 West 35th Street   Dept. OHJ
New York, NY 10011
(212) 675-0718
MO   RS/O
Company sells supplies to art restorers. Several
products are of special interest to those restoring
old houses: textile cleaner; Wishab and Absorene
wallpaper cleaners; Vulpex liquid soap for
cleaning stone and marble. Catalog, $5.00 —
please call or write for specifics and prices.

Taney Supply & Lumber Corp.
5130 Allendale Lane   Dept. OHJ
Taneytown, MD 21787
(301) 756-6671
MO   RS/O   DIST
Manufacturers of prebuilt wood stairways and
stairway parts. Will also do stair restoration and
custom work. Illustrated catalogue, $1.

Tatko Bros. Slate Co.
Dept. OHJ
Middle Granville, NY 12849
(518) 642-1640
DIST   MO   RS/O
Manufacturers of slate floor tile for in and outside
installation, Slate flagstone, structural and roofing
slate. Free literature.

Tec Specialties
PO Box 909   Dept. OHJ
Smyrna, GA 30081
MO
Reproduction clock dials in a variety of finishes
including "antique stained", "yello-aged", and
metal grey. Available in a variety of
manufacturers names and sizes. Free catalog.

Tennessee Fabricating Co.
2366 Prospect Street   Dept. OHJ
Memphis, TN 38106
(901) 948-3354
MO
Manufacturer of full line of aluminum and iron
ornamental castings. Reproductions of lawn
furniture, fountains, urns, planters. Complete
line of gates, fences, balconies and all residential
metal work. Will reproduce customer's designs or
create new designs. Booklet of patio furniture
and ornamental accessories $2.50. Full catalog of
architectural ornamental metal-work $5.00.

Terra Designs, Inc.
211 Jockey Hollow Rd.   Dept. OHJ
Bernardsville, NJ 07924
(201) 766-3577
MO   DIST
Hand-moulded, hand-painted ceramic tiles with
country charm. Designs include reproductions of
antique buttermolds, carousel animals and
weathervanes. Old-world tiles available in terra
cotta, earthtones, delft blue and multi-colored
handpainted styles. Catalog, $1.

Thermal Wall Insulating Shutters, Inc.
RD 1, Box 462-A   Dept. OHJ
Voorheesville, NY 12186
(518) 765-4020
MO   RS/O
Interior insulating shutter framing system. Core
of one-inch rigid insulation. The system slides,
swings or bifolds. Can be decorated with fabric,
wallpaper, paint, or wood veneer. Free literature.

Thermocrete Chimney Lining, Inc.
335 Mountain Road   Dept. OHJ
Stowe, VT 05672
(802) 253-9766
DIST
Thermocrete installs cast-in-place chimney lining
through franchised dealers. Seamless one-piece
masonry liner can reline old and damaged
chimneys with no major construction required.
Seals and insulates flues. Reduces risk of
chimney fire. Contact for free brochure, nearest
dealer, and free estimate.

● **Thibaut, Richard E., Inc.**
706 South 21st Street   Dept. OHJ
Irvington, NJ 07111
(201) 399-7888
DIST
Decorative wallcoverings and coordinating
fabrics. Mural collections, Early American,
Traditional. Authentic reproductions available for
restoration work. Mural folder & color brochures,
$2.00.

Thomas Antique Services
150 E. New Hampshire   Dept. OHJ
Southern Pines, NC 28387
(919) 692-6724
RS/O
Brass and copper polishing, furniture stripping
and refinishing, antique restoration. Brass
hardware, antique lighting fixtures, door
hardware, stained glass, and mantels. Large
selection of architectural antiques. Price list on
request.

Thoro System Products
7800 N.W. 38th Street   Dept. OHJ
Miami, FL 33166
(305) 592-2081
DIST
The Thoro system is a complete line of
waterproofing, maintenance, decorative, and
insulating products for concrete and masonry
surfaces. Free booklet.

Tile Distributors, Inc.
7 Kings Highway   Dept. OHJ
New Rochelle, NY 10801
(914) 633-7200
RS/O   MO
Carries unglazed white hexagonal, black and
white spiral, white unglazed random, 3/4-in. and
2-in. square unglazed white bathroom floor tiles;
3-in. x 6-in. & 6-in. x 6-in. white replacement wall
tile; glazed black wall trim; replacement ceramic
non-flange fixtures. Will research and try to
locate ceramic tile produced before 1940. No
literature, but can send specific samples in the
mail. Will ship prepaid orders. Can also call (212)
792-0900.

Timberpeg
Box 1500   Dept. OHJ
Claremont, NH 03743
(603) 542-7762
RS/O   DIST
Post and beam homes reflect traditional designs
yet integrate contemporary open spaces,
cathedral ceilings and greenhouse areas. The
colonial styled mortise and tenon pegged frame is
accented with natural wood finishes. Fully
insulated. Architectural design and engineering
are part of the package. Solar series models also.
Portfolio — $10.

Timeless Patterns
465 Colrain Rd.   Dept. OHJ
Greenfield, MA 01301
(413) 774-5742
MO   RS/O
Company sells patterns for 41 stencil designs.
High-quality Mylar patterns can be cut, or are
traceable for free-hand painting. Designs range
from traditional Early American and Victorian, to
original adaptations and contemporary. Includes
3 designs for stair treads, and 2 for hearth rugs.
Full catalog, $4. Will also do stencilling, locally.

Timesavers
PO Box 171A   Dept. OHJ
Wheeling, IL 60090
(312) 394-4818
MO   RS/O
A complete line of clock and watch parts:
movements, pendulums, dial hands, bobs,
cuckoo accessories, decals, decorative hardware,
and keys. Also, tools and supplies for repairing
clocks. Catalog, $2.

Tioga Mill Outlet
200 S. Hartman St.   Dept. OHJ
York, PA 17403
(717) 843-5139
RS/O   MO
Drapery and upholstery fabrics including
imported Lizere and damasks. Send $1.50 with
color preferences for swatches. Free brochure.

● **Tiresias, Inc.**
PO Box 1864   Dept. OHJ
Orangeburg, SC 29116
(803) 534-8478
RS/O
This company specializes in remilling old heart
pine timbers (from 250-400 years old) into heart
pine flooring, v-groove panelling, stair treads,
risers, beams, doors, and other assorted heart
pine products. Free literature.

Tomahawk Foundry
Rt. 4   Dept. OHJ
Rice Lake, WI 54868
(715) 234-4498
RS/O
This company has ten years' experience in
custom-casting parts for old stoves. Pattern
making available.

**Tomblinson, Harburn, Yurk and Assoc.,
Inc.**
705 Kelso St.   Dept. OHJ
Flint, MI 48506
(313) 767-5600
RS/O
An architectural firm involved in restoration and
preservation. Among the services offered are:
historical research, exterior stabilization,
photographic documentation, and measured
drawings. Free brochure.

Tool Works
111 8th Ave.   Dept. OHJ
New York, NY 10011
(212) 242-5815
MO
A complete line of hardware, woodworking tools
and supplies. Also original brass and bronze door
& cabinet hardware. Tool catalog available for $2.

Tootie's Tile & Trim
531 Cascade   Dept. OHJ
Bellaire, TX 77401
(713) 661-3523
MO
Over 200,000 pieces of new-old, stock ceramic tile
liners or feature strips used as decorative borders
in baths & kitchens. Approximately 30-40
selections including dozens of colors, patterns,
and textures. Art Deco reliefs a specialty. No
order too small. Design capabilities available. No
literature; write with specific needs.

● **Travis Tuck, Inc. — Metal Sculptor**
RFD Lamberts Cove Road   Dept. OHJ
Martha's Vineyard, MA 02568
(617) 693-3914
RS/O   MO
Custom metalwork studio, specializing in copper
weathervanes copper reproduction lamps,
hand-forged ironwork (chandeliers brackets,
gates, hardware), and tradesmen signs in hollow
copper repousse and hand-forged iron. All
custom work in copper, brass, or iron. No
literature: pieces are one-of-a-kind.

● **Tremont Nail Company**
P.O. Box 111   Dept. OHJ
Wareham, MA 02571
(617) 295-0038
RS/O   MO   DIST
In business since 1819, this company
manufactures old-fashioned cut nails that are
useful for restoration work. These decorative
antique nails include Wrought Head, Hinge, Rose
Head Clinch and Common; also the
DECOR-NAIL® and many others. A sample card
with 20 patterns of actual cut nails attached,
history and complete ordering information is
available for $3.50 ppd. Free brochure and price
list.

KEY TO ABBREVIATIONS

MO   **sells by Mail Order**

RS/O   **sells through Retail
             Store or Office**

DIST   **sells through
             Distributors**

ID   **sells only through
             Interior Designers
             or Architects**

Trow & Holden Co.
P.O. Box 475   Dept. OHJ
Barre, VT 05641
(800) 451-4349
MO   DIST   RS/O
Manufacturers of a complete line of stoneworking and masonry tools including pneumatic carving hammers, pneumatic drills, carbide tipped hand tools, and stone splitting tools. Free catalog and price list available upon request.

Troyer, Le Roy and Associates
415 Lincolnway East   Dept. OHJ
Mishawaka, IN 46544
(219) 259-9976
RS/O
Serves Indiana, Illinois, Ohio, and southern Michigan area with architectural restoration services. National register applications. Information on previous restoration projects available on request.

Trump R.T., & Co., Inc.
666 Bethlehem Pike   Dept. OHJ
Flourtown, PA 19031
(215) 233-1805
RS/O
A few museum quality, late 18th-century and pre-1820 fireplace mantels taken from demolished Philadelphia townhouses. Can be seen by appointment only. Located just outside of Philadelphia.

Turnbull's Lumber Company
P.O. Box 602   Dept. OHJ
Sumner, MI 48889
(517) 833-7089
MO   RS/O
Specialists in custom duplication of mouldings, gingerbread, architectural millwork. Also, suppliers of quality hardwoods at wholesale prices. Free flyer; please specify your interest.

Turncraft
PO Box 2429   Dept. OHJ
White City, OR 97503
(503) 826-2510
DIST
A full line of stock round columns, porch posts, railings and spindles. Also ornamental wood capitols. Free brochure.

The Twigs, Inc.
5700 Third Street   Dept. OHJ
San Francisco, CA 94124
(415) 822-1626
DIST
Hand-screened wallpapers and fabrics in 18th and 19th century designs (French, English & American). Upholstery fabrics and leathers, as well as imported products from Europe and the far east. Available to designers, architects, and large commercial clients through nationwide showroom representatives (or directly from their offices in San Francisco). They don't sell retail, but will sell to museums, historical societies, and qualified persons involved in historic restorations.

U

Unique Art Glass Co.
5060 Arsenal   Dept. OHJ
St. Louis, MO 63139
(314) 771-4840
MO   RS/O
Manufacturers, designers, and repair specialist of Art and Stained Glass windows and lamps, since 1880. Custom designed colored and beveled glass windows, and etched mirrors. Hand painted and stained Art Glass work. Bent glass pieces for Tiffany shades.

United Gilsonite Laboratories
Box 70   Dept. OHJ
Scranton, PA 18501
(717) 344-1202
DIST
UGL manufactures a complete line of products for home repair and maintenance, including ZAR "Rain Stain" for exterior surfaces, ZAR Clear Finishes and Stains, DRYLOCK masonry treatment products, caulks and sealants, paint and varnish removers, among others. Free descriptive literature. Three booklets at $.25 each — "The Finishing Touch", a beginners guide to wood finishing. "How to Waterproof Masonry Walls," and "Tips on Texturing."

• **United House Wrecking Corp.**
328 Selleck Street   Dept. OHJ
Stamford, CT 06902
(203) 348-5371
RS/O
Six acres of relics from old houses: mantels, stained glass, antiques, used furniture, antique reproductions of copper weathervanes, fabulous brass & copper reproductions. Free illustrated brochure available about the yard.

U.S. General Supply Corp.
100 Commercial Street   Dept. OHJ
Plainview, NY 11803
(516) 349-7282
MO
A first-rate mail order source for name-brand tools and hardware at lower prices. Catalog offers traditional tools — everything from drawknives and spokeshaves to mitre boxes and handsaws. Plus modern power tools for saving time. Catalog has over 6,000 items in 196 pages. Fully illustrated — $1.

U.S. Gypsum Company
101 South Wacker Drive   Dept. OHJ
Chicago, IL 60606
(312) 321-3863
DIST
Products produced by this major construction products company include plaster and plaster patching materials, textured paints, gypsum, dry wall, waterproofing paints, and thermal entry doors in classical styles. Free literature.

Universal Clamp Corp.
6905 Cedros Ave.   Dept. OHJ
Van Nuys, CA 91405
(213) 780-1015
MO   DIST
A variety of clamps for repairing and restoring antiques, cabinetmaking and fine woodwork. Produces the popular "805" Porta-Press frame jig for assembly of mitered frames and doors. Also, a salvage pry bar, an electric doweling machine, a mortise & tenon attachment for routers, and a lathe duplicator. Brochures & prices free with stamped, self addressed envelope.

Up Your Alley
784 South Sixth Street   Dept. OHJ
Philadelphia, PA 19147
(215) WA5-5597
MO
Ceramic tiles — Dutch, English, American — over 100 years old. For interior or exterior use. Photographs will be supplied on specific request.

Upland Stove Co., Inc.
PO Box 361   Dept. OHJ
Greene, NY 13778
(607) 656-4156
DIST
These are the manufacturers of the all-cast-iron Upland woodstoves. Four airtight models available: 2 box stoves and 2 combination fireplace/box stove models. Quality American-made construction and materials. Available in black, brown, green. Literature and information about distributors free on request.

V

Vecon Energy Systems Corp.
275 Circuit St.   Dept. OHJ
Hanover, MA 02339
(617) 871-3180
DIST
Manufacturer of "Magnetite Windows," an interior storm window which attaches magnetically to window frame. Free information.

Verine Products & Co.
Goldhanger   Dept. OHJ
Maldon, Essex, UK
(0621) 88611
RS/O   MO
From U.K. authentic reproductions in fiberglass of original 18th century Georgian mantelpieces, overdoors, Ionic and Doric columns, porticos and lead garden tubs and planters. Specify product interest. Literature — $5. Also, gas log or coal fires with brass or cast iron grates.

Vermont Iron
311 Prince St.   Dept. OHJ
Waterbury, VT 05676
(802) 244-5254
MO   RS/O
Manufacturer of a cast iron and wood bench line. The "Catamount" bench line consists of hardwood slats, class 30 grey cast iron, stainless steel hardware, solid bronze medallions, urethane paint on castings, and clear wood finish on slats. Benches are weather resistant for use indoors or outdoors, available in commercial or residential styles. Also available are swings, and woodstoves. Free literature.

Vermont Marble Co.
61 Main St.   Dept. OHJ
Proctor, VT 05765
(802) 459-3311
MO   RS/O
Manufacturer of 12-in. x 12-in. marble floor tiles, fireplaces, building veneers, and window sills. Free literature.

Vermont Soapstone Co.
Pond Rd. Box 77   Dept. OHJ
Perkinsville, VT 05151
(802) 263-5404
MO   RS/O
Custom-cut soapstone available for sinks, countertops, stovetops. Also handcrafted griddles, bedwarmers, etc. Brochure and price list — $.50.

• Vermont Structural Slate Co.
P.O. Box 98   Dept. OHJ
Fair Haven, VT 05743
(800) 343-1900
RS/O MO DIST
"Slate Roofs" — a handbook of data on the constructing and laying of all types of slate roofs. A 1926 reprint. Send $7.95. Besides roofing, company also fabricates slate flooring, sink tops, etc. Also has brownstone — typically used for replacement balustrades, cap, dentil course and lintels. Non-laminated stone with sufficient range of colors to match in restoration. Fact sheet, available: please specify. In VT, phone (802) 265-4933.

Vermont Weatherboard, Inc.
Box 536   Dept. OHJ
Hardwick, VT 05843
(802) 472-5513
MO DIST
Full thickness individual shiplapped boards for wall paneling and exterior siding, processed to authentically reproduce the natural texture of aged barnwood. Available in two grades and two colors — Sugarhouse Grey and Autumn Brown. For restoration and reproduction work. Moulding, stain, and wrought nails available. Free color literature.

Victorian Accents
163 Joralemon St.   Dept. OHJ
Brooklyn Heights, NY 11201
(212) 625-0079
MO RS/O
Selection of reproduction Victorian Christmas ornaments, decorations, and cards. Also, reproduction Victorian toys and children's books, stereoviewers and views, bandboxes, silver serving items, hard-to-find gifts and decorative accessories. Catalog, $1.

Victorian Building & Repair
RR 1B, Box 162-A   Dept. OHJ
Compton, IL 61318
(815) 538-7001
RS/O MO
General construction, repair, remodelling, and additions in a Victorian-complementary manner. Especially experienced in Victorian restorations, including wood siding, open porches, and millwork restoration. Design and duplication of sawn ornament. No literature; specific inquiries with SASE will be answered.

Victorian Collectibles Ltd.
6916 N. Santa Monica Blvd.   Dept. OHJ
Milwaukee, WI 53217
(414) 352-6910
MO RS/O
100% wool rugs and hand-painted ceiling canvases in 4 ornate patterns derived from late Victorian and Art Nouveau wallpapers. Also, coordinating plaster mouldings. From the Brillion Collection, c.1875 to 1910, they offer never-used original wallpapers for use in houses of significant historic interest. Several patterns from this collection are being reproduced for retail sales. Their Ripon Collection, c.1910 to 1962, of unused papers includes 'Oatmeal Paper,' and is offered to homeowners. Write for further details.

Victorian Crown, Ltd.
5901 SW Macadam Ave., Ste. 100   Dept. OHJ
Portland, OR 97201
(503) 227-4661
RS/O DIST
A source for Crown embossed wallcoverings: Anaglypta, supaglypta, vynaglypta, and lincrusta. They can be hung on the ceiling or walls, and finished to resemble metal, wood, or leather. Free literature.

Victorian D'Light
533 W. Windsor Road   Dept. OHJ
Glendale, CA 91204
(213) 956-5656
MO DIST
Company designs and manufactures electric, gas, and combination lamps and light fixtures of solid brass. Pieces designed and executed in turn-of-the-century manner, based on documented designs. Full-color catalog of 107 items that can be combined for the creation of 5000 different light fixtures. Catalog $3.

Victorian Glass Works
476 Main Street   Dept. OHJ
Ferndale, CA 95536
(707) 786-4237
RS/O
Restorers of antique furniture, complete rebuilding of wood components and all types of caning and rattan work. They also specialize in repairing and restoring most types of antique picture frames. No literature.

Victorian Glassworks
3760 Howard Ave.   Dept. OHJ
Kensington, MD 20895
(301) 942-8822
RS/O
A small company specializing in leaded art glass: contemporary, Victorian, Art Deco, and Art Nouveau. Specialists in small commercial jobs, and any size residential. Also restoration of glass panels and lamp shades, and custom etching. Information upon request.

Victorian House
128 N. Longwood   Dept. OHJ
Rockford, IL 61107
(815) 963-3351
RS/O
Interior designer and consultant serving southern Wisconsin and northern Illinois. Carries a line of solid mahogany reproduction Victorian furniture and turn-of-the-century oak furniture, wallpaper, lighting fixtures and antiques. Also, upholstery service. No literature.

• Victorian Interior Restoration
6374 Waterloo Rd.   Dept. OHJ
Atwater, OH 44201
(216) 947-3385
MO RS/O
A respected and competitively priced design and restoration service for homes, commercial structures, and museums. Serving the North-Central U.S.

• Victorian Lightcrafters, Ltd.
PO Box 332   Dept. OHJ
Slate Hill, NY 10973
(914) 355-1300
MO RS/O
Manufacturers of authentic design, solid brass reproduction Victorian and turn-of-the-century lighting fixtures and desk lamps. They also carry appropriate glass shades. Fixtures are handmade to order; polished and lacquered if desired. Illustrated catalog, $3., refundable on first order. Wholesale inquiries invited.

• Victorian Lighting Co.
PO Box 654   Dept. OHJ
Minneapolis, MN 55440
(612) 338-3636
MO RS/O
Manufacturers of solid brass period lighting. Reproduced by using 19th-century techniques and original designs. Design styles are from the period 1880s to the 1920s. Most fixtures are U.L. listed. Free "New Century Collection" lighting brochure; foldout lighting brochure, $1.50; Edition 1 catalog, $4. Store hours, Mon. to Sat., 10-4.

• Victorian Lighting Works, Inc.
Gamble Mill, 160 Dunlap St.   Dept. OHJ
Bellefonte, PA 16823
(814) 355-8449
MO DIST
Authentic, handcrafted reproductions of Victorian and turn-of-the-century electric and gas-style chandeliers and wall brackets. Fixtures are crafted in solid brass and available with a variety of shades. UL listed—send $3. for complete catalogue.

Victorian Reproductions Enterprises, Inc.
1601 Park Ave., South   Dept. OHJ
Minneapolis, MN 55404
(612) 338-3636
RS/O MO DIST
Suppliers of reproduction products for residential, commercial, restaurant projects. Glass or cloth lamp shades, foiled Tiffany-style shades & lighting parts. Hand-carved solid mahogany furniture, marble top tables, solid brass hardware, brass bathroom accessories, & custom duplication of original hardware. Lightning rods/weathervanes, stamped metal ceilings, chimney pots, cast-iron park benches, eastern white pine shingles. Catalog, edit. 1: Lighting, $4; Catalog, edit. 2: Furniture, etc., $3. New Century Coll. Lighting brochure, free. Large lighting brochure, $1.50.

• Village Forge
P.O. Box 1148   Dept. OHJ
Smithfield, NC 27577
(919) 934-2581
MO
Adaptations and reproductions in wrought iron of Early American lighting. Of special interest are the well-designed iron floor lamps. Illustrated brochure and price list — $1.

Village Lantern
P.O. Box 8J   Dept. OHJ
North Marshfield, MA 02059
(617) 834-8121
MO RS/O
Handmade pewter plate lanterns, sconces and chandeliers. Custom work in pewter plate, tin, brass or copper. Reproductions and restoration. Illustrated brochure and price list — $.50.

Vincent — Whitney Co.
PO Box 335   Dept. OHJ
Sausalito, CA 94966
(415) 332-3260
MO DIST
Firm specializes in hand-powered dumbwaiters. Capacities range from 5 to 250 lbs; priced from $500 to $1850. Also opener for operable clerestory windows. Free brochure; specify whether for residential or commercial use.

Vintage Lumber Co.
9507 Woodsboro Rd.   Dept. OHJ
Frederick, MD 21701
(301) 898-7859
RS/O   MO
Dismantler of barns, houses, and log houses from 18th, 19th and 20th century. They sell old lumber in rough form as well as resawn or remilled flooring, paneling and beams. Specializing in heart pine, chestnut, oak, white pine and poplar. They maintain a large stock of various lumber found in old buildings. Send for free literature.

Vintage Pine Co., Inc.
Box R   Dept. OHJ
Prospect, VA 23960
(804) 392-8050
MO
Heart pine plank flooring. Also Stair-treads, risers, and cabinet wood. Send $1 for brochure and price list.

Vintage Plumbing
17800 Minnehaha St.   Dept. OHJ
Granada Hills, CA 91344
(213) 368-1040
MO   RS/O
Old bathroom fixtures, i.e., toilets, showers, lavs, footed and sitz baths. Also accessories. Most items restored, but some in original condition. Faucets & handles not sold separately. Lots of free advice and reference info. Will restore old fixtures. Free flyer.

• Vintage Wood Works
Box 1157   Dept. 183
Fredericksburg, TX 78624
(512) 997-9513
MO
Produces a line of authentic Victorian Gingerbread Designs for interior and exterior use. Brackets, scroll-work running trims, fret work, gable eave treatments, porch railings, and signs are stocked in inventory for prompt shipment. Quotes are given for variations on standard designs, as well as for custom designs. All work is shop sanded, ready for painting. A sister company "Vintage Gazebos", produces two mail-order authentic Victorian gazebos. An illustrated catalog, $2.

Virtue, W.D., Co., Inc.
Box 126   Dept. OHJ
Summit, NJ 07901
(201) 273-6936
RS/O
Distributors of Gladding-McBean Terra-Cotta & other ceramic products. Terra cotta, brick, and ceramic veneer. Also, custom ceramics. Free brochure.

WSI Distributors
PO Box 1235   Dept. OHJ
St. Charles, MO 63302
(314) 946-5811
MO
Brass hardware including door, furniture, Hoosier, ice box, and desk hardware. Wood & porcelain casters, furniture locks. Also trunk repair supplies, fiber and wood chair seats, caning and weaving supplies, wood veneer, and wood ornaments — catalog, $2.

• Wagner, Albert J., & Son
3762 N. Clark Street   Dept. OHJ
Chicago, IL 60613
(312) 935-1414
RS/O
Established in 1894. Architectural sheet metal contractor working in ferrous and copper metals: cornice mold; inlaid cornice mold gutter; facade; and hip and ridge cap. Fabrication and installation of metal and glass gable end and hip style skylights. Specialty roofing (slate, title). Will travel. Call for appointment. No literature.

Walbrook Mill & Lumber Co., Inc.
2636 W. North Ave.   Dept. OHJ
Baltimore, MD 21216
(301) 462-2200
RS/O
A 65 year old family owned company. A complete mill — will reproduce anything made of wood — sashes, doors, mouldings, curved wood members, carved items, lathe turned items. Active in the restoration & renovation of homes and old commercial buildings. No literature.

• Walker, Dennis C.
P.O. Box 309   Dept. OHJ
Tallmadge, OH 44278
(216) 633-1081
RS/O
Hand-hewn barn beams, barn siding, roof slate, old hand planed beaded panelling. Also a large stock of architectural antiques: doors, wood mantels, wainscot and panelling, flooring, mouldings, plumbing fixtures, etc. Brochures available.

• Walker Industries
P.O. Box 129   Dept. OHJ
Bellevue, TN 37221
(615) 646-5084
MO
Full line of old-style bathroom fixtures, includes 7 styles of pull-chain toilets (19th century railroad-station lettered type to carved throne). Solid brass & copper vanity bowls and kitchen sinks. Solid copper bathtubs with brass clawfeet and wooden rims. All china fluted Victorian pedestal sink with oval basin & brass faucets. Color catalog $5.80 includes postage.

Wallin Forge
Route 1, Box 65   Dept. OHJ
Sparta, KY 41086
(606) 567-7201
RS/O   MO
Makes a wide range of custom handforged iron door hardware, boot scrapers, fireplace equipment, lighting fixtures, kitchen utensils, etc. No literature.

• Jack Wallis' Doors
Rt. 1, Box 22A   Dept. OHJ
Murray, KY 42071
(502) 489-2613
MO   RS/O
A large selection of handcrafted wood doors, with stained, etched, or bevelled glass inserts. Will also custom build any type door or glass. Also offer carved components and will custom make carvings in quantities. Color catalog, $3.

• Walsh Screen Products
24 East Third St.   Dept. OHJ
Mount Vernon, NY 10550
(914) 668-7811
MO   RS/O
Interior, rolled screens custom-made to fit almost any window. Ideal for casement windows. Free information.

Warner Company
108 South Des Plaines St.   Dept. OHJ
Chicago, IL 60606
(312) 372-3540
DIST
Designs from the Art Institute of Chicago Collection, based on actual English, French, Dutch, Italian and American textiles of the 16th, 17th, 18th and 19th centuries. They have been adapted for use in today's interiors. No literature.

Warren, William J. & Son, Inc.
300 South Holmes Street   Dept. OHJ
Ft. Collins, CO 80521
(303) 482-1976
RS/O
General contractor with extensive experience with old buildings, both residential and commercial. Also provides home inspection service. Will travel anywhere. Home inspection and roofing brochures, free.

• Washington Copper Works
South St.   Dept. OHJ
Washington, CT 06793
(203) 868-7527
RS/O   MO
Hand-fabricated lighting fixtures in styles compatible with the 18th and 19th centuries. Copper post lights, wall lanterns for indoors, outdoors, and entryways. Chandeliers & candelabras. Weatherproof kerosene lanterns, and an unusual selection of candle lanterns. Each original piece is hand-wrought, initialed and dated. U-L approved. 32 page illustrated catalog and price list, $2.00, refundable with an order.

Washington House of Reproductions
PO Box 246-Main St.   Dept. OHJ
Washington, VA 22747
(703) 675-3385
MO   RS/O
Reproductions of old lighting fixtures (many very reasonbly priced), particularly gas, in solid brass. Will also restore old fixtures — rebuild, clean, strip nickel plating, convert to electricity, and replace missing parts. Custom fixtures are our specialty.

Washington Stove Works
P.O. Box 687   Dept. OHJ
Everett, WA 98206
(206) 252-2148
DIST   RS/O
This company has been making stoves since 1875: Air-tight cast box heaters, decorative parlor stoves, cast iron Franklin stoves, wood and oil kitchen stoves, air-tight fireplace inserts and free standing stoves. Illustrated literature, $1.

KEY TO ABBREVIATIONS

MO   sells by Mail Order

RS/O   sells through Retail Store or Office

DIST   sells through Distributors

ID   sells only through Interior Designers or Architects

Watco - Dennis Corporation
1756 22nd Street   Dept. OH-82
Santa Monica, CA 90404
(213) 829-2226
DIST
Architectural finishing and maintenance products
for wood, concrete, masonry, tile and marble.
Super penetrating resin-oil finishes for furniture,
floors, interior and exterior wood surfaces are of
particular interest to the do-it-yourself person.
Free brochure.

● **Watercolors, Inc.**
    Dept. OHJ
Garrison on Hudson, NY 10524
(914) 424-3327
ID
Exclusive importer of authentic English
Edwardian bathroom fixtures and other
traditional faucet designs. Complete fittings for
U.S. specifications. Washbasin sets,
bathtub/shower sets, and bidet sets in chrome,
brass, gold and enamel finishes. Complete
catalog available through architects, designers, or
contractors.

Waverly Fabrics
58 West 40th St.   Dept. OHJ
New York, NY 10018
(212) 644-5890
DIST
Four Sturbridge Village collections: features
documentary patterns gathered from Europe, the
Near East and native American designs of the
19th century. The group consists of 13 prints, 13
multi-purpose fabrics and 3 all cotton damasks.
Victoria & Albert Museum Collection — A group
of 12 printed patterns are adaptations of
documents housed at the London Museum. Also
in their general line are some excellent large
design fabrics appropriate for Victorian draperies
and upholstery. Widely available moderately
priced at department and fabric stores, or write
for distributor.

J.P. Weaver Co.
2301 W. Victory Blvd.   Dept. OHJ
Burbank, CA 91506
(213) 841-5700
RS/O   MO
Manufacturers of composition ornaments since
1914. Over 6,500 ornaments for architectural
interiors, woodwork, furniture, frames, etc.,
made from the original European formula.
Flexible (will fit a radius or OG moulding) and
self-bonding, these ornaments are historically
authentic. Completed jobs include Sacramento
State Capitol restoration in California. Custom
designing and installation services. Literature and
catalog information, $1.

Weaver, W. T. & Sons, Inc.
1208 Wisconsin Ave., N.W.   Dept. OHJ
Washington, DC 20007
(202) 333-4200
RS/O   MO
Firm has been selling decorative hardware and
building supplies since 1889. Stock includes
porcelain and brass furniture hardware, knobs,
rim locks, front door hardware, shutter
hardware, full line of solid brass switchplates,
lavatory bowls, sconces, hooks, and decorative
ornaments and ceiling medallions (styrene).
Catalog $2.50. Literature on ceiling pieces is free.

● **See Product Dis-
plays Index on page
199 for more details.**

Webster Stove
3112 LaSalle   Dept. OHJ
St. Louis, MO 63104
(314) 772-0454
MO   DIST   RS/O
Manufacturers of highly decorative and functional
wood stoves. Antique looking by design, sturdy
built, safety and efficiency tested to U.L.
standards, these wood burners are available in 4
colors, with solid brass trim or nickel plating. 2
catalytically assisted models boost efficiency by
25%, cut wood consumption by 1/3, keep
chimney clean, and environment nearly pollution
free. Brochures, $1.

Webster's Landing Architectural Antiques
475-81 Oswego Blvd.   Dept. OHJ
Syracuse, NY 13202
(315) 425-0142
RS/O
Mantels in stock; beveled & leaded glass;
columns — large hotel or smaller home units;
paneling; light fixtures and chandeliers; balusters;
skylights; tiles; ornate doors and entries; ornate
hardware. No literature.

Welles Fireplace Company
287 East Houston St.   Dept. OHJ
New York, NY 10002
(212) 777-5440
RS/O
They service fireplaces in the metropolitan New
York area. Mantels installed; chimneys repaired,
cleaned and relined; gas and coal fireplaces
converted to woodburning. On-site consultation,
$35.00 deductible. Flyer on request.

Welsbach
240 Sargent Drive   Dept. OHJ
New Haven, CT 06511
(203) 789-1710
RS/O   DIST
This 100 year old company supplies street
lighting fixtures, brackets, and posts. Originally
designed for gas-lighting, these Victorian-styled
fixtures & posts are now available with
incandescent or high-intensity electric light
sources. They also make cast-aluminum
landscape furniture such as park benches,
bollards and gazebos. Complete illustrated
catalog available: Free to the trade; $2.00 for
consumer.

Welsh, Frank S.
859 Lancaster Ave.   Dept. OHJ
Bryn Mawr, PA 19010
(215) 525-3564
RS/O   MO
Historic paint color consultant. Professional
microscopic techniques used to investigate,
analyze, and evaluate the nature and original
color of historic architectural surface coatings.
Conducts on-site research for historic house
museums & adaptive restorations; plus lab
analysis of paint samples mailed in by old-house
owners who have already ordered the
PAINTPAMPHLET™ (available for $5).
Completed projects include: Philadelphia
Athenaeum; Abraham Lincoln's Home;
Monticello.

● **Wes-Pine Millwork, Inc.**
PO Box 1157   Dept. OHJ
West Hanover, MA 02339
(617) 878-2102
MO   DIST
"Self-storing" storm windows made of Ponderosa
pine and replacement sash — for double-hung
windows. True divided lights or insulating glass.
Custom and stock sizes. Free brochure.

● **West Barnstable Stove Shop**
Box 472, Rt. 149   Dept. OHJ
W. Barnstable, MA 02668
(617) 362-9913
RS/O   MO
This store buys, sells and restores antique wood
and coal stoves. Will do foundry, recasting,
nickel plating, and welding. Brochure available,
write or call with your needs.

Westal Contracting
1 Mayfair Road   Dept. OHJ
Eastchester, NY 10707
(914) 337-8733
RS/O
Excellent roofing company specializing in copper
work, seam roofs, slate — everything but wood
shingles & asphalt. Westchester, Rockland, and
NYC area.

Western Reserve Antique Furniture Kit
Box 206A   Dept. OHJ
Bath, OH 44210
MO   DIST
Reproductions of Shaker, New England, and
Pennsylvania Dutch furniture and house
accessories are available in either kit or assembled
and finished form. A newly expanded line is
pictured and fully described in the brochure
about Western Reserve New 'Connecti-Kit'.
Special order items can be built for customers
needing something not in regular catalog. Cost of
the brochure is $2.00.

Western Wood Doctor
PO Box 2146   Dept. OHJ
Fremont, CA 94536
(415) 796-4056
DIST   MO
Furniture restoration and preservation products:
tung oil, lemon oil, brass & copper cleaner,
furniture cleaner. Of special interest is their
refinisher. Free information.

Westlake Architectural Antiques
3315 Westlake Drive   Dept. OHJ
Austin, TX 78746
(512) 327-1110
RS/O   MO
Architectural antiques, American, and European
stained glass panels. Also bevelled, leaded, glass
doors, sidelights, wood doors, wood & marble
mantels. Returnable 200-page Xerox color
brochure — $4, postage charge.

Westport Housewrights
Box 95   Dept. OHJ
Westport Point, MA 02791
(617) 636-8943
RS/O
These builders reproduce complete 18th century
houses using post and beam construction or
stick-frame. Designed in collaboration with
owner, and they can reflect some compromise
between authentic styling and modern
necessity/convenience. Serving S.E. MA & RI.
Will provide representative photographs. No
literature.

Whitley Studios
Laurel Road, Box 69   Dept. OHJ
Solebury, PA 18963
(215) 297-8452
MO   RS/O
Restoration and replication of fine antique
furniture. Illustrated brochure on original
designed "Whitley Rocker," $5.00.

Whittemore-Durgin Glass Co.
Box 20650H   Dept. OHJ
Hanover, MA 02339
(617) 871-1790
RS/O   MO
Everything for the stained glass craftsman presented in an illustrated color catalog that is unusually helpful, and amusing. Also "Baroques" — pieces of stained glass onto which designs in black ceramic paint are fused. Can be used to create panels, or as replacements in windows. Antique-type window glass. Four retail stores: Rockland MA, Middlesex, NJ, E. Lyme CT, Peoria IL. Catalog $1.

Whole Kit & Kaboodle Co., Inc.
8 West 19th St.   Dept. OHJ
New York, NY 10011
(212) 675-8892
MO   RS/O
A large selection of inexpensive, pre-cut "Stencil Magic" stencils cut on durable, reuseable vinyl plastic. Selection includes Early Amer., Victorian, Contemporary, borders, florals, children's designs, Xmas, animals, and fruit & vegetables patterns. Acrylic stencil paints in 2 oz. and 4 oz. plastic squeeze bottles. Also, stencil brushes — small & medium. Brochure, $1.

Wiebold, Inc.
413 Terrace Place   Dept. OHJ
Terrace Park, OH 45174
(513) 831-2541
MO   RS/O
An art conservation lab specializing in the repair and restoration of paintings, frames, porcelain, and glass & metal objects. Free literature.

Wigen Restorations
R.D. No. 1, Box 281   Dept. OHJ
Cobleskill, NY 12043
(518) 234-7946
MO   RS/O
Will dismantle and move any house or barn. Dutch and New England barn frames available - will move to your location. Also small house frames, floor boards, old pine boards, weathered siding, mantels, etc. Free flyer.

● **Wiggins, D.B.**
Hale Road   Dept. OHJ
Tilton, NH 03276
(603) 286-3046
RS/O
Itinerant artists. Period interiors, painted and stencilled; murals and marbleizing — anything to do with paint. 15 years experience, second generation in antique business. Also quality restorations of existing designs. Write for free brochure.

Wikkmann House
Box 501   Dept. OHJ
Chatsworth, CA 91311
(213) 780-1015
MO
Home renovator and wood craftsman tools. Also a line of woodworking clamps; frame and door jigs. Of special interest is their pry bar — a tool to aid in structural dismantling without destroying timbers. Evenings — (213) 891-2564 or 349-5148. Pry bar info free. Catalog package $2.

● **See Product Displays Index on page 199 for more details.**

Willard Restorations, Inc.
141 Main St.   Dept. OHJ
Old Wethersfield, CT 06109
(203) 529-1401
RS/O
Architectural historians and skilled craftspeople offering consultation, planning, restoration, dismantling and re-erection of historic structures. Howard Willard, raised in a family of architectural historians, is dedicated to preserving early America's architectural heritage. Descriptive company literature free. Please call for individual consultation, or to arrange a speaking engagement.

Willems Painting & Decorating
731 Josephine Circle   Dept. OHJ
Green Bay, WI 54301
(414) 468-7228
RS/O
Traditional interior painting and paper services: Paper hanging, wood finishing, dry wall, color matching, wood graining, and spraying. No literature, but free estimates are given.

Willet Stained Glass Studio, Inc.
10 East Moreland Avenue   Dept. OHJ
Philadelphia, PA 19118
(215) 247-5721
MO   RS/O
One of the oldest glass studios in America. Stained and leaded glass pieces designed and executed to order. Also has extensive facilities for restoration of antique leaded glass. No literature; call for more information.

Williams & Hussey Machine Co.
Elm Street   Dept. OHJ
Milford, NH 03055
(603) 673-3446
MO   DIST   RS/O
Manufacturer of a small Molder Planer that is capable of planing up to fourteen inches wide, (by reversing). Ideal for renovating old homes as any molding can be reproduced exactly from any sketch or sample sent to us. Planes thicknesses up to 8'. Made of heavy cast iron with ground surfaces. Send for free brochure and price sheet.

Helen Williams—Delft Tiles
12643 Hortense Street   Dept. OHJ
North Hollywood, CA 91604
(213) 761-2756
RS/O   MO
17th and 18th century antique Dutch Delft tiles, in colors of blue, manganese, tortoise shell, white and polychrome. Also: English Liverpool tiles, 17th century Dutch firebacks and fire grates, Spanish and Portugese tiles. Free literature and price list with stamped, self-addressed envelope.

● **Williamsburg Blacksmiths, Inc.**
1 Buttonshop Road   Dept. OHJ
Williamsburg, MA 01096
(413) 268-7341
RS/O   MO   DIST
Authentic reproductions of Early American wrought iron hardware. All items are hand-finished and treated with a rust inhibitor. Catalog and price list, $2.50. Introductory brochure $.50.

Willis Lumber Co.
PO Box 84   Dept. OHJ
Washington C.H., OH 43160
(614) 335-2601
RS/O
A supplier of kiln-dried hardwood lumber, in several different grades. Free delivery to Ohio customers; will ship nationwide. Free catalog.

Wilson, H. Weber, Antiquarian
9701 Liberty Road   Dept. OHJ
Frederick, MD 21701
(301) 898-9565
MO   RS/O
Fine decorative components recycled from antique buildings. Stained and leaded glass a specialty: repairs, creations, windows and lamps bought, sold & traded. Also serves as consultant on projects involving new & antique decorative windows; available for lectures and seminars. Please write or call for free information and list of stained-glass publications.

Winans, Paul/Designer-Builder
2004 Woolsey St.   Dept. OHJ
Berkeley, CA 94703
(415) 843-4796
RS/O
Design & construction services in the San Francisco Bay Area. Specializing in renovation & restoration of old residential and commercial structures. Initial design plan through project completion. Stock and custom millwork available through this firm. Portfolio & references available during client's first consultation. No literature by mail.

Windham Millworks
PO Box 720   Dept. OHJ
North Windham, ME 04062
(207) 892-4055
RS/O
A source for stock wooden gutters. They'll do their own shipping to Southern Maine and New Hampshire. But they'll ship via UPS to other areas.

Windle Stained Glass Studio
PO Box 7321   Dept. OHJ
Jacksonville, NC 28540
(919) 346-9072
MO   RS/O
Custom design new stain glass windows. Also quality restoration and repair of old windows. Free brochure.

Windmill Interiors
2508 Laguna Vista Dr.   Dept. OHJ
Novato, CA 94947
(415) 897-8500
MO   RS/O
Manufacturer of plaster ceiling medallions in ornate Victorian designs. Also, reproductions of English cast-iron fireplace surrounds produced in plaster — for decoration only. Brochures, $.50 each, specify your interest.

Window Blanket Company, Inc.
Rt. 1, Box 107 Davis Lane   Dept. OHJ
Lenoir City, TN 37771
(615) 986-2115
MO   DIST
Insulated window curtains: Channel quilted tab-style window covering. Made of 100% polished cotton with soil-resistant finish. Filled with lightweight polyester fiberfill for sound-absorption and energy-savings. Fade resistant, water-repellent insulated cotton lining. Standard size 45" wide x 84" long. Custom lengths available. Easy to install on cafe or dowel rods. Free color brochure and fabric swatches.

Window Components Mfg.
3443 N.W. 107th St.   Dept. OHJ
Miami, FL 33167
(305) 688-2521
DIST
Replacement hardware for windows and doors. Mostly for modern installations, but many parts can be adapted. Selection includes casement operators and transom latches. Free catalog.

Window Grille Specialists
790 Cromwell Ave.   Dept. OH3
St. Paul, MN 55114
(612) 645-5736
MO
Supplier of hardwood grilles designed to give the appearance of traditional muntins. In rectangular or diamond patterns. Sample grille and catalog, $2.

Winterthur Museum
    Dept. OHJ
Winterthur, DE 19735
(302) 656-8591
RS/O
Decorative arts seminars are offered throughout the year. For information contact The Office of Advanced Studies.

Wolchonok, M. and Son, Inc.
155 E. 52 St.   Dept. OHJ
New York, NY 10022
(212) 755-2168
RS/O MO DIST
Two sister companies: Decorators Wholesale Hardware carries an extensive line of reproduction hardware by quality manufactures like Baldwin, Shepherd, Artistic Brass. Locksets, faucets, and casters available as well as most furniture hardware. Of particular interest is the second company, Legs-Legs-Legs, selling an extensive line of furniture legs and table pedestals: iron, brass, wood. Also, decorative carpet rods; many wood, iron and brass shelf brackets. Free descriptive literature available — specify interest and wholesale/retail.

● **Wolf Paints And Wallpapers**
771 Ninth Ave. (At 52nd St.)   Dept. OHJ
New York, NY 10019
(212) 245-7777
RS/O MO
An incredibly stocked paint store, with a large supply of hard-to-find finishes and supplies. Among the exotic items carried are: Graining brushes, specialty waxes like beeswax, crystalline shellac, Behlen wood finishes, casein paints, gold leaf and gilders supplies, wall canvas, and plaster patching materials. Will also handle mail orders. 54-page catalog shows much of their inventory. Catalog doesn't carry prices; must call for latest prices. Catalog is $2.00

Wollon, James Thomas, Jr., A.I.A.
600 Craigs Corner Road   Dept. OHJ
Havre de Grace, MD 21078
(301) 879-6748
RS/O
Architect, specializing in historic preservation, restoration, adaptation and additions to historic structures. Services range from consultation to full professional services; Historic Structures Reports; National Register nominations. Building types include residential, exhibit, commercial, religious. Resume and references on request.

Women's Woodwork
26 Adams St.   Dept. OHJ
Newton, MA 02160
(617) 964-6496
RS/O
House carpentry services — Victorian and old house restorations. Interior remodeling, designs, plans. Structural changes. House inspections by licensed builder. No literature; portfolio available, please call for an appointment.

Wood Designs
100 Jupiter St., PO Box 282   Dept. OHJ
Washington C.H., OH 43160
(614) 335-6367
RS/O
Custom made quality hardwood furniture, millwork, mouldings and panel doors for reproduction and restoration. Specialize in all hardwoods, including walnut, Honduras mahogany, cherry, and quarter-sawn oak. No lit. Call or write for free quotations.

Wood Masters, Inc.
87 Augusta Street   Dept. OHJ
South Amboy, NJ 08879
(201) 721-9111
MO RS/O
Manufacturers of architectural woodwork: Specialists in custom hardwood mouldings and butcher block tops in hard maple or red oak — in any size or thickness. For a prompt quote, mail sample or sketch of moulding & quantity needed. No literature.

Wood Moulding & Millwork Producers
PO Box 25278   Dept. OHJ
Portland, OR 97225
(503) 292-9288
DIST
Wood mouldings available in retail stores throughout the U.S. A brochure and order form describing wood moulding literature is free.

Wood and Stone, Inc.
7567 Gary Rd.   Dept. OHJ
Manassas, VA 22110
(703) 369-1236
MO DIST
Distributes a stone adhesive, AKEMI, for bonding together two pieces of stone, for filling natural faults, or for mending accidental breaks. AKEMI accepts iron oxide colors, so the restoration can be matched to any color stone. It can also be polished to a high gloss. Information sheet and price list free.

Woodbury Blacksmith & Forge Co.
P.O. Box 268   Dept. OHJ
Woodbury, CT 06798
(203) 263-5737
RS/O MO
Custom-made recreations of Colonial hardware, lighting devices, kitchen utensils, and fireplace equipment. Serving So. New England. Shipment can be arranged, but they have no literature. Custom orders by mail or phone. Catalog, $2.

● **Woodcare Corporation Sales & Technical Sales Svc.**
P.O. Box 92 H   Dept. OHJ
Butler, NJ 07405
(201) 838-9536
MO DIST
Products for refinishing, restoring, or reconditioning woodwork. Floors, furniture, aged wood, or metals. Beeswax finish reviver (in 4 shades) — a product designed to dissolve old wax and restore original finish. Also: metal polish, rust & tarnish remover, penetrating oil finishes, and varnish & paint removers. Free restoration guide.

Woodcraft Supply Corp.
41 Atlantic Ave., Box 4000   Dept. OHJ
Woburn, MA 01888
(617) 935-5860
RS/O MO
Woodworking hand tools, finishing supplies, hardware, and books on woodworking. Many high quality tools and supplies necessary for restoration — including cabinet scrapers. Also, carving tools and equipment, wooden and metal planes, wood-turning equipment, and supplies. Illustrated comprehensive color catalog — free.

Woodmart
PO Box 45   Dept. OHJ
Janesville, WI 53545
(608) 752-2816
MO RS/O
Chimney & flue brushes available made of steel or polypropyl 4-3/4'' to 14'' diameter round or 6 x 6'' to 14 x 14'' square. Information sent free with a stamped, self-addressed envelope only.

Woodstock Soapstone Co., Inc.
Route 4, Box 223/908   Dept. OHJ
Woodstock, VT 05091
(802) 672-5133
MO
Manufactures a classic 1867-design wood-burning parlour stove made of soapstone. Fine-textured soapstone panels with cast-iron mouldings. A pretty, formal stove, but also functional: 10-12 hour burning time, even heat. Literature package, free.

● **Woodstone Co.**
P.O. Box 223 Patch Road   Dept. OHJ
Westminster, VT 05158
(802) 722-4784
MO RS/O
Manufactures reproductions of period staircases, entrances, doors, wainscotting, cabinetry and furniture along with custom mouldings and wood turnings. Insulated foam-core wooden panel doors in traditional styles, multi-lite sidelites, straight & fanned transoms, and Palladian windows available with double & triple glazing. High quality natural & synthetic finishes available. Brochure, $1.

Woodworkers' Store, The
21801 Industrial Blvd.   Dept. OHJ
Rogers, MN 55374
(612) 428-4101
RS/O MO
A comprehensive source of supplies for the do-it-yourself person: hand tools, veneering supplies, picture framing, carved and embossed wood trim, books and plans, knobs & pulls, table and cabinet hinges, fine hardwood, finishing supplies. Stores also in Denver, Minneapolis, Cambridge (MA) and Seattle. 112 page catalog and price list — $1.00.

Worthington Trading Company
147 N. Main St.   Dept. OHJ
St. Charles, MO 63301
(314) 723-5862
MO RS/O
Retailers of woodburning stoves, Aladdin oil lamps, Hunter Ceiling Fans. High quality merchandise in traditional styles. Stoves: Esse Dragon, Petit Godin, Webster Oak, Cawley, Hearthstone Soapstone, & Elmira Cookstoves. Serving St. Louis metro area. Will ship many items in continental U.S. Literature includes booklet "Installing and Using Woodburning Stoves" $5.00.

Wrecking Bar of Atlanta
292 Moreland Ave., NE   Dept. OHJ
Atlanta, GA 30307
(404) 525-0468
RS/O
One of the nation's largest collections (18,000 sq. ft., 3 million dollar inventory) of authentic architectural antiques. Items include doors, mantels, statuary, columns, capitals, wrought iron, bevelled and stained glass, and lighting fixtures. Restoration design, and installation services available. Customers providing details of decorating/restoration projects will be sent photos of in-stock items for approval. Free literature.

● **Wrecking Bar, Inc.**
2601 McKinney Ave.   Dept. OHJ
Dallas, TX 75204
(214) 826-1717
RS/O MO
An ever-changing inventory of antique architectural elements, housed in an old 18,000-square-foot church. French, English and American classics: mantels, trumeaux, doors, entries, columns, stairway components, brackets, carvings, lighting, panelling, stained and bevelled glass, iron gates, and much more. All repaired and ready for shipping, anywhere. Please inquire for specific information and photographs.

Wrightsville Hardware
North Front Street   Dept. OHJ
Wrightsville, PA 17368
(717) 252-1561
RS/O MO DIST
Heavy duty cast iron blind and shutter hinges and fastenings. Stovepipe dampers and cast-iron stove lid lifter. Free illustrated brochures — please specify.

Wrisley, Robert T.
417 Childers Street   Dept. OHJ
Pulaski, TN 38478
MO RS/O
A one-man workshop in an old former church building. Will repair antiques (no stripping, refinishing, or chair-seat caning), especially those items requiring replacement carving. Also designs and builds custom furniture, mostly in reproduction styles. Stair handrail volutes and curved parts designed and carved. Free literature.

X

Xenia Foundry & Machine Co. Specialty Castings Dept.
PO Box 397   Dept. OHJ
Xenia, OH 45385
(513) 372-4481
RS/O
Founded in 1920, this family-owned business primarily makes industrial iron castings from 1 to 500 pounds. Specialty castings or one-of-a-kind pieces are a sideline. Skilled molders are capable of making stove parts, lawn or house ornamental pieces. If original object is unable to be used as a pattern, custom pattern making is available. Castings priced at time and material. No literature.

Y

Yankee Craftsman
357 Commonwealth Rd. Rt. 30   Dept. OHJ
Wayland, MA 01778
(617) 653-0031
MO RS/O
Yankee Craftsman deals primarily in the restoration and sale of authentic antique lighting fixtures. Tiffany, Handel and other leaded-glass repairs. Custom lighting designed and executed using old lamp parts. Fine quality custom-leaded shades. Restoration and sale of antique furniture. No catalog; specific information and photo furnished free in response to serious inquiries.

Ye Olde Mantel Shoppe
3800 N.E. Second Ave.   Dept. OHJ
Miami, FL 33137
(305) 576-0225
MO RS/O
Established in 1879, this company offers a complete line of domestic and imported mantels. Available in wood, metal, and porcelain. Will do custom designs. Also, fireplace accessories such as andirons, fenders, tools, and screens. Inquiries welcomed.

● **Yestershades**
3534 S.E. Hawthorne   Dept. OHJ
Portland, OR 97214
(503) 238-5755
MO RS/O
Handcrafted shades: Victorian styling in silks, satins, lace, and georgette. Trimmed with beads and silk fringes. Bases for sale separately. Custom work. Free brochure.

Yield House, Inc.
    Dept. OHJ
North Conway, NH 03860
(800) 258-4720
MO
Quality pine furniture, fully-finished or easy-to-assemble kits. Range of designs includes traditional, Early American, and classic Queen Anne. Furniture for every room in the home. Unique gifts & accessories. Free color catalog. In NH (800) 552-0320.

You Name It, Inc.
1959 Central Ave., Box 1013   Dept. OHJ
Middletown, OH 45042
(513) 424-1651
MO RS/O
Brokerage/consignment sales of antique, salvage & recycled building materials, houseparts, fixtures & hardware, furniture & accessories, period clothing, prints & original art, tools, etc. — primarily from SW Ohio. Free information.

● **See Product Displays Index on page 199 for more details.**

Z

Zetlin, Lorenz — Muralist
248 East 21st St.   Dept. OHJ
New York, NY 10010
(212) 473-3291
RS/O
Handpainted, custom murals, trompe l'oeil rendering. Aslo marbleizing — mantels, baseboards. Will do store fronts, exteriors, decorations, screens and window shades. Free illustrated flyer.

Zina Studios, Inc.
85 Purdy Avenue   Dept. OHJ
Port Chester, NY 10573
(914) 937-5661
MO DIST
Design and art studio, manufacturing wallcoverings and matching fabrics in custom colors, on a very high level. Reproductions are done for the restoration projects themselves, and they have permission to use them thereafter. Besides Camron-Stanford House, Zina Studios made several wallpapers for Chateau-sur-Mer, Newport, RI and other mansions in Newport. Free price list of museum reproduction papers.

Zynolyte Products Co.
18915 Laurel Park   Dept. OHJ
Compton, CA 90220
(213) 604-1333
DIST
Manufactures Klenk's Epoxy Enamel: a tub and tile finish, two-part epoxy coating for refinishing old sinks, tubs, ceramic tile, and appliances. Free leaflet.

KEY TO ABBREVIATIONS

MO   sells by **Mail Order**
RS/O   sells through **Retail Store or Office**
DIST   sells through **Distributors**
ID   sells only through **Interior Designers or Architects**

You'll get better service when contacting companies if you mention The Old-House Journal Catalog

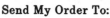

COMPANY LISTING BY STATE

ALABAMA

Alexander City — Robinson Iron Corporation
Birmingham — Lawler Machine & Foundry
Birmingham — Southern Heritage Metal Amenities, Ltd.
Eufaula — Jaxon Co., Inc.
Fairhope — Emperor Clock Co.
Huntsville — Giles & Kendall, Inc.
Montgomery — American Furniture Galleries
Montgomery — Martha M. House Furniture
Northport — Nutt, Craig, Fine Wood Works
Troy — Henderson Black & Greene, Inc.

ALASKA

Anchorage — Enerdynamics

ARIZONA

Phoenix — New Victorians of Arizona, Inc.
Pinetop — Crowfoot's Inc.
Tempe — Direct Safety Company

ARKANSAS

Eureka Springs — Corner Legacy
Fayetteville — Sunshine Architectural Woodworks
Fort Smith — Antique Bldrs. Hardware
Rogers — House of Webster
Stuttgart — Potlatch Corp. — Townsend Unit

CALIFORNIA

Alhambra — Bel-Air Door Co.
Alhambra — Leyva's Ornamental Staff & Stone
Anaheim — Heads Up
Arcata — Mad River Wood Works
Benicia — Bradbury & Bradbury Wallpapers
Berkeley — Architectural Emphasis, Inc.
Berkeley — Caning Shop
Berkeley — Jennings Lights of Yesterday
Berkeley — Ocean View Lighting and Home Accessories
Berkeley — The Sink Factory
Berkeley — Sunrise Specialty & Salvage Co.
Berkeley — Winans, Paul/Designer-Builder
Bethel Island — Lena's Antique Bathroom Fixtures
Burbank — J.P. Weaver Co.
Chatsworth — Wikkmann House
City of Industry — CasaBlanca Fan Co.
City of Industry — Peterson, Robert H., Co.
Compton — Zynolyte Products Co.
Corte Madera — Shades of the Past
Costa Mesa — Master's Stained and Etched Glass Studio
Covina — Barnard Chemical Co.
Culver City — Charles Barone, Inc.
Cupertino — Billard's Old Telephones
Davenport — Lundberg Studios
Del Mar — Mexico House
Durham — Feather River Wood and Glass Co.
El Cerrito — Brass & Iron Bed Co.
Escondido — Crowe Company
Eureka — North Pacific Joinery

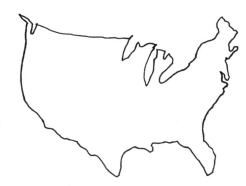

Eureka — Restoration Hardware
Ferndale — Victorian Glass Works
Fortuna — Hexagram
Fremont — Western Wood Doctor
Glendale — Plexacraft Metals Co.
Glendale — Victorian D'Light
Granada Hills — Vintage Plumbing
Gualala — Ritter & Son Hardware
Hollywood — Designer Resource
Holy City — Blue Frog Enterprises
Industry — Mansion Industries, Inc.
La Mesa — Burdoch Silk Lampshade Co.
Lafayette — Clocks, Etc.
Laguna Beach — Off The Wall
Laguna Hills — Russell & Company Victorian Bathrooms
Lincoln — Gladding, McBean & Co.
Long Beach — Guild, The
Long Beach — South Coast Shingle Co.
Los Angeles — Brass Bed Company of America
Los Angeles — Cane & Basket Supply Company
Los Angeles — Greg's Antique Lighting
Los Angeles — International Terra Cotta, Inc.
Los Angeles — Rumplestiltskin Designs
Los Angeles — Swan Brass Beds
Martell — Sierra Trading Co.
Mendocino — Hallelujah Redwood Products
Monrovia — Howard Products, Inc.
North Hollywood — Helen Williams—Delft Tiles
Novato — Windmill Interiors
Oakland — Bartley's Mill — Victorian Woodwork
Oakland — Classic Illumination
Oakland — Finishing Touch
Orange — Monier
Pasadena — Knickerbocker Guild
Rough & Ready — 19th Century Company
Sacramento — Dentelle de France
Sacramento — Sign of the Crab
San Diego — California Heritage Wood Products, Ltd.
San Diego — Ferris, Robert Donald, Architect, Inc.
San Diego — Howard Palmer, Inc.
San Diego — International Wood Products
San Diego — Keystone
San Diego — Szabo, George T., & Assoc., Inc.

San Francisco — Artistic License in San Francisco
San Francisco — Larry Boyce & Associates
San Francisco — Circast, Inc.
San Francisco — Haas Wood & Ivory Works
San Francisco — Illustrious Lighting
San Francisco — Meyer, Kenneth Co.
San Francisco — San Francisco Restorations, Inc.
San Francisco — San Francisco Victoriana
San Francisco — The Twigs, Inc.
San Jose — Amerian Woodworking
San Jose — Anglo-American Brass Co.
San Jose — Cedar Valley Shingle Systems
San Marcos — Mayer, Michael, Co.
San Mateo — A.S.L. Associates
San Mateo — Dura Strip of San Mateo
Sanger — Kings River Casting
Santa Barbara — Architectural Antique & Salvage Co. of Santa Barbara
Santa Barbara — Moriarty's Lamps
Santa Barbara — Rheinschild, S. Chris
Santa Monica — Watco - Dennis Corporation
Sausalito — Nowell's, Inc.
Sausalito — Vincent — Whitney Co.
Sherman Oaks — Canterbury Designs, Inc.
Sonoma — Artisan Woodworkers
South Gate — Artistic Brass
St. Helena — JMR Products
Torrance — Abaroot Mfg., Co.
Torrance — Antique Hardware Co.
Van Nuys — House of Moulding
Van Nuys — Universal Clamp Corp.
Ventura — Pemko Co.
Visalia — Boomer Resilvering
Watsonville — Beauti-home
Woodacre — Pagliacco Turning & Milling Architectural Wood Turning

COLORADO

Boulder — Boulder Stained Glass Studios
Boulder — Community Services Collaborative
Boulder — Jackson Bros.
Castle Rock — Iron Anvil Forge
Colorado Springs — Kingsway
Denver — Cherry Creek Ent. Inc.
Denver — Crown Glass Co.
Denver — Form and Texture — Architectural Ornamentation
Denver — Grammar of Ornament
Denver — Grandpa Snazzy's Hardware
Denver — Restoration Masonry
Denver — Silver Dollar Trading Co.
Ft. Collins — Warren, William J. & Son, Inc.
Grand Junction — Sunflower Studio
Ouray County — Cascade Mill & Glass Works
Silverton — Klinke & Lew Contractors
Silverton — Silverton Victorian Millworks

A company's name in boldface means they have placed a product display.

CONNECTICUT

Ashford — Jerard Paul Jordan Gallery
Bethel — Bix Process Systems, Inc.
Bloomfield — Mirror Patented Stove Pipe Co.
Branford — Breakfast Woodworks Louis
    Mackall & Partner
Branford — Smithy Hearth Products
Bristol — Blaschke Cabinet Glass
Bristol — New England Brassworks
Brooklyn — Native Wood Products, Inc.
Chester — Period Lighting Fixtures
Cornwall Bridge — Strobel Millwork
Cromwell — Custom House
Cromwell — Horton Brasses
Danielson — Pine & Palette Studio
East Lyme — S. & C. Huber, Accoutrements
Easton — Pollitt, E., AIA
Essex — Essex Forge
Fairfield — Stained Panes
Farmington — Black Wax — Pacific
    Engineering
Glastonbury — Cusson Sash Company
Glastonbury — Maurer & Shepherd, Joyners
Glastonbury — Parsons, W.H., Jr. &
    Associates
Hartford — Brewster's Lumberyard
Hartford — Hydrochemical Techniques, Inc.
Hartford — Swift & Sons, Inc.
Kent — Howland, John — Metalsmith
Manchester — Connecticut Cane & Reed Co.
Meriden — Colonial Casting Co., Inc.
Meriden — Orum Silver Co., Inc.
New Haven — Colonial Foundry & Mfg. Co.
New Haven — Welsbach
North Stonington — A.E.S. Firebacks
North Stonington — Olde New England
    Masonry
Norwalk — Architectural Woodworking
Norwalk — Gates Moore
Old Wethersfield — Willard Restorations, Inc.
**Plantsville — Southington Specialty Wood
    Co.**
Ridgefield — Gill Imports
Rocky Hill — M.R.S Industries, Inc.
Sharon — Litchfield House
Simsbury — Studio Workshop, Ltd.
Southbury — Henderson Lighting
Southington — The Brass Stencil
Southington — Canning, John
Stamford — Good Directions
Stamford — Preservation Development Group
Stamford — Stamford Wallpaper Co., Inc.
Stamford — United House Wrecking Corp.
Terryville — Colonial Lock Company
Unionville — Hayes Equipment Corp.
Washington — Washington Copper Works
West Suffield — Old-Home Building &
    Restoration
Wilton — Enlightened Restorations
Wilton — Kenneth Lynch & Sons, Inc.
Woodbridge — Mendel-Black Stone
    Restoration
Woodbury — Woodbury Blacksmith & Forge
    Co.

DELAWARE

Dover — Dover Furniture Stripping
Wilmington — History Store
Winterthur — Winterthur Museum

DISTRICT OF COLUMBIA

Washington — Acme Stove Company
Washington — Beck, Nelson of Wash. Inc.
Washington — The Brass Knob
Washington — Bucher & Cope Architects
Washington — Canal Co.
Washington — Cathedral Stone Company
Washington — The Ehrenkrantz
    Group/Building Conservation
    Technology
Washington — Weaver, W. T. & Sons, Inc.

FLORIDA

Gainesville — Aachen Designers
Gainesville — Hank, Dennis V.
Jasper — Quality Woodworks, Inc.
Key Largo — Backlund Moravian Tile Works
Key West — Elmore, Chris/ Architectural
    Design
Miami — Entol Industries, Inc.
Miami — Rich Woodturning and Stair Co.
Miami — Thoro System Products
Miami — Window Components Mfg.
Miami — Ye Olde Mantel Shoppe
Sanford — Florida Victoriani Architectural
    Antiques
West Palm Beach — JoEl Enterprises

GEORGIA

Adairsville — Oak Post Reproductions
Athens — Faucher, Evariste—Woodworker
Atlanta — Architectural Accents
**Atlanta — ByGone Era Architectural
    Antiques**
Atlanta — Conklin Tin Plate & Metal Co.
Atlanta — Estes-Simmons Silver Plating, Ltd.
Atlanta — Focal Point, Inc.
Atlanta — Hartmann-Sanders Column Co.
Atlanta — Hearth Realities
Atlanta — Hi-Art East
Atlanta — Legacy Pine Ltd.
Atlanta — Lesco Restorations, Inc.
Atlanta — Magnolia Hall
Atlanta — Period Pine
Atlanta — Red Baron's Peachtree Antique
    Emporium
Atlanta — Sandy Springs Galleries
Atlanta — Toby House
Atlanta — Wrecking Bar of Atlanta
Avondale Estates — Southeastern Art Glass
    Studio
Brunswick — Fuller O'Brien Paints
Dalton — Belcher, Robert W.
Decatur — Devenco Louver Products
Macon — Second Chance
Marietta — CasaBlanca Glass, Ltd.
Marietta — Rocker Shop of Marietta, GA
Marietta — W. P. Stephens Lumber Co.
Moultrie — Moultrie Manufacturing
    Company
Norcross — Norcross Galleries
Roswell — Gifford, D.K.
Savannah — Nostalgia, Inc.
Smyrna — Tec Specialties
Toccoa — Habersham Plantation Corp.

HAWAII

Aiea — Greg Monk Stained Glass

IDAHO

Boise — Remodelers & Renovators

ILLINOIS

Chicago — Architectural Terra Cotta and Tile,
    Ltd.
Chicago — Barclay Products Co.
Chicago — Bird — X, Inc.
Chicago — Consumer Supply Co.
Chicago — Decorators Supply Corp.
Chicago — Downstate Restorations
Chicago — Frog Tool Co., Ltd.
Chicago — Hasbrouck, W.R., Architect
    Historic Resources
Chicago — Historic Boulevard Services
Chicago — M — H Lamp & Fan Company
Chicago — Peerless Imported Rugs
Chicago — Reed Illinois Corp.
Chicago — Renovation Source, Inc., The
Chicago — Roman Marble Co.
Chicago — Salvage One
Chicago — Specialized Repair Service
Chicago — Standard Heating Parts, Inc.
Chicago — Stanley Galleries
Chicago — Sterline Manufacturing Corp.
Chicago — U.S. Gypsum Company
Chicago — Wagner, Albert J., & Son
Chicago — Warner Company
Compton — Victorian Building & Repair
Danville — Elliott Millwork Co.
Des Plaines — Chicago Faucet Co.
Elmhurst — Midwest Spiral Stair Company,
    Inc.
Evanston — Botti Studio of Architectural Arts
Evanston — Sarah Bustle Antiques, Ltd.
Freeport — Pyfer, E.W.
Galena — Bassett & Vollum Wallpapers
Gilberts — Abatron, Inc.
**Glen Ellyn — Easy Time Wood Refinishing
    Products Corp.**
Highland Park — Carpenter and Smith
    Restorations
Hinsdale — Newell Workshop
Joliet — Reproduction Distributors, Inc.
Joliet — Spiess, Greg
Lake Zurich — Illinois Bronze Paint Co.
Melrose Park — Cedar Gazebos, Inc.
Moline — Nixalite of America
Morton — Iron-A-Way, Inc.
Mount Carroll — Campbell Center
Mundelein — Cooper Stair Co.
Mundelein — Industrial Woodworking, Inc.
Naperville — Squaw Alley, Inc.
New Lenox — Johnson Bros. Specialties
Oswego — Jack's Upholstery & Caning
    Supplies
Pocahontas — Pocahontas Hardware & Glass
Prairie View — Hardwood Craftsman, Inc.
Rockford — Raleigh, Inc.
Rockford — Victorian House
Savanna — Facemakers, Inc.
Skokie — Braun, J.G. Co.
So. Holland — Kelly Plastering Co.
Springfield — Melotte-Morse Studios
St. Charles — Kyp-Go, Inc.
Wheeling — Timesavers
Wilmette — Perkowitz Window Fashions
Winnetka — Arch Associates/ Stephen
    Guerrant AIA

INDIANA

Auburn — **1890 Iron Fence Co.**
Auburn — Smith-Cornell Homestead, Inc.
Bloomington — Gaston Wood Finishes, Inc.
Bloomington — Indiana Mirror Resilvering
Gary — FerGene Studio
Indianapolis — Acquisition and Restoration
Corp.
Indianapolis — Brandt Bros. General
Contractors
Indianapolis — Haines Complete Building
Service
Jasper — Kimball Furniture Company
Jeffersonville — Gorsuch Foundry
Kokomo — Ragland Stained Glass
Lafayette — Architectural Emporium
Mishawaka — Troyer, Le Roy and Associates
Newburgh — Sunburst Stained Glass Co.
Noblesville — Sedgwick House
South Bend — J.C. Lauber Co.

IOWA

Ames — Jennings, Gottfried, Cheek/
Preservationists
Cedar Falls — Econol Stairway Lift Corp.
**Davenport — Amazon Vinegar & Pickling
Works Drygoods**
Davenport — Grilk Interiors
Des Moines — Knudsen, Mark
Dubuque — Adams Company
Iowa City — Max-Cast, Inc.
Iowa City — Oak Leaves Woodcarving Studio
Iowa Falls — Competition Chemicals, Inc.
Marshalltown — Marshalltown Trowel Co.
Monticello — Heritage Design

KANSAS

Colby — Butterfield Co.
Kansas City — Goldblatt Tool Co.
Kansas City — ProSoCo, Inc.
Manhattan — Landmark Company
Wichita — Lesco, Inc.

KENTUCKY

Berea — Berea College Student Craft
Industries
Campbellsville — Campbellsville Industries
**Covington — Stewart Manufacturing
Company**
Covington — Stripper, The
Lexington — Huskisson Masonry & Exterior
Building Restoration Co.
Lexington — Kentucky Ornamental Iron
Louisville — Bentley Bros.
Louisville — Devoe & Raynolds Co.
Louisville — Kentucky Wood Floors, Inc.
Louisville — Joe Ley Antiques, Inc.
Louisville — Lyemance International
Louisville — Morgan Woodworking Supplies

LOUISIANA

Baton Rouge — Spiral Manufacturing, Inc.
New Iberia — Iberia Millwork
New Orleans — Bank Architectural Antiques
New Orleans — Brass Connection, Inc.
New Orleans — Brass Menagerie
New Orleans — Gallier House Museum
New Orleans — Lachin, Albert & Assoc., Inc.
New Orleans — Preservation Resource Center
of New Orleans
New Orleans — Robinson Lumber Company
New Orleans — Strip Shop

MAINE

Brooks — Marsh Stream Enterprise
Fryeburg — Ram's Head Forge
Gray — Royal River Bricks Co., Inc.
Kennebunk — Cole, Diane Jackson
Liberty — Old Colony Crafts
North Windham — Windham Millworks
Pemaquid — Pemaquid Floorcloths
Phippsburg Center — Colonial Weavers
Portland — Jotul U.S.A., Inc.
Portland — Phoenix Studio, Inc.
Rockland — Mazzeo's Chimney Sweep
Suppliers
Rockport — Lea, James — Cabinetmaker
Sanford — Leeke, John — Woodworker
Sanford — Paints N Papers
**South Berwick — Maine Architectural
Millwork**
Thorndike — Bryant Stove Works
Union — Curry, Gerald — Cabinetmaker
West Brownfield — Fox Maple Tools
Wilton — Homestead Supply
Wiscasset — Friend, The
Yarmouth — Heritage Lanterns

MARYLAND

Aberdeen — Chemical Products Co., Inc.
Baltimore — Avalon Forge
Baltimore — Inner Harbor Lumber &
Hardware
Baltimore — G. Krug & Son, Inc.
Baltimore — Munsell Color
Baltimore — Readybuilt Products, Co.
Baltimore — Swiss Foundry, Inc.
Baltimore — Walbrook Mill & Lumber Co.,
Inc.
Boonsboro — Custom Sign Co.
Boyds — Finish Feeder Company
Brentwood — Giannetti Studios
College Park — Fine Woodworking Co.
Frederick — Vintage Lumber Co.
Frederick — Wilson, H. Weber, Antiquarian
**Hagerstown — Blaine Window Hardware,
Inc.**
Hagerstown — Duvinage Corporation
Havre de Grace — Wollon, James Thomas,
Jr., A.I.A.
Hyattsville — Beaumier Carpentry, Inc.
Kensington — Fireplace Mantel Shop, Inc.
Kensington — Fireplace Mantel Shop, Inc.
Kensington — H & M Stair Builders, Inc.
Kensington — Victorian Glassworks
Oxon Hill — Building Inspection Services,
Inc.
Potomac — Claxton Walker & Associates
Princess Anne — Ainsworth Development
Corp.

Rockville — Dell Corp.
Severna Park — Floorcloths Incorporated
Sharpsburg — Preservation Associates, Inc.
Silver Springs — Rollerwall, Inc.
Taneytown — Taney Supply & Lumber Corp.
Upper Falls — Paxton Hardware Ltd.
Williamsport — Cushwa, Victor & Sons Brick
Co.

MASSACHUSETTS

Adams — Mohawk Industries, Inc.
Adams — Old Stone Mill Corp.
Ayer — The Reggio Register Co.
Belchertown — Home Fabric Mills, Inc.
Blandford — Chester Granite Co.
Bolton — Bow House, Inc.
Boston — ARJ Assoc. — Reza Jahedi
Boston — Adams and Swett
Boston — Bench Manufacturing Co.
Boston — Charles St. Supply Co.
Boston — Consulting Services Group
S.P.N.E.A.
Boston — Dixon Bros. Woodworking
Boston — Faneuil Furniture Hardware
Boston — Johnson Paint Co.
Boston — Kenmore Industries
Boston — Period Furniture Hardware Co.,
Inc.
Boston — Perry, Edward K., Company
Bridgewater — Lemee's Fireplace Equipment
Brockton — Surrey Shoppe Interiors
Brookline — Castle Home Maintenance Co.
Boston Victoriana
Cambridge — City Lights
Cambridge — Lyn Hovey Studio, Inc.
Cambridge — Kruger Kruger Albenberg
Chelmsford — Elcanco
Cohasset — Cohasset Colonials by Hagerty
Colrain — Donald C. Stetson, Sr., Enterprises
Concord — Shaker Workshops
**Dorchester — Olde Bostonian Architectural
Antiques**
East Weymouth — Allied Resin Corp.
Fall River — Building Materials Inc.
Fitchburg — Skyline Engineers, Inc.
Fitchburg — Such Happiness, Inc.
Florence — Curran, Patrick J.
Gardner — Shingle Mill, Inc.
Great Barrington — Jenifer House
Greenfield — Richardson, Matthew
Coppersmith
Greenfield — Timeless Patterns
Groton — Country Bed Shop
Groton — Craftsman Lumber Co.
Groton — Old-Fashioned Milk Paint Co.
Hadley — 21st Century Antiques
Hanover — Hand-Stenciled Interiors
Hanover — Vecon Energy Systems Corp.
Hanover — Whittemore-Durgin Glass Co.
Harvard — Antique Color Supply, Inc.
Harvard — Cornucopia, Inc.
Hingham — Country Loft
Lawrence — Dee, John W. — Distinctive
Decorating
Leverett — Architectural Components
Lexington — Antiquaria
Lowell — Dovetail, Inc.
Mansfield — Acorn Manufacturing Co., Inc.
Marion — The Mechanick's Workbench
Marlborough — Butcher Polish Co.
**Martha's Vineyard — Travis Tuck, Inc. —
Metal Sculptor**

Medford — LaRoche Stained Glass
Medford — Pompei Stained Glass
New Bedford — Preservation Partnership
Newburyport — Anderson Reconstruction
Newton — Women's Woodwork
North Andover — Merrimack Valley Textile
Museum — Textile Conser. Cntr.
North Dartmouth — Cape Cod Cupola Co.,
Inc.
North Easton — Newstamp Lighting Co.
North Marshfield — Village Lantern
Northampton — Amherst Woodworking &
Supply
Northampton — Bernard Plating Works
Northampton — LaForte Design
Orleans — Guardian National House
Inspection and Warranty Corp.
Orleans — Olde Village Smithery
Rockport — London Venturers Company
Rowley — Cassidy Bros. Forge
Scituate — Faire Harbour Ltd.
Scituate — Peg Hall Studios
Shelburne Falls — Berkshire Porcelain Studios
Ltd.
Shrewsbury — Stencil School
Shutesbury — House Carpenters
Shutesbury — Sky Lodge Farm
South Boston — Coran — Sholes Industries
Southbridge — Hyde Manufacturing
Company
Stockbridge — Country Curtains
Taunton — NuBrite Chemical Co., Inc.
Turners Falls — Mill River Hammerworks
Tyngsboro — Seitz, Robert/Fine
Woodworking
Tyngsborough — Greenhalgh & Sons
**W. Barnstable — West Barnstable Stove
Shop**
W. Harwitz — Bullseyes Unltd.
W. Yarmouth — Mason & Sullivan Co.
Wakefield — A.J.P. Coppersmith
Wales — Country Comfort Stove Works
Wareham — Tremont Nail Company
Watertown — National Home Inspection
Service of New England, Inc.
**Watertown — New Boston
Building-Wrecking Co., Inc.**
Wayland — Yankee Craftsman
West Hanover — Wes-Pine Millwork, Inc.
Westport — Baker, A.W. Restorations, Inc.
Westport — Millham, Newton — Blacksmith
Westport — Newby, Simon
Westport Point — Westport Housewrights
**Williamsburg — Williamsburg Blacksmiths,
Inc.**
Wilmington — Duro Fiber Co.
Winchester — Hill, Allen Charles AIA
Woburn — Woodcraft Supply Corp.
Worcester — Hammerworks

MICHIGAN

Ann Arbor — Jefferson Art Lighting, Inc.
Battle Creek — O'Sullivan Co.
Belding — Country Roads, Inc.
Blissfield — Riverbend Timber Framing, Inc.
Dearborn — Greenfield Village and Henry
Ford Museum
East Lansing — Elbinger Laboratories, Inc.
Flint — Tomblinson, Harburn, Yurk and
Assoc., Inc.
Frankfort — Barap Specialties
Grand Rapids — Klise Manufacturing
Company
Grand Rapids — Past Patterns
Kalamazoo — Humphrey Products General
Gaslight Co.
Kingsford — Smith, F.E., Castings, Inc.
Lake Orion — Renaissance Marketing, Inc.
Lake Orion — Sunset Antiques, Inc.
Marshall — Conservatory, The
Mt. Clemens — Artistic Woodworking, Inc.
Niles — Kool-O-Matic Corp.
Niles — QRB Industries
Okemos — Kirk, M.A./Creative Designs
Southgate — Masters Picture Frame Co.
St. Johns — Custom Kitchen and Millwork
Stevensville — Sawdust Room
Sumner — Turnbull's Lumber Company
Traverse City — Menerey, E. W.
Ypsilanti — American General Products
Ypsilanti — Materials Unlimited
Zeeland — Howard Miller Clock Co.

MINNESOTA

**Brooklyn Park — Gage, Wm. E., Designer of
Homes**
Cold Spring — Old World Sewing Pattern
Co.
Dundas — Heirloom Enterprises
Grand Rapids — Charmaster Products Inc.
Minneapolis — Copper Sales, Inc.
Minneapolis — Durable Goods
Minneapolis — Nelson-Johnson Wood
Products, Inc.
Minneapolis — Ogren & Trigg Clock Service
Minneapolis — Renovation Concepts, Inc.
Minneapolis — Ring, J. Stained Glass, Inc.
Minneapolis — Victorian Lighting Co.
Minneapolis — Victorian Reproductions
Enterprises, Inc.
Richfield — Leo, Brian
Rochester — John Kruesel's General
Merchandise
Rogers — Woodworkers' Store, The
St. Paul — CW Design, Inc.
St. Paul — Industrial Fabrics Association
International
St. Paul — S H M Restorations
St. Paul — Window Grille Specialists
Warroad — Marvin Windows

MISSISSIPPI

Clermont Harbor — Morningstar
Jackson — Historical Replications, Inc.
Philadelphia — DeWeese Woodworking

MISSOURI

Hannibal — River City Restorations
Kansas City — Broadway Collection
Kansas City — Olde Theatre Architectural
Salvage Co.
Maryland Heights — Hope Co., Inc.
Nevada — Norman, W.F., Corporation
St. Charles — WSI Distributors
St. Charles — Worthington Trading Company
St. Louis — Art Directions
St. Louis — Brass & Copper Shop
St. Louis — Finishing Products
St. Louis — Frenzel Specialty Moulding Co.
St. Louis — Maggiem & Co.
St. Louis — McAvoy Antique Lighting
St. Louis — St. Louis Antique Lighting Co.
St. Louis — Shaw Marble & Tile Co., Inc.
St. Louis — Unique Art Glass Co.
St. Louis — Webster Stove
Webster Groves — Pedersen, Arthur Hall —
Design & Consulting Engineers

MONTANA

Missoula — Johnson, R.L. Interiors

NEBRASKA

Lincoln — Hydrozo Coatings Co.

NEW HAMPSHIRE

Acworth — Heating Research
Alexandria — Alexandria Wood Joinery
Alstead — Howard, David, Inc.
Canaan — Kraatz/Russell Glass
Claremont — Timberpeg
Concord — Stencil House
Dublin — Good Stenciling
Durham — Piscatagua Architectural
Woodwork, Co.
Epsom — Copper House
Exeter — Interior Decorations
Freedom — Iron Craft, Inc.
Gonic — Kane-Gonic Brick Corp.
Hillsboro — Millbranth, D.R.
Kingston — Curvoflite
**Manchester — Chimney Relining
International, Inc.**
Manchester — Richmond Doors
Marlow — Glass & Aluminum Construction
Services, Inc.
Meredith — Hood, R. and Co.
Merrimack — Staples, H. F. & Co., Inc.
Milford — Williams & Hussey Machine Co.
North Conway — Cornerstone Antiques
North Conway — Yield House, Inc.
Portsmouth — Nancy Borden, Period Textiles
Portsmouth — Dodge, Adams, and Roy, Ltd.
Portsmouth — Littlefield Lumber Co., Inc.
Stoddard — Carlisle Restoration Lumber
Tilton — Country Braid House
Tilton — Wiggins, D.B.

NEW JERSEY

Basking Ridge — Castle Burlingame
Bayonne — Muralo Company
Bernardsville — Terra Designs, Inc.
Bound Brook — AMC Housemaster Home
  Inspection Svc.
Bound Brook — House Master of America
Brielle — Hearth & Home Co.
Butler — Woodcare Corporation Sales &
  Technical Sales Svc.
Closter — Pasvalco
Collingswood — Bradford Consultants
E. Rutherford — Hoboken Wood Floors Corp.
Edison — E & B Marine Supply
Englewood — Authentic Lighting
Englewood — Englewood Hardware Co.
Englewood — Impex Assoc. Ltd., Inc.
Fair Haven — Roberts, Lee & Lynne
Fair Lawn — Bedlam Brass
Freehold — Bevel Right Mfg.
Harrison — Osborne, C. S. & Co.
Irvington — Thibaut, Richard E., Inc.
Jersey City — Novelty Trimming Works, Inc.
Leonia — Renaissance Decorative Hardware
  Co.
Midland Park — Archeological Research
  Consultants, Inc.
Montclair — Eklund, Jon Restorations
Montclair — Omnia Industries, Inc.
Montclair — Poor Richard's Service Co.
Montvale — Benjamin Moore Co.
Montvale — Minwax Company, Inc.
Moorestown — ART, Inc.
Mountainside — Mine Safety Appliance
  Corp.
Neptune — Studio Design, Inc., t/a Rainbow
  Art Glass
New Brunswick — Housewreckers, N.B. &
  Salvage Co.
New Brunswick — Stryker, Donald,
  Restorations
Newton — Historic Preservation
  Alternatives, Inc.
Northvale — Bendix Mouldings, Inc.
Palmyra — Littlewood, Craig
Paterson — Benjamin Eastwood Co.
Paterson — Center Lumber Company
Pennington — Lenape Products, Inc.
Pennington — Master Wood Carver
Rancocas Woods — Spencer, William, Inc.
Salem — Mannington Mills, Inc.
Sayreville — Balzamo, Joseph
Scotch Plains — Eastern Marble Supply Co.
Somerville — Alte, Jeff Roofing, Inc.
South Amboy — Wood Masters, Inc.
Summit — Virtue, W.D., Co., Inc.
Trenton — The Antique Restoration Co.
Trenton — Bailey Architectural Millwork
Union — King Energy Corp.
Union — Red Devil, Inc.
Union — Stair-Pak Products Co.
West Orange — Drill Construction Co., Inc.
Westfield — Old Colony Curtains
Westmont — W.N. Russell and Co.

NEW MEXICO

Santa Fe — Spanish Pueblo Doors

NEW YORK

Albany — American Boa, Inc. — Ventinox
Albany — Empire Stove & Furnace Co., Inc.
Albany — Preservation/Design Group, The
Amsterdam — Behlen, H. & Bros.
Bayside — Energy Etcetera
Binghamton — Binghamton Brick Co., Inc.
Briarcliff Manor — Bronze et al
Bronx — Constantine, Albert and Son, Inc.
Bronx — Englander Millwork Corp.
Bronx — Mittermeir, Frank Inc.
Bronx — J.H. Monteath Co.
Brooklyn — AA-Abbingdon, Inc.
Brooklyn — A.A. Used Boiler Supply Co.
Brooklyn — A.R.D.
Brooklyn — Ace Wire Brush Co.
Brooklyn — Air-Flo Window Contracting
  Corp.
Brooklyn — American Wood Column
Brooklyn — Antares Forge and Metalworks
Brooklyn — Arriaga, Nelson
Brooklyn — Artistry in Veneers, Inc.
Brooklyn — A Second Wind for Harmoniums
Brooklyn — Brooklyn Stone Renovating
Brooklyn — Brooklyn Tile Supply
Brooklyn — Burt Millwork Corp
Brooklyn — Chandelier Wharehouse
Brooklyn — City Barn Antiques
Brooklyn — Craftsmen Decorators
Brooklyn — Dimension Lumber Co.
Brooklyn — Fourth Avenue Stove &
  Appliance Corp.
Brooklyn — Gargoyles — New York
Brooklyn — Kaplan/Price Assoc. — Architects
Brooklyn — LaPointe, Chip, Cabinetmaker
Brooklyn — Louis Baldinger & Sons
Brooklyn — Mead Associates Woodworking,
  Inc.
Brooklyn — Morgan & Company
Brooklyn — Nast, Vivian
Brooklyn — Ohman, C.A.
Brooklyn — Old House Inspection Co., Inc.
Brooklyn — Old-House Journal
Brooklyn — Oliver Organ Co.
Brooklyn — Ornamental Design Studios
Brooklyn — P & G New and Used Plumbing
  Supply
Brooklyn — Piazza, Michael — Ornamental
  Plasterer
Brooklyn — Porcelli, Ernest
Brooklyn — Restorations
Brooklyn — Ross, Douglas — Woodworker
Brooklyn — Roy Electric Co., Inc.
Brooklyn — Security Home Inspection, Inc.
Brooklyn — Shadovitz Bros. Distributors, Inc.
Brooklyn — T.A.G. Preservation Consultation
Brooklyn Heights — Victorian Accents
Buffalo — Kittinger Company
Buffalo — Pratt & Lambert
Buffalo — Restoration Works, Inc.
Cambridge — Cambridge Textiles
Central Bridge — National SUPAFLU
  Systems, Inc.
Chappaqua — Decorative Hardware Studio
Clifton Park — Bradford Derustit Corp.
Cobleskill — Wigen Restorations
Cooperstown — Dean, James R.
Corona — George Studios
Cortland — Silberman, Allen
Deansboro — Old Lamplighter Shop
Deansboro — Schwartz's Forge & Metalworks
Deer Park — Armor Products
Douglaston — Manor Art Glass Studio
East Moriches — Dermit X. Corcoran Antique
  Services
East Nassau — Eastfield Village
Eastchester — Lieberman, Howard, P.E.
Eastchester — Westal Contracting

Elmsford — Crane Co.
Elmsford — Elon, Inc.
Farmingdale — National Guild of Professional
  Paperhangers, Inc.
Farmingdale — Old World Moulding &
  Finishing Co., Inc.
Florida — Sculptured Tiles
Garden City Park — S & W Framing
  Supplies, Inc.
Garnerville — Chromatic Paint Corp.
Garrison on Hudson — Watercolors, Inc.
Glen Cove — Artex Studio
Glendale, Queens — Shanker—Glendale
  Steel Corp.
Glenwood — International Building
  Components
Granville — Evergreen Slate Co.
Greene — Upland Stove Co., Inc.
Greenlawn — Stevens, John R., Associates
Hicksville — Modern Technical Tools &
  Supply Co.
Huntington Station — Fichet Lock Co.
Jamaica — Merit Moulding, Ltd.
Jeffersonville — Pfanstiel Hardware Co.
Kingston — Hurley Patentee Lighting
Larchmont — Cosmopolitan International
  Antiques
Lima — Country Stencilling
Long Island City — Decor International
  Wallcovering, Inc.
Long Island City — Eastern Safety Equipment
  Co.
Long Island City — Gould-Mesereau Co., Inc.
Long Island City — Mazza Frame and
  Furniture Co., Inc.
Mahopac — Industrial Window Corp.
Mattituck — Russell Restoration of Suffolk
Mecklenburg — Philip M. White & Associates
Middle Granville — Hilltop Slate Co.
Middle Granville — Tatko Bros. Slate Co.
Mount Vernon — Accurate Weatherstripping
  Co., Inc.
Mount Vernon — Rohlf's Stained & Leaded
  Glass
Mount Vernon — Walsh Screen Products
New Rochelle — Architectural Restoration
New Rochelle — Tile Distributors, Inc.
New York — Amsterdam Corporation
New York — Architectural Paneling, Inc.
New York — Architectural Sculpture
New York — Archive
New York — Bendheim, S.A. Co., Inc.
New York — Biagiotti, L.
New York — Brunschwig & Fils, Inc.
New York — Buecherl, Helmut
New York — Castle Roofing Co., Inc.
New York — Chandler — Royce
New York — City Knickerbocker, Inc.
New York — Collyer Associates, Inc.
New York — Country Floors, Inc.
New York — Couristan, Inc.
New York — Cowtan & Tout, Inc.
New York — Cyrus Clark Co., Inc.
New York — Dierickx, Mary B.
New York — Dotzel, Michael & Son Expert
  Metal Craftsman
New York — Evergreene Painting Studios,
  Inc.
New York — Garrett Wade Company
New York — Gem Monogram & Cut Glass
  Corp.
New York — Gibbs, James W. — Landscape
  Architect
New York — Glassmasters Guild
New York — Gold Leaf & Metallic Powders,
  Inc.
New York — Greenland Studio, Inc., The

New York — Guerin, P.E. Inc.
New York — Gurian's
New York — Hess Repairs
New York — Horowitz Sign Supplies
New York — Hunrath , Wm. Co., Inc.
New York — Import Specialists, Inc.
New York — Industrial Plastic Supply Co.
New York — Inglenook
New York — Jackson, Wm. H. Co.
New York — Janovic/Plaza, Inc.
New York — LEE JOFA
New York — Lovelia Enterprises, Inc.
New York — Mattia, Louis
New York — Mohawk Electric Supply Co., Inc.
New York — Mosca, Matthew
New York — Museum of the City of New York ·
New York — Navedo Woodcraft, Inc.
New York — New York Carved Arts Co.
New York — New York Flooring
New York — New York Marble Works, Inc.
New York — Paramount Exterminating Co.
New York — Patchmakers
New York — Patterson, Flynn, & Martin, Inc.
New York — Putnam Rolling Ladder Co., Inc.
New York — Quaker Lace Co.
New York — Rambusch
New York — Retinning & Copper Repair
New York — Sanders, David & Co.
New York — Scalamandre, Inc.
New York — Schumacher
New York — Sculpture Associates, Ltd.
New York — Sculpture House
New York — Sound Beginnings
New York — Standard Trimming Co.
New York — Stark Carpet Corp.
New York — Supradur Mfg. Corp.
New York — TALAS
New York — Tool Works
New York — Waverly Fabrics
New York — Welles Fireplace Company
New York — Whole Kit & Kaboodle Co., Inc.
New York — Wolchonok, M. and Son, Inc.
New York — Wolf Paints And Wallpapers
New York — Zetlin, Lorenz — Muralist
Nyack — Brasslight, Inc.
Nyack — Brown, T. Robins
Old Bethpage — Life Industries
Oneonta — Castings Unlimited
Ossining — Piccone, James Corrado, & Associates
Ozone Park — American Stair Builder
Plainview — U.S. General Supply Corp.
Port Chester — Zina Studios, Inc.
Port Jervis — Gillinder Brothers, Inc.
Port Washington — Hearthstone Tile Studio
Poughkeepsie — Sedgwick Machine Works, Inc.
Rego Park — Dentro Plumbing Specialties
Rochester — Pike Stained Glass Studios, Inc.
Rockville Centre — Gaudio Custom Furniture
Roslyn — Bienenfeld Ind. Inc.
Salt Point — Michael's Fine Colonial Products
Saugerties — Mangione Plaster and Tile and Stucco
Scarsdale — American Comfort Systems, Inc.
Shushan — Johnson, Walter H.
Slate Hill — Victorian Lightcrafters, Ltd.
Smithtown — Perma Ceram Enterprises, Inc.
Spring Valley — Lamb, J & R Studios
Syracuse — Jacobsen, Charles W., Inc.
Syracuse — Pelnik Wrecking Co., Inc.
Syracuse — Webster's Landing Architectural Antiques

Tarrytown — Restoration Workshop Nat Trust For Historic Preservation
Valley Steam — Croton, Evelyn — Architectural Antiques
Voorheesville — Thermal Wall Insulating Shutters, Inc.
Walden — D'Onofrio Restorative Studio
Warwick — Golden Age Glassworks
West Danby — Shelley Signs
West Nyack — Grant Hardware Company Div. of Grant Industries, Inc.
West Valley — Native American Hardwood Ltd.
Westbury — Nassau Flooring Corp.
Westfield — Crystal Mountain Prisms
Wyandanch — Cosmetic Restoration by SPRAYCO

NORTH CAROLINA

Asheville — Biltmore, Campbell, Smith Restorations, Inc.
Boone — Heritage Studios
Candler — Kayne, Steve & Son Custom Forged Hardware
Carrboro — Sutherland Welles Ltd.
Charlotte — Porcelain Restoration and Brass
Eden — King's Chandelier Co.
Greensboro — Greensboro Art Foundry & Machine Co.
Greenville — Carriage Trade Antiques & Art Gallery
Hickory — Carolina Leather House, Inc.
Hickory — Furniture Traditions, Inc.
Jacksonville — Windle Stained Glass Studio
Lexington — Mid-State Tile Company
Monroe — Littlejohn's
Pleasant Garden — Boren Clay Products Company
Raleigh — Dan Wilson & Company, Inc.
Raleigh — Gingerbread House
Salisbury — Norman's of Salisbury
Salisbury — Old Carolina Brick Co.
Smithfield — Village Forge
Southern Pines — Thomas Antique Services
Wilmington — Dorothy's Ruffled Originals

OHIO

Alliance — Deft Wood Finish Products
Atwater — Victorian Interior Restoration
Bath — Western Reserve Antique Furniture Kit
Cincinnati — Anderson Building Restoration
Cincinnati — Bona Decorative Hardware
Cincinnati — Colonial Tin Craft
Cincinnati — Huseman, Richard J. Co.
Cincinnati — Meierjohan — Wengler, Inc.
Cleveland — Antique Trunk Supply Co.
Cleveland — Astrup Company
Cleveland — Fischer & Jirouch Co.
Cleveland — Hexter, S. M. Company
Cleveland — Leichtung, Inc.
Cleveland — Newe Daisterre Glas
Cleveland — Taft Wood Products Co.
Columbus — Flue Works, Inc.
Columbus — Franklin Art Glass Studios
Columbus — Image Group, The
Columbus — Stencil Store
Dayton — Canal Works Architectural Antiques
Dayton — The Farm Forge
Findlay — Colonial Charm
Franklin — Architectural Reclamation, Inc.
Glenmont — Briar Hill Stone Co.

Kidron — Lehman Hardware & Appliances
Mansfield — Marshall Imports
Marysville — Larcomb & Wicht
Middletown — You Name It, Inc.
Millersburg — Rastetter Woolen Mill
New Lexington — Ludowici-Celadon Co.
Summitville — Summitville Tiles, Inc.
Tallmadge — Walker, Dennis C.
Terrace Park — Old World Restorations, Inc.
Terrace Park — Wiebold, Inc.
Troy — R.D.C. Enterprises
Uhrichsville — Superior Clay Corporation
Washington C.H. — Willis Lumber Co.
Washington C.H. — Wood Designs
Wellington — Century House Antiques
Worthington — Baker, Jim
Xenia — Xenia Foundry & Machine Co. Specialty Castings Dept.

OKLAHOMA

Carter — Elk Valley Woodworking Company
Oklahoma City — Structural Antiques

OREGON

Corvallis — Furniture Revival
Eugene — Old'N Ornate Wooden Reproductions
Portland — 1874 House
Portland — A-Ball Plumbing Supply
Portland — J.O. Holloway & Company
Portland — Hopkins, Sara — Restoration Stenciling
Portland — Ostrom Studios
Portland — Rejuvenation House Parts Co.
Portland — Restoration A Specialty
Portland — Victorian Crown, Ltd.
Portland — Wood Moulding & Millwork Producers
Portland — Yestershades
White City — Turncraft

PENNSYLVANIA

Adamstown — Pratt's House of Wicker
Allentown — Allentown Paint Mfg. Co., Inc.
Allentown — Lehigh Portland Cement Co.
Ardmore — Felber, Inc.
Ardmore — Finnaren & Haley, Inc.
Bangor — Pennsylvania Barnboard Company
Bellefonte — Victorian Lighting Works, Inc.
Bethlehem — Campbell, Marion
Bridgeport — Moser Brothers, Inc.
Broomall — Smolinsky, Ltd.
Bryn Mawr — Welsh, Frank S.
Bucks County — Heritage Rugs
Carlisle — Cumberland Woodcraft Co., Inc.
Cochranton — RUSCO
Derry — 18th Century Hardware Co.
Douglassville — Merritt's Antiques, Inc.
Drums — Drums Sash & Door Co., Inc.
Elizabethville — Restorations Unlimited, Inc.
Emmaus — Gerlachs of Lecha
Emmaus — Homespun Weavers
Erie — Lake Shore Markers
Exton — Ball and Ball
Flourtown — Trump R.T., & Co., Inc.
Ft. Littleton — JGR Enterprises, Inc.
Gettysburg — RAM's Forge
Gibsonia — Masonry Specialty Co.
Glenside — Schmidt, Edward P. — Cabinetmaker
Green Lane — Flaharty, David — Sculptor
Hanover — Rustic Home Hardware

Harrisburg — Tomas Spiers & Associates
Intercourse — Country Window, The
Kittanning — Continental Clay Company
Lancaster — Creatus
Lancaster — Lancaster Paint & Glass Co.
Lancaster — Saltbox
Landenberg — Lauria, Tony
Lansdale — American Olean Tile Company
Latrobe — Homecraft Veneer
Leesport — Loose, Thomas — Blacksmith/
  Whitesmith
Lima — Restoration Fraternity
Lionville — British-American Marketing
  Services, Ltd.
Lumberville — Delaware Quarries, Inc.
Marietta — Barnett, D. James — Blacksmith
Milford — Architectural Iron Company
**Montgomeryville — Philadelphia Resins
  Corp.**
Mountainhome — Oliver, Bradley C.
New Hope — Purcell, Francis J., II
Norristown — Stulb Paint & Chem. Co., Inc.
Paoli — The Country Iron Foundry
Pen Argyl — Bangor Cork Co., Inc.
Pen Argyl — Bedpost, The
Pen Argyl — Structural Slate Company
Penndel — Langhorne Carpet Co.
Perkasie — Perkasie Industries Corp.
Philadelphia — Aetna Stove Company
Philadelphia — Angelo Brothers Co.
**Philadelphia — Architectural Antiques
  Exchange**
Philadelphia — Bangkok Industries, Inc.
Philadelphia — Betsy's Place
Philadelphia — Clio Group, Inc.
Philadelphia — Gargoyles, Ltd.
Philadelphia — Holm, Alvin AIA Architect
Philadelphia — International Consultants,
  Inc.
Philadelphia — David M. LaPenta, Inc.
Philadelphia — Luigi Crystal
Philadelphia — McCloskey Varnish Co.
Philadelphia — Neri, C./Antiques
Philadelphia — Pennsylvania Firebacks, Inc.
Philadelphia — Progress Lighting
**Philadelphia — Roland Spivak's Custom
  Lighting, Pendulum Shop**
Philadelphia — Up Your Alley
Philadelphia — Willet Stained Glass Studio,
  Inc.
Pittsburgh — Heckler Bros.
Pittsburgh — Koppers Co.
Pittsburgh — Schwerd Manufacturing Co.
Reading — Baldwin Hardware Mfg. Corp.
**Robesonia — Rich Craft Custom Kitchens,
  Inc.**
Scranton — United Gilsonite Laboratories
**Sharon Hill — Quaker City Manufacturing
  Co.**
Shoemakersville — Glen - Gery Corporation
Solebury — Whitley Studios
Somerset — Somerset Door & Column Co.
Spring City — Spring City Electrical Mfg. Co
Stewartstown — Fypon, Inc.
Unionville — Lee Woodwork Systems
Warminster — Morgan Bockius Studios, Inc.
Warrington — Merit Metal Products Corp.
West Chester — Arden Forge
West Chester — Campbell-Lamps
West Chester — Dilworthtown Country Store
West Chester — Guthrie Hill Forge, Ltd.
West Chester — Monroe Coldren and Sons
Wrightsville — Wrightsville Hardware
Yardley — Dutch Products & Supply Co.
Yardley — Oberndorfer & Assoc.
York — Lewis, John N.
York — Tioga Mill Outlet

RHODE ISLAND

East Greenwich — Keddee Woodworkers
Newport — Rue de France
Rumford — Heirloom Rugs

SOUTH CAROLINA

Charleston — Charleston Battery Bench, Inc.
Charleston — Historic Charleston
  Reproductions
Florence — Driwood Moulding Company
Liberty — Flexi-Wall Systems
Orangeburg — Tiresias, Inc.

SOUTH DAKOTA

Sioux Falls — C & H Roofing

TENNESSEE

Bellevue — Walker Industries
Clarksville — Clarksville Foundry & Machine
  Works
Crossville — Cumberland General Store
Johnson City — Harris Manufacturing
  Company
Lenoir City — Window Blanket Company,
  Inc.
McMinnville — B & P Lamp Supply Co., Inc.
Memphis — Chapman Chemical Co.
Memphis — Graham's Lighting Fixtures
Memphis — Hunter Ceiling Fans
Memphis — Memphis Hardwood Flooring
  Co.
Memphis — Tennessee Fabricating Co.
Oneida — Hartco
Pulaski — Wrisley, Robert T.

TEXAS

Austin — Antique Street Lamps
Austin — Hanks Architectural Antiques
Austin — Westlake Architectural Antiques
Bedford — Creative Glass Works
Bellaire — Tootie's Tile & Trim
Blessing — Blessing Historical Foundation
Dallas — Bruce Hardwood Floors
Dallas — Century Glass Inc. of Dallas
Dallas — Renovation Products
Dallas — Wrecking Bar, Inc.
Flower Mound — Brass Fan Ceiling Fan Co.
Fort Worth — Bombay Company, The
Fredericksburg — Vintage Wood Works
Ft. Worth — Jones Interior Design
Galveston — Island City Wood Working Co.
Houston — Alcon Lightcraft Co.
Houston — American Ornamental
  Corporation
Houston — Architectural Archives
Houston — Berridge Manufacturing Co.
Houston — Chelsea Decorative Metal Co.
Houston — Emporium, The
Houston — Mel-Nor Marketing
Jefferson — Ceilings, Walls & More, Inc.
New Braunfels — Decorators Market, USA
Pearland — Boseman Veneer & Supply Co.
Spearman — Charolette Ford Trunks
Tyler — Brass Lion
Waco — Ideal Millwork Co.
Wharton — Heritage Home Designers

UTAH

Salt Lake City — Rosander's Wood Turning

VERMONT

Arlington — Chem-Clean Furniture
  Restoration Center
Arlington — Miles Lumber Co, Inc.
Barre — Trow & Holden Co.
Bennington — Energy Marketing Corporation
Brattleboro — Appropriate Technology Corp.
Burlington — Conant Custom Brass
Burlington — Depot Woodworking, Inc.
Burlington — Great Northern Woodworks,
  Inc.
Fair Haven — Hubbardton Forge Corp.
Fair Haven — Vermont Structural Slate Co.
Hardwick — Vermont Weatherboard, Inc.
Manchester — Bishop, Adele, Inc.
Montpelier — Great American Salvage
Montpelier — Northern Design General
  Contractors
Moretown — Congdon, Johns/Cabinetmaker
Moretown — Housejoiner, Ltd.
Perkinsville — Vermont Soapstone Co.
Poultney — Iron Horse Antiques, Inc.
Proctor — Vermont Marble Co.
Putney — Brown, Carol
Putney — Eddy, Ian — Blacksmith
Randolph, — Douglas Gest Restorations
Rutland — Rutland Products
Saxtons River — Agape Antiques
So. Strafford — Strafford Forge
South Woodstock — Barn People, The
Springfield — Lavoie, John F.
Stowe — Coalbrookdale Company
Stowe — Thermocrete Chimney Lining, Inc.
Sudbury — Mr. Slate - Smid Incorporated
W. Rupert — Authentic Designs Inc.
Waterbury — Vermont Iron
West Brattleboro — Broad-Axe Beam Co.
West Pawlet — Rising & Nelson Slate Co.
Westminster — Woodstone Co.
Wolcott — Smithy, The
Woodstock — Woodstock Soapstone Co., Inc.

VIRGINIA

Alexandria — Artifacts, Inc.
Bremo Bluff — Cain-Powers, Inc.
  Architectural Art Glass
**Charlottesville — Mountain Lumber
  Company**
Charlottesville — Swofford, Don A., Architect

Clarksville — Old Wagon Factory
Fairfax — Robson Worldwide Graining
Falls Church — Itinerant Artist
Fredericksburg — Joy Construction, Inc.
Hampton — Electric Glass Co.
Harrisonburg — Historic Windows
Harrisonburg — Shenandoah Manufacturing
  Co.
Louisa — Byrd Mill Studio
Lovingston — Braintree Woodworks
Lovingston — Buck Creek Bellows
Manassas — Wood and Stone, Inc.
Marion — Laura Copenhauer Industries, Inc.
Martinsville — Poxywood, Inc.
Mechanicsville — Durvin, Tom & Sons
Montebello — Blue Ridge Shingle Co.
Norfolk — Herman, Frederick, R.A.,
  Architect
Petersburg — Lisa — Victoria Brass Beds
Prospect — Vintage Pine Co., Inc.
Richmond — Biggs Company
**Richmond — Buckingham-Virginia Slate
  Corporation**
Richmond — Caravati, Louis J.
Richmond — Hendricks Tile Mfg. Co., Inc.
Richmond — Hudson Venetian Blind Service,
  Inc.

Richmond — Long, E. T., Inc.
Richmond — Moore, E.T., Jr. Co.
Richmond — Royal Windyne Limited
Riverton — Riverton Corporation
Springfield — PRG
Springfield — Preservation Resource Group
Washington — Peter Kramer/Cabinetmaker
Washington — Washington House of
    Reproductions
Williamsburg — Colonial Williamsburg
    Foundation Craft House
Williamsburg — Hobt, Murrel Dee, Architect

WASHINGTON

Bellevue — Dorz Mfg. Co.
Bellevue — Old And Elegant Distributing
Bellingham — Creative Openings
Edmonds — Sheppard Millwork, Inc.
Everett — Nord, E.A. Company
Everett — Washington Stove Works
Mercer Island — Hearth Shield
Puyallup — Gazebo and Porchworks
Redmond — Beveling Studio
Seattle — Daly's Wood Finishing Products
Seattle — Kaymar Wood Products, Inc.
Seattle — Light Fantastic
Seattle — Millwork Supply Company
Seattle — Norh Coast Chemical Co.
Seattle — Pacific Lamp & Stove Co.
Snohomish — Puget Sound Shake Brokers
Spokane — Jim & Barb's Antique Stoves
Stevenson — Essex Tree Service
Winlock — Shakertown Corporation

WEST VIRGINIA

Cowen — Leslie Brothers Lumber Company
Follansbee — Follansbee Steel
Hamlin — Contois Stained Glass Studio
Milton — Blenko Glass Co., Inc.
Parkersburg — Good Impressions Rubber
    Stamps
Williamstown — Fenton Art Glass Company

WISCONSIN

Beaver Dam — Malleable Iron Range Co.
De Pere — Auto Hoe, Inc.
Delafield — Sun Designs
Fond du Lac — Combination Door Co.
Franklin — American Building Restoration
Green Bay — Willems Painting & Decorating
Janesville — Woodmart
Madison — Gibbons, John — Cabinetmaker
Manitowoc — Goddard & Sons
Milwaukee — Brasslight Antique Lighting
Milwaukee — Casey Architectural Specialties
Milwaukee — Experi-Metals
Milwaukee — Millen Roofing Co.
Milwaukee — Orlandini Studios Ltd.
    Decorative Plaster Supply Co.
Milwaukee — Victorian Collectibles Ltd.
Oak Creek — Diedrich
    Chemicals-Restoration Technologies,
    Inc.
Oak Creek — McGivern, Barbara — Artist
Oshkosh — C—E Morgan
Racine — Dremel/Div. of Emerson Electric
Rice Lake — Tomahawk Foundry
Waukesha — Crawford's Old House Store
Wauwatosa — Building Conservation
Wisconsin Rapids — Preway, Inc.

CANADA

Delta, BC — Hart, Brian G./Architect
Elmira, Ontario — Elmira Stove Works
Ottawa, ONT — Architectural Antique
    Warehouse, The
Ottawa, OT — Cohen's Architectural
    Heritage
Ottawa, Ontario — Association for
    Preservation Technology
Ottawa, Ontario — Lee Valley Tools, Ltd.
Toronto, ON — Carson, Dunlop &
    Associates, Ltd.
Toronto, Ont. — Hulton, Roger L.
Vancouver, BC — Nye's Foundry Ltd.
Willowdale, ON — Steptoe and Wife
    Antiques Ltd.

ENGLAND

Horsmonden, Kent — Chilstone Garden
    Ornament
London, England — Colefax and Fowler
Maldon, Essex — Verine Products & Co.
Stoke-on-Trent, Engl — H & R Johnson Tile
    Ltd./ Highgate Tile Works

Index To Products & Services

Product Displays Index

Product Displays Index, cont'd

Notes

Notes

Notes